D1523859

How should we reason about what to do? The answer offered by most recent philosophy, as well as such disciplines as decision theory, welfare economics, and political science, is that we should select efficient means to our ends. However, if we ask how we should decide which ends or goals to aim at, these standard theoretical approaches are silent.

Henry Richardson argues that we can determine our ends rationally. He constructs a rich and original theory of how we can reason about what to seek for its own sake as a final end. Richardson defuses the counter-arguments for the limits of rational deliberation and develops interesting ideas about how his model might be extended to interpersonal deliberation of ends, taking him to the borders of political theory. Along the way Richardson offers illuminating discussions of, *inter alia,* Aristotle, Aquinas, Sidgwick, and Dewey, as well as the work of several contemporary philosophers.

This is a book of major importance to a broad swath of philosophers as well as social and political scientists.

Practical Reasoning about Final Ends

CAMBRIDGE STUDIES IN PHILOSOPHY

General editor Ernest Sosa

Advisory editors
Jonathan Dancy – University of Keele
Gilbert Harman – Princeton University
Frank Jackson – University of Melbourne
William G. Lycan – University of North Carolina, Chapel Hill
Sidney Shoemaker – Cornell University
Judith J. Thomson – Massachusetts Institute of Technology

Practical Reasoning about Final Ends

Henry S. Richardson

Georgetown University

CAMBRIDGE
UNIVERSITY PRESS

PUBLISHED BY THE PRESS SYNDICATE OF THE UNIVERSITY OF CAMBRIDGE
The Pitt Building, Trumpington Street, Cambridge CB2 1RP

CAMBRIDGE UNIVERSITY PRESS
The Edinburgh Building, Cambridge CB2 2RU, United Kingdom
40 West 20th Street, New York, NY 10011-4211, USA
10 Stamford Road, Oakleigh, Melbourne 3166, Australia

First published 1994
First paperback edition 1997

Printed in the United States of America

Library of Congress Cataloging-in-Publication Data is available.

A catalog record for this book is available from the British Library.

ISBN 0-521-46472-2 hardback
ISBN 0-521-57442-0 paperback

To my parents

Contents

Preface

Everyone has an interest in reasoning practically about ends. To fail to recognize its possibility is to miss the full potential for evaluating human pursuits and achieving practical wisdom, yet living wisely and discerning the true complexity of value should concern everyone. Both the centrality of the topic of deliberation about ends and the reasons why its potential rationality is not generally recognized have affected how this book has been written. Because of the broad human importance of the topic, I have aimed to write an accessible book. This may mean that in some places – in particular the long examples of Chapter X – the exposition moves too slowly for professional philosophers. In contrast, a few sections of the book establish preliminaries or address details that will mainly interest philosophers and may be skipped by others: §§5, 6, and 12. More generally, since the obstacles to recognizing the potential rationality of deliberation about ends are philosophical inventions, and since common sense already provides some evidence on its own that we do deliberate rationally about ends, only readers with some interest in philosophy are likely to be motivated to follow my arguments through to the end. They will include those readers who have sufficient philosophical curiosity about how the constructive argument against my opponents will go or about the precise shape the theory of deliberation about ends will take. They will also include readers who at the outset feel to some degree the force of the philosophically originated doubts (described in §2) about the possibility of rational deliberation of ends. Accordingly, although this book presumes no special knowledge, it does presume a degree of interest in matters philosophical.

Still, what orients my approach to this topic is the importance to human life of attaining a correct view about deliberation about ends, not a relish for philosophical controversy for its own sake. I claim that an individual's reasoning can establish new final ends, even a new ultimate end, for that individual. Since it has always been true that we can do this, and since our ability to do so is such a central feature of our lives, it would be surprising if the great philosophers wholly failed to recognize this. And in fact, I have no quarrel with Aristotle, say, or with Hume, each of whom may (with a bit of ingenuity) be interpreted so as to allow for rational deliberation of ends. I pick fights, rather, in the course of clearing away philosophical views that have impeded recognition of the possibility of rational deliberation about ends, as well as on the way to constructing a positive account about how we do so.

Via a bit of autobiography, I can better explain why it matters, in practice, that we all recognize that we can deliberate rationally about ends. My own involvement with this topic grew out of my astonishment that the formal models of decision making, such as cost–benefit analysis, that were taught to me in a Master's program in public policy should have been offered as the central techniques for policy deliberation. These techniques all assume that ends are somehow given externally, whether by the legislature or by the preferences of citizens as revealed in the market. Yet I was and am convinced that deliberation about policy, at whatever level, unavoidably involves settling upon new and more specific ends. Unless and until it is recognized that this establishment of new ends can be rational, policy making will remain too much in the sway of technical approaches that mask the play of factional interest and too closed to democratic deliberation. The same is true about the deliberation of democratic assemblies themselves. Although the political assembly is historically the home setting for deliberation, that is now hard to believe. Public disaffection with the supposed corruption and privileges of the legislators makes it difficult to imagine true political deliberation on the ends of policy; but the absence of productive political deliberation may be more a cause of this discontent than its effect. We have lost confidence, in general, in the possibility of deliberating rationally about ends. This faltering erodes trust in democracy, leading us to expect no more from politics than the jockeying for favor of organized interests.

Although my own concern with deliberation about ends thus initially arose from a preoccupation with the challenge of achieving the ideal of democracy, I decided that it was necessary first to take up the less complex problem of showing how an individual can deliberate rationally about ends. The latter was the project that sent me from public policy to philosophy more than a decade ago, and is the topic to which this book will confine itself. That the problem of rational deliberation of ends is simpler at the individual level cannot be shown a priori. I would reject any form of methodological individualism strong enough to imply that since political deliberation is a social fact it must be analyzed into facts about individuals in order to be understood. To the contrary, I see the value of understanding deliberation in terms of an inherently social background of action and argument. The reasons I have for thinking the problem of political deliberation more complex than its individual counterpart hinge to a considerable extent on my normative account of deliberation, here to be defended. Accordingly, I will not be able to set them out until Chapter XI. Although politics is the original context both of Western philosophical analysis of deliberation and of my own interest in the subject, I postpone addressing it so as to first get straight what is for me the simpler topic of an individual's deliberation about ends.

My first cut at this topic was a dissertation that built upon the writings of Aristotle and Kant. Although the outlines of the proposal this book develops were present in the dissertation, the example in §32 is the only significant part that survives here. Nonetheless, I am pleased to record again my great debt to my dissertation advisers, John Rawls and Hilary Putnam, who provided needed support, inspiration, and direction.

Since then, I have benefited from much institutional and individual generosity. The work on Sidgwick that forms the basis of §§18 and 19 was supported by summer grants from the National Endowment for the Humanities and Georgetown University. It first appeared as "Commensurability as a Prerequisite of Rational Choice: An Examination of Sidgwick's Position," in *History of Philosophy Quarterly* 8 (1991): 181–98. I am grateful for permission to print material adapted from that article here. My work on the specification relation benefited from a stimulating year as a Fellow in Ethics and the Professions at Harvard University and from further support from Georgetown. I also thank Princeton University Press for permission to adapt, as §§10 and 25, portions of my article "Specifying Norms as a Way to Resolve Concrete Ethical Problems," in *Philosophy and Public Affairs* 19 (1990): 279–310.

From the outset of my philosophical work on this subject, the most challenging support and the most generous flow of detailed comments and suggestions have come from Martha Nussbaum. Wayne Davis went over an earlier draft with a fine-tooth comb, saving me from many errors and offering important insight into the relationship between my view and coherentist theories in epistemology. Amy Gutmann and Terry Pinkard provided welcome advice and criticism pertaining to Part Five. I received helpful written comments on various portions of the manuscript from Steve Kuhn, Elijah Millgram, Thomas Pogge, Amélie Rorty, Geoffrey Sayre-McCord, Roy Sorensen, Michael Stocker, and Kenneth Winston.

Conversations and correspondence with Mark Lance, Christian Perring, Hilary Putnam, Nathan Salmon, Geoffrey Sayre-McCord, and Jennifer Whiting supplied me with particularly telling points and questions. My father helped me excise much needless jargon. I have also been greatly helped by a number of anonymous reviewers and by the participants in my seminars at Georgetown during 1992–3.

I was privileged to spend the academic year 1991–2 as a Fellow at the Woodrow Wilson International Center for Scholars. The Center provided a quiet tower office, perfect for writing a first full draft of this book. It also gathered a stimulating interdisciplinary community, without which Part Five's discussion of the situation of rape victims in Pakistan would not have been possible. For help with that aspect of my project, I am grateful to the late Elie Kedourie and to Ben Amini, Granville S. Austin, Pierre J. E. Cachia, Robert Frykenberg, Grace Goodell, Sylvia Haim Kedourie, Mahnaz Ispahani, and Fariba Thomson.

To my family, I am thankful for many kinds of help and support, going well beyond their willing tolerance of a writer's seclusion. The love of my wife, Mary Challinor, and my children, Benjamin and Hope, has provided me with shining examples of what is worth pursuing for its own sake, thereby answering for me the concrete question with which the body of this book begins.

Part One

Problem

I

Introduction

Despite its broad practical importance, the question whether we can reason practically about final ends may strike an archaic note. To show that relegating this question to the ersatz battleground of discarded philosophies would be a mistake, I begin by explaining my topic and its significance (§1). I then describe how some rather diffuse philosophical stances – ones that ultimately should be discarded – have made deliberating about ends seem impossible (§2). The reader will then request, and be granted, a preview of my argument as a whole and an indication of those more particular opponents against whom I will be arguing (§3). To explain the topic, I begin with an example.

§1. THE ISSUE

Having children is not for everyone a matter of deliberation. I do not simply mean that it can be the result of mistake or coercion. Far more commonly, it is blandly accepted as a natural, if not automatic, concomitant of marriage. What could be more traditional? Yet for some couples propagation is a matter of deliberate choice. Moral issues may impinge on this choice. An educated professional in an industrialized country, sufficiently worried that population growth will cause more pollution than the world can absorb, may refrain from having more than one child. The injustice and cruelty of the world may so disgust an impoverished citizen of a developing country that she refuses to bring a child into it. For others considering parenthood, the salient issues may be more personal. They may ask themselves whether they are ready to give up the spontaneity and thrill of footloose adventure so as to buckle down and support a family, be an example to children, and avoid orphaning them at an early age. Are they ready for the lifelong responsibility to another person, so less revocable than marriage? The peasant may worry about whether having another pair of hands in the fields will sufficiently offset having another

3

mouth to feed, and whether the authorities will fine the family for having more than its quota of children. Such are the questions that are apt to occur to someone, doubting the wisdom of well-worn ways, who begins to deliberate about whether to have a child.

All of these questions, including both those with moral overtones as well as those without, are practical questions, questions about what to do. There is no uniquely canonical way to phrase a practical question. It is often natural to say that one is deciding what one "should do," or wondering what one "ought to do," where this "should" and this "ought" are not anchored in any particular set of norms – moral, religious, social, or prudential – but rather stand *sans phrase*. Asking what is "to be done" similarly expresses openness to whatever reasons may seem relevant. We will also see that the general practical "ought" of these questions does not carry with it the presumption of complete and univocal advice sought when one asks, "What is the right thing to do in these circumstances?" A fleeting circumstance may occasion any of these sorts of practical questions, or they may take in concern with how one is to live a whole life. I may ask, for instance, what I am to do to mold my character to prepare for the likely frailty and dependence of old age. To be sure, some limits to deliberative questions – limitations we will be exploring in depth in Chapter III – center on the fact that deliberation starts from a practical question. As Aristotle noted, deliberation concerns "things that are in our power and can be done."[1] We do not deliberate about things past or about future events that we are sure are beyond our power to affect. "Practical deliberation" I take to be a redundant phrase.

That all deliberation is practical in the sense that it is concerned with what to do should not obscure the fact that we can deliberate in theoretical contexts. For instance, the scientist can deliberate about which strategy of experimentation to follow or which theory to bank his or her career upon. This deliberation can involve ends important to any scientific endeavor – ends, in brief, such as explanation, understanding, and knowledge. While conceptually it is one thing to decide what to do and another to decide what is true, in the practice of science these two activities merge.

Deliberation – thinking about what to do – can be a bad idea. Dangerous or fast-moving situations often call for rapid, resolute action and make hesitation a losing strategy. There are also less strategic and more substantive reasons not to deliberate in certain circumstances. Critical re-

---

1 Aristotle, *Nicomachean Ethics* (hereafter *N.E.*) 1112a29. Unless noted, all quotations from Aristotle will be from the revised Oxford translation (Aristotle 1984).

flection of the sort involved in deliberation can wither the fragile goodness of traditional or intimate practices, often crushed by self-consciousness (cf. Williams 1985, 148, 167–9). This incompatibility between certain goods and self-consciousness about them – whether in skills such as painting where it can lead to confusion or in sexual or ritual practices where it can lead to embarrassment – does not indict them as irrational. They might even be goods that a fully rational agent – whatever she is like – *would* endorse on ideally informed reflection. It's just that in any actual attempt to endorse them deliberately while engaging in them she trips over her own feet. In addition, it may be morally wrong to deliberate in certain cases. An excessively deliberative approach may involve "one thought too many." Williams influentially developed this sort of attack on impartial morality, with reference to the case of a person in a lifeboat who must choose between saving his or her spouse and saving a stranger (Williams 1981b, 16). A virtuous and loving spouse, Williams suggested, should straightaway prefer the spouse without stopping to reflect about whether favoring one's spouse is morally permitted.[2] Sometimes, deliberation is not appropriate. Returning to the issue of having children, we find a very different sort of moral limit on deliberation exemplified by those Catholic moralists who hold that since conception is by the grace of God, it is wrong to deliberate about whether or not to have children. Some present this as a special instance of the argument from the fragility of particular goods, here that of the union of man and wife in full openness to God's grace. Both contraception and active measures to increase fertility can be cast as attempts whose self-consciousness and aspiration to control interfere with this overriding good. For those who take this position, deliberating about whether to have children could properly take place only within the broader context of deciding whether to get married.

While deliberation is thus not always called for or even permissible, it is often necessary and apt. When it rightly occurs, it had better proceed rationally. Indeed, whether or not it is appropriate for the agent to deliberate in a given situation may depend upon whether he or she will be able to deliberate rationally. Because extreme fear can cloud judgment, deliberating in dangerous situations can be dangerous. You may have time to think up some tricky maneuver when the mugger asks for your wallet;

---

2 Naturally, many upholders of impartial morality leaped to answer this charge, some arguing that they do not hold morality to require the spouse to pause to deliberate (e.g., Herman 1984). My present purpose is not to enter into this controversy but just to note that both sides seem to accept the view that requiring deliberation of a certain kind would be an intrusion upon the integrity of the agent.

but if fear (and adrenaline) will addle your thinking, causing you to light on some such hare-brained response as trying to run, you would do best to train yourself to hand over your wallet automatically to any mugger who points a pistol your way. Setting out in general when deliberation is appropriate is not a sane task. It is a tricky and a substantively loaded matter. The presence of strong emotion, by itself, does not make deliberation dangerous; indeed, as I will be arguing in §27, even strong emotions such as fear can sometimes fruitfully focus deliberation. There will be no simple, hard-and-fast rules here. Whether deliberation in a given context offers the prospect of rationality, however, seems important to whether it is there appropriate.

This fact gives my topic, the possibility of deliberating rationally about ends or purposes, practical significance. For reasons that I will canvass briefly in the next section, many today seem convinced that we cannot deliberate rationally about ends. Perhaps only implicitly, via the sort of reasoning I have just laid out, they take this limitation to excuse them for not attempting to deliberate about ends. If the thesis of this book is correct, this unfortunately limits their lives. We can deliberate rationally about ends. Often, we must do so in order to reach a rationally defensible decision. To assume in a blanket fashion that rational deliberation cannot extend to adopting ends is wrongly to suppose that intellectual effort cannot be fruitfully brought to bear upon what matters to us most.

Thus, to return to our example, having children might well be conceived as an end – that is, as something for the sake of which actions are done.[3] It would even be reasonable to think of it as a final end – that is, as something for the sake of which an action is done or is to be done and for which the action would still be done even if no other advantage flowed from it. Having children might be considered intrinsically worthwhile, wholly apart from whether or not one's children will support one in one's old age or contribute to the establishment of world peace. To understand having children in this way is to place it within a complex practice – and not, say, as reduced to bodily acts of childbearing and feeding – whose goods can only be fully understood from within the concrete social traditions in terms of which it goes on (cf. MacIntyre 1984, 193–4). Rituals of baptism or redemption, balloons or chocolate cigars; reciprocal patterns of mutual kvetching about lack of sleep; and intricate stroller

---

3 The terminology set out in this paragraph, with its broad sense of "end," within the range of which "final end" is distinguished, is adapted (as I see it) from Aristotle: see Richardson 1992a. It will be developed more fully in §7.

dances for discreetly displaying parental pride are all examples of what may go into constituting what "having children" will mean in a given social context.

Yet this complexity, which stems from the way ends are embedded in layers of social practice affecting their interpretation and significance, also threatens to divert our attention from the ends themselves. Pursuing any one end yields many different goods and bads. This being so, someone who is convinced that we cannot deliberate rationally about ends will indeed truncate deliberation about whether or not to have children; but he need not simply say that this is a matter on which, the intellect being silent, gut feelings must decide. There remain various time-honored patterns of deliberation that assume the ends as given and nondeliberable, but that nonetheless attempt to cope with the ways they conflict when the pursuit of one good brings bads in its train or involves forsaking other goods. One method that may seem appropriate to the decision whether or not to have children is that of pros and cons. Benjamin Franklin summed up this form of "Moral Algebra" in a letter to Joseph Priestley (quoted in Bain 1865, 424–5):

In the affair of so much importance to you, wherein you ask my advice, I cannot, for want of sufficient premises, counsel you *what* to determine; but, if you please, I will tell you *how*. When those difficult cases occur, they are difficult, chiefly because, while we have them under consideration, all the reasons *pro* and *con* are not present to the mind at the same time; but sometimes one set present themselves, and at other times another, the first being out of sight. Hence the various purposes or inclinations that alternately prevail, and the uncertainty that perplexes us.

To get over this, my way is, to divide half a sheet of paper by a line into two columns; writing over the one *pro* and over the other *con*; then, during three or four days' consideration, I put down, under the different heads, short hints of the different motives, that at different times occur to me, *for* or *against* the measure. When I have thus got them altogether in one view, I endeavor to estimate their respective weights; and when I find two (one on each side) that seem equal, I strike them both out. If I find a reason *pro* equal to some *two* reasons *con*, I strike out the *three*. If I judge some two reasons *con* equal to some *three* reasons *pro*, I strike out the *five*; and thus proceeding, I find where the balance lies. . . . And though the weight of reasons cannot be taken with the precision of algebraic quantities, yet, when each is thus considered separately and comparatively, and the whole lies before me, I think I can judge better, and am less liable to take a false step; and, in fact, I have found great advantage from this kind of equation, in what may be termed *moral* or *prudential algebra*.

Franklin's remarkable confidence in his ability to weigh heterogeneous reasons against each other here shows up in his silence about any restrictions on the compared reasons that must be met for them to cancel one another out. Whether this hearty confidence in simple weighing amounts to much is a question I will address in Chapter V. If anything really can be weighed against anything else, then final ends, too, can be weighed.

For the slightly more modest weigher, who wants to think of reasons as being similar before crossing them out as offsetting, such a prudential algebra will encourage seeing activities as means to further ends rather than as themselves choiceworthy for their own sake. By this restricted version of the method, a simplified course of deliberation about whether to have children might go as follows: Children bring joy, but then again so does work, which competes with children for time commitment; hence, the two cancel each other out in joy. On income, by contrast, children are a net drain whereas work is the main source. Clearly, best not to have children! Here we want to respond that this deliberator has doubly missed the point. In coming to doubt whether it is best for him or her to have children (to use yet another locution for a general practical question), he or she has thrown into suspense a central aspect of his or her system of ends. To attempt then to respond to this situation by employing a prudential algebra that treats ends as fixed and has no place for their interpretation is to fail to take one's own questioning seriously. Someone wondering whether to have children should not presume that the qualities of joy that they bring can be offset in any simple way even by the joys of hard work well rewarded. Yet meditating on these qualitative differences moves in the opposite direction from collecting reasons under pro or con headings on a short list. Worse, Franklin's method does not invite the deliberator to ask whether having children is worth pursuing for its own sake. It encourages reducing all considerations to the same level, as commensurable pros and cons, ordered only in terms of "weight" and not in terms of what is to be sought for the sake of what. Nussbaum (1991) eloquently discusses the human costs of this sort of attitude. And in any case, taking the net effect on disposable income to settle this decision sidesteps the central issue and affronts the goods involved. Income is typically not a final end, but a means to other things – often, to supporting children. This deliberator should be trying to decide whether income will have that importance for them, or some other. If this deliberator treats the option of having children as itself merely a means to achieving other goods of the sort that might be listed in the column of pros, then perhaps he or she is in fact not ready for parenthood.

The more rigorous models of deliberation now standard in welfare economics and decision theory make explicit the setting aside of deliberation about ends that Franklin's algebra merely suggests. These modern approaches, which I will criticize in some detail in §15, assume as given a set of preferences or a "space" of goods. Given these, they can spin out sophisticated theorems expressing the requirements for coming up with, say, a complete ordering of one's preferences or for coping rationally with risk distributed across different dimensions of value. The case of whether to have children already suggests, however, that these wonderfully precise models cover only the less important part of deliberation. About what matters most – settling upon ends – they are largely silent. Sometimes they go beyond silence, explicitly ruling out the possibility of rational deliberation of ends, as in the following statement by one of the most famous theorists of this school, Maurice Allais (1979 [1953], 70):

> It cannot be too strongly emphasized *that there are no criteria for the rationality of ends as such other than the condition of consistency.* Ends are completely arbitrary. To prefer highly dispersed random outcomes may seem irrational to the prudent, but for somebody with this penchant, there is nothing irrational about it. This area is like that of tastes: they are what they are, and differ from one person to the next.

Yet many of their proponents tout these formal decision theories as "complete" accounts of practical reasoning, whose sometimes counterintuitive results must be accepted as the price of supreme theoretical unity. It is as if a fully consistent and effectively functioning word processing software program were accepted as delineating a complete theory of writing, despite its silence about what to write; or again, as if an atlas were accepted as giving a complete theory of travel, despite its silence about where to go.

Yes, such silence can be hard to avoid. Trying to explain why one pursues what one does take to be worth pursuing for its own sake ties the tongues of the most articulate. This is after all not accidental: It is part of the role of final ends to answer questions about why to do things. If they themselves are thrown into question, what can we say? I find myself in this predicament when called upon to explain why I love philosophy. On the one hand, pointing to what the activity of philosophy yields – such as intellectual excitement, clarity, continuing the evolution of a certain culture, and perhaps even remotely contributing to the public good – unsettles the claim that I value it for its own sake, apart from any other goods in which it results. On the other hand, picking out certain constituents of the activity of philosophy as I understand it – such as pursuing general questions about reason and the good – seems only to postpone the question why. For simply to describe the activity of philosophy more finely is not to answer a question about why it is to be pursued for its own sake.

Yet we do sometimes criticize intrinsic desires as irrational. In some of these cases, we do so on the grounds that desires involve a distinction that seems arbitrary, and for which we can imagine no adequate rationale (cf. Parfit 1984, 124). For example, consider Jack, who seeks out and values opportunities for medical research with anyone not named Henry. We can suppose something explains this quirk of Jack's, namely that a Henry in his second-grade class did something nasty to him, but that the residue of this past injury is neither so powerful that it would ruin Jack's enjoyment were he actually to do research with someone named Henry nor so prominent in his mind that he would cite this as his reason for not wanting a Henry as collaborator. If he were to work with a Henry, he would enjoy it and the quirk would disappear (cf. Millgram, forthcoming). Jack realizes that this may well be true: He simply doesn't want to work with a Henry. He has no other reason to avoid working with Henrys. Now, if the only researcher in the area who could work productively with Jack on the problems preoccupying him is named Henry, and Jack forgoes this opportunity, I think we will agree that he is being irrational in pursuing for its own sake only research work with other-named partners. He has no reason – or no good reason – to superimpose this arbitrary distinction within the category of goods that his research aims mark out. (This is what, in the jurisprudence of the United States Constitution, counts as "irrationality" under the Equal Protection Clause. A statute fails the standard of rationality if it imposes a distinction among citizens that has no realistically conceivable rationale.)[4]

Notice, to anticipate a theme that will be developed in Chapter VI, that this judgment of irrationality hinges on this agent having nothing to say about why all Henrys are special. His ability to give a discursive explanation gives out at that point. A theory of rational deliberation of ends must show that discursive rationality does not give out every time one reaches a final end. Consider the person who is indifferent to all but philosophical wisdom. She will knowingly forgo any amount of scientific or historical wisdom rather than give up even the smallest bit of philosophical insight. It is not that she believes that history or science are worthless inquiries. She does not believe the old story that philosophy is the

---

4 *F. S. Royster Guano Co.* v. *Virginia*, 253 U.S. 412, 415 [1920]. Compare also the "principle of individuation by justifiers" offered in Broome 1991, 103, discussed further in §15: "Outcomes should be distinguished as different if and only if they differ in a way that makes it rational to have a preference between them."

queen of the sciences. She simply values philosophical wisdom, and not the other forms of wisdom, for its own sake. And here we are tempted to say that this is just an aspect of human valuing, that the question why can be pursued only until one reaches a final end, valued for its own sake. Against this conclusion that reasoning runs out at final ends, however, I will be arguing (in §7) that it typically relies upon an overly simple understanding of what a final end is, and (in subsequent chapters) that the fact that final ends provide answers to what is sought for its own sake does not mean that rational deliberation cannot extend to adopting them. In any case, it would be rash to throw out as irrational the indifference to nonphilosophical wisdom just because it makes a distinction within a broader value category. The contrast between this case and Jack's highlights the substantive judgment involved in declaring a refusal to collaborate with a Henry irrational: Simply picking out Henrys as special is not a *good* reason. Picking out philosophy as special may be.

We also criticize the positive value categories that agents pick out – as opposed to distinctions within broader value categories – as being irrational. A well-known example is Rawls's grass-blade counter (Rawls 1971, 432–3). This imaginary person is one

whose only pleasure is to count blades of grass in various geometrically shaped areas such as park squares and well-trimmed lawns. He is otherwise intelligent and actually possesses unusual skills, since he manages to survive by solving difficult mathematical problems for a fee. . . . Naturally we would be surprised that such a person should exist. Faced with his case, we would try out other hypotheses. Perhaps he is peculiarly neurotic and in early life acquired an aversion to human fellowship. . . . But if we allow that his nature is to enjoy this activity and not to enjoy any other, and that there is no feasible way to alter his condition, then surely a rational plan for him will center around this activity.

That is, if we were to define the rationality of a life plan as taking all of an agent's intrinsic desires for granted, then this way of life may count as rational for him. Yet the example also tends to show that our judgments of rationality are not limited by this sort of assumption. If we are forced by a definition to grant the life plan rational, then we may still count the individual as irrational. Whether we do will depend importantly on how his ends are described. A grass-blade counter who recognizes his neurosis sufficiently to be able to say to himself that he must count to be happy (or to avoid depression) seems considerably more rational than one who simply says that he counts blades for its own sake. Perhaps the latter counter is beyond reasoning with; but if not, we will consider that there are rational grounds for getting him to change his mind about what he pursues for its own sake. It is not rational to take counting blades of grass as a final end.

Here, again, my point is just that we sometimes criticize intrinsic desires as irrational. I am not yet trying to set out the basis on which we do so. This may be quite narrow. We might, for instance, recognize a distinction between the grass-blade counter and the (actual) person who has collected 4,300 four-leaf clovers. What admirable persistence and luck we might see in the latter, what neurotic compulsion in the former! The distinction, here, slices finely (compare that noted by Parfit 1984, 123, between a good whim and a bad whim). Our judgments of the irrationality of intrinsic desires are freighted with substantive presuppositions; but that is just to be expected. Substantive rationality, which judges the rationality of someone's intrinsic commitments, must carry substantive baggage. Yet judgments of substantive irrationality are part of what a theory of rational deliberation should enable us to explain.

There is one more layer of potential irrationality. People sometimes inappropriately connect an activity with an end for the sake of which it is pursued. For example, suppose that we do decide that it is perfectly rational to value the collection of four-leaf clovers for its own sake. Even so, this does not mean that we would recognize it as rational to choose to have children solely in order to use their good eyesight, small hands, and free labor to speed up one's collection of four-leaf clovers. This is a bad reason to choose to have children. Its irrationality seems to consist in improperly ordering activities as means to ends. While the objection, here, may be partly a moral one, against using children as mere means, it is not entirely that. We would not equally object to the farmer who decided to have children in order to have additional hands to help with the harvest. Unlike having children to further a hobby of collecting four-leaf clovers, this is not crazy. We have the sense that having children ranks higher and stands more centrally in human activity than collecting good-luck charms (though not necessarily more centrally than keeping food on the table), and that, if anything, such hobbies should be regulated by reference to procreation (say, as a superstitious way of enhancing luck with fertility) but not the other way around. Again, I am intending here not to defend this sort of assumption, but simply to point out that this kind of ordering of final ends represents an additional basis on which we sometimes criticize as irrational someone's conception of what is intrinsically valuable.

This brief survey of ways in which we criticize the deliberations of others suggests that we at least implicitly believe that we can deliberate rationally about ends. To hold the explicit position that we cannot is to withdraw from criticizing agents in these ways. Despite the commonsense evidence that we can and do deliberate rationally about ends, however, a number of highly influential philosophical doctrines have narrowed our recognition (at least in the modern West) of the extent of practical reason. One of these philosophical obstacles to allowing for rational deliberation of ends has already been alluded to, for it builds upon the fact that final ends seem to be answers to the question why something is to be pursued, and hence not themselves subject to this questioning. This and the other important obstacles will be canvassed in the next section.

§2. OBSTACLES

Understanding the motivation of this book's argument requires being aware of the philosophical obstacles to recognizing that we deliberate rationally about ends. Obstacles to this recognition are not the same as opponents of my thesis. I see my overall tasks as first clearing away philosophical obstacles to allowing that we can set new final ends rationally and then constructing a positive account about how we can do so. As I will explain in the next section, in setting out my strategy of argument, more direct philosophical opponents will be encountered as I undertake these two tasks, negative and positive. Here I will simply sketch the main obstacles in preliminary fashion, leaving a more exact statement of the difficulties to the chapters that deal with them. As will be apparent, these are barriers to recognizing even a form of relative rationality (§4) – rationality relative to an individual's starting points, as end–means rationality is – in deliberation pertaining to ends. The principal obstacles are three: resistance to the idea that ends are subject to deliberation at all, insistence that rational deliberation must presume ends as criteria of decision rather than subjecting them to revision, and last-ditch conviction that an ultimate end, at least, lies by its very nature beyond the reach of practical reasoning to vary or adopt. I will call these the obstacles of scope, system, and source.

The first obstacle, the belief that practical questions about ends overstep the scope of deliberation altogether, let alone that of rational deliberation, in turn has a double origin in the Western philosophical tradition. It can arise from a contrast between description and prescription or as an analytic claim about the nature of deliberation.

The classic tag for these first two rationales for the first obstacle is Hume's dictum that "reason is, and ought only to be the slave of the passions, and can never pretend to any other office than to serve and obey them" (Hume 1986, II:iii:3, p. 415). Whether the view was Hume's need not concern us, and has been argued both ways by interpreters.[5] I will call the view "pseudo-Humean." The core of the pseudo-Humean position is the claim that while reason is concerned with ascertaining the truth of statements or beliefs, desires are not such as to be true or false. Although reason can get a grip on factual and logical questions, it cannot, on this view, settle purely prescriptive ones. For this reason, Hume wrote, " 'Tis not contrary to reason to prefer the destruction of the whole world to the scratching of my finger" (Hume 1986, II:iii:3, p. 416). This bit of Hume, at least, tends to indicate that he would allow for no rational criticism of Jack's aversion to Henrys, counting blades of grass, or having children so that they can help collect clovers. The negative lesson of the alignment of ends with intrinsic desires on the prescriptive side of things is bolstered, on the pseudo-Humean account, by a motivational point. The passions, while not true or false, are nonetheless depicted as the masters of reason. The passions provide motivation and direction; reason's task is to do their bidding. The passions get instrumental reasoning – reasoning from end to means – going.

That deliberation must always begin from some end, if understood distributively, that is, as holding strictly of each episode of deliberation, may be thought to provide a third reason why deliberation's scope cannot include setting or revising final ends. As I have noted, this limitation may be regarded as an analytic truth about deliberation. Deliberation, it might be held, is essentially the selection of means to some end. Here, the best-known classical tag for the view is Aristotle's statement that "we deliberate not about ends but about what contributes to ends" (*N.E.* 1112b11–12). As in the case of Hume, it is debated whether Aristotle really intended this claim to rule out deliberation about ends of the sort I defend.[6] In any case, as this recent translation acknowledges, deliberation may include ascertaining the constituent components of some end as well as assessing alternative causal means to it. Either way, however, deliberation must begin from some end. This fact tempts us, therefore, to see that end as setting the bounds on the deliberation to which it gives rise.

For these three kinds of reason, then, many doubt that deliberation can extend to ends. Since ends are seen as essentially prescriptive, they are not

---

5 For a postrevisionist interpretation according to which Hume really does, after all, take the strong instrumentalist position I am calling "pseudo-Humean," see Piper 1988–9. I do not find Piper's textual case wholly compelling.

6 For my sketch of how Aristotelian practical reasoning can settle on new final ends, see Richardson 1988. Tuozzo 1991, however, may be right that this reasoning cannot come under the rubric of Aristotle's *bouleusis*, traditionally translated "deliberation."

subject to the constraint of fitting with the facts. Since our ends (as expressed in intrinsic desires) are what motivate us, they set the limits on practical reasoning rather than being subject to limits themselves. And since deliberation naturally reflects these inherent metaphysical (or epistemological) and psychological facts, it is incoherent to speak of deliberating about whether a given item is a final end. Final ends fall outside deliberation's scope.

But wait: What happens when ends conflict? Here the latter-day pseudo-Humean may initially seem more accepting of deliberation about ends than is Hume, for contemporary economics and decision theory squarely face the pervasive contingent conflicts among ends and desires. Here some further scope for the criticism of desires emerges; however, there simultaneously arises a second obstacle to deliberation about ends, one which focuses on the sort of rational system required in order to resolve practical conflicts rationally.

This second obstacle, that of system, can be explained more simply than the first. It revolves around the idea that commensurability is a prerequisite of rational choice, an idea that underlies the appeal of the maximizing formulas of contemporary utilitarianism and rational choice theory. Things would work out very simply indeed if there were at bottom but one kind of intrinsic value – pleasure, say – in terms of which all value could be measured together, or commensurated. Then rational choice would concern itself with maximizing that "commensurans," as I will call the commensurating value or good. The existence of serious practical conflicts tends to undercut the plausibility of such a simple value monism. Still, it may seem that resolving such conflicts rationally depends upon weighing the conflicting values on a single scale and choosing that option which yields the best score thereon. In deciding whether to have children, for instance, one may feel torn between being entirely devoted to one's work and experiencing the intimate love of parenthood. This choice might be made rationally if, for example, each of these values could be adequately assessed as a contribution to one's happiness; for then one could decide whether or not to have children in terms of which option would lead to greater happiness. Since this approach depends upon treating the commensurating end – here, happiness – as the one final end relevant for this choice, the idea that commensurability is a prerequisite of rational choice seems to rule out rational deliberation of ends. Practical rationality, on this account, depends upon holding some end fixed for each choice so as to commensurate the values that compete in that choice. Practical rationality thereby resists any thoroughgoing deliberation of ends.

15

Still, this insistence on commensurability obviously leaves room for a considerable amount of systematization. It may take deliberative work, or at least practical reasoning of some kind, in order to arrive at a clear view of the commensurating end(s). This will be especially true if there is just one commensurans – pleasure, happiness, utility, or what have you – in terms of which all competing values are to be weighed. Some deliberation about subordinate ends therefore seems compatible with this picture. Deliberation about the single ultimate end that serves to commensurate all subordinate considerations, however, has no place on this picture. This observation brings us to the threshold of the third obstacle.

The third obstacle to recognizing rational deliberation of ends, the source obstacle, concerns the notion of an ultimate end and its place in deliberation. While there might be ways in which we might deliberate rationally about subordinate ends, we must always lean, it might be thought, on some more final end that is held fixed. Ends provide the framework within which we deliberate. Without some end held fixed, deliberation will lack a target. These reflections lead to the conclusion that an ultimate end is an end from which no episode of deliberation can abstract. An ultimate end, it is suggested, is the source of rational valuation: It is the ultimately fixed background against which all deliberation necessarily proceeds insofar as it is rational. The last proviso is important, for it indicates how an ultimate end can be viewed as the necessary aim of rational deliberation and yet have substantive content, for those acting irrationally may fail to pursue it.[7] Echoing the gerundives of Aristotle and of Aquinas, this view holds that the ultimate end is to be pursued by the rational agent. It is the nature of the ultimate end, on this view, to be the necessary touchstone of rational choice. It is perhaps even the source of value also in a more literal sense, giving rise to all of the value in subordinate ends and pursuits. Be that as it may, the ultimate end itself, on this conception, clearly cannot be thrown into question by rational deliberation. Many modern thinkers who allow for some rational systematization of conflicting subordinate values or aims nonetheless deny the possibility of rational deliberation of ends on account of the source obstacle. Their resistance will not be fully overcome unless we can show that rational deliberation can extend to the level of the ultimate end.

In seeking to overcome these philosophical barriers to recognizing ra-

---

7 There might be certain very broad readings of "the good," "desire-satisfaction," or "happiness" that make it analytically true that all deliberate human action aims at one of them. Perhaps the interpretations of these that would make these claims come out true would make them uninteresting (cf. Stocker 1979, Velleman 1992).

16

tional deliberation about ends, this book aims to establish that we *can* deliberate rationally about ends. There are two aspects to this effort, critical and constructive. The influence of the three obstacles just set out must be diagnosed more precisely, their philosophical import clearly delineated, and their implications undercut. This counterattack will already show that rational deliberation of ends is possible, in a sense; for it will show that there is no contradiction in supposing that rational deliberation extends to ends. The effect of these obstacles on philosophical and popular imagination, however, makes it equally necessary to set out constructively and in a general way *how* we can deliberate rationally about ends. Unless an alternative, positive picture of deliberation is put in the place of the instrumentalist ones that now hold sway (especially in the form criticized in §15), merely establishing the logical possibility of rational deliberation of ends will carry no conviction. My opponents will rightly want to know how this deliberation will go; and the skepticism that their arguments have engendered will still prevent many from realizing the possibilities of rationality that exist. Accordingly, the bulk of this book will be devoted to explaining how we may deliberate rationally about ends. As a constructive suggestion, this theory takes account of general but perhaps contingent facts about the nature of human beings and their societies, about human psychology including the ways we reflect and the ways judgment and emotion interact in our thinking, and about the ways in which our various ends and commitments tend to clash. Although my proposal idealizes in certain ways, I aim not so much to establish a pure ideal for the perfectly rational deliberator as to indicate to actual persons how they – you and I – can deliberate rationally about ends. The idealizations that I employ will mainly concern how rational deliberation can extend to ultimate ends (in Chapter X) and how a rational bridging of deep cultural disagreement over ends can overcome the myriad concrete divergences that result from contrasting upbringings (in Chapter XIV). In both of these cases, we may rightly be more pessimistic than in the general case of rational deliberation of ends about whether the possibilities for rationality that I defend will actually be realized in our practices. Again, though, I have striven to present possibilities that could be realized, given what we know about human nature and society.

I am by no means such an optimist as to think that even a wide acceptance that the possibilities for rationality that I describe are real will do much to realize them. The nonphilosophical obstacles of interest, perversity, vice, and stupidity will remain the most obdurate ones. If the philosophical case for the possibility of rational deliberation of ends has practical importance, that is more likely because we already do deliberate rationally about ends than because recognizing the possibility will cause us to deliberate more rationally. If, as I believe, we do often deliberate rationally about ends, we will gain in self-understanding if we recognize this about ourselves. These gains will especially improve politics, by correcting for the pervasive subjectivism of currently influential understandings of democratic participation.

If we do in fact sometimes deliberate rationally about ends, then why cannot my argument take the short form of an argument from existence to possibility (*ab esse ad posse*)? Because the terrain of rationality is too contested to allow any case history to be acknowledged by all as an instance of rational deliberation. Unless the philosophical obstacles are cleared away and a positive account of deliberation of ends put in their place, rational deliberation of ends will not be recognized for what it is. I seek to lay out its practical possibility, its accessibility to actual agents, in a way that clearly undercuts or overcomes the philosophical obstacles. Accordingly, my use of realistic cases of deliberation as evidence for certain kinds of possibility will go hand in hand with developing a theory about how we may deliberate rationally about ends.

§3. STRATEGY AND OPPONENTS

While the whole of this book is devoted to defending the possibility of rational deliberation of ends, different parts of it may be of relatively greater interest to different readers, depending upon which obstacles to this possibility they find the most daunting or impressive. After some further discussion of practical reasoning in general in the following chapter, the main parts of the book take up these obstacles in turn. Part Two addresses the scope obstacle, attacking the view that we cannot deliberate about ends at all. Part Three examines the system obstacle. It undercuts the position that we cannot deliberate rationally when final ends conflict because rational choice depends upon commensurability, putting in its place an ideal of reflective coherence. Part Four then overcomes the source obstacle by showing that deliberation along these latter lines can extend to ultimate ends as well. It is left to Part Five to deal with a new, fourth obstacle that arises as a reaction against my positive proposals about deliberation, which turn on a parallel with theory building. The worry that then arises is: What if an individual is committed, not just to incommensurable ends, but to incommensurable conceptions of final ends? To address this problem, Part Five delves into deliberation among people who deeply disagree, to see what light this sheds on the case of a single person with such radically divergent attachments.

To give you, my readers, a somewhat fuller preview of the argument, to guide you to chapters that touch on subjects that may be of interest to you even apart from my overall thesis, and to indicate whom I will take on as direct opponents, let me indicate in more detail the work of the chapters to come.

In Chapter II, I set out the general understanding of practical reasoning that frames this study. I explain that while I do not take it to imply objectivity, and work within what may be relativized to an agent's commitments, I nonetheless leave the door open to truth and objectivity. The focus is on what should count as reasoning, rather than on what reason (the purported faculty) can accomplish. Practical reasoning is distinguished from practical inference, the reconstruction of whose "logic" being a task I renounce. In so doing, I attack views, such as that of Audi (1989), that build their account of practical reasoning around the "practical syllogism." Once this assimilation is blocked, it becomes easier to defang the scope obstacle.

Part Two takes up the two main variants of the scope obstacle separately. After first analyzing the notion of an end, Chapter III confronts the analytic aspect of this first obstacle, allocating it its grain of truth, but arguing that ends are subject to deliberation. As §9 argues, my assessment of the scope of rational deliberation must accept internalism about reasons for action, according to which reasons must be intelligibly linked back to initial motivations, in a generalized form. I do not, therefore, count an "internalist" such as Bernard Williams as an opponent.[8] On this footing, Chapter IV then takes up the motivational aspect of the scope obstacle, and shows how practical reasoning can set up new ends. My claim there is that this process has just as good a claim to rationality as ordinary end–means reasoning.

To neutralize the objection to rational deliberation of ends that arises out of the idea that commensurability is a prerequisite of rational choice, Part Three first locates the power of this idea in a particular ideal of practical system. It then undercuts this ideal and replaces it with another.

---

8 While some might count the Williams of "Internal and External Reasons" (Williams 1981a) as a neo-Humean because of his purported opposition to Kant, it has never been clear to me how Williams would exclude Kant's incentive of pure respect for the moral law – self-produced by a rational concept though it be (Kant 1964a, Ak. 401n.) – from the set of initial motivations. Since, as I see it, Williams's quite general internalism does not even exclude Kant's view, I see no great danger in accepting it.

The ideal of practical system I attack was most explicitly developed in Sidgwick 1981 [1907], and it is Sidgwick's argument I reconstruct and then undercut. Something like his ideal, however, attracts many utilitarians and consequentialists to this day. In the course of setting out the form of value commensurability relevant to deliberation in Chapter V, I have occasion to attack those, such as Harsanyi (1977), who mistake the preference-based theories of the economist and the standard decision theorist for accounts of deliberation. I will show that these accounts are useless in deliberation, except as convenient ways of packaging information about attitudes toward risk. On the basis of an examination of the notion of a tragic choice, this chapter also argues that, on the relevant definition, and contrary to the hopes of theorists such as Broome (1991), incommensurable values exist. Does this mean that rational choice is impossible in some cases? Chapter VI reconstructs the argument that it would (this argument was already outlined in §2). There are various ways this argument can be undercut. My own strategy is to develop an alternative conception of practical systematization, which begins by replacing Sidgwick's leading metaphor of an appeal to a higher authority with the metaphor of first-personal reflection.

The next two chapters fill in this alternative account of systematization. Chapter VII explores the complicated notion of practical coherence, distinguishing its many aspects. Contrary to Bittner 1989, for example, I argue that strong practical coherence is not a peremptory, a priori requirement of rationality; but I do show that a strong pragmatic case can be made for building mutual support among ends. Chapter VIII presents the core of my positive account of rational deliberation of ends, namely the holistic standard of rationality appropriate in the revision and specification of ends. The relevant kind of holism[9] is introduced by means of Dewey's salutary and archetypally pragmatist emphasis on the revisability of ends. While Dewey's holism is shown to be insufficiently accepting of theory, and case-based weighting theories of deliberation such as that presented in Hurley 1989, which presume as fixed a list of basic values, are insufficiently holistic, the operation of specification, as defined in Chapter IV, enables us to combine the virtues of each sort of view.

Part Four addresses the last of the initial obstacles by showing that

---

9 Throughout this book, unless discussing specific theses of W. V. O. Quine or Donald Davidson, I mean "holism" in a quite general and loose sense, to refer to an absence of segmentation and a mutual relevance of all members of the whole. I do not, in other words, intend it in the more specific and demanding senses attacked by Fodor and Lepore 1992.

rational deliberation can extend to establishing ultimate ends. Since I am still working within relative rationality and within a generalized internalism, this establishment is in a sense relativized to the individual deliberator's initial commitments. It will be important, therefore, to show the range of objective criticism potentially allowed for by this way of setting ultimate ends. For this reason, Chapter X shows how rational deliberation can track the philosophical argumentation of two widely differing views: Aristotle's account of the human good and Rawls's theory of justice. My opponents in this Part include those – whom I cannot name but am confident exist – who believe that the restrictions of internalism and relative rationality sharply limit the scope for rational criticism of ends. They also include philosophers – such as Aristotle and Kant as tendentiously but illuminatingly described by Korsgaard (1986a) – who see an ultimate end as a source of value, and hence only as an item from which deliberation can begin. Against this understanding, Chapter IX puts forward a competing analysis of the idea of an ultimate end, one that straightforwardly extends Chapter III's analysis of the notion of a final end.

As I noted above, Part Five moves from the personal to the interpersonal plane, mainly for defensive reasons. Since the possibility of rational deliberation of ends, on my view, depends upon the individual building a coherent theory of his or her ends, the question arises whether a person of deeply divided cultural commitments can deliberate rationally about ends. Since this is an objection against my original proposal, I do not here face direct opponents. In developing my position, however, I oppose the influential argument of Davidson (1986c) to the effect that one cannot make sense of the idea of conceptual incommensurability. To the contrary, I do make sense of it. On the other side, however, I argue against cultural relativist writings such as Feyerabend 1978 and neo-Nietzschean positions such as that of Foucault 1977, that conceptual incommensurability is not a bar to rational deliberation – at least not when the incommensurable views are both held by one person, the form of the problem that I am forced to address in defending my position. My abstract claims in Part Five are tested by reference to the possibilities for reasonable dialogue between a liberal Westerner and an orthodox Sunni Muslim judge about the treatment of women who bring rape complaints in Pakistan.

II

Practical reasoning

Setting out to show that we can deliberate rationally about ends, it behooves me to articulate what I take to be the marks of whether a given course of deliberation is rational or not, and more generally what I have in mind by "practical reasoning." The terrain of rationality being what is contested, there is no noncontroversial way to lay out these marks. There is no core concept of rationality shared between me and my opponents, such that simply setting out a counterexample to their limited view would force them to recognize that we can deliberate rationally about ends. Yet I shall not simply concede them the word "rational," and accept some other term – perhaps "reasonable" – to cover well carried out deliberation of ends.[1] This fact provides one of my main motivations for taking the more indirect route of first clearing away the three philosophical obstacles to allowing for this possibility. Although the marks of rationality that I develop here may accordingly be expected to beg some questions, they do not provide the first premises of my argument. I set them out nonetheless in order that the reader may better understand the goal towards which this book is directed. For similar reasons, I want to situate (practical) reasoning as I understand it in relation to issues of objectivity and truth (§4) and to explain that although it cannot usefully be captured by a "logic of practical inference" (§5), the general practical "ought" does give it some logical structure (§6).

§4. MARKS OF REASONING

I call reasoning "practical" if it concerns what to do. Sorting out the contribution of different psychological faculties is not my con-

---

1 While Rawls's distinction between the Reasonable and the Rational might be thought to suggest this tack, in fact his notion of the Rational allows for some deliberation about

cern.[2] To determine whether a given psychological process has proceeded rationally, we do not need to know what aspects of it were contributed by which faculty. All the less so if we are skeptical about there being any hard-and-fast ways to divide the psyche into, say, reason on the one hand and the passions on the other. Recent philosophical and empirical work on the emotions, for instance, has tended to show that they combine desiderative, evaluative, and cognitive aspects in complex ways. In short, the question about whether deliberation has proceeded rationally differs from Hume's question about whether reason (the faculty) is inert or not. Given the difficulties of separating the faculties, the former is a better question.[3] Even in relation to whether or not deliberation has proceeded rationally, I aim to provide neither necessary nor sufficient conditions. Instead, my goal is to construct an account of how we might deliberate rationally about ends. Since, as I have said above, I do not regard deliberating rationally as itself the ultimate end – and a fortiori not deliberating rationally about ends – I leave open whether rational deliberation always requires deliberation about ends of the sort I defend.

My aim, then, is to argue that there is something we can do, despite the obstacles to recognizing that we can, namely to deliberate rationally concerning final ends. In setting aside the ambition of providing necessary or sufficient conditions for the use of "rational," my project contrasts with those that aim to provide an analysis of "rational." An important recent example of the latter is Gibbard 1990, which develops an "expressivist" analysis of "rational" analogous to (although more developed than) familiar emotivist analyses of "right." The central idea of Gibbard's theory is that to think something rational is to express one's commitment to norms that permit it. Now, although I will be careful to present an account of rational deliberation more compatible with objective truth about what

---

ends: see Rawls 1971, 419–20. For Rawls, the Reasonable is distinguished not by its extension to ends but by its being built around moral constraints (constraints of right): see Rawls 1980, 528.

2 In my relative unconcern with allocating roles to subparts of the psyche, I claim an affinity with Aristotle, who – especially in the area of human action – was quite informal and ad hoc about the ways it is useful to analyze the psyche for the task at hand (cf. Richardson 1992b). Sometimes, in fact, his silence about such matters is quite frustrating for those who would insist upon knowing which part of the soul is contributing what operation: Think of the difficulties of sorting out the respective contributions of moral virtue and practical wisdom given the description of their joint work in Book VI of the *Nicomachean Ethics*.

3 Contrast, also, the questions, how deliberative reasoning can be causally efficacious (cf. Velleman 1989) and how reasoning can guide thought (Wittgenstein 1958, Anscombe 1989, Audi 1989).

is or is not rational than Gibbard's expressivism, I do not think of such an analysis of "rational" as a primary opponent. While some of the details of Gibbard's theory are inimical to recognizing the possibility of rational deliberation of ends, his overall expressivism is not.[4] For the most part, I simply avoid discussing alternative analyses of "rational." Just as Rawls lets the sense of the term "justice" emerge from his developing theory, I prefer to let the sense of "rational," as I understand it, emerge from my developing theory.

In relation to objectivity, my argument that we can deliberate rationally about ends aims lower than many previous ones so as to have a better chance of hitting the mark. Past philosophers who have tried to defend this possibility have tended to merge this effort with the far more demanding one of listing the "rational ends," the ends endorsed by rationality for all agents. In other words, working to establish that we can deliberate rationally about ends gets hitched to trying to say in advance what the outcome of that deliberation will be for all rational agents – namely to endorse a particular conception of the ultimate end favored by the philosopher. In fact, the argument often seems to take roughly the following form: "We can deliberate rationally about ends because look: Rationality endorses X as the ultimate end valid for all agents." I am not at all hostile to such attempts. Setting aside their tendency to hypostatize rationality, I have no general ground for believing that they all must fail, and I wish them well. I have not, however, found any of those that I have looked at to be rationally compelling. Accordingly, I am unable to endorse any such argument. My suspension of judgment on this question allows me then to note an important strategic consideration. Philosophical reaction to the "rationalists" who have defended particular conceptions of the ultimate end as required or established by reason has mainly attacked their specific conclusions. Reasons are put forward why pleasure, or utility, or autonomy are not rationally valid as ultimate ends for all people. The smoke of the intellectual battle obscures the more basic question of whether it is possible to deliberate rationally about ends.

Some of those who embrace skepticism about rational deliberation of ends leap to this conclusion from the assertion that no particular conception of the ultimate end can be established as rationally required or valid for all agents. For example, Gauthier, having rightly noted that the ideal

---

4 Gibbard's view does needlessly restrict the possibility of deliberating about ends in its assumption that norms are either particular or absolute (see §10) and in its pervasive reliance on a form of pragmatism that licenses inarticulateness about ultimate ends (as in Dewey's pragmatism, discussed in §23).

of rationality (in some sense) applies to all alike, then identified what he called "the modern Western view of man":

To characterize a person as rational is not to relate him to any order, or system, or framework, which would constrain his activities. It is not, as Plato thought, to relate man to the Good. It is not, as Saint Thomas thought, to relate man to God. It is not, as Kant thought, to relate man to the Kingdom of Ends. To characterize a person as rational is not then to determine his ends either positively, in terms of a goal or goals to be sought, or negatively, in terms of beings (such as other persons) to be respected (1990 [1975], 210–11).

Passing whether Gauthier's negative judgment on prior efforts was too categorical, look at what he took to follow from it:

Given [the] supposition [of this modern Western view], the strict answer to the question, What must a person do, solely in virtue of being rational? is: Nothing. Reason of itself determines no actions. The modern Western view of man implies at least part of the Humean view of reason, that it is the slave of the passions. Reason takes the ends of our activities as given, and determines the means to those ends.

But Gauthier was wrong: That there is no end established by reason for all persons does not imply that, for each individual, reason is confined to determining means. A parallel hastiness is exemplified by Allais, who explains the italicized vehemence of his skepticism about rational deliberation of ends, quoted in §1, by noting that "in an epoch in which totalitarian tendencies are rife, no language is too strong to denounce the propensity of many of our contemporaries for branding as *irrational* any behavior that is not to their taste" (Allais 1979 [1953], 135). But again, to show that an individual can deliberate rationally about ends is not yet to show that there are objective ends valid for all agents, let alone to impose these. Clearing away the tendency to draw these mistaken inferences takes a first step toward recognizing the possibility that we can deliberate rationally about ends. As I will explain, we can develop a conception of rational deliberation of ends that sets aside (for the nonce) the ambition of universality across agents. Once we regain a clear grasp of how we may deliberate rationally about ends – who knows? – perhaps then we will be in a better position to determine whether there is an objectively valid or true or rationally required end on which all rational deliberation should converge.

In the meantime, however, my strategy dictates that I stick within what might be called "relative rationality."[5] In this respect, the proposal that I

---

5 Darwall, from whom I borrow the term "relative rationality," equates it with a conception

will be defending parallels the instrumentalist models that I oppose. I will not try to argue that certain ends are recommended by objective reason. Like the accounts of decision theorists and welfare economists, my account will start with individuals with a given set of practical commitments (in their case, preferences; in mine, ends). In each case, we describe a set of principles or guidelines covering the agent's deliberation from those starting points. The accounts are "relative," in that a course of deliberation endorsed as rational for one agent – either by mine or by my instrumentalist opponents' – will not necessarily be endorsed as rational or even be a realistic possibility for some other agent. Much will depend upon what the initial commitments are. In the case of decision theory, different choices will be endorsed for the agent who intrinsically prefers engaging in a gamble than for one who does not. My account will involve a similar dependence of the endorsed path of deliberation on the agent's initial commitments, sufficient to allow that rationally deliberating individuals might reasonably disagree about what to do in given circumstances. I will show that even accepting such a dependence on initial commitments (or ends), rational deliberation can adopt and revise even ultimate ends. While the divergent initial commitments of different agents will undoubtedly affect the content of the ultimate ends they end up with through the exercise of rational deliberation, I will show that this relativity does not prevent rational deliberation from reaching the level of ultimate ends. (There may be some tendency to think of an "ultimate end" as "an end endorsed by reason as valid for all agents." I propose a competing understanding of "ultimate end" in §29.)

It is important to reiterate, however, that I work within relative rationality purely for strategic reasons. I do not rule out the possibility of showing that certain ends are valid or required for all rational agents. I can allow that relative rationality, even when it extends to defending a conception of an ultimate end for an individual, may not exhaust the content of practical rationality. Partly for this reason, I focus above all on the rationality of the way in which someone deliberates. The central question will be the adverbial one: Is this a way in which someone might rationally deliberate? Just as one might rationally deliberate about how efficiently to achieve some irrational end, so too one might rationally deliberate, from a set of unacceptable or crazy initial commitments, in a way that determines what one's ultimate end should be. The question

of rationality limited to end–means reasoning: see Darwall 1983, 104, 207. As will be seen, I use the term more broadly, but analogously.

whether the process of deliberation from the initial starting points has been rational certainly does not exhaust the scope for possible criticism, and may not exhaust the content of what rationality dictates. I claim only that the process of rational deliberation from initial commitments is not limited to picking means to ends or preferences taken as given and fixed, but can extend to adopting ends, even ultimate ones. If such a process then draws further criticism because, on account of its initial commitments, it ends up endorsing ends that reason cannot countenance, all the better, from my point of view. It is for the strategic reasons I have outlined that I do not want to fall into the trap of having my positive argument depend on an effort to show which ends reason can and cannot support, for everyone.

Being agnostic about objective ends, my argument should be welcomed by two kinds of reader. First, there are those who, like Gauthier, deny the existence of objective, rational ends, yet unlike him chafe against the restrictions of an instrumentalist conception of practical reasoning. As I noted in §2, the three obstacles inhibit recognizing even a relative rationality in deliberation about ends. Second, there are the believers in objective ends. While they may be confident that certain ends are rationally supportable for all persons, they may not be so sure about how this may be done. In leaving the door open to objectivity, I mean in particular to be offering these believers a theory about how rationally to defend and elaborate the objective ends they believe in.

Beyond being compatible with a robust account of objective ends, in other words, my view leaves open a place into which such an account can step. This will become obvious in Chapter X, where I will discuss the opportunities for reasoning available to deliberators with roughly Aristotelian and Kantian (or Rawlsian) initial commitments. Although I imagine these virtuous agents simply as ordinary people shaped in one or another of these traditions, these philosophers initially put forward their views as objective. In working with these philosophical views in that chapter, I will in effect show that my account of relative rationality can stretch to incorporate the structures of objective criticism of a wide variety of types. Rather than using premises about rationality to argue that acting morally or being virtuous is rationally required, I will there be using well-developed moral theories to establish the possibility that we can deliberate rationally about ultimate ends. If one of these theories is true, then it will have been shown that we can deliberate rationally to objective results. In this respect, my argument serves as a Trojan horse, smuggling potentially objective elements inside the stronghold of relative rationality.

Even within relative rationality, we must ask about truth. Are there true and false answers about whether a given agent should refine or revise her ends in a certain way in a certain situation? If so, then how must an account of rational deliberation respect this fact? If not, then what makes it an account of rationality, except simple stipulation?

Answering these questions would be simpler if the process of rational deliberation were wholly independent of its content, for then a straightforward realist picture would apply. Think again of the person deciding whether or not to have children. If it would be best for him or her to have children, then a rational process of deliberation ought to lead him or her to that conclusion; if not, not. What would make deliberation rational, on this picture, would above all be its tendency to settle practical questions when and as appropriate.[6] Such a realist tack in giving an account of relative rationality lets the answers govern the process, by and large. (The opposite, more "idealist" approach, which would identify practical reasoning with certain processes of inference, and hence endorse whatever answers result from these processes given appropriate inputs, will be addressed in the following section.)

The realist strategy for developing standards of rationality fits naturally with assimilating deliberation to self-discovery. For relative rationality, it is tempting to suppose that the right answers would be supplied by the agent's beliefs and desires in combination. To deliberate rationally would then be to discover what one should do by inspecting one's belief-desire reasons to find the strongest. If self-discovery of this sort provided a fully adequate metaphor for deliberation about what to do, then models of rational deliberation could be developed in some simple relationship to the right answer about what the individual ought to do. Problems for the realist strategy, however, begin to appear when we notice the limitations of the model of discovery.

Self-discovery is a part, but only a part, of what is going on in deliberation. Pursuing practical coherence among one's various commitments, in the ways I will elaborate, is the best way to discover what we ought

---

6 If the question is a borderline question, such that we cannot know which the right answer is, that is a reason our theory of rational deliberation should not settle the question, either (cf. Sorensen 1991b). To be sure, there will be atypically structured choices – such as the Allais paradox (Allais 1979) or the Newcomb problem (Lewis 1981), which have bedeviled decision theorists – in which policies of deliberation that generally yield correct (individually relative) results go awry. Realists might cast their theory of rational deliberation in terms of a set of guidelines that work out for the best in the general run of cases rather than simply declaring that the rational course of deliberation is the one which in each instance yields the correct answer about what to do.

to do. An essential part of this process is discovering – whether anew or just in more detail – what our ends are. In some cases, this can be a matter of discovering new ends that we have recently developed (cf. Millgram, forthcoming). The metaphor of discovery as self-observation, however, does not fully fit the nature of deliberation. As I will argue in more detail in §§20 and 26, deliberation is one of those subjects that is "Socratic," in Rawls's sense (Rawls 1971, 49). That is, it is a subject marked by the central role it accords critical reflection. Especially for the case of an individual's relative rationality, there is no distinction between participant and observer. The deliberator is at one and the same time the discoverer and the discovered. For the existentialist hero the distance between these two aspects perhaps reduces to nil: He simply acts. For the rest of us, there is often sufficient conceptual space between our will and our commitments for the metaphor of reflection to be literally correct: We go back and forth between putting forward proposed actions and checking them against our ends.[7] Socratic reflection reverberates between commitments and proposals in a continuous effort to determine what one should do. Oriented by this normative task, it will generate revisions in the agent's commitments justified in terms of what one should do (as we will amply see in later chapters).

A striking example of Socratic reflection, in this sense, is Leonard Savage's response to the Allais paradox. I present it here partly because it nicely shows how Socratic reflection goes more deeply than end–means reasoning. At issue in the paradox is the sure-thing principle, central to modern decision theory, which affirms that each outcome is evaluated independently of other outcomes not realized. If this principle fails, it would be impossible to retain the additive form that allows decision theory to indicate how to maximize "utility" in situations involving risk (for a clear exposition, see Broome 1991, ch. 5). To generate the Allais paradox, subjects are asked to declare their preferences in two pairs of lotteries:

1. $500,000 for certain.
2. 10 percent chance of $2,500,000; 89 percent chance of $500,000; 1 percent chance of $0.

3. 11 percent chance of $500,000; 89 percent chance of $0.
4. 10 percent chance of $2,500,000; 90 percent chance of $0.

---

7 Not all reflection deserving of the name is Socratic. Velleman 1989 develops a theory of practical reflection that starts off from a sophisticated development of this mirror imagery. Central to his reflecting agent, however, is not so much the attempt to figure out what he should do as the desire to be intelligible to himself.

As Savage reports (1954, 102)

> Many people prefer Gamble 1 to Gamble 2, because, speaking qualitatively, they do not find the chance of winning a *very* large fortune in place of receiving a large fortune outright adequate compensation for even a small risk of being left in the status quo. Many of the same people prefer Gamble 4 to Gamble 3; because, speaking qualitatively, the chance of winning is nearly the same in both gambles, so the one with the much larger prize seems preferable.

But such preferences violate the sure-thing principle, and hence cannot be represented by a utility function. In addressing this difficulty, Savage notes, in effect, the importance of Socratic reflection in normative disciplines such as decision theory: "In general, a person who has tentatively accepted a normative theory must conscientiously study situations in which the theory seems to lead him astray; he must decide for each by reflection – deduction will typically be of little relevance – whether to retain his initial impression of the situation or to accept the implications of the theory for it" (102). Savage illustrates this methodological principle by presenting his own reaction to the Allais paradox. At first, he says, his intuitive reaction was the common one that generates the paradox. On reflection, however, he found a way of re-presenting the hypothetical gambles that both made it more obvious why the ordinary reactions violate the sure-thing principle and changed his preference between 3 and 4. Allais's lotteries could be conducted using 100 numbered tickets, distributed as follows:

		tkt # 1	tkts 2–11	tkts 12–100
I.	1.	5	5	5
	2.	0	25	5
II.	3.	5	5	0
	4.	0	25	0

In light of this new way of conceiving of the problem, Savage says, his intuitive reaction changed. "It seems to me," he commented, "that in reversing my preference between Gambles 3 and 4 I have corrected an error" (103). Allais, by contrast (true to his generally deferential attitude toward particular preferences), instead rejected the sure-thing principle.

As Socratic reflection, therefore, deliberation can reshape the agent's commitments – both those norms within which relative rationality works and those norms by which it works. And if this reflectiveness is a common feature of our deliberations – as I think it is – then it does not make sense to follow the simple realist's strategy in giving an account of practical reasoning. The processes of rational deliberation so centrally influence what ought to be done (relative to the agent's commitments) that one cannot expect to be able to define those procedures simply in terms of what is likely to yield true answers about what ought to be done (relative to the agent's commitments). The norms delineating relative rationality are not fully independent of the norms on which it works.

Self-construction in this Socratic sense by no means contradicts any claim that statements about what one ought to do, or is to do, have truth-values. To the contrary, it may simply indicate that what one ought to do, or is to do, depends (at least in some central cases) upon what deep self-examination or thorough reflection would endorse. "Invention" and "construction" refer, here, not to the arbitrary filling in of truth-value gaps, but to the agent's necessary participation in settling what it is she is to do. This element of self-construction means that beyond helping one arrive at the right answer about what to do, reflective deliberation may also influence what the right answer is.

This reflective interdependence between substantive normative commitments and core ideas of rationality makes it impossible to escape the fact that an enterprise such as mine is normative all the way down. Contrary to prevailing opinion, as sheltered by the three obstacles, I aim to show that a certain way of going on (deliberating about ends) would be rational if done in a certain way. Lest this effort be misunderstood as simply a verbal flanking maneuver designed to capture the word "rational," I shall now set out in a preliminary way the general marks of rationality, as relevant to deliberation, to which I will hold my own account responsible. It is my hope that many of my opponents would agree with this list. A somewhat fuller account of the marks of rationality may be found in §18.

In brief, I take the principal marks of the rationality of a process of thinking to be (1) potential discursiveness or public expressibility, (2) orderliness, and (3) the absence of such general defects of thinking as inconsistency, vicious circularity, excessive close-mindedness, and one-sidedness.

In being at least potentially expressible in words, a course of deliberation that is rational is one that can be assessed and explained, justified and criticized – publicly, it goes without saying (cf. Habermas 1984, 9). It contrasts with a course of reasoning that relies on intuitive leaps not subject to this sort of public check. Although I will be stressing (in §27) that deliberation of ends needs certain sorts of "intuitive" or emotional input, I will take pains to point out that considerations that arise in this way can still be expressed in words. This sort of potential discursiveness is generally

31

important to whether a succession of mental states counts as a course of reasoning. Recall that I am here characterizing the features of "rational" as applied to a course of deliberation. Different considerations would be involved in interpreting "rational" as applied to the action chosen in a given case.

Deliberating rationally also contrasts with floundering about on some question of practice. Rational deliberation, in other words, involves a modicum of order. This feature is the valid residue of the idea that reasoning must have a "method." As we have seen, the Socratic aspect of deliberation makes it implausible that practical reasoning could simply be identified with a given set of procedures thought likely to yield right answers. While confidence that explicit methods of inquiry might be laid out has waned somewhat since Descartes's day, the idea that a process of reasoning should be at least minimally methodical has remained with us. It would be exaggerating to hold that this requirement implies that individuals deliberating rationally from the same starting points will reach identical conclusions. There are too many optional choices along the way, too many points at which alternatives are rationally indifferent, for this result to follow. Just as excellent chess playing from a given initial position need not converge on a single result required by excellence in chess, not all rational deliberation from a given starting point need converge on a unique answer about what is to be done as the alternative required by reason. A step can be guided by reasoning even though not uniquely. (The temptation to think otherwise may result from a confusion between a step in reasoning and a logical inference: cf. Harman 1986 and Anscombe 1989 on the difference, to which I will come in the next section.) Which initial steps are taken, and the order in which steps are taken, may reasonably affect which result is rationally supported in the end. Practical reasoning, that is to say, has a historical structure. Its order reveals itself not simply as an instance of a timeless pattern, but also in a temporal series of steps. While a theorist (such as myself) may sometimes licitly idealize away this temporal order in the attempt to clarify or recommend some particular pattern, some series of notional steps, the importance of temporal order must be remembered when we set our expectations for practical reasoning. We are left, then, with this vague feature of the orderliness of thinking in time, which makes the presence of intelligible patterns of thought an important mark of rationality.

The absence of general vices of thinking is also a crucial mark of its rationality (cf. Sorensen 1991a); however, this feature will play a less central role in my account than might be expected. Part of the burden of

Chapter VII will be to explain that the absence of the general cognitive vice of inconsistency does not suffice to describe even the skeleton of the virtue of practical coherence. While a more robust notion of practical coherence will figure centrally in my argument – in fact, just because it figures centrally in my argument – I want to avoid building it into rationality by definition. The connection will be forged indirectly, via a general pragmatic argument and via the features of discursiveness and orderliness.

§5. PRACTICAL INFERENCE

Historically the most influential account of practical reasoning casts it in apparently deductive form, namely the Aristotelian idea of the "practical syllogism." We shall see, however, that this cannot generally work deductively (nor was it intended to by Aristotle). In this section I will argue that it is a mistake to try to assimilate the whole of practical reasoning to deductive argument of any kind. Further, given the importance of Socratic reflection noted in the last section, it is equally a mistake to try to mimic the logical necessity involved in deductive argument by developing a special logic of practical inference. Deductively valid or otherwise indefeasible schemas of practical argument can be put forward only at the cost of making most instances of them unsound or inaccessible to deliberating agents. This century's long-standing philosophical debate over whether practical reasoning has a special logic or form distinct from theoretical reasoning is, I will be suggesting, principally a confused version of the debate about whether we can reason about final ends. Accordingly, while views that treat the practical syllogism more loosely as a defeasible inference pattern help explain one way to build connections of mutual support (see §21), it will be more important to envision the alternative structure of practical reasoning that proceeds independently of the practical syllogism.

The practical syllogisms that philosophers have used in an attempt to push practical reasoning toward the deductively valid have varied considerably in their form (for a brief survey, see Audi 1989, 86–8). Most of them take roughly the following form: (1) the first (or "major") premise mentions some end of the agent; (2) the second (or "minor") notes that an action of a given type is a way of realizing or achieving that end; and (3) the conclusion is that the agent does or should do an action of that type. If a practical syllogism of this form were the model of all practical reasoning, it would be very hard to see how deliberation could significantly extend to ends. Because it holds that practical reasoning begins from some end to which the agent is committed, it reinforces the motivational version of the scope obstacle. Because chains of practical reasoning would still have to start from some first end, this model also supports the source obstacle (§2): While there might be one or more ultimate ends from which one could deliberate about intermediate ends, reasoning would have to take the former for granted, and concern itself only with how to realize it or them. Thus Audi, who does defend the view that the practical syllogism serves as the model for practical reasoning, rightly admits that he is thereby committed to the position "that practical reasoning is very broadly a kind of means–end reasoning" (1989, 146). Thinking of the practical syllogism as *the* pattern of deliberation puts one into this box. To find a way out of the box, one must avoid giving such importance to the practical syllogism.

To avoid being forced to see all practical reasoning as end–means reasoning, it will not suffice to wield the distinction, standard in this literature, between two supposedly different types of practical syllogism, end–means and rule–case. The former is the type set out in the last paragraph. On the latter, (1) the first premise states that when one is in circumstances C, one should do an act of type A; (2) the second notes that one is in circumstances C; and (3) the conclusion is that the action of type A is to be done. Since a rule–case syllogism seems not to need to mention an end, perhaps reasoning along those lines could circumvent the obstacles to deliberation about ends. Yet, as I will be explaining more fully in §9, I believe it necessary to work within a broad version of the view (motivational internalism about reasons) that implies that the "first premises" of practical reasoning have motivational importance for the agent. On this supposition, and given the analysis of "end" that I will provide in §7, the distinction between these two sorts of "syllogism" will recede. Although I will therefore not make positive use of this distinction between the two types of practical syllogism, their possible logical validity and usefulness as schemas for deliberation must be assessed separately.[8]

A rule–case syllogism can yield new practical commitments when new factual premises come along. Consider the following case: Suppose that

---

8 The basic Aristotelian schema has been put to other uses as well. Von Wright, for instance, emphasized its importance in explaining and interpreting human action – lately even conceding that "practical inference" may have been a misleading label for his development of the practical syllogism (von Wright 1989, 804). Broadie, by contrast, explains how Aristotle's use of it may be understood as an analysis of the conceptual structure of an intention or deliberate choice (*prohairesis*: Broadie 1991, 226) rather than an action.

my boss has decided suddenly and unilaterally to cancel the morning coffee break, and that on the basis of bitter experience I had formed the general policy that when my boss does something arbitrary, it is always best just to lay low and hope that he will reverse his dictate on his own. Canceling coffee time is obviously arbitrary; whence it follows that I had best be patient. Of course it should be emphasized that there is an art to the correct discernment of relevant features of situations. Whether the boss's ban was truly arbitrary or really reflected a paternalistic concern for the health of the caffeine addicts in the office, for instance, will require some nuanced judgment. All this may be admitted by the defender of the syllogistic model, who can still insist that the model represents the structure of the agent's reasoning, whether insightful or myopic. Either way, the agent subsumes a new case under a standing rule.

Although the rule–case syllogism undeniably fits the way we deliberate in some cases, it would be a gross mistake to suppose that it covered most of our practical reasoning. Few instances of practical reasoning to a conclusion about a particular case could proceed deductively. The most general reason is that it is very hard to frame a useful and plausible practical norm that truly has the logical form of a universal generalization. I surely do not believe that it is best to meet my boss's arbitrariness with patience in all conceivable situations. If he threatened to set fire to my tie, I would rightly think it best to challenge him, with force if necessary. The problem here is analogous to that of finding "absolutes" in morality (cf. Richardson 1990c) or "basic valuations" in preference theory (that is, preferential comparisons that hold no matter what: cf. Sen 1984, 62–4; Lance, forthcoming). Since deliberation concerns what is to be done in particular circumstances, logical entailment of an instance by a rule requires that the rule be a true universal generalization across cases. This is needed for the inference to work as a "Peripatetic syllogism," which takes the following form:[9]

In all cases, if circumstances C hold, then do A.
Circumstances C hold in this case.
Therefore:
Do A in this case.

That one could conceivably face a case in which cruel fortune, or an evil demon, or an alien from another planet had so arranged things that if one

---

9 In calling this syllogism with singular middle term and conclusion "Peripatetic," I follow Łukasiewicz 1951, ch. I, §§1–3. This label signals his view that this syllogism, though often attributed to Aristotle and his school, especially in the practical context, was not one of the ones that Aristotle himself catalogued.

stuck by some purported rule then disaster would ensue makes it difficult to suppose that many of our practical norms are true universal generalizations.

One might try to get around this difficulty by hedging the norm's description of the relevant circumstances appropriately, including provisos such as "assuming my boss's arbitrariness is relevantly similar to the instances of it I have faced in the past," or "so long as nothing really weird happens" in a complex description of circumstances C. The trouble is that even if hedges of this sort enabled us to frame genuinely acceptable universal generalizations, it would also make the norms containing them so vague that it becomes hard to imagine reasoning with them. Truth so often being stranger than fiction, we manifestly lack criteria for determining whether things are proceeding normally or whether something weird is happening. This being so, it strains credulity to suppose that we have a faculty of judgment that somehow enables us to "discern" whether things are normal, so that we can then go on to apply the rule deductively. It starts to appear that a less logically tight model of practical reasoning will better fit the ways we do reason.

Before giving up on a deductive schema, however, my opponent may propose another type of hedging. It is all-purpose, and does not attempt to specify excusing or canceling situations in any factual detail. I have in mind a proviso sometimes associated with the modifier "prima facie," namely: "so long as there is no reason to act otherwise." This sort of hedge was influentially developed by W. D. Ross as a way of being faithful to the complexity of our commonsense moral beliefs. A prima facie duty in Ross's sense is one that states our "actual duty" so long as no other prima facie duty conflicts with it; however, when duties conflict, as he put it (quoting his own translation of Aristotle), "the decision rests with perception" (Ross 1930, 42). Since another, more evidentiary sense of "prima facie" has become current, I suggest the term "possum duty" for Ross's idea. A possum duty is a real animal all right, but one that when faced with a conflict (even with a member of its own species) rolls over and plays dead.[10] More generally, a "possum norm" is one framed so as to state a recommendation only for the case in which it conflicts with no other norms. Now since, as the next section will begin to lay out, there

---

10 Lest this terminology seem unfair to Ross, I hasten to point out that a possum so responding is not really dead, only prima facie dead. It still, for example, breathes out carbon dioxide. Similarly, a Rossian "prima facie duty" that has come into conflict with another of its kind may still exude emotional consequences and delimit the permissible options in indirect ways; it simply gives up its live claim on directly guiding action.

are many possible interpretations of the idea of a "conflict," there are correspondingly many possible variations of the "possum" qualifier. Ross, for one, clearly intended to include as a conflict disturbing the deductive application of the rule any case in which it was contingently impossible to fulfill both of two obligations – as when one cannot both arrive at one's lunch meeting at the promised time and save the person drowning in the canal (Ross 1930, 18). Possum practical norms certainly make more plausible candidates for universal generalizations than the ones that would result from removing this hedge. For one thing, this all-purpose qualification can take care of many of the problems mentioned in the last paragraph. In the last example of me and my boss it was perhaps implicit that I have a policy of avoiding having my clothes burned up while I am wearing them, a policy that there conflicts with my generally quiescent approach to office relations. If this is so, then the "possum" hedge frees me to exercise my nuanced discernment to decide which of the two conflicting norms to follow. Since such hidden hedges are pervasive in our commitments, however, it will turn out that such discernment, and not the "syllogistic" aspect of Ross's model, will end up doing most of the deliberative work.

I conclude that if constrained to being logically valid, the rule–case syllogism is of little use in our deliberation, because it is rare that the premises of such syllogisms are both true and more committal than possum norms. I will now argue that a similar conclusion holds of the end–means form: Those versions that fit our deliberation are not deductively valid, while the valid forms do not fit our deliberation. Let us begin with end–means "syllogisms" that faithfully represent ordinary reasoning.

Aristotle's own realistic examples of the "practical syllogism" famously fail to be deductively valid. Consider one of the most notorious and elaborate of these, from chapter 7 of the *Movement of Animals* (701a17–19):

I need a covering, a coat is a covering: I need a coat.
What I need I ought to make, I need a coat: I make a coat.

The second of these little "syllogisms" (Aristotle does not there call them that) illustrates the problem noted above about finding a plausible universal generalization to serve as a major premise in a sound and valid practical syllogism. We need many things that it would not be sane to think of making: sexual fulfillment, for instance, or sunshine. The first "syllogism," however, presents what looks like a distinct pattern, an end–means syllogism (Allan 1955 exaggerated the difference). This type, too, lacks deductive validity. I need a covering, to be sure; but I do not need every covering that exists, or even one of each type. Any sufficient means will do. When the weather is cold or I am in public, I always need some covering. Often, however, I will have a choice about what to use to clothe myself and whether to do so with one thick jacket or with a sweater and a windbreaker. Accordingly, one can at best infer a disjunction: "I need a cloak or a jacket or a barrel or. . . ." It seems that Aristotle recognized this lack of deductive tightness in the sorts of practical syllogism that he offered. Aristotle's practical syllogisms should generally be understood as implicitly invoking an offstage principle of selection among alternative means, directing one to pick the easiest and best (*N.E.* III.3, 1112b17; cf. Nussbaum 1978, essay 4). This fits the way we actually reason, but it is not deductively valid.

One might try to spell out needed hedges so as to endow the sufficient means schema with deductive validity. Black, for instance, suggests adding premises to the effect that the selected means is not "more trouble than it is worth" and is "preferable to any other action available for achieving" the end (Black 1989, 414). But this is the work of deliberation, to assess a proposed action in light of its impact on other ends and its relative capacity to satisfy the end initially proposed. Once it has endorsed an action as both the best means to an end and not productive of too much countervailing bad, then deliberation has largely done. The schema filled out as Black suggests becomes valid, but as a way of formalizing the conclusion rather than proceeding with deliberation.

To convert the end–means pattern into something like a deductively valid one along lines apparently more useful in deliberation, one might instead assert the necessity of a given type of means. G. H. von Wright, for one, built a whole study of "practical inference" around a necessary-means schema, as exemplified by the following case (von Wright 1983, 2):

One wants to make the hut habitable.
Unless the hut is heated, it will not become habitable.
Therefore the hut must be heated.

As it stands, of course, this schema is not logically valid. The move from "wants" to "must" is certainly open to question.[11] But suppose that the

---

11 Von Wright tries out a conditionalizing paraphrase of "must" that deprives the inference of much of its usefulness in yielding new conclusions; but other variations might be tried with "intend" in both the first premise and conclusion, for instance. For the schema to be logically valid, however, the attitude (intentional operator) that appears in first premise and conclusion would also have to be closed under believed logical implication. For

necessary-means schema could be supplied with deductive validity or something like it. Even so, I want to suggest, it falls flat as a general model for deliberation because middle premises of the needed form will only rarely be true. For the pattern to be deductively valid, the "unless" would have to stand for a relation at least as strong as the logical "if . . . then": "if the hut is not heated, then it will not become habitable."[12] As von Wright himself points out, however, the temperature might rise by itself (due to global warming, we might imagine). Alternatively, its owner might drink enough vodka not to feel the cold, or else buy a down comforter. There are all sorts of possibilities, and there almost always are. Means that used to be thought "necessary" are proven not to be by advances in technology. To bear a child, it used to be necessary first to ovulate – until in vitro fertilization came along. One might try to spell out a hedge to account for such possibilities, such as "relative to current technology . . . "; but we have seen already with rule–case syllogisms the problems with hedges invoking normalcy. Deliberation must often probe the boundaries of what is necessary, rather than simply taking them for granted. Acquiescence in what current technology can provide at reasonable cost should not be built into deliberation as a matter of logic!

Even if practical reasoning loosely fits a "syllogistic" form, then, it cannot usefully be formalized as having a "logic" of its own. Anscombe nicely lays out this conclusion in her criticism of von Wright (Anscombe 1989). Validity, she argues, goes with logical necessity, which exists only in deductive argument. Deductive logic is relevant to practical reasoning in much the same way that it is to theoretical reasoning. Consider the following example:

If the stove is lit, the hut will be heated.
If the hut is heated, it will be habitable.

The deductive chain formed by these two conditionals is a logical tie that can be put to use quite differently, depending on whether one's aim is (a) to make the hut habitable (say for one's family), (b) to ensure that the hut

argument that intending to A does not entail intending to do everything that one believes to follow from A, see Robins 1984 and Bratman 1987, 123, 135.

12 The precise nature of the needed conditional would be hard to pin down. The ordinary notion of a necessary means implies that if I do heat the hut, it will become habitable. Some degree of counterfactual tracking may also be implied: If I did not heat it, it would not become habitable. This issue is messy, in part because of difficulties about specifying the truth-conditions of "future contingents." On the relation between deliberation and the alleged contingency of the future, consult the literature stemming from Aristotle's classic discussion in *On Interpretation*, ch. 9; e.g., Broadie 1987.

is uninhabitable (if it is one's enemy's), (c) to explain how the hut became habitable, or (d) to predict its becoming so. The end, Anscombe insists, stands outside any valid syllogism of use in practical reasoning. On this ground, she objects to von Wright's insertion of "I want" or "I intend" into the first premise. On her picture, by contrast, one simply has ordinary syllogisms of the above sort, which turn out to be "practical" – or of use in practical reasoning – just in case the logical conclusion ("the hut will be habitable") or its negation is desired or aimed at and, in particular, is good.

Anscombe's way of putting things, however, still assigns too big a role to the practical syllogism. It wrongly encourages the thought that determining means to an end and determining the end are wholly nonoverlapping and contrasting activities. It suggests the following picture: We aim at some good and reason how to achieve it, checking the sufficiency of our means by running backward through ordinary "syllogisms" about the relevant empirical facts. If we assess the good aimed at, we do so quite differently. There would be no such thing as a distinctive form of practical reasoning only if there were no rational deliberation of ends. Anscombe herself raises this issue with the following question (Anscombe 1989, 403):

May not someone be criticizable for pursuing a certain end, thus characterizable as a sort of good of his, where and when it is quite inappropriate for him to do so, or by means inimical to other ends which he ought to have?
This can be made out only if man has a last end which governs all.

This leap to the necessity of some ultimate end by reference to which to assess intermediate ends might be justified, as we have seen, if practical reasoning did have to have the structure of a syllogism that always began from some end; but it does not. It seems, then, that Anscombe has only halfway learned the lesson of her own argument that there is no such thing as a valid practical syllogism of distinct form. Since practical reasoning does not generally take this form, it must take some other; and perhaps opportunities for criticizing ends will permeate this alternative form, rather than flowing only from a presumed ultimate end. Yes, the end stands outside the only sort of logically valid syllogism broadly relevant to practical reasoning; but it is not at all external to practical reasoning itself. Once we see (in later chapters) how practical reasoning can integrate deliberation of ends, we will see how it differs from theoretical reasoning plus an end: not that it has a distinct "logic," but that it proceeds differently nonetheless.

Like Anscombe, I have not meant to deny that deductive inference is ever useful in the course of practical reasoning. My point is the more modest one that practical reasoning is far from exhausted by deductive inference. Most deliberation that we count as rational resists formalization.[13]

§6. PRACTICAL "OUGHTS"

Although lacking a logic all of its own, in the sense of a special form of inference valid only in the practical realm, practical reasoning nonetheless has some important features "logical" in the broader sense that they reflect features of a central concept, the general practical "ought." As a first step toward a more detailed positive account of practical reasoning, philosophers, at least, will demand a clearer understanding of this "ought." This is the "ought" *sans phrase* described in §1, which is involved when one decides what one ought to do – or, more simply, what to do. Situating this "ought" is important, for it is clear that there are wide differences among the sorts of conflict tolerable for different aspects of our psychology. Desires we expect to conflict all the time: We often want to have our cake (uneaten) and want to eat it too. As has often been pointed out (e.g., by Williams 1973), desires do not "agglomerate." By this is meant, for instance, that these two desires do not imply a single desire that the cake both remain uneaten and be eaten. Moral obligations, by contrast, are thought by many to be subject to the demands of agglomeration. So, too, is the philosopher's strict notion of what one ought to do, "all things considered." We need to determine how the deliberative "ought" stands in relation to these other ideas. Since it may be thought relevantly similar to the moral "ought," and since moral conflicts have been intensively studied, we may begin with this analogous topic.

Some situations appear to present a *moral dilemma*, that is, a conflict of moral requirements that is morally unresolvable because neither of the conflicting obligations overrides the other (I follow Sinnott-Armstrong 1988). Schematically, a typical moral conflict involves the "incompossibility" of two obligations, which might be spelled out as follows:

(1) Action *a* is obligatory.
(2) Action *b* is obligatory.

---

13 This conclusion is similar to that of Harman's (1986) characterization of the limited importance of deductive logic for reasoning in general; and like him, I will turn to coherence, more richly characterized, as a central constraint on the "changes in view" effected by reasoning.

(3) Although it is possible to do *a* or to do *b*, it is not possible to do both *a* and *b*.

Where one of these obligations overrides or negates the other, the conflict is resolvable; where it is not, and each obligation remains nonoverridden, one faces a true moral dilemma. It is clear that only unresolvable conflicts among values or ends seriously threaten rationality: Prima facie moral and practical conflicts that may be resolved because one norm overrides another are both pervasive and relatively unproblematic.

It is important for Chapter V's discussion of value incommensurability that moral and practical dilemmas may arise from a single principle. Take the principle that forbids breaking promises. Quirks of circumstance can convert two innocently and reasonably made promises, whose mutual interference was not easily foreseen, into a moral conflict (Ross 1939). Less likely, but conceivably, the considerations might in addition be so symmetrically arrayed that there remains no rational basis for resolving the conflict (Marcus 1980). The possibility of clashing, symmetrical obligations arising from a single principle is perhaps most horrifyingly exemplified by the situation that lends the title to the novel and movie *Sophie's Choice*: A mother arriving at a Nazi death camp must choose which of her children to save and which to allow the guards to take to its death (cf. Greenspan 1983). Arguably, the important obligations, here, are the ones the mother has to *each* child; plausibly, there might be no difference between the children that could imply that one of these particular obligations overrides the other (if one arose, it could be imagined away). A coin flip might settle the practical question of what child to choose, but this does not seem to be a *moral* basis for resolving the difficulty.

The most influential and widely discussed argument for the rational intolerability of moral dilemmas invokes the idea of agglomeration already introduced and the Kantian idea that "ought" implies "can." With the addition of these two principles, the existence of a moral dilemma, in the sense defined, can be shown to imply a contradiction. The relevant agglomeration principle (a "deontic" one, as it applies to duties) may be set out as follows:

(4) If each of two actions is obligatory, then doing both is obligatory.

Correspondingly, the principle that "ought" implies "can" may be expressed in the following way:

(5) An action is obligatory only if it is possible.

From these and elements (1) and (2) of the schema for a moral dilemma, one may logically obtain:

(6) It is possible to do both *a* and *b*.

But (6) contradicts (3), which denies that it is possible to do both, so not all of the premises can be true. This does not tell us which one is false, however; and since both the principle that "ought" implies "can" and the deontic agglomeration principle are open to attack, logic alone fails to rule out moral dilemmas.

The plausibility of each of these principles depends heavily upon the interpretation given to the sense of obligation or "ought" involved (cf. Sinnott-Armstrong 1988). I want first to set out how those who defend the existence of moral dilemmas distinguish senses of (or contexts for) "ought," and then to say how I will be understanding the practical "ought" in relation to these senses.

All recent defenders of the existence of moral dilemmas, so far as I know, share the general strategy of distinguishing a heavy-duty sense of "ought" that states the unique thing that the agent should do, taking everything into account, from a less demanding "ought." The latter is supposed to represent neither a merely overridable or prima facie obligation nor a merely apparent obligation that might be concluded not to exist once all the relevant facts were taken into account. While not claiming to set out in a unique fashion what is to be done, the weaker "ought" is supposed to represent a real, nonoverridden moral requirement. This general strategy has been pursued in a wide variety of ways. Some (e.g., van Fraasen 1973) set out the difference directly in terms of whether something like the agglomeration principle applies. Williams (1973), more critical of the systematizing hopes of ethical theory, marks the difference as that between a practical "ought," which he explains in terms of the advice-soliciting question, "What ought I to do?" and a moral "ought" that admits dilemmas. Sinnott-Armstrong, whom I have been following, distinguishes the two relevant senses of "ought" in terms of the notion of one moral requirement overriding another. His heavy-duty "ought" is the overriding "ought," which beats anything it could conceivably conflict with: It clearly does not admit of dilemmas. Overridden "oughts," as in prima facie duties neutralized by conflict, do not make for a serious dilemma either. A nonoverridden "ought" does. Philippa Foot (1983) distinguishes types of moral "ought" in yet another interestingly different way. While the differences of detail among these ways of separating senses of "ought" rightly occupy moral philosophers, for present purposes what matters is what they share. In seeking to make sense of the possibility of moral dilemmas, each philosopher feels compelled to cordon off the relevant sense of "ought" both from a more demanding one that excludes conflict and from a minimal one that trivializes it. For my own pursuit of questions of practical deliberation, I will follow a similar strategy.

The practical "ought" with which I mean to be concerned, like the moral "ought" according to the defenders of moral dilemmas, occupies an intermediate position between a heavy-duty, fully agglomerating "ought" and a more whimsical "ought" that merely reflects the existence of desires, wants, or reasons. On the one hand, I want to make clear that I am not undertaking to investigate what might be called the *complete systematic "ought,"* which, presupposing a complete ordering of alternatives, states the unique thing that the agent ought to do in each circumstance, all things considered. The practical question, "What ought I to do?" orients my inquiry; but Williams was mistaken to hear uniqueness in that question. Sometimes the best advice will be equivocal or frustrating. Although completeness is a virtue in a system of practical norms, it is not an overriding one, nor does our very use of normative language presuppose it. "Well," might come the answer from a suitably magisterial adviser to someone faced by the well-known clash (in Sartre 1975), "you ought to stay with your mother, but you also ought to go fight with the Resistance; and there's nothing to say about the fact that you cannot do both except that you should feel angst either way!" So to respond is neither to misuse language nor to abuse the position of confidant. To be sure, we are tempted to read in qualifiers such as "from the point of view of filial duty . . . from the point of view of patriotic duty . . . but *really* what ought I to do?" Yet the licitness of the above answer to Sartre's student shows that the practical question does not necessarily carry the force of the "really," if this connotes agglomeration.

Far from its being clear that our very use of practical language contains the philosopher's rarefied notion of "what ought to be done, all things considered," there is serious doubt about whether it is licensed by ordinary speech at all. Some argue that our notions of goodness and of what ought to be done always bespeak a partial point of view, one that always reflects some particular norm or set of norms (cf. Foot 1983; Garcia 1987; Gibbard 1990). Things are good from one point of view or other, or in one respect or other; things ought to be done to fulfill requirements of fidelity, or self-interest, or patriotism; but, this position holds, there is no such notion as goodness or what ought to be done divorced from such a substantive perspective. Others, of course, hold that the complete systematic "ought"

44

pervades our language. Without taking a position on this controversy, I simply note that its existence undercuts the claim that the complete systematic "ought" is the only practical "ought."

In focusing on the possibilities of rational deliberation of ends, we are looking at the process of deciding what to do. Since we need to examine the process of arriving at a decision, more than the decisions to be reached, we do not need to limit ourselves to the complete systematic "ought" or any other practical "ought" purporting to state the decision, the thing that is to be done. We are looking at deliberation, reasoning about what to do, without presupposing that it will always produce decisive results. Just as juries can deliberate, and deliberate well, without reaching a verdict, so too can we all deliberate, and deliberate well, without reaching a decision about what to do. At other times, our deliberation makes some progress in narrowing down our options, but leaves us with more than one to choose from. For instance, in purchasing a car I will eliminate many as too costly, others as too flashy, and still others as too unreliable. Once I am done eliminating, I may be left with a few models whose virtues are so different as to leave me unable to decide which is best. Although I might then flip a coin, I won't think that I "ought" to abide by the toss; indeed, I often smoke out considerations I haven't been able to articulate by tossing a coin to see if I find the result comfortable. Deliberation about what one ought to do, then, often fails to reach a unique answer, even when the live alternatives are significantly different. The deliberative "ought" presupposes neither completeness (an answer to every question about what to do) nor uniqueness (exactly one answer to every question about what to do).

That this is so does not imply that there is not a true answer to what we ought to choose. The position that rational deliberation is compatible with incompleteness and indeterminacy does not imply a noncognitivist or antirealist position regarding reasons for action. That is because it is common for our reasoning to be faced with borderline cases, in the strict sense of situations in which no conceivable further research could settle the question. Yet the existence of borderline cases, in this sense, does not imply that the borderline proposition lacks a truth-value (Sorensen 1988). The way it is rational to deliberate is naturally tailored to the necessary limitations of our knowledge. It would not be rational to beat our heads against the wall of a true borderline question: While that effort might make us bald, it would not help at arriving at the right answer about whether a borderline bald person is bald or not. Similarly with borderline practical questions.

As soon as it has been made clear that one is not speaking of the complete systematic "ought," it should become apparent that practical conflicts – conflicts about what one ought to do – are not only possible but pervasive. As Foot has noted, "it makes perfectly good sense to say, when pressing business has given one overriding reason to go to town, that one nevertheless *ought* to be at home nursing one's awful cold" (Foot 1983, 383). Again, so long as one does not have in mind the complete systematic "ought," one could here sensibly say that one also ought to go to town. As Foot notes, these propositions are perfectly consistent, and their "consistency is easily explicable on a 'because of this . . . , but because of that . . .' basis" (391). Agglomeration fails: the mere fact that one ought to attend one's meeting and one ought to stay home in bed does not imply that one ought to do both.

Part Two

Scope

III

Ends in deliberation

Our discussion of whether and in what respects deliberation may extend to ends will naturally be advanced by a deeper consideration of the notion of an end (§7). Once this is clarified, I will be able to answer the analytic version of the scope obstacle by showing that deliberation can concern ends (§8). I will also be able to set out more precisely the reasoning underlying the motivational version of the scope obstacle (§9).

§7. ENDS AND FINAL ENDS

Part One's statement of the issue already helped fix the sense of "end" relevant to my argument. We have in mind an item that figures centrally in deliberation about what to do, whether simply by framing problems for the deliberator or also as being subject to deliberation. The three obstacles provide additional hints: The scope obstacle indicates (1) that although ends are relevant in deliberation, it is not obvious that they are what deliberation is about, and (2) that ends are intimately connected with motivation – as, say, ordinary beliefs or logical principles are not. The system obstacle credibly implies that ends are multiple and conflict with one another, giving rise to serious question about which should cede place. The source obstacle allows that some ends are more "final" than others, in that they are recognized as regulating or overriding other ends, at least in certain contexts. Even if there is not a single ultimate end that governs various subordinate ends, ends can be arranged in such a hierarchy. To avoid begging the question against believers in the obstacles, I will set out an account of the notion of an end that captures all of these general features. This account will make my argument easier, but not by clandestinely implying that my opponents' claims are false. Instead, it will help reveal a richer potential structure than they envisage. While I lay this out, I nonetheless will respect both the ordinary notion of an end (such as it is) and the typical ways in which ends noncontroversially figure in deliberation. My account is of broadly Aristotelian inspiration.[1]

An end is an aim of action. It is something for the sake of which an action is to be done. The normative aspect is cradled in the phrase "for the sake." Of course, ordinary speech usually replaces this stilted phrase with something plainer – often with a simple infinitive construction. In this form, ends figure in the most basic sort of action explanations. "Why did the chicken cross the road? To get to the other side!" "In order to get to the other side," we might explain, just in case someone did not get it. An end, in this broad sense, states a goal. The chicken fixes its gaze firmly on the far curb as it dodges the traffic, correcting its course so as to head toward the far side again after the cars spin it around, just as an archer adjusts the tension in his bowstring in order to be sure to hit his target (cf. Aristotle, N.E. 1094a23–5, 1138b22–3). Since getting to the other side need not be a final end (sought for its own sake), this sense of "end" is indeed broad. It is the one I will build upon, nonetheless. Neither the identification of ends with goals nor the visual metaphor of aiming should be taken to imply that all ends are physically, temporally, or even conceptually separate from the actions done for their sake. One can play a violin part in order to play one's part in a symphony, and (though this is getting ahead of my story) one can lie basking in the sun for its own sake. We need, then, an account of the normative aspect of ends broad enough to provide for the metaphorical equivalent of aiming even in contexts in which literal aiming cannot occur.

In part because I think of ends as embedding a normative element, I will in some parts of this book shift back and forth between speaking of ends and norms. A "norm" I think of simply as a principle – an item with propositional content – which has at least potential normative significance. Within relative rationality, a norm to which an agent is committed has normative significance. It is worth noting at this point, however, that ends, as commonly articulated, do not have a fully propositional form. "To get to the other side" is an infinitive construction, not a sentence. A corresponding norm – an "end-norm," we could call it – would be: "I (the chicken) should do something in order to get to the other side." In what follows, however, I will generally speak more informally of "ends,"

---

1 See Richardson 1992a for a detailed interpretation of Aristotle's notion of an end of action and his distinction among ends, final ends, and ultimate ends. Richardson 1992b interprets Aristotle's account of the relation between ends and action.

letting the context indicate whether ends (strictly speaking) or end-norms are in question.

The idea of a "reason for action," recently a favorite of philosophers, might seem to help elucidate the notion of an end; but this appearance is misleading. As often used, the notion of "a reason" is indeed supposed to refer to the sort of combination of motivational commitment and justification that one finds with ends (cf., e.g., Darwall 1983, 80–5). In particular, if we restrict our attention to what would be elicited by the questions, "What was his reason for doing that?" and "What is his reason for intending to do that?" we will come closer to the notion of an end (I will have more to say about intentions in a moment). Nonetheless, the notion of an agent's reason for action, if that simply involves the concatenation of motivation and justification in a form of which the agent is aware, remains too broad to identify with that of an end.[2] In addition, the idea of justification that the notion of an agent's reason for action embeds is liable to send us circling back to ends. It is likely that when we inquire about the justificatory or normative aspect of the relevant kind of reasons, it will be explained that they are "belief-desire" reasons (e.g., Davidson 1980, Essay 1). These involve (roughly) something wanted plus the belief that the action will provide it. In other words, a "belief-desire reason" is a complex of end and means, an implicit practical syllogism of the sort discussed in §5. If so, we need the notion of an end in order to analyze that of an agent's reason for action. Perhaps such interdependence among these basic concepts is to be expected. Understanding practical justification in terms of belief-desire reasons, it will be noticed, at least adds a reference to two psychological states (belief and desire) which may help us understand the role of ends in the psychology of action. I will now argue, however, that the notions of an end and of a "belief-desire reason" diverge.

An end names a process or state of affairs in terms of which the agent values some action. The agent may refer to the end in modulating his or her action (as does the dodging chicken), and the theorist may refer to it in individuating and explaining actions. Although a desire may be for the

---

2 Thus consider the possibility urged by Kant, that a good person can justifiably act from pure respect for the moral law, an incentive that does not constitute an end (Kant 1964a, Ak. 401n.). Respect is the motive from which (*aus welche*) action or pure good will is done, but according to Kant it is not the end for the sake of which (*um welches willen*) such actions are done. While the categorical imperative can figure in ends, such as that of moral self-perfection, it does not have this role in the incentive of respect.

occurrence of this same process or state of affairs, as a psychological entity in its own right it suggests a different path of modulation and explanation. A desire is a particular psychological state with motivational efficacy. Whatever causal influence it has may be only imperfectly correlated with its specifiable content. Building an account of action around desires leads naturally in the direction of assessing the causal force or "strength" of desires, especially when they compete – that is, to an account that focuses on desires' causal role as psychological particulars (e.g., Audi 1973). The chicken wants to cross the road, but also wants to avoid getting hit by a car. When these desires are equally strong, odd and occasionally self-defeating results can emerge, as when the chicken stands hesitating in the middle of the road, not being able to decide whether to press on to the other side or to retreat to the safe curb from which it started. Although this kind of analysis of action in terms of competing desires is empirically important, it differs from one that focuses on ends. A sign of this is that to speak of a conflict among ends in similarly quantitative, causal language, one would have to speak in circumlocutions, about the "strength with which an end is held" or the "strength of the agent's commitment to the end." We evaluate ends more naturally in terms of their choiceworthiness. This difference is related to the fact that although one simply *has* desires, one *adopts* or *pursues* ends. Although this linguistic fact does not prove that we are any freer in the latter case, it does reinforce this difference of nuance: that desires are relatively more apt to be thought of in terms of the inner states that they are, ends more in terms of the objects that form their intentional contents.

To provide an account of "end" that follows up on this difference of nuance, we need to look more deeply at how ends are aims. This aiming clearly implies some form of modulation, as I have noted, which presumably will support counterfactuals of some sort; for example, "If the target had moved we would have adjusted the aim." Attachment to a given end indicates something about how the agent would act were certain circumstances to obtain. Although the agent does not embrace a detailed contingency plan in committing herself to an end, she does make probable some definite counterfactuals about what she would do if she faced certain forks in the road (and if she were not coerced, weak-willed, or fickle). Which ones? We have noticed that the content of ends has relative prominence: But how? Clearly, their content must refer to something valued by the agent, whether intrinsically (for itself) or extrinsically (for the sake of something else). This means that the relevant counterfactuals will include not only those pertaining to whether the state of affairs referred to by the end will come to pass, but also those pertaining to whether the agent values it. An end, as we may put it in more old-fashioned words, is pursued as a good. (In this, it overlaps with an object of desire.) Simple examples of this sort of counterfactual control or regulation will involve mistakes: I reach for the cup in order to drink, but would not do so if I knew it was empty (or full of poison). More complex cases – and ones that will be central to my argument throughout this book – involve clashes of various degrees among ends. As the system obstacle anticipates, these clashes will be common. It is apparent that the schematic notion of what the agent finds valuable or pursues as good merely holds open a place into which a substantive conception of the good can step. Obviously, the very idea of an end cannot protect one from all value conflicts; neither, however, does commitment to an end typically amount to a commitment come what may. The structure of mutual regulation of ends needs to be filled in somehow before it can be very useful. In what follows, I aim to elaborate two main ways that this structure gets developed. First, in the remainder of this section and in §29 I will show how the simple notion of counterfactual control can be extended so as to build a hierarchy of ends. Second, in §§20 and 26 I will develop the theme of reflective endorsement by the agent, which so far merely lies implicit in the notion of "what the agent finds valuable."

The simple notion of an end cannot bear the full burden of the evaluative status of the goal: We need now to invoke the idea of a *final end*. In describing ends as aims, I have so far avoided saying whether they are sought for their own sakes or not. The drink I presumably want in order to assuage my thirst, not just to have a drink in my hand. Why the chicken wants to get to the other side we will never know, but it is probably not a final end for the fowl. A final end, sought for its own sake, is valued in itself. This implies something about the evaluative (and not just the causal) context. Since final ends provide fundamental reasons for action, the practical implications of a final end must go beyond ruling certain options out. A final end must in addition indicate something positive about when the agent would act.[3] What? We can see in the idea that a final end is

---

3 We cannot, therefore, understand a final end solely as "providing a *filter of admissibility* for options," to quote the core of the analysis of intention in Bratman 1987, 33. Bratman separates this planning and deliberative layer from what he views as an underlying layer of belief-desire reasons. By eschewing such a separation of levels, I make such a formal theory of rationality relatively difficult and make a substantive theory of rationality, which delves into the reasons that "underlie," less avoidable; but since my aim is to show how substantive practical rationality is *possible*, I have no choice but to short-circuit the separation of values and plans the way that ends do.

valued "in itself" a first-stage filling in of the placeholder idea we arrived at above, the idea that an end is pursued as good. What the agent finds valuable about a final end is itself. Aristotle suggested the relevant sort of counterfactual. He explains his claim that virtue and pleasure are final ends by noting that "we choose indeed [each of them] for themselves (for if nothing resulted from them we should still choose each of them)" (*N.E.* I.7, 1097b3–4). This parenthetical counterfactual test asks us to isolate the good or object of pursuit described in the end from any others that flow from it (whether normally or by necessity) and to determine whether we would choose it on its own. If we would, then we reaffirm that our description of the end marks out something we consider valuable. If we would not brush our teeth unless it prevented tooth decay or gingivitis, we do not hold tooth brushing to be a final end. If we would listen to Brahms even if no other value resulted, then listening to Brahms is one of our final ends.

Aristotle's counterfactual test can serve as part of a more general account of when one end is sought for the sake of another. End x is sought for the sake of end y only if x would still be sought even if the only value to be realized in so doing would be (that described by) y – setting aside even the advantages of x itself insofar as they are not conceptually carried by y. On Aristotle's view, for example, virtue and pleasure are also sought for the sake of happiness. If so, the test implies that one would (rightly) seek virtue and pleasure even if happiness were all that resulted from so doing. Whether an end is someone's final end may be settled by a special case of this test, the reflexive case in which $x = y$: end x is a final end only if it would still be sought even if the only value to be realized in so doing would be (that described by) x. Generalizing the test in this way helps explain what has puzzled many, namely how Aristotle can think that some ends can be sought both for their own sakes and for the sake of something else. These intermediate final ends will (in part) be ends that yield positive answers on both the reflexive and the non-reflexive applications of the counterfactual test.

It is a striking fact about the "pursuit for the sake of x" relation, as found in Aristotle and the subsequent tradition, that it is antisymmetrical; that is, although an object can be sought for its own sake, distinct objects cannot each be sought for the sake of the other. But why not? If pleasure is choiceworthy for its own sake, and so is virtue, then why wouldn't a result of either be enough to make the other worth choosing? The answer, I suggest, is that the bare counterfactual condition is not a sufficient condition of "pursuit for the sake of x" (hence my "only if" in the last paragraph). What fills in for the "x" must also be reflectively accepted by the agent as appropriately regulating the manner and extent of the pursuit. In this way, the notion that one end is sought for the sake of another fills in the initial idea that an end is pursued as valuable. The other end for the sake of which it is sought must not only be recognized as valuable by the agent, but also as helpful to indicating what it is about the first end that is valuable. The second end cannot do this unless its regulation of the first is appropriate. Whether it is or not is a substantive question, not merely a formal one. The full Aristotelian analysis of "S pursues x for the sake of y," then, is, first, that S would pursue x even if the only value realized in so doing would be (that described by) y; and, second, that S reflectively accepts y as appropriately regulating x (and not vice versa unless $x = y$).

A vivid Aristotelian example of a more final end regulating a less final one by qualifying the latter's pursuit is his appeal to the idea of the fine to help define the virtue of generosity or liberality in *N.E.* IV.1, with regard both to the sources and to the uses of money. The generous man "will take from the right sources, e.g. from his own possessions" (1120a31–b1), whereas the greedy may be led to acquire wealth from pimping, usury, robbery, and gambling (1121b31–1122a11). Since the wasteful do not aim at what is fine, "sometimes they make rich those who should be poor, and will give nothing to people of respectable character" (1121b4–6). In these ways, the fine regulates the virtue of generosity, not by overriding it, but by helping specify that wherein generous action consists. A rough account of generosity might refer only to moderate donation of money; but moderate donation that ignored the distinction between the fine and the base would not, it appears, be truly generous.

We can now get a little clearer about the antisymmetry of "pursuit for the sake of x." For example, take Professor Bates, who values having a powerful computer partly for its own sake. He delights in the sheer speed of the machine on his desk, and would purchase a powerful one even if he had no great need for it. He also values his writing (at least in part) for its own sake, and he does his writing on his computer. In his case, he values the computer also for the sake of his writing. On the analysis we are pursuing, this implies that in his quest for more and more computing power he will modulate and specify what he does by looking to the aim of writing. He will favor aspects of computing power (such as dynamic memory) that aid his writing over those (such as floating-decimal calculation capacity) that do not. If this is all there is to the structure of his pursuits, he will not do the opposite. He will not, for instance, embark on a book project simply as a way to exercise the vast computing power sitting on his desk (or even to rationalize getting more). But now the question arises whether he could not also accept the reverse direction of regulation. Would it be incoherent to suggest that he also sometimes designs research projects in particular ways just so that he has an excuse to get a faster hard disk? Would it be inconsistent of him to accept both directions of regulation? Although the answer is that bidirectional regulation of this sort is clearly possible, this need not disturb the general and traditional point about the antisymmetry of pursuit. On a given occasion or in a given respect, either the writing or the computing power regulates. Where a given computer feature or aspect of his writing project is clearly necessary both for enjoying computing power and for pursuing the writing project he has in mind, neither end need be seen as regulating the other. Regulation of one end by the other will exist only with respect to those features of the computer that cannot be given a rationale except in terms of the writing project, and vice versa for features of the writing. Accordingly, it will remain true that in any given respect, if x is pursued for the sake of y, then y is not pursued for the sake of x (unless $x = y$).[4] Frequently, one may reasonably abstract from these details and speak more generally of the relative place of certain ends in one's life. When Aristotle speaks of virtue as regulating pleasure, he may be understood as speaking loosely in this way about the general pattern of one's life. It is not that pleasure is never, in any respect, to inform one's specification or pursuit of virtue. Rather, in general, one's pleasures ought to be the proper ones, molded by virtue; and one's detailed account of virtues such as generosity should not generally be governed by an eye fixed on pleasure.

The regulatory structure of an agent's pursuit makes up his or her "conception of the good." A conception of the good is neither as simple as a formula, such as "virtuous pleasure"; nor again (pace Rawls) is a fully worked-out "life plan" required. Rather, a rougher description of the ends to which an agent looks, and how some of them regulate others, would seem closer to what is meant by a "conception of the good." In

---

4 This solution generalizes an idea in Kirwan 1967. Kirwan introduced a quantifier over occasions in order to explain how Aristotle could think that a given end could be sought both for its own sake and for the sake of another end. By using the counterfactual test to explain this aspect of the Aristotelian view, I avoid falling back on such a quantifier for this purpose, and thus get a real hierarchy of ends going. Generalizing from occasions to respects, however, I find such an additional quantifier useful instead for explaining the antisymmetry of regulation.

addition, in the structure that is well regulated as far as the agent is concerned we have at least the skeleton of an answer to the question what it means to pursue ends as good (cf. Velleman 1992). For a fuller answer, I again have to ask the reader's patience: Part Four will develop the additional regulatory structure that comes with the idea of an ultimate end, while Chapter XIV will argue that the sort of account I have developed at least invites objective constraint.

The idea that ends can be sought for the sake of further ends adds a layer of complexity to the ordinary empirical connection between having an aim or end and deliberating along certain lines. A desire, and an intention that corresponds to it, simply states an object: "to get something to drink," for instance. A hierarchy arranged by the relation of pursuit for the sake of an end can yield complex intentional objects, of the form "to get something to drink in order to regain my voice." By articulating the reasons underlying the first-order object of intention or desire, an end allows for a more discriminating regulation of which options are considered. In the example, the end will help control which drink I select (something honeyed); and if someone unexpectedly offers me a throat lozenge I may well stop trying to find a drink. The counterfactual that I have been taking to be part of the analysis of an end also plays a role in deliberation. Indeed, the end whose content implies a certain counterfactual may often have its effect on an agent's deliberation via the agent's thinking in terms of that very counterfactual. When suddenly offered the lozenge, I may stop and think if all I really wanted that drink for was to soothe my voice, or whether I would also like a drink to slake my thirst. If I decide that I would like a drink also for that reason, I may accept the lozenge and keep looking for the bar.

§8. DELIBERATION CAN BE OF ENDS

To understand pursuit for the sake of an end in terms of the counterfactual cum regulatory analysis of the last section is to begin to make room for deliberation of ends. By showing how a complexly ordered hierarchy of ends might not only be possible but also practically important, this analysis offers an alternative both to simply figuring out how to satisfy a given desire by end–means reasoning and to balancing clashing desires/ends in an intuitive fashion. Neither of these standard models affords interesting room for deliberation of ends, for the first takes the ends simply as given by desire, while the second tempts one to think of there being a single end, desire-satisfaction, that is to be maximized when desires conflict. On my analysis, by contrast, there is ample room for agents to consider whether ends that they have subordinated to other ends are in fact appropriately regulated by them. Accordingly, if this analysis is correct, it ought to be possible to deliberate about ends.

Thus encouraged, we may now face the analytic version of the scope obstacle, which might be expressed in one of two ways. The first begins from something it takes to be a fact about the occasions of deliberation, namely that when we deliberate, we always start from some end. This orienting end, the suggestion is, sets the limits of that particular course of deliberation. Of course, on some other occasion deliberation from some other end may bring the first end into question; but in either case, deliberation is bounded, on this view, by the end from which it sets out. In the words of Ross's misleading but influential translation of Aristotle, "we deliberate not about ends but about means" (*N.E.* 1112b11–12). The second analytic version of the scope obstacle simply takes it to be a conceptual fact about "deliberation" that ends are not the sort of thing we deliberate about. We deliberate about what to do, not about what ends to have. Although I will now criticize these negative arguments, I will also try to identify the kernel of truth that each contains.

"We deliberate not about ends but about means." Is a given course of deliberation limited by the end from which it began, so that all deliberation can be construed as figuring out means (instrumental or constitutive) to that end? If it were a conceptual truth that deliberation were thus limited, then the phenomena of deliberation should reflect this fact. They do not. Consider the case of Charlene, whose lifelong dream has been to become surgeon general of the United States (C. Everett Koop having been her childhood hero). Naturally, she aims to go to medical school when she finishes college; and she also aims to be a successful doctor – in particular, one who has a wide reputation for brilliance and integrity. These understandings of her intermediate ends reflect her ideas about how to achieve her dream. She is now deciding what courses she should take. Organic Chemistry is a must, she finds out. But she also discovers, to her horror, that those who do not cheat in Organic Chemistry all do poorly in it. And Charlene knows that her grades so far are too marginal for her to get into a decent medical school without having a top grade in Organic. Repulsed by her friends' suggestion that she simply go along with the common practice of cheating, she begins to have second thoughts about her commitment to medicine. If this is the sort of person that becomes a doctor in our society, she wonders, does she really want to spend her life with them? Would a good reputation with doctors, of the sort required

for being put forward as surgeon general, be worth much? Although she had previously rejected law school out of hand, that option begins to look more and more attractive to her. These perhaps exaggerated reflections lead her to examine her options further. She decides that her mediocre performance so far in college has been due to her difficulties with science classes, whereas in history and especially philosophy, the prototypical pre-law classes, she has done quite well. She begins to see the writ upon the wall: Law school is in her future. She shifts her attention to figuring out what she needs to do to get into law school.

A typical course of deliberation? Surely. In this brief example, I have not tried to set out what might make her revision of her aim rational – there will be plenty of occasion for such examples later. The more basic question for the moment is whether this is "a given piece of deliberation" (see Sherman 1989, 71, 82) or rather several adjacent ones? I naturally have tried to describe the case fairly seamlessly. Charlene could certainly run through this course of thinking in one climactic afternoon. Those who see deliberation as limited to ascertaining means, however, may want to break the case into two or more stages. A simple way of dividing it up would be to see one episode of deliberation guided by the juvenile dream of becoming surgeon general, which reaches a dead end in which she abandons this aim; and a second course of deliberation that restarts from the alternative end of getting into law school. But this description omits her pivotal comparison of these two objectives, when she decides which of them to pursue. A tripartite division could cast this middle step as a course of deliberation about how to remain a person of integrity, which step explains why she drops the medical goal and shifts to the legal one. But recall that as her initial ends were described, integrity figured merely as a means to becoming surgeon general. How does integrity become the end against which her initially most final end comes to be judged? The three parts cannot be linked together to represent Charlene's deliberations as a single chain of reasoning. That they cannot will obviously not upset the nonbeliever in deliberation about ends, but it does highlight the cost of holding onto the assumption that deliberation is limited to means: It obscures the unity of a course of deliberation such as Charlene's.

The regulative aspect of my analysis of ends, by contrast, helps reveal the unity of Charlene's deliberation. What she discovers – aided by her revulsion – is not a hidden end absent at the beginning, but the fact that she cannot abide that the goal of becoming surgeon general should regulate (and here delimit) her aim of being a person of integrity. (She need not decide that the regulation should go the other way.) On this basis having decided that this medical goal is not her most final end, she begins to wonder whether her detailed understanding of success should be governed by her specifically medical ambitions. Introspecting, she notices a factual pattern in her performance that suggests an alternative specification of success compatible – so she now thinks – with remaining regulated by integrity. In this way, as I would see it, she revises her conception of the good.

If one is allowed to look beneath the surface for an overarching end structuring a course of deliberation, then cannot my opponent postulate some end that remains constant, guiding Charlene throughout? That is, instead of partitioning her deliberation, as discussed above, my opponent might hypothesize the existence of some still abstract end that can remain constant through it: that of maximizing her career satisfaction, perhaps, or that of achieving success without compromising integrity. Her deliberation would then be cast as assessing alternative means to this abstract end. I reply that although many instances of deliberation may be like this, Charlene's need not be. Take a contrasting case, that of someone casting about for what to do before lunch. Here, the hypothesis that some such hidden end is present, such as enjoyment or productivity, may help explain why the agent runs so systematically through the options. We can fully understand Charlene's initial deliberation, however, in terms of her aim of becoming surgeon general. Hence, there is no corresponding empirical basis for assuming that the broader end must have been present all along. This branch of the first obstacle, which focuses on the limitations of a given episode of deliberation, confounds what gets deliberation going with what sets its bounds.

"We deliberate about what to do, not about what ends to have." Strictly speaking, this is true. That deliberation is essentially concerned with what to do, and is in that sense practical reasoning, is a point that I have embraced from the outset. We can deliberate, and have practical reasons, only about what to do.[5] To have an intention, and similarly to have an end, is not something that we do, any more than having a belief is. While we can do things to influence our ends and intentions, our committing ourselves to them is not an action in any normal sense, either. Accordingly, my opponents conclude, our framing of intentions and our commitment to ends are purely mental phenomena that fall outside the purview of deliberation.

This negative argument overstates a merely verbal point. It is true that

---

5 For the restrictive force of this fact, see the response to Kavka 1983 in Bratman 1987.

we deliberate *about* what to do, and not (primarily) *about* what ends we should have. But this is largely a matter of linguistic convention. To defer to it, it would be more than sufficient simply to say that deliberation is *of* ends. I will not always be so fastidious. That the limitation of deliberation to being about what to do is a merely linguistic one can be seen in the fact that, by the kind of reasoning put forward in the last paragraph, we can equally well show that we do not deliberate about means to our ends. Thus, we deliberate only about what to do; but selecting an action as a means to a given end is not something that we "do," in any normal sense. Rather, it is a purely mental phenomenon, a way of seeing some action in relation to an end to which we are committed. In Charlene's case, for instance, she is not deliberating about the best means to career success: She is deliberating about whether to sign up for premed or prelaw courses. It would be absurd to conclude from this that deliberation is not concerned with selecting means to ends.

The only substantive point lying behind the fastidious verbal one is that in saying what deliberation is about, we must focus upon some connection with what the agent is to do. This requirement hardly limits us, however, for what we do is normally to undertake certain actions as a means to or otherwise for the sake of some end. We sometimes wander aimlessly and do things for no reason, but not usually. Ordinarily, then, both end and means come bundled together within the envelope of what we do. Keeping the end constant, changing the means changes the action. It is equally true that keeping the instrumental steps constant, varying the end can yield actions different in kind. Marrying someone for money differs radically in value and consequences from marrying for love; yet the same steps need be taken to decorate the church and exchange rings. To be sure, if we examine the instrumental steps closely enough, we will see the imprint of the differing ends. The kiss that seals the ceremony may be expected to have more passion in the one case than in the other, for instance. But end and means are more important to an action's identity than any list of physical features. Thus, even if it would be possible to give an exhaustive description of all of the ways in which the action is behaviorally or physically different as a result of its being done for the sake of a different end, it would be a rash reductionist who thought that this list of otherwise disconnected facts about pressure on the lips, time spent fingering the engagement ring, and so on, could usefully be substituted in all explanatory and deliberative contexts for the description including the end. In deciding or explaining, a central question is whether the person is marrying for (the sake of) love or not. Ends are important to individuating and classifying actions, not least from a deliberator's point of view.

Since many of the subtle qualitative differences in the ways we do things are bound up with the ends for the sake of which they are done, framing ends is part and parcel of articulating what is to be done. We deliberate about ends (and about future intentions) all the time, because acting for the sake of an end (and with a future intention) is a pervasive and essential feature of what we do. What we do, and what we choose, is to-do-x-for-the-sake-of-y.[6] Since, as just argued, ends importantly define or individuate actions, we have general reason, independently of the present controversy about the scope of deliberation, to allow that *what is to be done*, deliberation's subject matter, may be analyzed in this way. We deliberate, then, about what to do; and deliberation takes within its purview all essential features of the ways we act, including the ends for the sake of which we act. To revise the statement of the restriction of the scope of deliberation to reflect our discussion, it should read: We deliberate about what to do, and about ends only insofar as they articulate what to do by indicating how action is to be regulated.

§9. ACCEPTING INTERNALISM

As briefly characterized in §2, the pseudo-Humean position starts by separating reason from motivation and "is" from "ought." Taking the psychological separation first, consider how it affects the way both reason and motivation get understood. The sharp division between the faculties of reason and desire generates a corresponding divide between the items they manipulate. Reason works with ideas, which have representative content. Desire is expressed by passions, which do not. As Hume exaggeratedly puts this point (1986, 415):

A passion is an original existence, or, if you will, modification of existence, and contains not any representative quality, which renders it a copy of any other existence or modification. When I am angry, I am actually possest with the passion, and in that emotion have no more a reference to any other object, than when I am thirsty, or sick, or more than five foot high. 'Tis impossible, therefore, that this passion can be oppos'd by, or be contradictory to truth and reason; since this

---

6 As Sarah Broadie has illuminatingly suggested, we may see Aristotle's practical syllogism, not as a rigid pattern for deliberation but rather as an analysis of the structure of the "rational choice" (*prohairesis*) that concludes deliberation (Broadie 1991, 226).

contradiction consists in the disagreement of ideas, consider'd as copies, with those objects, which they represent.

Reason is held to be motivationally inert on its own, and desires and other forms of motivation are held to enjoy neither truth nor falsity. If reasoning is limited to determining what is true or false, it follows that reasoning cannot determine what desires one is to have. If reason neither moves us (by giving rise to motivation in a causal fashion) nor implies how we ought to be moved (by deriving a desire), then surely it cannot in any way tell us what ends to have. It cannot do so "on its own," that is, but only insofar as it begins from the ends implied by desires or other motivating elements that are present at the outset. While reasoning may supply the minor premise of the practical syllogism, pertaining to the "possible," desire (or, more broadly, the passions) must supply the major premise, indicating what end is to be sought.

In the last paragraph's quotation, Hume makes a more radical claim than the pseudo-Humean needs. Few would now be persuaded by the suggestion that desires, passions, and emotions completely lack "any representative quality." These mental entities are best understood as having propositional objects in some sense. One may be angry *that* the philosopher exaggerates just as one may desire *that* he tone down his rhetoric to the bland level that passes for clarity. If Hume's point is instead seen as turning on the narrower claim that passions, unlike beliefs, lack truth-values, it will be recognized as a stronger one. This view is often spelled out as follows: By applying canons of logic and scientific method, reason can help us approximate true belief by aligning our views with the facts. The facts, here, are the "truth makers," and nothing parallel exists for desires. Intrinsic desires, like moral commitments, are prescriptive: While they may have "propositional content," the propositions involved concern how the world ought to be, not how the world is.

This way of building the pseudo-Humean position from the semantic separation of "is" and "ought" generates a distinctive version of the scope obstacle. A representative statement of the alleged restrictive implications of keeping this distinction in view is Herbert Simon's (1983, 6–7):

The principle of 'no conclusions without premises' puts forever beyond reach normative statements (statements containing an essential *should*) whose derivation is independent of inputs that also contain *should*'s. None of the rules of inference that have gained acceptance are capable of generating normative outputs purely from descriptive inputs. The corollary to 'no conclusions without premises' is 'no *ought*'s from *is*'s alone.' Thus, whereas reason may provide powerful help in finding means to reach our ends, it has little to say about the ends themselves.

Just as passions must provide motivations, so too they must provide the "oughts" with which reasoning begins. The ends, in other words, must on this view be given at the outset.

There are obviously many ways to attack this pseudo-Humean position. One, to which I will contribute indirectly, is to begin to break down the separation of reason and passion. Another would be to attack the view that an "ought" cannot be derived from an "is." A more frontal plan of attack would be to criticize the assumption that reasoning is limited to determining what is true or false.[7] Perhaps reasoning also includes determining what to desire. Although I sympathize with these efforts, I fear that in the context of a study such as this one, aiming to show that we can deliberate rationally about ends, such an approach would beg the question at issue by bringing into play a different definition of rationality. Accordingly, to keep my argument focused against my opponents, I will proceed more cautiously and indirectly. Although in the end my conclusions may imply that reasoning is not limited to determining what is true or false, I will not start out by challenging this part of the pseudo-Humean position. Instead, I aim to work within its framework, at least initially, to see what leeway it allows. Similarly, I will not try to claim that an "ought" may be derived from an "is," but will instead question the restriction of reasoning involving "oughts" to the sort of syllogistic pattern that Simon appears to have in mind. Accordingly, I suggest that we start by exploring what reasoning can accomplish even if it cannot work "on its own" – by accepting, that is, a generalized form of internalism.

The relevant form of internalism is a restriction upon an agent's possible motivating reasons for action. As we saw in §7, although the notion of a reason for action is broader than that of an end, it resembles it in involving both a motivational aspect and a normative aspect or "ought." Pseudo-Humeans reasonably characterize an agent's practical reasoning as arriving at circumstantially specific motivating reasons for action. They deny that reason can produce these conclusions on its own, on the grounds that it cannot generate the motivational aspect of the reason by itself. They allow, however, that reasoning can generate such conclusions if it starts from an

---

7 The separation of reason and passion has been called into question by, e.g., A. Rorty 1982 and Nussbaum, forthcoming. On the derivation of "ought" from "is," see Searle 1964 and the more general discussion in Putnam 1981. The assumption that reasoning is limited to determining what is true and false is flagged in Hare 1981, 216.

initial motivating reason. To yield practical conclusions, ones that state motivating reasons, an agent's deliberations must maintain an appropriate connection to initial reason. This connection must allow motivation available at the outset to transfer to the conclusion. An internalist about an agent's (motivating) reasons for action holds that they all must bear some such connection back to an initial motivation. As we will see, however, much will hang on the precise characterization of the needed connection and of the "initial" set of motivations.

By allowing for rational connections that broaden the set of motivating reasons, the pseudo-Humean here allows for some practical reasoning. This concession is not an accidental peculiarity of their view. Although I will be building on this concession, this will not produce merely an ad hominem argument, for the sort of practical reasoning that they allow ought to be recognized by all: end–means or "instrumental" reasoning. It was allowed by Hume. End–means reasoning, aimed at selecting sufficient means on the basis of a correct understanding of the relevant causal facts, can undercut a "passion" – that is, a specific motivating reason – when it comes up against serious obstacles. When the agent is luckier, presumably, such reasoning will yield more specific or more timely motivating reasons than those from which it started. In yielding conclusions about which means to take (or not to take) in the circumstances, instrumental reasoning plainly is not acting "on its own." In the relevant Humean or pseudo-Humean sense, it is acting in concert with desire, which provides the initial end. That this is reasoning seems relatively noncontroversial. The prima facie irrationality of willing an end while failing to will any means sufficient to it is often remarked (for a recent discussion, see Darwall 1983, 14–15). It is similarly irrational to select as a means something known not to be causally sufficient to yield the desired end. If I go to the market with the aim of coming back with enough food to feed myself and my mother for a month, I deliberate badly if I choose to trade my only asset (a cow) for five beans (which I know not to possess abnormal causal powers). The deliberation yielding this conclusion is irrational: It chooses as a means to the end from which it started something plainly neither sufficient to achieve it nor as close to being sufficient as I could have come. In these various forms, then, instrumental reasoning needs to be recognized even by the pseudo-Humean.

What kinds of connection can instrumental reasoning forge between initial motivations and motivating reasons? Containing end–means reasoning within a deductive framework would yield a very narrow internalist restriction; but as I argued in §5, ordinary instrumental reasoning cannot be given a deductive reconstruction. Accordingly, such a narrow internalism would leave out most of what ordinarily counts as end–means reasoning and much of what ought to count as reasoning of that sort. If the pseudo-Humean upholders of the scope obstacle want to accommodate the forms of instrumental reasoning that actually occur, therefore, they will need to be more liberal than this about the connection required for the transfer of motivation. For motivation does actually transfer by all the variegated paths of end–means reasoning.

Two further questions are important in specifying the relevant internalism: what the relevant initial set is, and when the initial time is. The relevant set of motivations is all of the agent's, not just the motivation or end with which a given path of deliberation explicitly begins (cf. Williams 1981a). This can be shown by reference to a pattern of end–means reasoning commonly recognized as rational. Deliberating about how to achieve a given end, we decide that there is no reasonable way to achieve it, and forsake its pursuit (cf. Broadie 1991, 241). Now at first blush, this might seem to be a possibility wholly at odds with an internalist restriction on reasons. My passions spur me to pursue instant fame, but after canvassing the ways that this might be achieved, my reason says no. Despite this anti-Humean appearance, however, the internalist can domesticate this pattern of reasoning by explaining that the "no" draws its force from others of the agent's motivations. This is in fact what seems to be going on in most such cases. For instance, I note that I could get on the front pages by committing a horrible crime; but I rule this means out as "too high a price to pay" for fame. A more literal price could be paid to a publicist, who might in turn bribe the editors of newspapers and magazines, but that, too, is too much to pay. In both of these responses, the reference to "price" indicates the relevance of other ends with which that of fame competes. The first option is ruled out by the competing end of integrity or virtue, and probably also by a concern about what my family life would be like after achieving grisly fame. In the second, the reference to cost does not invoke the retention of money as a final end; instead, monetary cost figures as a stand-in for all the various goods that could be purchased. This latter, extremely common pattern of reasoning pits all of the ends or motivations connected with goods traded on the market against the end that initiated the deliberation. I know of no way of demonstrating that all of an agent's ends or motives are always relevant initial material for the internalist, but it seems arbitrary to stop anywhere short of the entire set. This potential holism of the motivational constraint will be important for the constructive suggestions of Parts Three and Four, where I will show how much deliberation of ends may be built from the resolution of conflicts among them.

In that connection, it is also important to note that the notion of an "initial motivation" is rather fluid and dynamic. In a complex process of practical reasoning, new motivations may arise. Even if they do not arise as the result of reason working "on its own," they can arise when reason works together with antecedent desires or produces self-discovery. Later it will be important to distinguish among these sources of new motivation; but for now the point is that the internalist constraint should allow for them. The pseudo-Humean reasons for internalism privilege no particular initial stage. To the contrary, they hinge on the alleged motivational inertness of reason, and accept motivations however and whenever they arise. All upholders of the motivational version of the scope obstacle should share this stance, for cases we would noncontroversially recognize as cases of reasoning incorporate the input of desires that arise in the course of it. Suppose, for instance, that I begin to canvass the ways of driving from Venice to Florence, my initial desire being to visit those two cities. In doing so, I notice that one route would take me through Ravenna. As I begin to read about the Byzantine mosaics there, I begin to conceive a desire to visit Ravenna as well. Accordingly, I proceed to settle on a specific Venice–Ravenna–Florence route. Surely the fact that the desire to visit Ravenna did not arise until part way through this planning process should not be taken to prevent its contributing to a new motivating reason. Furthermore, it is not necessary for motivations to persist throughout a process of reasoning for them to make themselves felt in the conclusion. To continue the example, if I subsequently become so excited about the prospect of visiting the Uffizi in Florence, so worried about having enough time to let it sink in, and so bored with Byzantium as a result of taking an art history course that I lose all interest in stopping at Ravenna, it may still be reasonable for me to retain the Venice–Ravenna–Florence route as I try to figure out whether to take a train or rent a car. The latter decision may be rationally made, with proper respect for internalist scruples about the origin of reasons for action, even though it is affected by the residue of a defunct desire. In this respect, ordinary notions of practical rationality build in some deference to our limitations of time and mental energy: They do not require that all reasoning constantly be refreshed as desires change. (On rationality in reconsideration, see Bratman 1987.)

The internalist constraint that is acceptable, therefore, and that I will accept for the sake of argument, holds simply that an agent's reasons for action must derive from motivations that the agent has or had (for a comparably broad definition of internalism, cf. Korsgaard 1986b, 19). That, at least, is as tightly as I have been able to describe the appropriate internalist constraint thus far. In the following section, my aim is to describe another path by which motivations may be connected with antecedent motivations, one that can compete with and supplement the end–means pattern. By exploiting the flexibility of this path – the specifying path – I will be able to show that deliberation can extend to ends, even (eventually) ultimate ends, and can do so compatibly with the loose internalist constraint just articulated.

IV

Specifying ends

The last chapter's conclusion that deliberation is of ends may be thought a purely verbal victory. "Yes," it may be admitted, "there is no contradiction in saying that we can deliberate about or 'of' ends; but that does not mean that deliberation that modifies ends can be rational." While Part Three will show how deliberation of ends can be rationally constrained, we first need to confront the pseudo-Humean side of the scope obstacle, which gives the fundamental philosophical motivation for thinking that deliberation cannot rationally determine ends. Having accepted a generalized internalism about reasons for action, I cannot take a dismissive way with this opponent.

§10. SPECIFICATION DEFINED

This section will define the relation of specification, as it holds between two ends or norms, which will be seen to mark out an alternative both to deductive application of a rule and to end–means reasoning.[1] As we saw in §5, the hope that practical reasoning might be given a deductive reconstruction is a chimerical distraction. Once we fully accept that a deductive approach is not available, it becomes open to us to recognize that the ends and norms with which we begin are not "absolute" in logical

---

1 This section recasts a portion of Richardson 1990c. My appreciation of the importance of specifying ends owes much to Wiggins 1980a; see also Kolnai 1978, 46. In Chapter X I will lay out the way in which Aristotle developed the idea by recasting the *Nicomachean Ethics* as progressively specifying the good. See also *Topics* III.6, 120a6–32. Specification is presumably also akin to what Aquinas means by "determination of certain generalities" in *Summa Theologica* I–II, Q. 95, Art. 2 (Aquinas 1981, Vol. II, 1014). Unfortunately, Aquinas says little about this process of reasoning there. MacDonald 1991, which discusses specification in relation to Aquinas, draws more from Wiggins 1980a and other recent interpreters of Aristotle – including Cooper 1975 and Nussbaum 1986, 297 – than from Aquinas, in this respect.

form. By this I mean that they need not be strictly universal with respect to the domain of possible acts the way the major premise of a Peripatetic syllogism (defined in §5) must be. A schematic example of a logically absolute end-norm (a norm embedding an end) that fits this bill is the following:

(i)   Everything necessary to achieve E is to be done.

In somewhat prolix fashion, this schematic end-norm might be reworded as follows to bring out its logically universal form:

(i') For all actions x, if doing x is necessary to achieving end E, then x is to be done.

In the obvious way, this end-norm can be applied to entail particular conclusions via a Peripatetic syllogism. Yet if deductive reconstruction of practical reasoning is generally unavailable, it becomes both acceptable and plausible to allow norms that implicitly begin with a "generally speaking" instead of an "always" or a "for all actions." For example:

(i*) For most actions x, if doing x is necessary to achieving end E, then x is to be done.

More naturally and in line with the last chapter's conclusion on the scope of deliberation, one might say "within reason, if doing x . . . ," but we don't want to beg too many questions, here.

   The possibility of logically nonabsolute norms is important to the significance of specification, as I will define it. Specifying an end will involve spelling out the ways or circumstances in which it is to be pursued, and the like. If it is logically absolute in that it is to be pursued in *all* circumstances, then specification could add nothing not already implicit in it. If the initial norm were absolute (strictly universal over the domain of possible acts), then a specification that stood alongside it would be otiose, since it would already be implied in the initial norm, and could be omitted as an unnecessary step in a deductive argument to a practical conclusion. For example, if we began with "always do whatever is required for personal success," then "always dress in the way required for personal success" would be redundant. What matters, here, are the many empirical facts about what is required for success, which might or might not involve narrow wardrobe limitations, and not the more specific content of the latter end. If the more specific norm replaced the one it specifies, however, the result would be an implied exception logically incompatible with the initial norm's universal command, jeopardizing the transfer of motivation

70

through specification. Accordingly, to conceive of motivation continuing through a course of specification that does useful work, one must suppose that the norms being specified are not logically absolute in the way required for application via a Peripatetic syllogism.

This supposition poses no difficulty, for our ends are not plausibly viewed as formally absolute in this way. Rather, as we have seen in criticizing syllogistic models in §5, they are typically qualified, at least implicitly, by variants of "generally" or "for the most part."[2] Although the kind of looseness our norms allow is often thought of as making implicit room for exceptions, another way of regarding it is to use Kant's notion of "latitude." This idea, which he develops most fully in expressing the kind of looseness built into the "obligatory ends" of beneficence and self-perfection, is different insofar as it suggests that the exact extent and nature of the duty may require further specification. Thus, in presenting the positive duty of beneficence, Kant presents it as not specifying when, exactly, one must help others, what one must do to help them, or to what degree one must sacrifice one's own welfare in doing so. Nonetheless, there is an "imperfect" duty to do *something* for the sake of helping others (Kant 1964b *Tugendlehre*, Introduction, secs. 7–8). I believe that our common beliefs about beneficence are similarly latitudinarian; and other ends are even more obviously qualified in this way. To be sure, not all philosophers make room in their thinking for nonabsolute norms. For instance, Gibbard's catalogue of types of norms (1990, 94) glaringly omits the possibility of nonabsolute norms. In addition, many philosophical debates begin by supposing that norms are logically absolute. A philosopher may think, for example, that a political regime must do everything it can to promote liberty *and* everything it can to promote equality, and end up having to cope with the resulting conflict (see §33). Yet most ends, including these political ideals, fall short of requiring that we do everything possible that can be done in their service. A serious commitment to the end of liberty does not imply that one must shield pornographers or reduce government regulation to an absolute minimum. That ends are sometimes expressed simply by single abstract nouns ("liberty," "equality") or by infinitive phrases ("to succeed in business," "to live up to my ideal of courage") makes their latitude obvious. In these quite ordinary formulations, ends are logically indefinite as to whether one must do everything

2 This is true even of commonsense moral principles. Cf. Scanlon 1988, in Seanor and Fotion 1988, 134. Hare, responding to Scanlon in ibid., 263, poses the challenge that I am now addressing of how a norm can be seen as "the same" before and after revision.

that contributes to them. To reach an absolute norm of the form of (i'), these ends would have to be expanded by adding "for all acts x, if x is necessary to achieve [the end in question]." Yet as we saw in §5, it is not true that holding an end commits one to pursuing all means necessary to maximizing one's chances of achieving it, or even some means sufficient to achieving it. Our ends, in short, leave logical room for specification. In the following definition of specification, to avoid confusion on this score, I will avoid the more ambiguous substantive or infinitive forms and consider only ends expressed as norms — only end-norms — that spell out whether or not this latitude exists.

Defining the specification relation more precisely will require some preliminary definitions of component notions. Although usefully specifying ends supposes that they are not absolute, it will be convenient to define the relation of specification by reference to artificially tightened versions of these end-norms that, unlike an end-norm that begins with "generally" or "for most actions," can have well-defined and presumably bivalent conditions of satisfaction. The *absolute counterpart* of a norm of the form of (i⋆) is one that restores it to the form of (i') by replacing the hedging "for *most* actions" with the absolute "for *all* actions."[3] The detailed way in which the satisfaction of a norm is to be understood will presumably depend upon the *type* of norm involved, that is, upon whether it is an end, permission, requirement, or prohibition. In general, we can say that an *instance* of an absolute norm is an alternative action that satisfies it. Intuitively, an instance of an end is an example of an action that achieves or actualizes it; an instance of a permission is an example of what is permitted; and an instance of a prohibition is an example of avoiding what is prohibited. Given the generality of my account, it would be wrong to try for too much precision in the notion of satisfaction that underlies this extended usage of the term "instance." (See the instructive worrying of this notion of satisfaction in Wittgenstein 1958, Part 1, secs. 437–9.)

On the basis of these other definitions, I now define *specification*, considered as a relation between two end-norms, as follows:

End-norm p is a specification of end-norm q (or: p specifies q) if and only if
  (a) every possible instance of the absolute counterpart of p would count as an instance of the absolute counterpart of q (in other words, any act that satisfies p's absolute counterpart also satisfies q's absolute counterpart);

3 If a norm is already absolute, then its absolute counterpart is itself. I remind the reader that the absoluteness I have in mind is a matter of logical form, not epistemic basis.

(b) p qualifies q substantively (and not just by converting universal quantifiers to existential ones) by adding clauses describing what the action or end is or where, when, why, how, by what means, by whom, or to whom the action is to be done or the end is to be pursued; and

(c) none of these added clauses in p is substantively irrelevant to q.

Several comments are in order. First, by referring to the absolute counterpart of the specified norm, clause (b) enables specification to be defined in terms of the ordinary notion of containment without requiring that specification proceed from absolute norms.[4] It can therefore rule out making an exception by disjunction. That is, if the original end-norm says, "Generally speaking, when I have received great benefits from someone that were not simply my due, I am to do whatever is necessary to express my gratitude to him or her," this cannot be specified to read, "Generally speaking, when I have received great benefits from someone that were not simply my due, I am to do whatever is necessary *either* to expressing my gratitude to him or her *or to surreptitiously aiding his or her child*."[5] An act that satisfied the second end-norm by aiding the child could fail to satisfy the first end-norm's absolute counterpart. Second, clause (b) implies that the sense in which a specification is more "specific" than what it specifies goes beyond the "subset" requirement of clause (a), ruling, for instance, that a move from "Do what is necessary to achieve success" to "Do one of the things necessary to achieve success" is not a specification. Setting a brick is not a way to build a house. Specification proceeds by setting out substantive qualifications that add information about the scope of applicability of the norm or the nature of the act enjoined or the end aimed at. Sometimes it will do all three at once. For instance, "Within reason, do what is necessary to improve my chances of getting into medical school" might become "Generally speaking, while I am at school, do whatever morally acceptable acts are necessary to assuring myself a reasonable chance of getting into a premier East Coast medical school." Third, while clause (a) rules out specification by disjunction, clause (c)

4 Specification might begin from an absolute norm – and for this reason some instances of deductive application are also instances of superfluous specification – but it need not.

5 This restriction on the logical means available in specification is rather narrowly drawn. One might achieve much the same effect by putting the "exception" into the circumstances: "Generally speaking, when I have received great benefits from someone that were not simply my due, and when I do not have an opportunity to aid his or her child surreptitiously, I am to do whatever is necessary to express my gratitude." This norm, however, is of narrower scope than that in which the exception is by disjunction; in particular, the former does not say what one's duty is in those circumstances in which one does have this opportunity, whereas the latter explicitly leaves the agent two options in those cases.

rules out some forms of specification by conjunction. For instance, it blocks taking "to promote the health of my patients and to write a great opera" as a specification of the end of promoting the health of one's patients. The element referring to opera is (presumably!) irrelevant to the patients' health. There is no pretense, here, that any account of relevance can be innocent of substantive normative presuppositions. The notion of "substantive relevance" here flags both this fact and the contrast with the kind of practical relevance that every norm may have with every other because of the possibility of contingent conflicts between them.

Finally, note that the definition of specification as a relation between two end-norms makes no mention of any temporal or justificatory priority between the two. Although I will be suggesting that making our norms more specific is perhaps the most important tactic in resolving practical conflicts, it is also important that we sometimes *revise* an end-norm, for what we consider to be good reasons, in a way that will not count as a specification of it. Sometimes we move to a *less* specific formulation of an end-norm, for instance. Even here, however, the notion of specification can be useful, depending upon the nature of the grounds for claiming that this change is a rational one. In many of these cases, our appeal in changing an end-norm is to a deeper or more general end-norm that underlay it, which we now claim to understand better, and for which we provide a new specification. From the point of view of determining the scope of deliberation, however, the specifying direction has special importance, as we shall see.

§11. MOTIVATIONAL TRANSFER

Having accepted internalism, I must bow to the ways in which motivation is intelligibly transmitted from initial commitments. I will argue that transfer of motivation along the path of specification is at least as intelligible and likely as transfer of motivation from end to means. I concede at the outset that in either case, considerations can arise that defeat this transfer. It may be too inconvenient and noisy to use a howitzer as a means to kill a mosquito. And just because one wants to eat an egg doesn't mean that one wants to eat a rotten egg. In each case, judgment, informed by other considerations, is needed. In arguing this parity, I will first set out the reasons for thinking that transfer of motivation along the path of specification is intelligible and then speak more generally to the parity of specifications and means in deliberation.

Aristotle's cloak "syllogism" (§5) has already familiarized us with the point that our motivation focuses quite naturally on a specific way of achieving some more general end. In some cases, as in that example, the specification of the end ("I need a cloak") will be a transparently expedient one, the cloak simply being the sort of covering that lies ready to hand. Getting any other kind of covering would require too much trouble and expense, and hence conflict with a host of other ends via the agent's money and time budgets. But if this agent had been in Scandinavia, she might just as well have lit on the idea of a fur coat. In other cases, the specification will represent what the agent will justifiably recognize and accept as an authentic and appropriate expression of his end that improves upon and can replace henceforth his earlier, vaguer expression. Either way, however, it will be readily understandable why, if the agent is committed to the more abstract end, he will act on the more specific one. Fulfilling the more specific end is a *way* of fulfilling the more abstract one, in the double senses marked out by the subset and substantive qualification clauses of the definition of specification.

That the agent must light upon a *way* to do what she aims at is equally necessary as that she ascertain some *means* to what she aims at. Charlene's underlying aim was said, at the end of §8, to be that of professional success. Her deliberation will not get anywhere, however, unless she first specifies that aim to some degree. Even if she wants to deliberate by determining what would maximize her chances of professional success, undifferentiated as to profession, she will have to articulate and define what she means by professional success so as to be able to make the comparisons needed. She will need some basis for determining what *counts* as "professional success" in each of the varied professions, and to what degree. Is making partner in a law firm comparable with being accepted as a partner in a medical practice? Such questions will abound. Furthermore, this effort at articulating her notion of "professional success" – again, even if in service of a consequentialist, maximizing model – cannot usefully proceed simply by claiming to lay out the "concept" of "professional success." It is a concept that is variously interpreted, and is certainly contested (whether or not "essentially" so) among the members of the different professions. Thus, those in business are reputed to place the emphasis on earnings as the mark of success, while those in civil service may emphasize influence and contribution to the social good, and those in medicine stress help to patients and recognition by peers. Even if there were an objective fact of the matter about what "professional success" specifically *is*, Charlene would still need to decide whether, once specified in that way, "professional success" captures what she is after. The deliberative problem of specification, in other

75

words, cannot be evaded in this case by an appeal to conceptual analysis. Both this reflective aspect and the nonabsolute character of our norms ensure that judgment has a role in deliberation.

It may be objected that by picking an end as amorphous as Charlene's "underlying" one, I have exaggerated the need for specifying ends. Sometimes ends will be specific enough that there is no further need for interpretation. Might not a corporate manager simply maximize profit, for example, or a tennis pro maximize wins? It is true that there are many ends that, unlike professional success, admit of a quite natural measure. Even with these, however, a need for specification might arise. Does the manager seek to maximize profit understood as the difference between gross revenue and expenditure, or as a rate of return on shareholders' equity? Does the tennis pro want the biggest number of wins, the highest possible win–loss ratio, or the greatest number of Grand Slam trophies? In addition, Wayne Davis has suggested to me the importance of winning legally, prettily, and handily. Each of these specifications will support importantly different courses of action.

Still, the objector is correct that there will be occasions on which there is no pressing practical need to specify an end. I am simply arguing, however, that specifying ends is on a par with selecting means.[6] This conclusion can stand unscathed, for it is also sometimes unnecessary to deliberate about means to one's end. Sometimes they simply lie ready to hand. Although Aristotle imagines it being necessary to make a cloak, the real-time order of thought might go: "I need a covering. Here's a cloak. A cloak is a covering: I'll take it!" In such a case, the cloak is selected as a covering neither on account of an explicit path of specification that explains why the end is narrowed to cloaks nor on the basis of an account of how a cloak is the best means to covering oneself. In such cases, the initial end (or intention) is sufficiently specific already that awareness of the situation of action suffices to indicate what should be done. As Aristotle puts it, in such cases "perception" – not deliberation – supplies the link between the end and the action (*On the Movement of Animals*, ch. 7; cf. Charles 1984, 96). In other words, once a norm is sufficiently specific – a proviso for which no general criteria could be given – we may say that it is the norm in virtue of which the act is to be done even though its logically nonabsolute form prevents us from deducing from it that the action is to be done.

6 Both end and means can be too specific – so specific, for example, that no available action corresponds.

If a specific end can give rise to action without further deliberation, then specifying ends can be all the deliberation that one needs. A quite typical pattern of deliberation omits the selection among alternative means to a given end. Think of this as the case of a limited menu. A menu offers a few set alternatives, indicating the discrete and distinct courses of action open to the agent. Sometimes it takes deliberative work to discern what these options are; that is no small part of practical wisdom; yet it may be accomplished while the agent's aims remain quite up in the air. Once the ends are satisfactorily specified, it will often simply become obvious which menu option is best, namely the only one that satisfies them. Here's an example that abbreviates the discernment phase: "What would I like to eat? Something highly seasoned. That is, something hot rather than simply aromatic. Ah, there's a curry on the menu, the only spicy, hot dish on offer: I'll have that, please." My point is not that the options chosen are not means to the end settled upon: The curry dish may be viewed as a means to (as a vehicle for) spicy taste sensations. Rather, the point is simply that once the end has been deliberatively specified, it is sufficiently obvious which of the available options to take that no further stage of deliberation is required to determine which of the options is a better means to the end as specified. Moreover, sometimes the options we face are sufficiently complex in their internal regulative structure that selecting one just is to select a specification of some final end (a cloak *is* a covering).

§12. SPECIFICATION, JUDGMENT, AND AGENCY

In this section, I will briefly telegraph how the specification relation helps resolve some problems that have long bedeviled philosophical accounts of agency. The specification relation explicitly allows for ends and norms that are logically nonabsolute, because implicitly qualified with "generally speaking" or "in most cases." As a result, as I will now argue, specification allows for a kind of looseness important to maintaining a distinctive regulatory role for ends in practical judgment.

How is doing something to satisfy an end one has adopted different from simply doing something? What is it to adopt an end as something to be done? Accounts that explain this basic notion's role in deliberation and choice by invoking an inferentially tight version of the practical syllogism – a Peripatetic syllogism, for instance – run into a host of problems that cast doubt on the very idea of having an end. These problems concern akrasia or failure to act on one's ends, paradoxes – which I will expound in a moment – of derived obligation or commitment, and related difficulties in making sense of the residue of conflicts. The basic form of all these problems is this: If one does not do what may be inferred from an end to which one is allegedly committed, then one's commitment to this end has been rebutted (by *modus tollens*); but if one must do everything that follows from an end, where is the room for judgment or moderation? My suggestion is that the specification relation provides a needed conceptual buffer by showing how the content of ends can be related to action in a nondeductive fashion.

That some such looseness is needed is a point made by Bratman in addressing the parallel issue of the relationship between intentions and what we intentionally do. He presents the following example: If I know that in running a marathon I will wear down my sneakers, and if these sneakers are of sentimental value to me (as a gift from my wife) but are the only ones that are sufficiently broken in for me to wear, then when I run the marathon I wear them down intentionally, even though I had no intention to wear them down (Bratman 1987, 123). His general claim is that intentions play a systematic role in our planning, disposing us to channel our deliberations in certain ways. It is on the basis of these more systematic considerations that we should attribute intentions. In this case, the intention to run the race shows up in my disposition to deliberate about how to get to the starting line on time, but no corresponding tendency to deliberate about how to wear down my sneakers (125). Nonetheless, I certainly do not wear the sneakers down by mistake. Doing so lies within what Bratman calls the "motivational potential" of the running intention. As he frames this notion, "A is in the motivational potential of my intention to B, given my desires and beliefs, just in case it is possible for me intentionally to A in the course of executing my intention to B" (119–20). In this way he frames the needed "buffer" that insulates the considerations of systematic coherence that apply to intentions from the more complex criteria that seem to be involved in our attributions of intentional action (124). Without such a buffer, the effort to build a set of practically coherent intentions would be eroded by the conflicting demands of what we must admit that we intentionally do. Parallel points apply to ends.

The specification relation sets up a conceptual buffer that works with a more intelligible notion of "motivational potential" than Bratman's.[7]

---

7 Since my account does not directly compete with Bratman's, I would simply recommend to him some narrowed version of the notion of "motivational potential" like that to be defended in the text. Perhaps he had in mind something of the sort all along. Admittedly, the case of wearing down the sneakers involves a foreseeable consequence of running the

Although one can intentionally trim one's nails in the course of listening to a concert, doing so does not intuitively seem part of the motivational potential of the intention to hear a symphony. This is because, I submit, this sort of personal hygiene is not relevant to musical appreciation. To be sure, this judgment of irrelevance is a substantive one, depending upon my having some antecedent understanding of the nature and value of symphonic music. Things might come out differently regarding listening to *Bolero* while having sex or to new wave music while bathing. These might amount to distinctive *ways* of appreciating the music in question, as opposed merely to creative scheduling, which is all that seems to be involved in the case of the nail-trimming concertgoer. Given the omnipresent demands of time, any activity is within the "motivational potential" of any other, in Bratman's extended sense, if it can be done simultaneously with it. Making sense of the nail-trimming concertgoer, however, will require reference to the end of personal hygiene (or of having trimmed nails) as well as the end of musical appreciation. Because of the looseness possible in developing and appealing to nonabsolute norms, practical judgment does have a role. Its nature is the subject of Chapter VIII.

If ends were rules absolute in logical form, then (given suitable factual premises) they would imply specific directives about what was to be done in particular situations. This possibility of proceeding deductively would then give rise not only to the general problem of judgment but also to two more specific problems mentioned above: those of explaining akrasia and avoiding untoward implications of derived commitments. These latter two problems have in common the delicacy of explaining the residue of an end or norm that is in some sense overridden.

By the problem of akrasia I mean in the first instance simply the difficulty posed by the fact that one can have an end and yet not act upon it when a situation arises in which it can (best) be fulfilled. Take the absolute end-norm, "always to do whatever I can for the sake of helping others when doing so would not result in a severe sacrifice of my own welfare." If I fail to promote someone else's welfare in some situation in which doing so would not amount to any significant sacrifice on my part, and I know that, then this failure provides prima facie evidence against attributing this absolute end to me. If the attribution of ends to me must always be amended to reflect what I actually do, and if this amendment

race rather than a way of running the race: Specification does not mark out the only channel along which motivation runs.

process is wholly determined by this matching effort, however, then the attributed ends will cease to do any explanatory work. They will become so many idling wheels.

Paradoxes of derived obligation represent another way in which the implications of a commitment to a norm can seem to reach too far. These paradoxes have long been known by philosophers working on the logic of "ought." In the present context, the question is whether practical commitment is properly transmitted by (or remains "closed" under) logical implication. Closure under logical implication gives rise to a number of apparent paradoxes. One of the best-known is the so-called Good Samaritan paradox (Prior 1954; Aqvist 1967). A related example is the following:

(1) If S cheats on her lover, she ought to cheat on her lover secretly.
(2) S cheats on her lover.

Hence,

(3) S ought to cheat on her lover secretly.
(4) It is logically necessary that, if S cheats on her lover secretly, then S cheats on her lover.

Hence, if one's obligations (or practical commitments) extend to what follows logically from one's other obligations (or practical commitments) – that is, if obligation is closed under logical implication – then:

(5) S ought to cheat on her lover.

Such amorous advice was not intended, however, by those concerned with avoiding unnecessary hurt!

The requirement of secrecy in cheating on one's lover is like a requirement of reparation. It kicks in only when another norm is being violated. It is this other norm ("Do not cheat on your lover") that makes (5) paradoxical. Yet how can this norm "hang around," in the face of its flagrant violation, in such a way as to reinforce the idea that if one does cheat, one should at least do so secretly? (I do not mean to endorse this particular way of mitigating the ills of betrayal.) A first step is to recognize that a more ordinary way of expressing (1) would incorporate this background norm against cheating:

(1*) S should not cheat on her lover, but if she does, she should at least cheat on her lover secretly.

80

This way of expressing the requirement of secrecy explains why the "ought" in the second half remains within the consequent by making manifest its role as a norm of reparation or mitigation. This norm is not derived from some more general norm of secrecy in personal relations. Instead, (1★) anticipates a potential breach of its first line of defense. To understand how its second, compensatory line of defense affects the paradox, we should look more generally at the question of the residue of conflicts among norms.

Especially in the sorts of tragic conflict to be discussed in §17, there is reason to think that overridden norms leave two sorts of residue. Both were explicitly and to a degree allowed for by W. D. Ross in his exposition of prima facie or possum duties.[8] Practical residue would include resultant duties to make reparations, to apologize, or to mitigate the harm caused by one's infraction. Despite Ross's intentions, however, it has never been easy to see just how possum norms are supposed to give rise to residue in cases in which they are playing dead. The source of trouble is the fact that these norms are seen as both fixed and logically absolute or inflexible.

By contrast, the specification relation allows for a continuous development of the agent's normative view despite the fact that the initial norms are not absolute, being qualified by a "generally speaking" or equivalent. To be sure, if logical contradiction were all that mattered, then such norms could never seriously conflict. Yet practical conflict goes well beyond logical contradiction (§5), and an agent has reason to seek mutual support among her ends going beyond removing contradictions (§22). She accordingly has reason to build coherence among her nonabsolute norms by specifying them appropriately. Removing a conflict by specifying one of the norms does not mean that its initial form must be renounced. It can, without logical contradiction, "hang around" to guide future deliberation about related cases. Specifically, it can "hang around" to guide deliberation about what reparation or mitigation is appropriate, given how the conflict was resolved.

To illustrate this possibility in a somewhat more complex context, I will return to the "paradoxes" of derived obligation to show how the operation of specification can help resolve them. Here, I will suggest, residue shows up in the way in which an action is done when norms

8 Ross 1930, 28; see above, §5. Ross called the emotional residue of conflicts "compunction." Subsequent literature has debated whether the appropriate feeling is sometimes the stronger one of guilt: see Williams 1973; Greenspan 1983; Nussbaum 1986, chs. 2 & 3; Stocker 1990, 28–32.

conflict. In the example of cheating secretly, it appears that the general norm against cheating on one's lover comes up against some unexpressed end of desire that leads the agent to want to cheat. On a purely moral reading of this case, our moral disapproval of S's cheating can easily persist no matter what she does. To get a practical parallel, let us take an akratic version. Indeed, if S's rationale for the conditional norm (1) is well expressed by (1*), then it is plausible that her betrayal would be akratic. She thinks she should not cheat on her lover, but in some sense cannot help herself. The seriousness of her continuing endorsement of the abstract prohibition on cheating will then show up in her acceptance of burdensome secrecy, and no doubt in guilty feelings, as well. The situation is like a clash between two norms. Something – either another norm or, as in S's case, an irresistible urge – induces her to violate a given norm. The contest is not simply an either–or, however: Having violated this norm does not mean that its demands disappear. Here, they remain present in the way in which S is to act, given that she is cheating on her lover. Her action is specified in a way that (presumably) responds to one of the underlying rationales of the ban on cheating, namely the aim of avoiding hurting one's lover's feelings. If, as the specification relation allows, these norms are all nonabsolute, then there is no logical contradiction in her general commitment to fidelity coexisting with her desire to cheat in this way. This may not be the ideally rational situation, but it is a possible and a comprehensible one.

§13. ADOPTING NEW ENDS IN DELIBERATION

The preceding three sections have put forward and bolstered the conclusion that the pseudo-Humean internalist must allow specification as a licit kind of connection between an initial end and deliberation's conclusion. What I will now show is that specification can set up new final ends.

That new final ends can result from specification is a possibility that lies implicit in the conjunction of §7's analysis of the notion of a final end and §10's definition of specification. Here is a quick preview: Whether an aim is a final end is determined by facts about the circumstances under which it would be sought. Specification can set out these circumstances. A final end is an end that would be sought even if no other good resulted and that is reflectively accepted as appropriately self-regulating. Starting from a nonfinal end, deliberation might specify that this end is to be sought even when no other good results and in a way mainly responsible to its own regulation. If this specification is accepted on reflection, the end would thereby be promoted to a final end. To flesh out this argument, I will illustrate concretely how specification can qualify an end so as to convert it into a final end.

Deliberation can put forward as a final end something that had not been initially accepted even as a nonfinal end. New nonfinal ends can arise variously in deliberation. Since nonfinal ends are simply aims, without qualification as to that for the sake of which they are sought, they shift all the time in deliberation. Learning to play music on the piano is a different end than simply learning to play music, even though it is a specification of it. If the more specific of the two is the conclusion of practical reasoning, then it will describe an end newly formed in deliberation. Yet though new, it is not entirely novel – as its being a specification of a previous aim indicates. To explain how novel nonfinal ends can arise, we can recur to ordinary end–means reasoning. Under odd circumstances, almost anything can be a means to anything else: For instance, a politician might decide that becoming involved in an effort to help the homeless would be a good means to getting elected, especially on account of its being a high-profile issue that allows for good photo opportunities. Involvement in this issue – so distant in content from the project of getting himself elected – thus becomes a new aim, a new nonfinal end from which further deliberation proceeds. For deliberation to adopt as a final end something that had not even been an aim, then, two steps are needed. Instrumental reasoning can generate it as a nonfinal end, and specification can promote it to the status of a final end.

To make the latter move, specification must cover hypothetical circumstances. Although this possibility is encompassed within the definition of specification, it is worth emphasizing just how natural a role for deliberation this is. Consider Dewey's famous view that "deliberation is a dramatic rehearsal (in imagination) of various competing possible lines of action" (Dewey 1967 [1922], 132–3). As he there describes it,

Deliberation is an experiment in finding out what the various lines of possible action are really like. It is an experiment in making various combinations of selected elements of habits and impulses, to see what the resultant action would be like if it were entered upon. But the trial is in imagination, not in overt fact. . . . Each conflicting habit and impulse takes its turn in projecting itself upon the screen of imagination. It unrolls a picture of its future history, of the career it would have if it were given head.

We do not have to believe either that Dewey is in all points correct about deliberation or that he has stated the whole truth about it in order to agree that deliberation involves thinking about what things would be like if we acted in certain ways. Such mental "experiment" is naturally an important source of specifications.

For a concrete case in which deliberation's dramatic rehearsal of the possibilities elevates a nonfinal end into a final one, let us continue the story of the politician of two paragraphs back, who decides that helping the homeless would be a useful means to getting elected. Recall that this involvement with the homeless is a new aim for him, one that had first occurred to him in surveying the potential issue stances helpful in campaigning. As he pursues this possibility in imagination, he considers what sort of work with the homeless would be best for getting elected. From that point of view, it would be best to have a few encounters with seedy but nonetheless fairly pleasant-looking street people, ones lacking horrible deformities that would distract the television viewer from the intelligent and concerned look on the candidate's face as he tours the sidewalks. These visits should be brief, so as not to take too much time away from campaigning. He imagines sending his advance men out to the streets to find homeless men and women with the right look, asking them questions to assess whether they would say obscene things when the cameras were rolling. At this point, the thought of his own machinations suddenly disgusts him. The situation of these people is horrible; it is unjust the way society treats them; and for him even to contemplate fastidiously picking and choosing which ones to be seen with shocks him, showing him to what depths he has sunk in his effort be get elected. These new feelings are a sign that he has already learned something from this little deliberative experiment (in a way to be explored more fully in §27). It is not that he always aims to be magnanimous and just, or even to avoid being crass; it is simply that this particular way of using the poor strikes him as unacceptably cynical. No, he decides, he will refuse to specify the sort of involvement he has with the homeless so as to maximize his chances of getting elected. He will bravely go out into the streets, inviting the reporters along, and chance whatever sorts of encounters with the homeless that occur. What's more, he decides that the plight of the homeless demands more than a token effort from him. Accordingly, he will not even calibrate the amount of time he spends working to help the homeless by reference to the end of getting elected. Although he will not give up the latter entirely so as to devote himself to working full time in a soup kitchen, he decides he will sign up as a bona fide volunteer with one of the local groups targeted at helping the homeless. This specification of helping the homeless is as far as he feels he needs to go to avoid being a total cynic about it. He resolves that he will continue with this group whether or not he is elected, and to use his political office, if elected, to work for justice for the homeless. What was a mere means is thus transformed into an independent project in the course of his deliberation.

Having emphasized the realism of this example, I now need to interpret it in several respects. To begin with, let me highlight how a new final end has been adopted. Helping with the homeless, which first appeared as a mere means, is specified so as to assert that the way it is pursued is not to be regulated by the end of getting elected. Once the politician has reached that conclusion, he no longer pursues involvement with the homeless solely for the sake of electoral victory. The resolution about specifying when or at what times he will work with the homeless indicates, further, that he would pursue that project even if no other good resulted. At least, it indicates that he would do so independently of whether it aided in his campaign. To consolidate the conclusion that this volunteer work is now a final end for him, we would need to know whether he would pursue it even if no other good were thereby realized; however, he has already provided us strong grounds for an affirmative answer to this more general question by committing himself to helping the homeless even when doing so would interfere with the end to which that project was initially a mere means. Another point about this example that needs emphasis is that while it pursues the specification of a single nonfinal end until it is promoted to a final one, other ends become relevant along the way, especially those of avoiding crass cynicism and promoting social justice, which latter comes into the story rather obliquely. These provide further motivation for the politician's decision. As I argued in §9, the pseudo-Humean internalist must admit that all of the agent's desires and ends are relevant sources of motivation for a deliberate decision. Although I won't try to spell out exactly how each of these additional ends is connected to the politician's decision, we can see that in the decision to become involved with the homeless, cynicism, too, gets specified. That is, he reflectively affirms his commitment not to be boorish in that particular way. In sum, although the politician does not renounce the end of getting elected, he does refuse to accept the idea that it appropriately regulates the end of helping the homeless. With the motivation that still attaches to the nonfinal end of helping the homeless, which gets reinforced by the concern with justice, the politician is free to decide that he will pursue the project of helping them for its own sake.

While my version of the politician's deliberation alluded to these additional ends to suggest a rationale for his conclusion, we can fit his reasoning within the internalist restriction even without invoking these other ends. From this point of view, the issues are more strictly causal. Instrumental reasoning generates "becoming involved with the homeless" as a nonfinal end to which motivation thus transfers. Whether or not motivation should transfer to a nonfinal end, it very commonly does (cf. Mill 1979, IV:6, 36). Specification of that nonfinal end, which preserves that motivation, promotes it to a final end, sought for its own sake. By these two steps, a new final end is adopted – a final end that corresponds to no antecedent aim of the agent's. Taking specification of an end to be a sort of practical reasoning on a par with end–means reasoning, we have shown that practical reasoning can extend to adopting new final ends. Now, however, it will be questioned whether this course of specification really is a course of reasoning. To show that it is, and to incorporate a more explicit place for the supporting ends and emotions that are part of the politician's story, we must turn to the ways in which deliberation can build upon and contribute to a systematic practical theory or conception of the good.

Part Three

System

V

Value incommensurability

It appears to be widely assumed that to respond rationally to cases of value conflict is in effect to weigh or balance the importance of the values involved, and that weighing or balancing cannot be rational unless there is a common measure of value according to which it proceeds. Understood in the right way, the answer to the question whether or not values are or must all be commensurable in that way will determine what sorts of deliberation are possible and useful. If values are all commensurable in the right way, then one need not devote a lot of attention in deliberation to refining one's conception of them severally, and should better concentrate on weighing how instances of them contribute to the commensurating value (the commensurans, as I will call it). If values are all commensurable in the right way, then deliberation may take on a well-understood and much studied form, that of maximization; while the commensurans itself, if it has the status of being that in terms of which the value of everything else is assessed, will seem a source of value beyond calling into question in deliberation. If values are not so commensurable, then prospects for coping rationally with decisions in which they clash may seem correspondingly dim. Either way, therefore, the commensurability issue lurks as a reef upon which hopes for rational deliberation of ends seem likely to be wrecked: If values are commensurable in the relevant sense, then maximizing good consequences, according to some end taken for granted, is the order of the day; whereas if values are not commensurable in this sense, then rational deliberation seems often impossible. Although this worry may be vivid enough already, many of its defining terms and component arguments still lie obscured from clear view. We must first of all sort out the relevant from the irrelevant sorts of value commensurability. Once this has been done, it will also be important (in §17) to take a look around and notice that value commensurability of the relevant sort does not hold across the board.

§14. COMMENSURABILITY IN DELIBERATION

One reason to take up value commensurability first is that it can be hard to keep discussion of this topic going at its own level.[1] Instead, it tends to wander in either of two directions. For the buoyantly optimistic, all that matters is that we can, in fact, compare options, whether simple or complex. Discussion of commensurability, for these thinkers, floats up to the surface of our preferences or primitive comparative judgments, bobbing there without concern about what goes on underneath the surface. We can compare apples and oranges; what else do you need to know? On the lighter side, then, there is this tendency to reduce commensurability to comparability. For those who think that our practical reasoning needs a firmer anchor, by contrast, discussion tends to get dragged down to the bottom level, that of the ontology of value. (After all, the mere fact that we can form a comparative judgment says nothing, it will be protested, about whether that judgment is rational, well grounded, or even groundable.) Whether this bottom is bedrock on which to build, sedimentary ooze in which to get stuck, or jagged reef on which to be torn apart, it will seem to those pulled in this direction that the possibility of value commensurability must rest, at bottom, on the ontological monism of value. That is, for this heavier style of thinking, value commensurability cannot be made out unless, in some important sense, values really are one in kind. They can be made commensurable only by reference to some one "substantive super-value," which in fact turns out to be all that really is valuable in its own right, other things being valuable only insofar as they instantiate or participate in it (otherwise, how could it claim to commensurate the various competing values?). Yet, as will readily be seen, this is but another way to trivialize the issue of value commensurability. If all instances of value are really instances of the same sort of thing – for instance, if everything that is valuable is so as being pleasure-making – then the very idea of a plurality of values becomes dissolved. Once one has thereby given up value pluralism in favor of an ontologically grounded value monism, there is not any need for *co*measurability, the measurement of one value in terms of another. All one then will need is an accurate assessment of how much of the one value there is. By defending the existence of an important sort of value incommensurability at the end

---

1 I owe much to conversations with Michael Stocker about the problem discussed in this paragraph. The dichotomy it begins to call in question is presented as exhaustive by Griffin 1991, 101–2, from whence the quotation later in the paragraph is taken.

of this chapter, I will be indirectly undercutting any form of value monism strong enough to make commensurability otiose in this way. But the central issue for us concerns, not value theory, but the shape of deliberation. For this purpose, we need to understand value commensurability as a notion poised between surface judgments on the one hand and bottom-level ontology on the other. Only this form of commensurability could interestingly underwrite maximization; this sort I shall show not to be a prerequisite of rational choice.

In the present chapter, then, I will proceed as follows. In §15, I will examine the superficial form of commensurability that rests measurement solely on the comparisons that we can in fact make. The sense in which this notion does involve measurement will be set out and shown not to be of much use in typical cases of deliberation, for it reflects rather than guides decisions in most cases. The sort of commensurability at stake in the question whether commensurability is a prerequisite of rational choice will be defined in §16. Commensurability of this deliberative sort would swim along between the surface and the bottom. Once this notion of value commensurability has been understood and distinguished, §17 will present evidence for the existence of widespread value incommensurability. The need to make sense of the difference between the mere plurality of types of good or value and their incommensurability is an important reason to pursue the true intermediate notion. If commensurability implied monism, then plurality would imply incommensurability; yet it seems not to. The chapter's final section will explore the difference. In general, we might expect there to be some divergence between the sorts of value or good that exist and the mental resources we have for thinking about them.

§15. PREFERENCE-BASED COMMENSURABILITY

A powerful modern theory appears to bolster the idea that to deliberate rationally is to maximize some good or some index of goodness: expected utility theory. According to this view, a general form of which underlies accounts of consumer choice in descriptive economics, individual welfare in welfare economics, and contemporary decision theory, rationality imposes on the individual only a few quite schematic requirements of order.[2]

---

2 I depart from the usual convention of referring to these axioms as "consistency" axioms. The requirements on preferences that are typically referred to as "consistency" constraints (asymmetry, transitivity, completeness, etc.) are needed, not to avoid logical inconsistency, but to define a binary relation of preference that yields an ordering.

If these are met, then well-established theorems show us that the individual's preferences can be represented in terms of a "utility function," and his or her rationality summed up in terms of maximizing the index that function embodies, traditionally called "utility." If this is what practical rationality amounts to, then it seems to imply value commensurability. It also has no place for deliberation of ends. The relation between ends and means has no specific place in this model at all, which directly concerns the choice of "alternative outcomes" and – as we shall see below – *excludes* consideration of whether these outcomes are valued for their own sakes or instead as means. Preferences, not ends, are the basis of this view. In this section, I will argue that this distinctive modern approach presents merely an illusion of commensurability and is so ill suited as a model for deliberation that it should cede that ground to other views. However valuable it may be as a way of organizing information about consumer demand or attitudes toward risk (and in these areas too its contribution is debated), the preference-based theory of rationality is woefully deficient as an account of deliberation.[3]

To bring the preference-based view into focus, it is above all necessary to distinguish different interpretations of utility, only one of which fits it. As first philosophically used, "utility" was connected – both by Bentham and (equivocally) by J. S. Mill – with pleasure, a distinctive and allegedly measurable state of mind. It was dissociated from mere "usefulness," which, as Mill foresaw, would become associated in the popular imagination with the joyless labors of a Mr. Gradgrind (cf. Nussbaum 1991). As Mill also saw, the idea of "usefulness" remains too indeterminately instrumental – allowing so many ways to fill in "useful for _____" – to serve as the basis of any systematic theory of morality or practice. For this reason, he presents utility/happiness/pleasure frankly as the "summum bonum" or highest good, the ultimate end at which all actions aim. In the wake of strong criticism of this particular identification of the content of the good, contemporary discussions have generally given up the attempt to interpret utility via some single substantive end.

In its place stand two additional sorts of interpretation of utility (cf. Sen 1985; Hansson 1981; Gärdenfors and Sahlin 1988). On the first, the so-called *realistic* interpretation, the notion of utility is still intended to capture an individual's overall well-being or welfare. Instead of being identified

---

3 Hampton, forthcoming, powerfully argues to a similar conclusion, under the assumption that the expected utility theorist seeks to work within Humean limitations on reasoning. I argue, in effect, that even bending these limits will not save the preference-based theory.

with some supposedly homogeneous good, such as pleasure, however, utility is conceived as an index of overall well-being, which in turn is taken by some in this school to consist of a complex arrangement of many necessary goods and (undoubtedly) some optional ones (see, e.g., Griffin 1986; also Mill 1979, ch. 2, para. 11). Others defending a "realistic" interpretation, tied above all to the individual's good, simply take utility as an index of that good, while attempting to avoid committing themselves to any particular view of its content (e.g., Broome 1991).

On the second, *formalistic* interpretation, "utility" is again the name of an index, but in this case an index constructed from an individual's preferences. This is the interpretation that prevails in expected utility theory, where it originally arose (in reaction to the St. Petersburg paradox) as a way of reflecting the fact that no one would pay an unlimited amount of money to participate in a gamble of infinite expected monetary value (see the historical sketch in Savage 1954, 91–8). It is an approach shared between those who take the probabilities of alternative outcomes as fixed and objective, as in the classic presentation of Von Neumann and Morgenstern (1980 [1953]), and those in the tradition of Ramsey (1931) and Savage (1954) who make room for subjective assessment of probabilities. Preference itself is understood, not primarily in psychological terms, but rather formally, as a (two-place) relation, xPy, between alternative outcomes or states of affairs x and y (or, in the case of Jeffrey 1983, between propositions describing the same). An agent's overt behavior (verbal or otherwise) is – wrongly! – taken in this tradition to be an unproblematic source "revealing" preferences. The requirements of rationality are viewed as embodied in a number of seemingly innocuous axioms that are imposed on the preferences thus revealed. The first of these simply sets out in rigorous fashion what is meant by a "preference ordering." First, the relation must be *asymmetrical*: If x is preferred to y then it is not the case that y is preferred to x.[4] Second, the relation should be *transitive*: If x is preferred to y and y is preferred to z, then x is preferred to z. If these axioms are met by the preference relation, then the relation begins to indicate an ordering among the alternatives. Additional axioms are needed to ensure that the preferences can be represented by a numerical index or "utility function." Let the set of alternatives be expanded by adding all probabilistically weighted combinations of the "simple" outcomes, called

---

4 It is important to emphasize the asymmetry axiom, as von Wright 1963 does, in order to explain why the notion of "consistency" among preferences, as typically used, can only mean "consistency, given that the axioms that ought to govern preferences are met." See also Sen 1984.

"lotteries." Suppose that the preferences respond to these weightings in a *continuous* fashion and that a higher chance of a better outcome is always preferred to a lower chance at it (*"monotonicity"*). Suppose further that this ordering over the expanded set of alternatives is *complete*, in that every alternative is ranked as preferred, dispreferred, or indifferent to every other. Finally, suppose that one can always *substitute* into a compound lottery – one with many stages – elements that are indifferent, irrespective of context, and that all multistage lotteries can be *reduced* to simple ones. If all of these assumptions hold, then well-established theorems show that the set of preferences can be represented by any of a well-defined family of numerical functions. That is, if preference rankings are orderly in this way, then the pattern of rankings can be indicated by assigning a single number to each alternative, and supposing that the subject acts as if to maximize this index. Obviously enough, the rank order will remain the same even if each of the assigned numbers were multiplied by 729. Although thus not fixed at a unique cardinal level, the resulting numbers are what are known, under the formalistic interpretation, as the "utilities" associated with each alternative.

Although the realistic interpretation is not now my central target, let me say briefly why I will not dwell on it. In its relatively noncommittal stance toward the content of the good, this version of utility theory leaves most of the work of deliberation of ends undone. If ends can be determined via rational deliberation, then this process would importantly complete the work of such theories, and would provide what they need in order to be fully articulate in advising practice. By recognizing the potential complexity of the good, however, and the naturalness of regarding it as involving multiple component goods, the realistic interpretation of utility as well-being leaves open the possibility of important incommensurabilities *within* utility (a crucial vulnerability of, e.g., Broome 1991). Accordingly, the realistic interpretation leaves largely to one side both the guiding question of this study and the particular question this chapter is addressing. That is not to say that its claim to state even necessary conditions of rationality is well founded. Amartya Sen, in particular, has developed a powerful critique of the realistic interpretation's link between rationality and self-interest, asking whether it is really irrational to sacrifice one's own well-being for that of one's loved ones or neighbors (Sen 1982). (Here the typical dodge of the formalistic interpretation – the claim that if the agent really prefers the sacrifice, then the utility function will reflect that – is not open to the realistic interpretation, which claims to represent, however schematically, the content of an individual's welfare. If healthy

94

ties of friendship and civility are components of an individual's well-being, this would have to be shown on other grounds.) Sen's criticism cuts to the core of this type of utility theory which, lacking any definite commitments about the content of the individual's good, boils down to the claim that individual rationality consists in maximizing (or achieving a satisfactory level in) one's own welfare. Since this claim is dubious for this reason and since it does not speak to the question of deliberation of ends, I will leave it aside.

At first blush, the formalistic interpretation seems equally useless in deliberation. Since the utility index, on this proposal, derives from preferences among alternatives (however those are supposed to be revealed), and reflects only the ranking of those alternatives previously arrived at by the agent, it must follow deliberation. How can it precede it? As one commentator puts it, "On this view, utilities can never form a *reason* why someone makes a choice, but are rather to be construed as a way of *describing* a set of given choices" (Hansson 1981, 188). Furthermore, in setting aside matters of end and means, this approach stands silent on central matters of deliberation. As even my pseudo-Humean opponents admit, and as is clear from experience, deliberation does importantly involve the effort to pursue ends and select means. Of course, one might want to say that such considerations stand behind the preference ranking; but as we shall see, the idea that reasons "stand behind" the ranking will pose a dilemma for the formalistic interpretation. And if these reasons stand behind the ranking, rather than being exhibited in the ranking, then a course of reasoning limited to noting where in the rank order a specific outcome falls will not count as a case of deliberation of the familiar means–end sort. Although few doubt that rationality involves some commitment to will reasonable means to one's ends, the formalistic, preference-based model we are now considering has no place for this principle. To sum up the prima facie indictment, the formalistic approach seems a poor model for deliberation because it presupposes the ranking of alternatives that can only be the result of (thorough) deliberation and because it treats the individual's will as a black box, from which rankings emerge one knows not how, rather than trying to discern some structure (whether means–end or some other structure) in the reasoning leading to that ranking.[5]

---

5 The silence of traditional expected utility theory about end–means reasoning stems also from the fact that its basic input is a subject's preferences among states of affairs, irrespective of whether or not the subject, as agent, has any power to bring about that state (cf. von Wright 1963, 16, 25). The Newcomb problem dramatizes this fact (Nozick 1970; Campbell and Sowden 1985). To restore the focus of deliberation on what we *do*, Lewis 1981

Despite the appearance that the formalistic interpretation, whatever its merits in other theoretical uses, cannot serve as a theory of deliberation, there are those who insist that it can. Consider the following oft-quoted statement of Harsanyi's (1977, 381):

A Bayesian need not have any special desire to maximize his expected utility per se. Rather, he simply wants to act in accordance with a few very important rationality axioms; and he knows that this fact has the inevitable mathematical *implication* of making his behavior equivalent to expected-utility maximization. As long as he obeys these rationality axioms, he simply cannot help acting *as if* he assigned numerical *utilities*, at least implicitly, to alternative possible outcomes of his behavior.

Since this passage takes up the perspective of an agent contemplating future behavior, it clearly stakes a claim on deliberation. Importantly, what is regarded as controlling deliberation is not the ranking itself, in any direct way, but instead the schematic axioms of rational choice theory. Obviously, these by themselves indicate no behavior to be acceptable or not; it is these together with the agent's existing ranking (perhaps as already revealed in past behavior) that can have the kind of behavioral implications that Harsanyi has in mind. One is expected to act "consistently" with one's other preferences.

Anyone using the expected utility theory in this way must allow the agent to change his or her mind, whether as a result of learning or for any other reason. Preferences revealed in the past or taken for granted at the outset will have no implications for future decisions if they do not remain fixed. Yet clearly an important function of deliberation is to form and revise preferences; and about this process the preference theorist has little or nothing to say. The situation is comparable to the role of the principle of noncontradiction in empirical reasoning. The imperative of avoiding contradictions rarely dictates which of competing revisions to make in one's views.

Still, what if over a given range of choices an individual's general preference structure did remain fixed? Would the preference theory be useful in characterizing her deliberation in that domain? If some preferences be accepted as fixed, one can then determine whether choosing a given alternative is or is not consistent with those and the axioms (cf. Hansson 1981, 188). What I will now argue is that even on this restrictive as-

suggests a form of "causal decision theory," which adds another layer, a set of hypotheses about how states of the world will depend upon what the agent does. In what follows, in pursuing the question whether a preference-based theory is of any use in deliberation, you can suppose that this sophistication be added, if you like. It avails little.

sumption, settling new decisions by means of the preference axioms is not a sensible approach to deliberation. Concrete considerations that arise in the context of choice are likely to block the effort to use fixed preferences to settle new practical questions.

For example, suppose that Teresa has in the past acted upon a general preference for sending her children to parochial schools over secular private schools, and secular private schools over public schools. As she has thought of it hitherto, this preference pattern could be explained in terms of a rough descending weighting of three goods: spiritual education, strong academics, and ties of friendship with the neighborhood children, who are mostly in public school. If this general ranking is held fixed, then consistency would suggest that if her youngest child, Francis, were to get into a parochial school, she should not send him to public school. We may stipulate that Teresa has not and will not change her mind about her general preferences. While the example fairly bristles with potential issues for Teresa to consider, four stand out in her mind. First, she regards Francis as a child of extraordinary spiritual depth. Already an acolyte, Francis seems of priestly temper. Her feeling that Francis is already on firm spiritual footing leads Teresa to question whether it is crucial to send him to the parochial school. Second, she feels that Francis will be less likely than his elder brothers to be led astray by the sometimes rowdy neighborhood children who are in the public schools. Third, she does not want Francis to be overshadowed by his boisterous older brothers, who are still in the parochial school. Finally, the cost even of a Catholic school education is straining the family budget; public school would be a relief in that respect. In the face of these considerations, it seems downright silly to confront Teresa with the supposed demands of transitivity, as these appear to be projected from her past decisions. The point is this: Even holding the general preference-ranking fixed, that does not imply that she prefers that Francis go to parochial school. Both her preference for parochial schools over other ones and her ranking of the underlying goods involved are ones that hold "in general" and "other things equal." In Francis's case, she can justify an exception from this general pattern because other things are not equal.

While I chose this heavily value-laden example for the sake of vividness, the difficulties it poses for projecting requirements on future decisions from past choices are ones that arise quite generally. They are three. First, since the formalistic interpretation specifically disavows any attempt to express the reasons behind any decision, it is always possible that further reasons, hitherto unexpressed, could disturb the projection of the previous ranking. In Teresa's case, the reasons standing behind the parochial school preference get refined in a way that affects its application: not to assure her sons a religious education (that being taken care of on Sundays) but to bolster their spiritual commitment. In addition, a new reason arises, applicable only to Francis, namely the concern about his being overshadowed. Second, as already exhibited in these same considerations, there are myriad relations of interference, support, substitution, and complementarity among the various goods to which Teresa's ranking is responsive. Just as particular gustatory effects underlie the fact that peanut butter and jelly complement each other, so particular facts of personality underlie the fact that, for Francis, friendship with the neighborhood children and a continuing spiritual education will go (relatively) well together. When any new combination among these goods is put forward, these organic relations among them will typically prevent a straightforward projection of their value from past cases. The wider context (Francis's personality and church activities, his being the youngest) always is relevant. Finally, there is the fact that all alternatives must compete for the agent's time and resources. It is relevant not only that the family budget is strained but also (and countervailingly) that it would give Teresa more time to work if all three boys had the same school schedule. We may label these three general problems those of (i) lurking reasons, (ii) organic effects, and (iii) budget constraints. The first always threatens to provide a rationale for departing from the requirements of a projection of past preferences via the axioms, while the second and third upset projection by undercutting the separability of goods on which it relies.

These three problems imply that the attempt to convert preference-based utility theory into a theory of deliberative rationality will fail. It will fail, whether the attempt is to extend past decisions by analogy or merely to decide similar cases similarly. In the former case, going beyond the simple reproduction of past decisions depends upon a factoring of options that have been ranked in the past into component goods that can be separately weighted. Armed with such weights, the decision maker can then look to future options to see how much of each of these goods would result, and calculate the utility of the options accordingly. Organic effects (substitution and complementarity) and budget constraints block this kind of projection. So stymied, a defender of preference-based deliberation might insist that at least cases that are similar to past ones in all relevant respects must be decided in the same way. But the problem of lurking reasons prevents even this way of using the axioms to constrain deliberation. As the particularities of Francis suggest, a present case might be exactly like past ones in terms of the list of goods *as factored so far*, but involve peculiarities that should lead the agent to refine the list of goods still further. Thus, Teresa further factors *spiritual education* into *religious instruction* and *support of spiritual commitment*.

The recalcitrantly optimistic preference-based theorist might see behind the notion of lurking reasons a ray of hope: If only all these reasons could be brought out of the shadows! In fact, this problem might be seen also to underlie the other two. That is, the existence of substitution and complementarity effects might be taken to indicate that one had not yet reached a fully satisfactory factoring of goods. One had discriminated tasting peanut butter from tasting jelly, but had failed to include on the list the distinct value of tasting peanut-butter-and-jelly. Teresa had listed spiritual education, strong academics, and friendship with neighboring children, but had failed to discriminate between friendships with neighboring children that facilitated bad behavior and those that did not. The taste reasons lurk because they are intrinsically hard to articulate (although if the wine lover's way with adjectives were shared by writers on food generally, perhaps this obstacle could be overcome). In Teresa's case, there is a more discrete and easily statable lurking reason, namely the aim to keep her children from being corrupted by the neighborhood delinquents. Now it might be held, as it was by G. E. Moore, that goodness comes in organic wholes, not always susceptible of final analysis into atomic elements. By simply raising the problems of organic effects, budget constraints, and lurking reasons, however, I have done nothing to establish a value theory such as Moore's. Accordingly, for all I have said, the preference theorist may still hope to provide a final factoring, a final array of the dimensions of value (for each agent) such that no reasons lurk and no holistic effects remain unaccounted for.

To arrive at preferences behind which no reasons lurk was the explicit aim of von Wright's original "logic of preference." Von Wright distinguished between "extrinsic" preferences, preferences behind which further reasons might lurk, as when Teresa prefers one kind of school to another *because* of the various goods resulting, from "intrinsic" preferences, preferences that represent primitive and bare differential likings by the agent (von Wright 1963, 15). The preference-based theorist may retreat to intrinsic preferences of this sort in an effort to avoid the three kinds of problems I have set out. This move, however, brings two other sorts of problem in its train. First, it further diminishes the role within preference theory for ordinary end–means reasoning. The more usual formalistic interpretation of preferences, which allows that reasons may lurk, leaves room for acquiring preferences for something as a means to something else. This new, extrinsic preference will then affect the utility function. Von Wright's approach, by contrast, rules out this latter sort of preference (von Wright 1963, 23). One reason he did so is that including preferences for things as means to something intrinsically preferred will yield a kind of double counting. Becoming wealthy, for example, may gain undue status because of its figuring as a means to many intrinsically preferred conditions. Von Wright's move was to purge the theory of this sort of distortion by sticking with intrinsic preferences. Accordingly, end–means considerations will not be part of the reasoned revision of preferences, if any, that the theory allows. When A is intrinsically preferred to B, it is not preferred as being a better means to end E, or for any other reason, for that matter; for the whole point of intrinsic preferences is that they are not backed up by underlying reasons. They stand only on their own. Accordingly, preference-based deliberation that avoided projection problems by resting on intrinsic preferences would be confined to determining which option ranked highest in the utility scale. The effort to satisfy this "as if" end would replace the determination of effective or reasonable means to particular given ends. Such a model would mark a radical departure from our ordinary reasoning practices.

Second, it is clear that to expose and to capture explicitly all of the reasons that might lurk in organic effects, budget constraints, and otherwise, the preference theorist will be driven in the direction of complete descriptions of the alternative futures involved (supposing that to be a coherent notion).[6] This was already the conclusion that Kenneth J. Arrow had reached in his pioneering work on social choice theory in the 1950s. As he wrote in a 1958 paper, the problems of "interdependence of values" (organic wholes) and "jointness of resource limitations" (budget constraints) lead us

to a universal theory of choice where each decision is effectively a choice among total life histories. Such a theory is certainly impractical at our present state of knowledge, as we are forced to compartmentalize the different aspects of life, decisions in each area being treated in some sense independently. But at least we must be aware that such a breakup of the totality may be defective for either or both of the reasons cited above (Arrow 1984, 57).

6 Actually, it is not clear that pressing toward an ultimately refined description of alternatives will be uniformly helpful in dealing with this problem. An agent's inability to cope with discriminations that are too fine may present another source of difficulty. See, e.g., Quinn 1990, and Aizpurua et al. 1990.

More recently this realization has spread among philosophers sympathetic to the preference-based theory (see, e.g., Hardin 1988, 173). A somewhat reluctant member of this group is James Griffin, who develops a nuanced and complex account of human well-being in the confidence that certain goods will be important aspects of any agent's good, but rests this structure on the notion of a fully informed, yet "basic, unbacked" preferential comparison between "lives" (Griffin 1986, 36, 103; Griffin 1991, 110).

As has been widely noted, this move toward an "exhaustive" description of the alternatives, leaving no crannies uncovered in which reasons could lurk, provides a way of rebuffing all apparent counterexamples to the central axioms of utility theory, such as transitivity.[7] All relevant aspects of the context of choice – aspects that threaten the independence of the goods as factored by the utility function – can in principle be built into a richer description of the alternatives. For instance, in the Allais paradox described in §4, conformity to the axioms may be restored if the agents distinguish between (a) ending up with nothing when they might have had a fortune for certain and (b) ending up with nothing when all they ever had was a long shot (Broome 1991, 98; cf. Sen 1985).

There is a serious worry that "saving" the axioms by constantly reindividuating or redescribing the alternatives will make the theory vacuous, neither falsifiable nor violable (see also Hurley 1989, ch. 4). For *some* difference may always be found between any two alternatives. To prevent a total trivialization of the theory, however, it might be possible to suppose that only differences that *make* a difference were allowed to matter. These could be conceived as differences that – from some unspecified objective perspective – are relevant to justifying a preference (as Broome suggests: 103). This is to reject the idea of "intrinsic" preferences in favor of "extrinsic" ones that *can* be backed by a reason, and further to import objective constraints on ends at odds with the theory's remote Humean roots. Alternatively, and more in line with that tradition, only those differences that the agent sincerely regards as making an intrinsic difference might be

---

7 Defending the soundness of the transitivity requirement by moving towards intrinsic preferences over maximally specific alternatives is in some tension with the need to *explain* the requirement of transitivity. Darwall (1983, 71) notes that since mere arbitrary "picking" need not be transitive, the requirement that preferences be transitive "is most intelligible if preferences are themselves to be based on judgments about the support of reasons, and therefore, on reasons themselves." Perhaps this point can be reconciled with that in the text by supposing that the reason no reasons lurk behind intrinsic preferences is that they have already been accounted for in the formation of that preference. This response would reinforce the conclusion that preferences, on the formalistic interpretation, are postdeliberative.

counted (cf. Hampton forthcoming). Yet even with one of these limitations in place, the examples of Teresa and the Allais gambles already suggest that an adequate individuation or factoring of alternatives will lie so far in the direction of Arrow's alternative comprehensive futures as to prevent the theory from being useful in deliberation. Further, as considerations get overlaid in contexts of choice, the need to discriminate ever more finely among alternatives will begin to snowball. As one newly distinguishes two alternatives that had seemed of the same type, one will face distinct situations depending upon which of them were available. The distinctions will multiply.

By this long route we have arrived back at our first-blush conclusion about the formalistic interpretation. A ranking that adequately individuates the alternatives, so that the axioms will really apply, can only be the result of completed deliberation – of an ideally, and practically impossibly, completed deliberation about all practical questions that one could possibly ever face in one's lifetime. The ranking cannot be a standard useful *in* deliberation. Nothing in this preference-based model tells the individual how to refine the description of goods, how to discriminate relevant features of alternatives, so as to remain in the good graces of the axioms. To do these things is to articulate the reasons that still lurk, and that the preference model, on the formalistic interpretation, seeks to eliminate. Accordingly, we return to our opening statement that preference-based utility is not a form of commensurability useful in making choices but rather a way of representing choices, once made. Saving the action-guiding role of the formalistic model by supposing some finally complete articulation of reasons, of dimensions of value or goodness, and of discriminations therein, is like telling Seurat that in order to place all the figures in his masterly afternoon scene of the Grande Jatte, all he has to do is first determine where to put all the points of paint on the canvas. The solution may be logically coherent, but it is totally impracticable, and puts the cart before the horse. If our practical knowledge were perfect, we would already know what to do.

It is not merely ignorance that prevents agents from working with a final specification of reasons when they deliberate. It is also one of deliberation's tasks – and here I speak even of end–means deliberation – to *revise* the initial set of reasons from which it starts, if only by making further discriminations, as exemplified above in the case of Teresa. Sometimes this revision will count as a reasoned change of mind, rather than a discovery of what one really preferred all along. To omit this preference-transforming stage of deliberation is to miss much. In particular, one must

102

not overlook the fact that in deliberation one may find reason to discriminate anew among goods. To rule this out by supposing that somehow – in "constitutive" practices of interpretation or in a stipulated "context" (cf. Rawling 1990) – the factorization of reasons is given at the outset therefore conflicts with the aim of reconstructing the notion that one option is, all things considered, preferred to another. A debate bounded by a stipulated context of this sort ends before all things have been considered.

It is true, then, that preference-based models can overcome the threats to numerical representation that are posed by organic effects, budget constraints, and lurking reasons. By ramifying the description of the alternatives, they can retain a commensurating form. Commensurability of this sort, however, is purchased at the price of making this model useless as an account of individual deliberation.

§16. DELIBERATIVE COMMENSURABILITY

It is plain from the last section's argument that a form of value commensurability useful in deliberation cannot depend on a final factoring of reasons. A commensurability immune to being upset by lurking reasons because already reflecting all one's reasons is not a commensurability helpful in deciding what to do. In fact, I will now suggest, for value commensurability to be useful in deliberation, it must stake a claim to stand in for heterogeneous reasons whose practical implications have not been fully worked out. A commensurans that could usefully measure value for the deliberator must be capable of representing the force and direction of reasons that have not been fully articulated and that could be quite distinct in kind. If there were such a commensurating value that could in this strong sense embrace all other values within it, then the directive to maximize it would indeed be highly useful in deliberation. But we need first of all to define more carefully what this sort of deliberative commensurability might be, and then to examine various ways in which a commensurans might claim to represent the force of subordinate reasons.

That there is a plurality of qualitatively distinct goods and values is simply obvious (cf. Stocker 1990). Even corralling all goods or values within the bounds of one "type" does not tame plurality sufficiently to establish deliberative commensurability (cf. Richardson 1990a). For instance, neither coextensive hedonism, according to which all goods are pleasures, nor even the stronger claim that the good is pleasure, imply that values are deliberatively commensurable. Each of these claims can be true despite there being deep qualitative differences among pleasures. Indeed, unless the hedonist's claim is supposed to be quite revisionary of ordinary beliefs, the general diversity of goods will simply get included under the umbrella of pleasure. Even within what is ordinarily understood as pleasure there are vast qualitative differences. The refined pleasure of discovering and remedying a hidden fallacy in one's reasoning has little in common with the relaxed pleasure of basking in the sun or with the flushed pleasure of flirtation – or so it seems, at any rate. Accordingly, it remains a serious question whether pleasure (even ordinarily understood) is a single dimension in the relevant sense.

The sort of commensurability we are after would enable the agent, without distortion or other fault, to represent all of the considerations pertaining to some choice in terms of some single dimension – whether in terms of cardinal numbers, an interval scale, or a mere ordinal ranking – *before* deciding how to choose. The commensurans is to serve as the measure in terms of which the agent makes a choice, by maximizing along its dimension, and not merely as a summary of the choices the agent has made. In light of these remarks, I can now define the relevant sort of value commensurability, beginning with its most modest version:

(D1) Two values (or goods) are deliberatively commensurable with respect to a given choice if and only if there is some single norm (or good) such that the considerations put forward by those two values (or goods) for and against choosing each of the available options may be adequately arrayed prior to the choice (for purposes of deliberation) simply in terms of the greater or lesser satisfaction of that norm (or instantiation of that good).

This definition represents a basic building block toward the total commensurability that would allow deliberation to proceed solely by maximizing.[8] The features of this devoutly wished touchstone may be set out in terms of the following definition:

(D2) Strong deliberative commensurability obtains if and only if there is some single norm (or good) such that all the considerations for and against choosing any option in any situation may be adequately arrayed prior to the choice

8 My definition of "commensurability" differs from Stocker's (1990, 176). Stocker takes "commensurability" to imply the existence of a common cardinal unit of measurement. In my own definition of commensurability, however, I have not required that "the more and the less" be expressed in terms of a cardinal unit. Ordinal comparison will suffice. Stocker also mentions "inter-substitivity or fungibility," which amounts to a denial of plurality. My "commensurability" is intermediate between his "commensurability" and his "fungibility." I have learned much from his discussion of these issues.

(for purposes of deliberation) simply in terms of the greater or lesser satisfaction of that norm (or instantiation of that good).

This idea of "strong total commensurability" asserts that the elementary pairwise form of commensurability holds across all values and choices. There are obviously a number of ways in which strong commensurability might fail while yet leaving important sorts of commensurability in the field. In particular, if commensurability is not achieved by reference to the same commensurans in each choice, but can nonetheless be achieved for every choice, then the following sort of commensurability applies:[9]

(D3) Weak commensurability obtains if and only if all the considerations for and against choosing any option in any situation may be adequately arrayed prior to the choice (for purposes of deliberation) simply in terms of the greater or lesser satisfaction of some single norm (or instantiation of some good), though not necessarily the same norm (or good) for each choice.

While it is also possible that commensurability might not extend to all choices, or might not embrace all goods or values, I will define only the two variants set out above.

The heart of each of my definitions of value commensurability is the requirement of the adequate array or representation of the relevant considerations. The stipulation that this representation of the pros and cons be possible before the choice is made is a substantive demand. Merely concocting a rule that arbitrarily assigned numbers to alternatives or considerations and then told one to choose the option with the highest number would not effect deliberative commensurability, because these numbers would not reflect the real weight of the relevant reasons for action. Deliberative commensurability is not a simply mathematical fact. For instance, the requirement of adequate representation implies that commensuration may be asymmetrical: just because standard A serves to make B and C commensurable does not imply that either B or C could be taken as commensurating the other two. Commensurability is not simply a matter of establishing numerical trade-offs among different items. What is needed in addition is some reliable way of representing reasons: This is what deliberative commensurability offers.

Unfortunately, what it takes to represent reasons adequately is terribly hard to come to grips with without already presupposing some conception of commensurability and incommensurability. Since I aim to use the former to explain the latter, however, I must explain what it is for a measure

---

9 The distinction between what I am calling strong and weak commensurability was set out in Wiggins 1980b, 256–7; it was further developed by Williams 1981b, 77.

adequately to represent the force of reasons. I will attempt to do so in three distinct and mutually reinforcing ways. First, in the remainder of the present section, I will set out abstractly some possible relations between the commensurans and the goods or values it purports to measure that would ensure adequate representation. Second, in §17, I will work in the opposite direction by describing some cases of tragic choice, where the tragedy seems to reside in the fact that there is no one dimension in terms of which the competing considerations may be adequately arrayed. (It will prove fruitful, in approaching the phenomena of tragedy, to have in mind the abstract conditions under which adequate representation would and would not fail; for without these it is too hard to distinguish choices that are tragic from banal cases of trade-offs.) Each of these ways of getting at the idea of the adequate representation of considerations will indicate that not every unifying theory can rightly be seen as commensurating. In Chapter IX, I will elaborate on this insight by showing that an ultimate end need not commensurate the goods that are sought for its sake.

In order to explore the relations between measure and measured that would allow for adequate representation, I will assume for the sake of argument that the candidate commensurans is itself homogeneous, and varies only in degree. We must remember, in other words, that it is in terms only of the greater or lesser score on this one scale that the plural considerations are to be arrayed. Accordingly, if I sometimes speak, in the remainder of this section, of pleasure as a possible commensurans, it should be understood that I mean pleasure as Bentham conceived of it, as varying only in degree, and not pleasure as Plato or John Stuart Mill understood it, as containing important qualitative distinctions. (Of course, one could concede that there are important qualitative distinctions among pleasures, and nonetheless put forward *quantity* of pleasure as a measure meant to commensurate, possibly among other plural items, its many types.)

A seemingly minimal condition for adequate representation is that the measure must ordinally track the strength of the various subordinate considerations; that is, if a purported commensurans is to "represent" the force of plural values, then its ranking of alternatives must respond in the right way to quantitative variations in those values. What I have in mind parallels the rules of "dominance" or "Pareto improvement." We may informally state the *ordinal tracking condition* as follows:

A purported commensurans ordinally tracks the force of subordinate values or goods just in case, whenever one of the latter increases in force, and all other subordinate considerations remain unchanged, the commensurans registers a higher score (or a score that is no lower: see below).

Consider one of Kant's simple cases, in which someone is trying to decide between giving the money in his pocket to a homeless beggar and using it to buy a theater ticket; and suppose that the considerations on either side are roughly balanced in the scales of some proposed commensurans. If we keep other factors constant and increase the urgency of the homeless person's need – perhaps he is also blind, or on the verge of freezing to death – then the purported commensurans should tilt more strongly in favor of giving the money away. Similarly, if we keep the homeless person's need constant and vary the quality and excitement of the theatrical performance, the commensurating index should also vary accordingly. The reason for supposing that the considerations were roughly balanced at the outset was that even if the "measure" is merely ordinal, variations of this sort should typically show up in reversals of overall judgment.

While ordinal tracking may seem an innocuous requirement, it is doubtful whether it is even a necessary condition of adequate representation, whatever exactly that might mean. As emphasized in §15, relations of substitution and complementarity are rife among the plural goods or values. In the context of goods, as opposed to preferences, this phenomenon is traditionally labeled that of "organic wholes" (cf. Moore 1902). Tea with milk is (arguably) better than plain tea, and so is tea with lemon; but tea with milk and lemon is worse than any of the above. In the example of helping the homeless person versus going to the theater, if we imagine this as a choice faced by someone walking through Times Square on the way to a Broadway theater – rather than as a choice presented wholly in the abstract – then "organic" interaction will obviously be possible even between alternatives. If the homeless person is writhing in pain, perhaps the recent memory of this sight would spoil the theatergoer's enjoyment of the Neil Simon comedy of manners he was intending to see. If, on the other hand, the play is a politically progressive dramatic exposé of the plight of the homeless, any guilt about passing the beggar by might be assuaged by the smug thought that merely to attend such a play is to do one's part for the homeless. In framing a realistic minimal condition of ordinal tracking, therefore, we must suppose not only that other goods or values remain fixed but also that "organic" or interactive effects are not operating. Since, however, things can rarely be safely assumed to be equal in this sense, it seems likely that any purported failure of ordinal tracking could be excused as due to organic effects. That one of the component goods has increased (lemon from 0 to 1, say) does not imply that the value of the whole has not decreased (cf. Stocker 1990, 302). For this reason, ordinal tracking may not be necessary for adequate representation of plural values.

In any case, ordinal tracking is not a *sufficient* basis for "adequate representation." The most important reason why not is that the ordinal tracking condition either imposes an overall ranking more complete than we would be willing to endorse or else it leaves the overall ranking so incomplete that it hardly amounts to a "measure" at all. Which of these problems arises depends upon how, more precisely, the ordinal tracking condition is spelled out.

A strong version of the ordinal tracking condition would require that the overall ranking place any item higher that was better in any respect.[10] A higher ranking on any one component dimension would imply a higher overall ranking. But this strong a requirement flies in the face of the sort of incompleteness we are often happy to allow in our value comparisons (cf. Sen 1984, 4). The dimension of overall evaluation may be truly fuzzy or imprecise, and hence might not be sensitive to every variation in subordinate considerations. For example, even if it were true that Descartes's *Meditations* were worse than Wittgenstein's *Tractatus* in no respect and better than it in at least one respect, it is not clear that we would translate this partial superiority into an overall judgment that the former is the better book. Since neither of these philosophers is currently applying for any job or grant, there is no need for our overall evaluation of these books to seek specious precision. Similarly, while Beethoven in 1800 was not a worse composer than Mozart in 1780, and Mozart in 1780 was not a worse composer than Beethoven in 1823, Beethoven in 1800 was less great a composer than he was in 1823. What this may indicate, however, is that our ordinary judgments of the overall quality of philosophical works or composers do not proceed by reference to a single commensurating dimension. The fact that we are able to say that the later Beethoven was more sublime than the earlier indicates that there are detailed considerations about their value that matter to us. By demanding completeness in cases in which our reflection leaves us unclear how to rank, the strong form of the ordinal tracking condition would misrepresent what matters in these complex comparisons.

A weak version of the ordinal tracking requirement would ask only

10 My discussion in this paragraph draws upon ideas presented by Derek Parfit in a seminar at Harvard University in March 1989. See also Raz 1986, 325 (quoting a similar point of J. L. Mackie's).

that an option ranked no lower than another on any dimension not be ranked lower than it overall. On this laxer standard, superiority on any set of dimensions need not translate into superiority overall. While this requirement is certainly one that any purported commensurans must meet if it is to adequately represent subordinate goods or values, it is so lax that it hardly seems adequate to constitute a measure at all. In fact, it could be met by an "index" that declared all alternatives to be mutually indifferent. It certainly would allow for a large degree of incompleteness. From the point of view of an advocate of commensurability, however, the presence of significant incompleteness indicates a vulnerability, since if all considerations could really be boiled down to a single dimension, it is not clear why any incompleteness should remain. The omnipresent vagueness of our concepts provides no excuse: while vagueness in the notion of baldness may make it impossible to pick the exact numbers of hairs one must lose to be bald, the possibility of counting hairs (on a given person's head) nonetheless should enable us, albeit in a somewhat artificial sense, to say whether he has become more bald or (nowadays) less bald.

Unless we have some way of explaining how the measure manages to track the plural considerations it commensurates, the suspicion will remain that it is a mere index, luckily coincident with the evaluations examined so far, but not a reliable guide to practice. To overcome this doubt, and to surmount the other weaknesses of relying solely upon the ordinal tracking condition, a measure that purports to commensurate should bear a relation to what it measures that helps explain *how* it can adequately represent these plural considerations on a single scale. This explanatory relation might either leave the apparent plurality of goods intact or else end up implying that, despite appearances, there is really only one sort of good. The three ways that I will now discuss of explaining how a purported commensurans can adequately represent subordinate considerations are also ways of specifying what it is for it to represent them adequately.

Source. If the commensurating good is in some way the source or cause or origin of the value of everything else, then its ability to represent this value would be no mystery. This idea has been developed in quite different ways. In Aquinas, for instance, God is quite literally the source of all value, and all things are good insofar as they have being and hence participate in Him. A quite different way of making out a commensurability claim of this sort would be to work via a motivational monism of the sort underlying Kant's position that all material goods are commensurable, because all material desires spring, at bottom, from one and the same "life force" (Kant 1956, I.I.3, §3; Ak. 23). If, in addition, the (subjective) value of the object of desire is fairly represented by a desire's strength, then happiness, conceived simply as the satisfaction of material desire, will commensurate subjective aims. These desires and their objects may be as varied as one pleases; it is their contest for influence that is reduced to a quantitative matter. Admittedly, this sort of motivational monism is implausible, even in the restricted form Kant puts it forward. It is also independently doubtful that the contest among motivations can faithfully be reduced to competition between desires of different strengths (cf. Mele 1984). Nevertheless, in our own day, this homogeneity of desire is built into the quantitative models of many behaviorists, for whom what matters is the degree of conditioning and counter-conditioning that has occurred (cf. Brandt 1979).

Inherence. Instead of pointing to a causal connection to explain how a measure can adequately represent subordinate values, the defender of commensurability may instead assert a conceptual connection. For example, he may assert what Nussbaum, in attacking such views, has called "metricity," namely, "the claim that in each situation of choice there is some one value, varying only in quantity, that is common to all the alternatives, and that the rational chooser weighs the alternatives using this single standard" (Nussbaum 1990, 56). Note, first of all, that this notion is quite close to what I have called "weak commensurability," if we assume that responsibly using this standard requires that it adequately represent all the other considerations relevant to the choice. What metricity adds to weak commensurability is the assertion that the measured value somehow inheres in or is instantiated by each of the alternatives. How, then, can metricity adequately represent subordinate values? In the course of answering this question, further conceptual ties between these and the chosen metric may be alleged. For instance, G. E. Moore held that goodness itself was a nonnatural property that inhered in all good things, that could be intuited in the course of deliberation, and that it responded to the presence of subordinate valued features in a way respecting the complexities of organic wholes (indeed, our understanding of organic wholes owes much to Moore's investigations). If this were correct, then the claim of this nonnatural property to adequately reflect all subordinate considerations rests on two legs: first, the fact that in its very meaning it represents an overall evaluation of the goodness of the thing in question, and second, that it at least in theory can respond in quite complex ways to the presence of subordinate valued properties.

Reduction. Finally, there is at least conceptual space for a view that would hold that although there are plural values or goods, they can be reduced to one kind of value or good, or are identical to it. Such a view might be set out analogously to many mind–brain identity theories, which admit the prima facie distinctness of mental and neurophysiological events, but claim to be able to reduce the former to the latter in the strict sense that any particular instance of the former just is a particular instance of the latter. Although I am not aware of anyone who has put forward such a view about goodness or values, it might be aided by a reformist attitude toward what we ordinarily think of as good or valuable. For instance, if the plural goods are first held all to be mental states of various flavors, it may then be at least plausible to try to claim that each of these different states just is a state of pleasure.

There are at least three ways, then, in which a measure might succeed in adequately representing the considerations embodied in plural goods or values. The measure might (1) refer to a source of the goodness or the value of these plural items, (2) inhere in them in addition to tracking them, or (3) refer to something to which they can all be reduced. None of these relations assures that the representation of these plural goods or values will be proof against criticism; however, my discussion at the moment remains on the more primitive plane of trying to gloss what is to be meant by "adequate representation." We cannot sensibly adjudicate claims about adequate representation of plural goods or values in terms of a single measure without first being clearer what we mean by this. In this section, I have put forward, in an abstract way, these three ways of bolstering a claim to adequate representation by beefing up the connection between the measure and what it measures. We must now turn to the phenomena of tragic conflict to learn more about the notion of adequate representation by looking at cases in which it fails. To the extent that this failure is necessary, it will also provide stronger grounds for being dubious about any of the three routes to commensurability just canvassed.

§17. TRAGEDY AND INCOMMENSURABILITY

It would be foolish to try to refute here all possible attempts at constructing an adequately representing value commensurability. Fortunately, nothing in the overall argument of this book requires that I do that. While my positive proposal about deliberation of ends proceeds without relying upon or constructing any form of value commensurability, it is not incompatible with the existence of commensurability, either. Nonetheless, the need for an alternative account of deliberation such as the one I will propose will be all the stronger if value commensurability is not possible, for the mainstream maximizing pictures (such as those discussed in §15) generally do presuppose some kind of deliberative commensurability. Accordingly, in this section I will present some general reasons to doubt that any such value commensurability can be constructed with the values that are ours.

This last qualification is important. It would be easy enough to imagine a set of goods or values that could be adequately represented by a single standard. In suggesting that value commensurability is beyond our reach, I am supposing that one must work within the very general sort of internalist constraint articulated in §9. This implies that in assessing what is practically rational, one must start within the actual values of human beings, rather than allowing one's sense of the possibilities to be influenced by merely conceivable constellations of values.

What makes some conflicts of values tragic if others are banal and undisruptive? For instance, I might like to own a car that was both a high-performing sports car and very economical in its use of fuel. The fact that, as things stand, I must sacrifice one or the other of these attributes seems hardly tragic. The goods or values involved do not seem sufficiently "important" or "central" – to well-being, or to any normal person's conception of the good – to be the stuff of tragedy. In addition, neither of these goods, by itself, seems essential to living well or to flourishing as a human being. One can live perfectly well without owning a car at all. There is no duty to get a car, either. For similar reasons, discontinuities in what one would be willing to trade with what, arising from the difference between necessities and optional goods, neither make out a kind of value incommensurability (as I have defined the term) nor support any sense of tragedy. This is important to bring out, for the word "incommensurability" is sometimes used to refer to such discontinuities (Griffin 1991, 111, notes the distinction). For example, there may be a quantity of food such that, if I have less available to me, no number of musical compact disks would entice me to give up getting a decent meal instead. There may also be a higher quantity of food such that I could not and would not want to eat more, and would gladly forgo the entire excess for even a single disk of Zamfir on the pan pipes. Even when two types of good, each necessary for life and each discontinuously traded with merely optional goods, come into conflict with each other, this may not be tragic. Famine and drought, for instance, may require the peasant to choose between drinking scarce water and using it to irrigate a parched field. Although these circumstances, like Oedipus's ignorance, may be tragic, the choice is not. The reason, it seems, is that it is possible to construct a weak representative commensurans for this choice by looking to the desired effect of drinking water and eating vegetables, namely staying alive. In testing whether there are cases that disrupt the use of a commensurans in deliberation, we must look to whether the choice itself is tragic.

While discontinuity combined with inevitable, severe loss does not suffice to make a choice tragic, what of divergence of perspective combined with inevitable, severe loss (cf. Nagel 1979; Nussbaum 1986, chs. 2 & 3)? This would be one way to describe the paradigmatically tragic choice of Agamemnon, who faced a conflict between his love for his daughter Iphigenia and the clamorous demands of his political role, his responsibility for the Argive sailors and their mission to Troy. In his case, as Aeschylus describes it, severe loss is inevitable and there seems no way to reconcile the competing viewpoints of fatherhood and ruler. Accordingly, it looks as though the combination of divergence of perspective and inevitability of severe loss may account for the tragedy of a choice. Yet since divergence of points of view is perhaps to be explained, in turn, in terms of an underlying value incommensurability, we must probe more deeply.

Imagine the situation of Thomas, a young assistant to the powerful president of a small country. The president, although initially elected democratically, has arrogated more and more power to himself. This now-dictatorial leader could still be brought down and democracy restored if Thomas would reveal to the press the details (known only to him) of how the president systematically has been diverting state funds to a numbered bank account in Switzerland at a pace that will soon bankrupt the nation. To make this information public would be the right thing to do, and would greatly benefit the citizenry; but Thomas also knows that if he leaks the information then the president will retaliate by confiscating the property of Thomas's family. Does Thomas face a tragic choice? I think not. Consider how differently we would evaluate his position in retrospect, depending on which choice he makes. If he sacrifices his belongings, then indeed we will say that it is tragic that he had to make this sacrifice in doing good, and that it was correspondingly noble or supererogatory for him to do so. If, however, Thomas decides to keep mum, while we may say that it is tragic for the country that there was no one in high places with the courage to do the right thing, we will not automatically say that this was a tragic choice that Thomas made or faced.

To be sure, we might recognize an element of tragedy in the choice

Thomas faces if he actually struggles with his conscience about what to do. An internal struggle in Thomas's case would indicate that instead of simply taking the easy and self-serving option (as considerations of self-interest prompt), he had, like Agamemnon, actually tried to weigh the competing demands of supporting his family and protecting the national treasury. If he had a way of ranking these claims, or of making them mutually commensurable, then again his choice would not seem tragic; but if his choosing is burdened by his being unsure how he should weigh these competing demands, then it takes on a more tragic quality. A process of elimination therefore tends to suggest that tragic choices distinctively involve goods or values that are apparently incommensurable in the sense that concerns us, namely in that it is not possible adequately to represent their importance in deliberation in terms of any single scale.

That these competing values correspond to broadly different perspectives or represent contrasting strategies for systematizing moral or practical demands does indeed add depth to the tragedy. Nussbaum's illuminating analysis of the *Agamemnon* brings out this fact (Nussbaum 1986, ch. 2). Yet it remains important that for an agent to be facing a tragic choice (as opposed simply to being in a tragic situation), it is at least necessary for him or her to recognize (or to be able to recognize) the validity of each of the claims that clash, each of the values that pull in opposite directions. In that sense, there is a perspective that the agent must occupy, or must be able to occupy, which is in some way receptive to each side. In this respect, the *Agamemnon* contrasts with the *Antigone*. In burying her brother, whose body lies exposed as that of a traitor to his city, Antigone seeks to do the right thing by the lights of traditional religion and family obligation; that in doing so she courts disaster in terms of her self-interest and – if Creon is to be believed – threatens the social order are facts that seem not to trouble her greatly. Creon, responsible for ruling the city, is, initially at least, receptive only to considerations of public welfare and impatient with the requirements of religion. The tragic choice in this play, however, is not that faced by Antigone when she decided to bury Polyneices. Rather, it is that faced by Creon, who must decide whether to carry out the threat of his burial ban by executing Antigone, his niece and his son's betrothed. And the tragedy of this choice comes to the fore toward the end of the play, as Creon does become receptive to Antigone's warnings about impiety and apprehends that his preferring the social welfare has brought about the death of his son and wife. Even with Agamemnon the salient fact is not that he occupies one perspective to the total exclusion of the other but that he cannot find a way adequately to

114

represent the concerns of one in terms of the other. Once he begins to favor the political perspective, Nussbaum argues (42), he cannot even fully see his daughter for who she is and for the rebuke to his fatherhood that she represents. Agamemnon's seeing Iphigenia as a sacrificial goat rather than as an accusative daughter is an emblematic failure of adequate representation of the kind required for deliberative commensurability as I have defined it. The perspective from which Agamemnon attempts to commensurate the competing considerations thus grotesquely fails in this task. By allowing himself to attempt to weigh all the considerations on the political scale, Agamemnon shields himself from a full realization of the tragic dimensions of his choice.

This partial analysis of the phenomena of tragic choices indicates that they are situations in which important losses are inevitable but in which there is no way to arrive at a complacent decision by commensurating the losses involved in terms of an adequately representative measure. The agent faced with a tragic choice cannot hide behind the banner of maximizing the good or minimizing losses. (Indeed, Nussbaum 1986, ch. 3, brings out how welfare maximization is but one of the values in conflict in Creon's situation.) If this analysis is correct, then from the existence of tragic choices, which is hard to deny, it follows that there are incommensurable values.

Against this partial analysis of tragic choice, however, it might be objected that at least one famous case, briefly mentioned in §6, involves a choice between two goods that are – or could be supposed to be – the same in kind. I have in mind the choice brutally imposed upon the mother of two young children, in *Sophie's Choice*. A Nazi doctor tells her that he will divert one of the children from the gas chambers, but only if she first decides which one to save. The choice he poses seems particularly cruel, and not just because it forces Sophie to abandon one of her children to death. Its tragedy and cruelty also resides in its forcing her to choose which child to doom. The difficulty of this choice has nothing to do with different moral principles being in play for the different children. So far as we know, each has an equal claim on life and on its mother's love. At the level of general principles of obligation, therefore, there is no incommensurability in Sophie's situation. Nonetheless, I submit that incommensurability of value is essential to the tragedy of her having to choose. It shows up at a different level, namely in terms of what is valuable about each of the children. It is a distinguishing feature of love, including parental love, that it cherishes the particular and unique features of the beloved. This form of particularism will survive as a relevant feature of

115

Sophie's choice even if the philosopher asks us to suppose that they are genetically identical twins. Despite their genetic identity, they will have developed distinct virtues and charms. In addition, their mother will have had distinct experiences with each that will become woven into her cherishing the child. These have such a central place in making their mother's love what it is that to overlook these particularities is to fail to regard the children with love. For this reason, adopting a simple commensurating rule to make this choice – either by declaring that each child "obviously" is to be weighed equally or by trying to calculate which has the greater life expectancy (if, say, they were not twins, or if one of them had a cold) – would be to employ a rule that fails from the mother's point of view adequately to represent what is valuable about these children. A stranger with no bonds of love or friendship toward these children might reasonably flip a coin to decide between them. Although he would be troubled about being forced to serve as a device for selecting randomly which child dies, he does not face a tragic choice. For Sophie, with her love for each child's particularities, by contrast, the fact that she cannot adequately represent each child's value on a single scale is what makes the choosing tragic.[11] This would remain true even if love carried no moral obligations of its own, so that the scale of a more general beneficence represented the only morally relevant obligation: She would then say that the obliging standard is one that fails adequately to represent the values that concern her.

This particularism is not peculiar to modern, post-Romantic conceptions of love, such as those found by Nussbaum in Proust and Henry James (Nussbaum 1990). Consider the particular details of shared experience and memory that work the pivotal scenes of recognition in ancient Greek literature: Penelope tests Odysseus by reference to the olivewood bed he carved; Orestes proves himself to his sister Iphigenia (in *Iphigenia in Tauris*) by reminding her of the tapestry she wove and the bath perfumes she received as a wedding present. In the latter play, moreover, Iphigenia appeals to each of her friends in the Chorus individually for their loyalty and help in the following terms:

> But if we do escape, then we shall work
> For your deliverance, for you and you

11 Greenspan 1983, which introduced Sophie's choice into philosophical discussion, suggests that "the moral code yields *no* particular recommendations" for a case like Sophie's, "rather than two which conflict" (117). If love gives rise to obligations of its own, then this suggestion gives insufficient importance to the lack of fungibility of the children.

116

To share our happiness at home in Hellas
And you and you. Holding your hand, I ask you –
Kissing your cheek. Clasping your knees, I ask you –
And you I ask by love of your two parents.
And you by love of the child you left behind.

(Euripides 1960, ll. 1067–73)

In fact, the particularism of this appeal to friends – appealing to each separately and on the grounds of a distinct particular fact – contrasts with the universalism of the appeal to sympathy made by Goethe's Iphigenia in his version of the same story: Romanticism can also mean overlooking quotidian particularities under the influence of a broader ideal. Yet valuing one's children, one's spouse, one's lover, or one's friends in terms of their "unique" qualities and of the particular experiences one has shared with them is a perennial feature of human love.

While the particularism of personal love is the best antidote to the commensurating mentality (in ways that Nussbaum's writings have beautifully elaborated), my use of it here is somewhat more modest. I referred to it not to sweep away all attempts at commensurability, but to bolster my claim that cases of tragic choice are cases in which it is not possible to make the values in play commensurable in a way that adequately represents their import. Once we understand Sophie's choice in these terms, we see that it actually reflects the existence of incommensurable values.

Stepping back from tragedy, we should expect that the more pervasive value incommensurability is, the more likely will be conflict about what to do. Many of the most compelling examples of practical conflict exhibit value incommensurability. If I face a choice between more pay and less pay for the same work, and other things are equal, then it would be hard to understand how I could be in a quandary about which offer to accept; but if the lower-paying job is safe but sedentary and the higher-paying job is dangerous but exciting, then it will be easier to understand how I could feel torn. As this homely little example reminds us, the incommensurable pulls on us need not be dramatically different or tragically incompatible – need not be the sort of "existential" clash between being faithful to one's mother and being a courageous citizen that Sartre exploited (Sartre 1975) – in order to be understandable as conflicts. When the values involved are heterogeneous even though trivial, we are not surprised if the agent has difficulty reconciling their allures (cf. Stocker 1990). Where values are incommensurable, it is easy to understand how conflicts among them can resist ready adjudication.

The existence of incommensurable values spells the death not only of

Sidgwick's dreams for practical science, but also of accounts of practical reasoning, such as that of Broome 1991, that attempt to transfer the facile post hoc commensurability of preference theory to the realm of goods. If the goods or values in competition in a given choice cannot adequately be represented on a single scale, their interaction in the case at hand must be sorted out in deliberation. In the terminology of §15, reasons lurk that resist ready representation. In the case of preference theory, the relation of preference can simply be *defined* by the postulates of transitivity, independence, and so on. But no theorist has adequate license to postulate (as Broome does) that the idea of goodness satisfies these axioms.[12] Absent some strongly objective and reforming theory of the good – of a sort to which Broome and other utilitarians attempting to remain noncommittal about the content of the good do not aspire – the existence of tragic choices gives us sufficient reason to conclude that what is good or valuable does not obey these postulates. The existence of tragic conflicts combines with the fact, discussed in §6, that irresolvable practical conflicts cannot be ruled out on grounds of logic, to suggest that the incommensurability of values will often mean that there is no answer to the question, Which alternative is better? That is, in the jargon, there will be incompleteness in the "betterness" relation. Preference theory can construct commensurability ad lib because it is a practically meaningless. Once one shifts to talking about what is really valuable or good, however (even if only in terms of what an individual takes to be valuable or good), the claim to guide deliberation cancels this freedom to postulate. If commensurability of goods, whether of Sidgwick's old-fashioned substantive sort or of Broome's newfangled axiomatic sort, is a bust, the question becomes whether rational resolution of deep value conflicts is possible at all.

12 Actually, Broome recognizes that incommensurability among goods may be a problem for his theory; but it is one he assumes away for the sake of building his theory: see 1991, 93.

VI

Is commensurability a prerequisite of rational choice?

The aim of avoiding value conflicts (on which more in Chapter VII) provides a strong motivation to systematize and unify our practical and moral concerns. The task for the current chapter is to show that despite this, there is no need for this systematization to take the form of unification around a single commensurating standard. More generally, I will argue that rational choice even within a limited domain does not require a partial commensurability that applies to that domain. By "commensurability," as applied to values or goods, I will henceforth generally have in mind the sort of deliberative commensurability defined in §16. I will argue that such commensurability is not necessary even if systematization is. In the present chapter I will simply diagnose the narrow-mindedness that leads many to think that commensurating is the only rational way to systematize. It will be the task of Chapters VII–X to develop the alternative mode of systematizing.

§18. THE ARGUMENT THAT COMMENSURABILITY IS A PREREQUISITE OF RATIONAL CHOICE

Suppose, to adapt one of Kant's examples, that you have to decide between continuing to listen to an enlightening philosophy lecture and departing to join your family for dinner (Kant 1956, I.I.i.3, Ak. 23).[1] Can you arrive at your decision rationally without finding a way to commensurate the values involved? It seems to be widely assumed, both among philosophers and popularly, that you cannot. That is, it seems to be widely held that

(CPR) In order for it to be possible to choose between two alternatives rationally, the goods or values they involve must be deliberatively commensurable.

---

1 This section and the next are adapted from Richardson 1991.

According to Kant, one must be able to weigh philosophy and family, or wisdom and society, on a single scale in order to choose rationally whether to stay at the lecture. From such humble origins, an impressive argument for the rational necessity of strong deliberative commensurability (§16, [D2]) is born.

In our own time, it is hard to find explicit arguments in defense of the claim that deliberative commensurability is a prerequisite of rational choice (CPR). It rather seems to be taken for granted in most of the literature on decision theory and practical reasoning, as part and parcel of an attachment to maximization. Preference-based or postchoice versions of commensurability are not generally well distinguished from value-based or prechoice versions. Insofar as there is a literature on whether or not goods are commensurable, it is focused on preference-based commensurability. Accordingly, to find strong arguments for CPR, it is necessary to turn to the nineteenth century. The arguments of which I am aware are both by prominent utilitarians, John Stuart Mill and Henry Sidgwick. In their hands, CPR is an important prop of utilitarianism: Commensurability is a prerequisite of rationality, and what can commensurate except the utilitarian standard, which asks one to maximize the sum of social happiness?

Mill presents a compressed argument for CPR in the last chapter of his *System of Logic* (Mill 1911). Imitating the opening of Aristotle's *Nicomachean Ethics*, Mill suggests that while each "Art" (read: *technē*) has an end that defines it and that it takes for granted, each is also to be subordinated to a general, and architectonic, "Art of Life" (VI:12:6). For this general Art, as well, there must be first principles or ends that serve as "first principles of Conduct." But since plural principles can lead to conflicting advice (VI:12:7),

> there must be some standard by which to determine the goodness or badness, absolute and comparative, of ends or objects of desire. And whatever that standard is, there can be but one: for if there were several ultimate principles of conduct, the same conduct might be approved by one of those principles and condemned by another; and there would be needed some more general principle as umpire between them.

Mill regards the existence of such conflicting advice as intolerable – though not on purely logical grounds, but rather because it would indicate that one had failed to articulate the first principles of a proper science of practice.

Mill, of course, takes happiness to be an ultimate end that serves as the needed single standard. Yet he takes pains to insist that in so doing he is not denying the plurality of values. Happiness, he writes, "is the justification, and ought to be the controller, of all ends, but is not itself the sole end" (VI:12:7). Thus, there are other ends distinct from happiness that have a place in our deliberations. Mill explains the ability of happiness to adequately represent the reasons embodied by those other ends by referring to the fact that the "justification" of their value and the "controlling" of their pursuit rightly falls to happiness. This is not the place to speculate about exactly what Mill means by these phrases. In §16 I have set out a number of relations between plural values and the commensurans that might fit Mill's view. The present point is just that he really does set up happiness as a commensurans, in my sense of the term.

While Mill's argument for CPR is suggestive, it is at best a sketch. It does not spell out exactly why conflict is intolerable, why the metaphor of a "common umpire" is appropriate, why the umpire must take the form of a single measure that relevantly varies only in quantity, or why one might not resolve conflicts either by denying plurality altogether or by invoking an all-purpose tie breaker. For answers to these questions, we should turn to the argument offered by Henry Sidgwick, a utilitarian philosopher a generation later than Mill, whose *Methods of Ethics* (Sidgwick 1981: hereafter *ME*) is an unsurpassed effort at utilitarian systematization. In this section, I will reconstruct Sidgwick's argument at length. This is worth doing for there is much we have to learn from it, both about what to imitate and about what to avoid.

The main goal of Sidgwick's book is to see to what extent reason can adjudicate between three "methods of ethics" – three competing conceptions of the ultimate end of action: egoistic hedonism, hedonistic utilitarianism, and a form of intuitionism that holds that "the practically ultimate end of moral action is often the Rightness of the action itself" (*ME* I.i.2, p. 4). He eliminates intuitionism as a separate contender, but notoriously ends by declaring that reason cannot decide between egoistic and utilitarian hedonism: this is the "dualism of practical reason."

Although Sidgwick sometimes seems to allow that egoistic hedonism and utilitarianism appeal to broadly different types of reasons for action, he is clear that each proceeds within an overall rubric of practical rationality or reasonableness. Accordingly, he often treats as interchangeable the terms "reasonableness," "rationality," and "rightness." " 'Acting rationally' is," he writes, "merely another phrase for 'doing what we see to be right' " (*ME* III.xiii.2, p. 375; cf. I.vi.1, p. 77 and III.xi.3, pp. 343–4). This implies that the commensurability he sees effected by either egoistic hedonism or by utilitarianism – which he conceives in strictly quantitative terms – is not limited in its range to a set of specifically "moral" considerations. In addition, each of these two "methods" obviously posits strong

121

commensurability, in that each puts forward a single commensurans in terms of which every choice is to be made. For these reasons, Sidgwick's ethical views are clearly relevant to our study of practical reasoning.

Since Sidgwick conceived each of the two hedonistic "methods" as putting forward an "ultimate end," it appears that the relation that he sees between the hedonistic commensurans and the considerations it systematizes is a teleological one. By this I mean not merely that the items commensurated are assessed as causal means to pleasure, nor just that they have weight proportional to their tendency to produce pleasure, but also that they are sought, ultimately, for the sake of pleasure. Positing that the commensurans is the ultimate end is a dramatic way of claiming that this measure captures the force of all of the considerations it arrays. Since the commensurability that Sidgwick envisions is strong, unrestricted in domain, and embodies teleological claims, his defense of CPR is all the more striking – and, if successful, all the more powerful.

Sidgwick's argument will be seen, in the end, to hinge upon a challenge to the opponent of CPR to think of some alternative way of systematizing practical considerations. What gives this challenge force, however – and what makes Sidgwick's argument so deep – are his conditions on an adequate conception of practical reason, which tend to show that systematization is necessary, and his epistemological views, which indicate why any systematization of our practical ends would have to involve commensurability.

A. The postulates of practical rationality

There are grounds for thinking that Sidgwick held that a full systematization of reasons for action is per se a prerequisite of rationality (cf. Schneewind 1977, 234–5.). Sidgwick wrote of "the one impulse (as human as any) which it is the special function of the philosopher to direct and satisfy: the effort after a complete and reasoned synthesis of practical principles."[2] He despairingly admits at the end of the *Methods* that the dualism – the undecidable contest between the "methods" of egoism and utilitarianism – makes it seem necessary to abandon this aim of "rationalizing [the sphere of morality] completely" (*ME*, Concl. §5, p. 508; cf. §1, p. 498). While some coincidence in the recommendations of the two

2 Sidgwick, "Review of Grote's *Examination of the Utilitarian Philosophy*," *Academy*, 1 April 1871; quoted in Schneewind 1977, 191. I am deeply indebted to Schneewind's comprehensive study.

methods may be hoped for, cases of conflict will nonetheless occur. In those cases, Sidgwick writes, "practical reason, being divided against itself, would cease to be a motive on either side; the conflict would have to be decided by the comparative preponderance of one or other of two groups of non-rational impulses" (*ME*, Concl. §5, p. 508). It sometimes seems, therefore, that Sidgwick understands the full systematization of the sphere of practical reason as being in itself a prerequisite of rational choice, and that this has something to do with whether a choice involving conflicting reasons can be settled on rational grounds. But does rationality require such a synthesis? The later Wittgenstein taught us that such "needs" for system, though deep, are to be resisted (see Wittgenstein 1958, Pt. I, §107, commenting on the requirement of "perfect order" alluded to in §98). Does it really undercut rationality to let a contest between principles, otherwise undecidable on rational grounds, be decided by the weight of present aims – or by "intuition"? The purported necessary connection between rationality and systematization needs to be defended.

Sidgwick's defense of this connection can be set out in terms of what I will reconstruct as his five postulates of practical rationality. They are the following:

(P1) *Discursiveness:* All rational claims must rest upon or reside in statable principles (the "first principles of practical reason").

(P2) *Respect for subordinate reasons:* The first principles of practical reason must provide for a way to represent (and delimit) the considerations put forward by the various principles of common sense.

(P3) *Practical coherence:* The first principles of practical reason must not only be logically consistent but also practically coherent, in that they must not ever give conflicting advice.

(P4) *Completeness with respect to conflicts:* When subordinate practical principles give conflicting advice, the first principles of practical reason must determine which advice should be followed.[3]

(P5) *Superior validity of the grounds of adjudication:* In order for a practical principle to resolve a conflict between practical principles rationally, it must be of wider domain of valid application than the principles in conflict and must be capable of overriding their claims to enjoy that wider domain.

Of these postulates, (P1) and (P5) have an epistemological character, setting out the conditions on the adequately rational statement or explanation

---

3 Note that this completeness requirement does not extend so far as completeness requirements for preference orderings normally do, since incompleteness with respect to questions for which no practical conflict arises (such as certain questions about day-to-day minutiae) need have no rational answer.

of reasons; (P3) and (P4) bespeak a more purely practical concern with conflicts; and (P2) links the two former sorts of postulate together by characterizing the sorts of reasons that there are, adumbrating that they tend to come into conflict. I will approach Sidgwick's defense of these postulates via his criticism of certain intuitionist approaches.

In *ME* I.viii, Sidgwick distinguishes three "phases" of intuitionism, Perceptional, Dogmatic, and Philosophical (§4, p. 102). Perceptional intuitionism is the view that "the particular case can be satisfactorily settled by conscience without reference to general rules" (§2, p. 99). This view Sidgwick finds inadequate, on the grounds that it mistakes the nature of conscience and fails to provide for a way to arrive at any kind of consistency among judgments either within or across individuals. For both of these reasons, a satisfactory conception of practical reason, Sidgwick believes, must meet the discursiveness requirement of (P1). (In fact, he believes that practical requirements must rest on self-evident principles; but his argument for CPR does not directly depend upon this further claim.)

In Sidgwick's view, the various principles of common sense express genuine (ethical) reasons for action. Dogmatic intuitionism goes farther, holding "that we can discern certain general rules with really clear and finally valid intuition" (§3, p. 101). This view Sidgwick associates with the intuitionist conception of the ultimate end mentioned above, namely that acting in a certain way is taken to be "unconditionally prescribed without regard to ulterior consequences" (§1, p. 98). He takes this form of intuitionism very seriously, making a great effort in Book III to lay out the diverse ethical content of common sense in as orderly a way as possible. Since, however, there are innumerable ways in which the application of a general rule to a given case either yields unacceptable results or conflicts with some other rule, the purported "intuitions" of common sense cannot, in Sidgwick's view, be taken as an adequate guide to practice. Accordingly, these commonsense considerations must be respected, but subordinated to a set of first principles, as stated in (P2).

As this conception of regulative first principles already implies, Sidgwick believes that an adequate epistemology of practice must be a form of what he calls philosophical intuitionism (§4; cf. III.xiii), namely a consistent set of (self-evident) axioms capable of averting these conflicts, limiting the application of the subordinate principles where necessary, and exhibiting on their face the "why" of conduct – as ultimate ends, for instance, do. But this is getting ahead of our story. The first role for the first principles of any philosophical intuitionism is simply to avert practical conflicts.

In practice, as Sidgwick affirms, any two norms can conflict. Sidgwick asserts in the opening chapter of the *Methods* that "we cannot, of course, regard as valid reasonings that lead to conflicting conclusions; and I therefore assume as a fundamental postulate of Ethics, that so far as two methods conflict, one or other of them must be modified or rejected" (*ME* I.i.3, p. 6). Characteristically substituting "practical reason" for "ethics" a few pages later, he notes that "it is, as was said, a postulate of Practical Reason, that two conflicting rules of action cannot both be reasonable" (*ME* I.i.5, p. 12). That avoiding conflict was a necessary condition of rationality would be obvious, uncontroversial, and of relatively little import if it meant only that one must purge one's principles of *logical* inconsistencies. But Sidgwick has in mind *practical* conflicts, clashes that may arise given that certain contingent facts obtain.

That this is his meaning may be shown by reference to the "dualism of practical reason," mentioned above. Egoism and utilitarianism already represent Sidgwick's best efforts at systematizing commonsense so as to avert more particular conflicts. (He holds that while utilitarianism fits common sense better than does egoism, the latter is more easily constructed out of self-evident axioms [*ME*, Concl. §1; cf. Schneewind 1977, 359].) Because each individual is likely to feel the conflicting pulls of these two systematizing principles, the conflict between them is not merely an academic concern. Yet although the point is contested (cf. Richardson 1991, n. 26), Sidgwick apparently does not think that the serious incompatibility between them – which threatens the aim of "rationalizing" the practical sphere – is a logical inconsistency, for he seriously considers the postulation of a benevolent God who brings it about that their recommendations coincide as one way to avoid the problems of the dualism (*ME*, Concl. §4). Accordingly, Sidgwick seems to be committed to a postulate such as (P3), which rules out contingent conflicts.

Why not allow that in those cases in which the two methods – or indeed any two reasonable principles – conflict, following either one would be rational (cf. Parfit 1984, 461–2; also Levi 1986)? That is, why not, contrary to (P4), allow for some incompleteness in one's overall ranking, admitting that one cannot say that each option is equally good, but only that neither overrides the other? On this suggestion, it is not that the two conclusions are declared equally reasonable, in any robust sense; they are just both reasonable, and neither overrides the other. The defense of completeness (P4) that I would supply on Sidgwick's behalf is suggested by his concern (noted at the outset of this section) with whether reason is a motive. He analyzes " '*X* ought to be done' . . . as a 'dictate' or 'precept' of reason" (*ME* I.iii.3, p. 34). Sidgwick's lack of differentiation between ethics and rationality bespeaks the unity of reason, and this talk of "reason" as moving or dictating, in contrast to talk of there being "reasons" for either alternative, strongly suggests that when reason is divided against itself it fails to generate any 'oughts' at all. If "doing X would be rational," in turn, is glossed in Sidgwickian fashion as "X ought to be done" (cf. *ME* I.iii.4, p. 35), then simply declaring each of two conflicting courses to be "rational" would be a Pyrrhic victory. Alternatively, of course – or in addition – we might simply suppose that Sidgwick takes completeness to be an independent condition on a conception of rationality.

Although (P4) will prove indispensable to Sidgwick's argument for *strong* commensurability, it is not necessary to his argument for CPR. As can be seen from its role in the dualism, this requirement for the complete resolution of conflicts presses in the direction of the singleness of the first principle. It is the singleness of the commensurating principle that gives rise to strong commensurability. Weak commensurability, by contrast, does not require singleness; but a rational need for even weak commensurability is enough for CPR. That Sidgwick's argument for weak commensurability could be recast to go through without (P4) is due to the crucial contribution of the one remaining postulate. Before I can set out Sidgwick's defense of (P5), I must explain the technical notion of "superior validity" that it involves. Let me preface this bit of Sidgwickian arcana by considering a recent proposed solution to the dualism of practical reason.

Although we can now see why rationality might require the adjudication of all conflicts, the question still remains why this would have to be by appeal to a single, still higher principle. For the dualism, Derek Parfit has suggested an alternative (Parfit 1984, 462–3). Suppose that there were a third "method" of ethics (or rationality), of as good credentials as egoism and utilitarianism (Parfit has in mind what he calls the "present-aim theory," which lacks egoism's temporal neutrality). If there were three competing conceptions, then one would have good reason to follow any two (or three) of them that coincided in their recommendations. This way of settling the conflicts that arise from the dualism could obviously be generalized to cope with all conflicts among principles.

Sidgwick would decline to accept Parfit's help, here. That he would is indicated by the prominence in his thinking of the judicial metaphor of an appeal to a higher authority. When divergences arise within common-sense morality, he writes, "an appeal is necessarily made to some higher principle" (*ME* IV.iv.1, p. 466; cf. IV.ii, p. 421). As Schneewind has shown in admirable detail, Sidgwick's effort to systematize commonsense morality is largely a search for principles "superior in validity" to those of common sense in that they are both capable of overriding them and more general in scope. Sidgwick contrasts a principle that is "absolutely valid" with one that "need[s] to be controlled and completed by some more comprehensive principle" (*ME* IV.ii, p. 420; cf. Schneewind 1977, ch. 9). He approaches this notion of superior validity via his concern with dogmatic intuitionism and its claim that the multiple considerations of common sense enjoy self-evident validity or correctness. Since these many principles conflict, however, they cannot each be regarded as self-evidently valid without qualification. Nonetheless, by (P2), the reasons they represent must be respected to the extent possible. Normally, this would mean not simply rejecting either of two principles that are in conflict. The alternative, it seems, is to find some way to restrict the scope of application of these principles so that they are kept out of each other's way: benevolence towards one's friends, implacable justice to strangers, for instance. Of course, Sidgwick finds all such attempts to rationalize common sense wanting unless they converge upon the utilitarian principle as that which determines the proper scope of all subordinate principles. The point for now, however, is that (P5) builds on the discursiveness requirement of (P1) in insisting that any scope restriction that allows subordinate principles to be respected in a qualified form cannot simply be ad hoc but must be explicable.

It is here that we return to the "philosophical intuitionism" mentioned above. In criticizing dogmatic intuitionism (at *ME* I.viii.4, p. 102), Sidgwick articulates this requirement of rational explanation:

Even granting that [moral] rules can be so defined as perfectly to fit together and cover the whole field of human conduct, without coming into conflict and without leaving any practical questions unanswered, – still the resulting code seems an accidental aggregate of precepts, which stands in need of some rational synthesis. In short, without being disposed to deny that conduct commonly judged to be right is so, we may yet require some deeper explanation *why* it is so.

Sidgwick's idea seems to be that this explanation must be set out in a reason that (a) is of greater scope than the two subordinated principles because it concerns itself with what should happen on both sides of the scope restriction (in our example, with both friends and strangers), and (b) can soundly or appropriately override each of the two subordinated principles, in that it plausibly rebuts their claim to a wider scope. It is the combination of greater scope of application and relative overridingness that makes for "superior validity." Neither of these elements is susceptible of a purely formal characterization. The scope of "justice for friends" is not affected by the fact that it could be rephrased as "For all people x, if x is a friend then be just to him or her." Whether one norm soundly overrides another is even more obviously a substantive matter.

Principles of superior validity thus can sit in judgment over lesser principles, overruling them when necessary and settling their boundaries. The informal coincidence principle to which Parfit appeals fails on both counts to serve as an adequate court of appeal: It is neither as general in scope as the principles of unlimited scope that it purports to mediate, nor could it be taken to override either one of them. It is not as general, in that it applies only in cases where the two principles conflict. It does not plausibly override either of the two, in that it carries no claim to superior warrant or status.

B. Why rationality requires systematization

We may now put together Sidgwick's postulates of practical rationality in order to show why practical rationality requires systematization in terms of a single, supreme principle. The argument begins with some assumptions, already aired in our discussion of the dualism, about the pervasiveness of conflicts among reasons that, by (P2), practical rationality must respect:

(1) Any two practical principles that overlap in domain will sometimes give conflicting advice (unless one specifies or implies the other; but we will ignore this complication below).
(2) Common sense contains many principles that overlap in domain.
(3) Therefore, by (1) and (2), the principles of common sense will sometimes give conflicting advice.
(4) Therefore, by (P3), the principles of common sense cannot be accepted as being the first principles of practical reason.
(5) Together, (4), (P2), and (P4) imply that the first principles of practical reason must adjudicate the conflicts that arise among commonsense principles in a way that both determines what ought to be done and provides a way to represent (and delimit) the considerations that the conflicting principles put forward.
(6) By (P5), these adjudicating principles must validly enjoy a scope wider than the principles between which they claim to adjudicate.
(7) But any two practical principles, even higher-order ones that seem capable of adjudicating subordinate conflicts, will sometimes overlap in their domain of practical application unless they are each delimited by some further principle of still wider domain.
(8) Therefore, by (1), (6), (7), and (P3), there is at most one first principle of practical reason, which is of unlimited domain.
(9) Therefore, by (8) and (P1), if reason is to have any practical claims, there

must be exactly one first principle of practical reason, of unlimited domain (*singleness*).

(10) Therefore, by (9) and (5), if reason is to have any practical claims, there must be a single first principle of practical reason that systematizes the principles subordinate to it in a way that adjudicates all the conflicts that arise among them (*systematization*).

In this argument, the pervasive possibility of practical conflicts, their intolerability, and the requirement of superior validity combine to make a single, systematizing first principle a necessity of practical rationality. It might be thought that CPR is already implied in this conclusion. In fact, however, there is important further work that Sidgwick's argument must do to explain why, on his assumptions, systematization requires commensurability.

C. *Why systematization requires commensurability*

To imagine how systematization in terms of a single first principle might be possible without commensurability in any real sense, consider the status of alternative actions in a "two-level" utilitarian view, as in Hare 1981. At the level of "intuitive thinking" are expressed many important moral reasons for action. Agents are supposed to act on these reasons most of the time, inasmuch as they often are not in a position to calculate what would actually maximize utility. At the intuitive level, the reasons for and against a given action cannot be adequately arrayed in terms of the greater or lesser satisfaction of a single norm. If not, then (D1), the definition of "deliberative commensurability" set out in §16, implies that commensurability does not obtain among alternative actions. Now, as Hare emphasizes, these intuitive-level principles often come into conflict, seemingly forcing upon us the idea of a higher, "critical level" of moral reflection at which these conflicts can be adjudicated. At this level, the independent force of commonsense reasons for action melts away, and one can confront the alternatives armed solely with the utilitarian principle. The latter is grounded solely in the "logic" of moral language, not in its ability to systematize common sense.

Yet it was crucial to Sidgwick's argument for the necessity of systematization, as reconstructed in the last section, that the force of subordinate, commonsense reasons does not evaporate in this fashion. The adjudicating principles that enter at step (5) are thought of as representing as well as delimiting the force of the subordinate reasons, not as shifting to a plane of debate at which the subordinate reasons are held to be no longer relevant. Therefore, Sidgwick cannot infer commensurability from the singleness of the systematizing principle by claiming that its level of satisfaction is the only consideration that counts. Whether commensurability is required by a form of systematization that takes subordinate reasons seriously in the way required by (P2), then, hinges upon the way in which these subordinate reasons are arrayed by the single first principle.

In Sidgwick's view, as I have already hinted, it is the teleological relationship between the supreme principle and what it regulates that turns it into a genuine commensurans. It remains to be shown why this view of what the supreme rational principle must be is not just a teleological prejudice. There are two aspects to the explanation I will put forward on Sidgwick's behalf. First, Sidgwick simply issues a challenge (cf. Rawls 1971, 556–7). In defending his hedonistic conception of the ultimate end, he concludes by saying that if it "be rejected, it remains to consider whether we can frame any other coherent account of the good." More fundamentally, he goes on (at *ME* III.xiv.4, p. 406) to ask,

If we are not to systematise human activities by taking Universal Happiness as their common end, on what other principles are we to systematise them? It should be observed that these principles must not only enable us to compare among themselves the values of the different non-hedonistic ends which we have been considering, but must also provide a common standard for comparing these values with that of Happiness. . . . For we have a practical need of determining not only whether we should pursue Truth rather than Beauty, or Freedom or some ideal constitution of society rather than either . . . but also how far we should follow any of these lines of endeavor, when we foresee among its consequences the pains of human or other sentient beings, or even the loss of pleasures that might otherwise have been enjoyed by them.

How else can one systematize such final ends as Truth and Freedom, except by making them commensurable in terms of a single ultimate end? Second, on the understanding of the teleological relation bequeathed to the tradition by Aristotle (as interpreted in §7), the delimiting role required by systematization is built into the idea of an end. An end delimits by determining in what range of counterfactual circumstances an action done for its sake would and would not be choiceworthy or reasonable to do. For instance, if justice is sought for the sake of utility, then (a) it is sought only insofar as (in those situations in which) it is productive of utility, and (b) the idea of utility must capture at least an important part of the motivating reasons for pursuing justice (as Mill tried to show in ch. 5 of *Utilitarianism*) or otherwise appropriately regulate the pursuit of justice. An action described in a certain way is an end in itself (is a final end) just in case, considered solely in terms of that description, it would count as reasonable or choiceworthy. But what if the action also falls under a different description, according to which it would be unreasonable to do it, or unworthy of choice? The obvious response is to look for an end that is *more* final, in the sense that (being wider in scope) it can take account of a wider range of descriptions of action and of circumstances, and so better delimit the conditions under which an action satisfying the initial description is deemed reasonable or choiceworthy. And since, as we have seen, any two principles can come into conflict, one would need eventually to seek an end *ultimate* in the sense that, being unlimited in scope, it does not admit of further delimitation, and being overriding, it does not require it.

If this ultimate end is to serve to resolve all conflicts, it must be such as to avoid giving rise to conflicts itself. It seems possible that an ultimate end that is one in definition could nonetheless be so complex that a competition among its components could prevent it from serving to resolve all practical conflicts. (This would certainly be the case, for instance, on the crude "inclusivist" reading of Aristotle's conception of the ultimate end, eudaimonia, according to which it just is a collection of all intrinsic goods.) Accordingly, to ensure that the systematizing end does not itself give rise to the sort of practical conflicts declared unacceptable by (P3), it must be simple in some appropriate sense. The requisite simplicity will have been achieved just in case the considerations embodied in the ultimate end may all be expressed in terms of "the more and the less," that is, in terms of its greater or lesser satisfaction. I will call an end that meets this condition *homogeneous.* Sidgwick did not squarely face the possibility that the ultimate end might be qualitatively complex. His candidate for an ultimate end, namely pleasure, he thinks of as homogeneous in this sense. Protesting against one interpretation of Mill's distinction between "higher" and "lower" pleasures, Sidgwick writes that "to work out consistently the method that takes pleasure as the sole ultimate end of rational conduct, Bentham's proposition must be accepted, and all *qualitative* comparison of pleasures must really resolve itself into the quantitative" (*ME* I.vii.2, p. 94).

Accordingly, the half of Sidgwick's argument that connects systematization with commensurability may be set out as follows:

(11) Among the principles of common sense are many that are properly construed as putting forward final ends.

(12) (*The Challenge*) There is no way to adjudicate conflicts among final ends by appeal to a single first principle of unlimited scope and in a way that represents (and delimits) the claims of each end except in terms of a single ultimate end.

(13) An ultimate end is either homogeneous (in the sense that the considerations that it embodies may all be expressed in terms of its greater or lesser satisfaction) or else qualitatively complex.

(14) If an ultimate end is qualitatively complex, its elements may give rise to conflicting advice.

(15) Therefore, by (13), (14), and (P3), if an ultimate end is to serve as the first principle of practical reason, it must be homogeneous.

(16) Therefore, by (10), (11), (12), and (15), if reason is to have any practical claims, then there must be a single ultimate end, the greater or lesser satisfaction of which serves to adjudicate all the conflicts that arise among subordinate ends and principles.

(17) Therefore, by (16) and (D1) and (D2) (see §16), if reason is to have any practical claims, then there must be a single supreme principle that establishes strong commensurability among all reasons for action.

From such a strong conclusion, CPR follows trivially: If it is to be possible to choose between two items rationally, then they must be commensurable. Sidgwick, of course, remains somewhat uncertain about whether reason does have any practical claims, as it is divided against itself.

§19. ACCEPTING SYSTEMATIZATION

The argument that Sidgwick built on the basis of Mill's is subtle, deep, and powerful. On the one hand, it shows how CPR might be established on the basis of an appeal to widely held, if often implicit, conditions on practical rationality. On the other hand, one of the great advantages of setting his argument out in detail is that one can see where it might be challenged. In particular, each of the postulates of practical rationality upon which the argument depends is open to question. Not all of these possible avenues of attack are useful to my theory of deliberation, however. For one thing, even if the postulate of completeness with respect to conflicts (P4) is dropped, a revised argument could still succeed in establishing CPR on the basis of weak commensurability. In fact, I will accept at least for the sake of argument each of the first four postulates, focusing my attack on the fifth, the requirement of superior validity in an adjudicating principle. Bringing out the centrality of this last postulate is the great achievement of Sidgwick's argument. To more fully appreciate its importance, let us consider both how the other postulates might be questioned and why a theory of practical deliberation should retain them, at least in qualified form.

To anticipate one of the qualifications that I will want to make, let me note an important reservation about the terms of Sidgwick's discussion. Sidgwick seeks to put ethics on the secure path of science. To do so, he tries to find principles of superior validity that can serve as the "first principles" of that science. In adopting the traditional language of "first principles," from which practical advice is to be deduced, Sidgwick suggests a foundationalist or antiholist conception of moral reasoning with which I will take issue, on which all justification must flow from self-evident first principles. Accordingly, although I will accept most of his postulates, I will insist that we understand the phrase "first principles" that appears in them in a looser way, as indicating simply the leading or organizing principles of one's systematizing theory, principles that are "first" in perhaps only an expository sense.

Certain present-day intuitionists would object to Sidgwick's conception of practical reason as essentially discursive. Some of these philosophers would allow statable principles some role in deliberation, but would see a need for intuition or perception to resolve conflicts among them. These philosophers would reject the discursiveness postulate (P1) because, together with (P3), the requirement of practical consistency, it implies that conflict between principles can be resolved only on the basis of an appeal to some further principle. One way to deny this is to adopt an intuitionism such as Ross's. He held that there were self-evident principles that set forth the moral reasons for acting, but that there was no discursive method, no further set of priority principles, and no rules of procedure that might determine how to resolve the conflict (Ross 1930). On this view, the first principles of moral reasoning, at least, do reflect the multiple considerations of common sense, to some extent satisfying the second postulate (P2). This sort of view could easily be generalized from moral reasoning to practical reasoning as a whole. A more radical intuitionist challenge would come from a direction that Sidgwick would call "ultra-intuitional" (*ME* I.viii.2, p. 100), namely from those who would reject (P1) and (P2) simply on the grounds that statable principles are useless or inadequate in expressing rational grounds for action. On this view, it is a mistake even to speak of "first principles" as crystallizing the myriad considerations relevant to each case of choice. Rather, even the subordinate principles are, at best, rules of thumb that should always be subject to the discerning correction of a deliberator sensitive to each situation's particular features. The reason that deliberation is everywhere dependent upon the discerning perceiver, on one version of this view, is that statable rules are never adequate for expressing the claims upon us. This being so, to demand

133

discursiveness is to demand falsification. This "ultra-intuitional" view is important, for in its militant assertion of the importance of perception across the board, it puts forward as a virtue what seems, in a view such as Ross's, to be a failing, namely the exhaustion of discursively stable grounds. In addition, the idea of a discerning and patient effort to respond to the particularities of a situation certainly is attractive, in practical reasoning in general as well as in morals. As we will see in §25, however, accepting the importance of discernment does not entail giving up on the discursiveness of reasons.[4]

There may still arise conflicts that are difficult, if not impossible, to settle upon rational grounds. In §6, I emphasized that rationally unresolvable conflicts are *possible*. Here, however, the point to note is that the discursiveness postulate simply conditions *rational* claims. That conflicts that are not resolvable rationally might be resolved by other means – by "intuition," by the agent's preference, or by a coin toss – is hardly news; rational grounds, however, are discursively stable ones. What this means may be brought out by reference to Marcus's case, referred to in §6, of balanced promises that turn out, through no fault of the agent, to conflict. Let us assume that you simultaneously promised two people that you would help each of them. Unforeseeably, however, it turns out that you cannot fulfill both of these promises. Let the other facts be as symmetrical as you like. Then, says Marcus, there can be "no moral grounds" – and indeed, no practical grounds – for preferring keeping one of the promises to keeping the other (Marcus 1980, 125). Suppose, now, that a Rossian intuitionist claimed that, even in such a case, a decision would be forthcoming from "perception." This would indicate the arbitrariness of perception's dictates in this instance. If there are grounds to prefer one alternative over the other, then this must be because of some feature that one of the alternatives has that the other lacks. If so, as Christopher Gowans has argued, we are implicitly endorsing a priority rule according to which that feature is decisive in such conflicts (Gowans 1987, 27–8). The demand that some nonparticular feature – however highly concrete – be there to be stated is, to be sure, just the discursiveness requirement in another guise. Still, Marcus's case at least serves to remind nonintuitionists of the reasons they hold to the discursiveness postulate.

Before leaving intuitionism, it is perhaps worth noting that the demand

4 Thus, while the "ultra-intuitional" picture sometimes seems to be implied in the writings of Martha Nussbaum – e.g., in Essays 5 and 6 of Nussbaum 1990 – in fact her overall view is more complex, more hospitable to discursive rationality, and more akin to the one I develop: see the "Introduction" to ibid.

for discursive expression does not conflict with the claim (analyzed in §17) that unique particular features of individuals can have supreme value. Although this particularity cannot be fully expressed discursively, the practical and moral importance of the attachment to a particular person can be captured in a principle. It is for this reason that requiring discursive expression of claims does not amount to denying the importance of love for particular beings. This accommodation of particulars will not suffice, of course, to explain how a competition between attachments to two particular persons might be settled, as when one truly loves two persons, and, as the Lovin' Spoonful put it, must "finally decide, say yes to one, and let the other one ride." In such cases, we do fall back on comparing traits and compatibilities, while suspecting that these thoughts cannot exhaust the content of our hearts. Yet it is one thing to say that we have reasons about which we happen to be in the dark, and quite another to assert that we have "reasons" that, because of their nature as embodied in particulars, cannot in principle be discursively expressed. Accordingly, we suspect that one reason it's not often easy to make up one's mind in such cases is that we lack reasons or grounds for doing so. And again, our discursiveness postulate is simply a restriction on what will count as a ground for rational decision.

In stark contrast to the intuitionists, extreme moral or practical monists would reject the requirement of respect for subordinate reasons (P2), claiming that there are none. They imagine a single principle applying to practice without any need to take the measure of any other considerations. Of course, if there is only one principle that counts, then it will be trivially true that all relevant considerations can be expressed in terms of it. Accordingly, by the definitions of §16, this counts as a form of commensurability; but it is an uninteresting form. As I noted there, it makes more sense to think of commensurability as providing a way of coping with the plurality of goods or values. To be sure, one might admit the existence of plural values and goods and yet deny that one's systematization need respect them. Since my position commits me (along with Sidgwick) to respect for subordinate reasons, I cannot allow this way out. Further, to take this position is already to give up on deliberative commensurability, as I have defined it, for this implies that the single measure adequately represents the considerations that are made commensurable. Adequate representation of the subordinate considerations, though hard to define, is surely a form of respect for them.

Although practical conflicts are not impossible (§6), their avoidance is an important goal for a moral or practical theory. Accordingly, the pos-

135

tulates pertaining to practical consistency and to resolving the conflicts that do arise express important rational ideals. This we may take for now as an obvious point of agreement with Sidgwick: It will be argued on the merits in the following chapter. As I will also argue there, however, there are some cases in which we ought to recognize that we face an intractable conflict, one that we cannot resolve without severely compromising the integrity of our commitments. If this is also correct, then the postulates pertaining to conflict avoidance and resolution must be softened somewhat. Instead of stating necessary conditions for what can count as a "first principle" of morals or practice – a notion that, as signaled above, I in any case intend to transform into an expository one – the postulates must simply state ideals of rationality for the theorist. Still, accepting these postulates as ideals, we can rephrase the question that guides our present chapter in the following way: Can one make a fully rational decision between alternatives involving competing, distinct values or goods without commensurating them?

Against even my qualified acquiescence in these ideals of conflict avoidance and resolution, it might be objected that it is crazy to try to unite all practical concerns into a single, coherent system. Does the argument for CPR depend upon the general currency in our thought of the sort of general systematic "ought," subject to agglomeration (§6)? I do not believe that it does. I have already noted that if the completeness requirement were dropped, the argument would still establish the rational necessity of *weak* commensurability. Now consider that the argument as a whole might be confined in its scope to a certain class of reasons, therefore ending up defending only a partial weak commensurability. Nonetheless, the claim would remain that in a given case of choice, in order to settle in a rational way the competing claims of any subset of the plural goods that are vying with one another in that case, these goods must be made commensurable. Thus, suppose that one held that there is no notion of the overall good, only distinct virtues of character such as courage, temperance, and generosity; and suppose that one is called upon to decide between alternative generous acts, such as holding a wedding feast for one's best friend's daughter and donating money to Oxfam. Confined now to a single choice invoking only one of the types of value that the opponent admits to exist, the defender of the necessity of a weak, partial commensurability will still claim that in order to make this decision rationally, the relevant considerations must all be weighed on a single scale (in this case, presumably, the scale of generosity). Although this argument for the necessity of a partial commensurability is capable of adapting to whatever compartmentalization of considerations the opponent to system has in mind, it is nonetheless importantly damaging to the alternative, holist view of deliberation I want to recommend. From the point of view of my concern with rational deliberation, then, Sidgwick's argument for CPR thus survives the renunciation of the hope for a total system.

From the point of view of the theory of deliberation, the crucial question is therefore whether systematization – however partial and weak (or case-by-case) it is – requires commensurability. To show that it does not, I will begin by attacking the idea that conflicts are to be settled by appeal to a principle of superior validity.

§20. DELIBERATION WITHOUT AN UMPIRE

Uncovering the pivotal role played by the requirement that conflicts must be resolved by norms of superior validity, as stated in (P5), is the most novel and exciting result of our investigation of Sidgwick's argument for the necessity of commensurability as a prerequisite of rational choice (CPR). This requirement, whether put forward on its own or as part of the test for a principle's self-evidence, is crucial both to the pressure toward unified system that builds up in the first half of Sidgwick's argument and to the plausibility of the Challenge at step (12). Although Sidgwick develops the requirement of superior validity with characteristic explicitness and thoroughness, it is clear that Mill's simple argument for CPR presupposes something like it. Accordingly, if this requirement is dropped, the leading argument for the necessity of commensurability collapses.

The idea that the adjudicating grounds must be at once firmer and broader, more strongly overriding and more general, is built into the metaphor of an appeal to a higher authority. In questioning the requirement of superior validity in the present section, I will therefore also be questioning the aptness of this figure of speech. After having done so I will propose and defend an alternative metaphor for conflict resolution.

Sidgwick's additional background assumption that the claims of practical reason must rest upon self-evident first principles gives the notion of an appeal to a higher authority an almost irresistible attraction. When these two elements are joined, the superior-validity requirement emerges as a corollary of a vision of ethical or practical theory as a hierarchical, deductive system: With self-evident principles at the apex, and more particular theorems deduced from these via factual assumptions, all authority flows from its most general principles. This is a rationalist's dream for practical theory – and not just that of any rationalist, but specifically of one that would proceed *more geometrico*, attempting to deduce results from unquestionable axioms. Since such a strong rationalist would likely have little taste for dispensing conflicting advice, it is likely that he will be led towards a genuinely pyramidal ideal, in which all flows, somehow, from *one* self-evident first principle. Such seems to have been Sidgwick's dream, and a part of the philosophical intuitionism to which he adhered (cf. *ME* I.vi.1, 77n.; and compare Mill 1911, I:12:4–5). In the end it proved no more accessible to him than the ghosts he sought at innumerable seances.

Sidgwick's mistake, and that of a whole related tradition of thought about practical reasoning, is to suppose that the self-evident starting points must stand as the few, highly general axioms from which all else may be deduced – and in terms of which all conflicts among subordinate norms may be definitively settled. This supposition I will now undercut. Sidgwick's misguided demand for an axiomatic practical science stems from his yoking together two features, generality and overridingness (or, perhaps, generality and warrant), that in fact can vary independently. Among normative judgments that stand most firm are some quite concrete, even particular ones – about the evil of the Holocaust and of the My Lai massacre, about the admirable character of Mother Teresa's work with the poor and sick of Calcutta, about the injustice of Idi Amin's rule, and so on. Similarly, an author may be more firmly attached to the project of writing a particular book than to any one description of his or her ends in so doing – so much so, that if one of those candidate ends were to imply that he or she had better go into the entertainment business instead (that being where real fame is achieved in this country), then he or she would likely find that writing the book was an attachment that overrode this end. In both the moral and practical arenas, then, the most concrete propositions are among the firmest. Conversely, it is so difficult to frame satisfactory general principles for ethics or for practice that we are constantly indicating our doubts about them by hedging them in one way or another. In short, generality is not even positively correlated with overridingness or superior warrant, let alone necessarily linked with it. This conclusion accords with Aristotle's remark that "among statements about conduct those which are general apply more widely, but those which are particular are more true" (*N.E.* II.7, 1107a29–31). Sidgwick's notion of superior validity thus combines two elements that are logically independent. Revealingly, Sidgwick takes a standard line on Aristotle that quite ignores this remark and yields an interpretation more in line with his own fusion of these two elements (*ME* I.viii.2, 99n.).

The metaphor of an appeal to a higher authority misrepresents not only the structure of our practical commitments but also human psychology. As applied to an individual deliberator, all metaphors built on judicial process seem too narrow in their relevance, excessively segmented, and overly rigid. It is only in the cartoons that an angelic version of oneself whispers in one ear while a devilish version of oneself whispers in the other, leaving one's actual self in the middle to decide which one to obey. In the *Republic*, Plato, assuming that one part of the soul could not conflict with itself, did use certain sorts of practical conflict as evidence that one should distinguish parts of the soul. Yet in *De Anima* III.9, Aristotle rightly countered that if one took susceptibility to conflicts as a sufficient reason for distinguishing parts, one would end up with a wild proliferation of parts of the soul (cf. Richardson 1992b, 382–3). In this respect, Aristotle's psychology anticipated Marcus's point that monism is not proof against conflict. This being so, talk of "parts" of the soul, whether after the fashion of Plato, Aristotle, or Freud, will not usefully cover the whole range of an individual's deliberative problems.

More importantly, whatever the merits of a segmentation of the psyche for the purposes of psychological explanation, it clashes with the way deliberation feels from the inside. It would be an oddly self-dissociated person who generally felt as distanced from his competing desires and commitments as a judge is supposed to be from the parties who come before her. Sometimes, of course, one does feel assailed by one's desires and commitments. One's addiction to coffee sings in a siren voice that he despises and yet must hear. Another's conscience nags about the use of pirated software, bringing a message to which he would rather not have to listen. Yet surely this is not the normal lot of a healthy and sane individual! We sometimes would wish to dissociate ourselves from one or another of our desires or commitments, but usually our involvement with them is so intimate that if we were a judge we would have to recuse ourselves for likely bias in the case at hand. How can you decide a case fairly when you are sleeping with both the plaintiff and the defendant?

The final fault with the metaphor of a judicial appeal, as applied to individual deliberation, is that it fails to take account of the fluidity of the "parties."[5] The judge in a court of law adjudicates a controversy largely defined by the separate identities of the parties and the particular past event – car accident, breach of contract, or murder – that brought them into

---

5 In developing the metaphor of adjudication, Darwall (1983, 94–8) asserts that the "pool of claimants" may be enlarged. He can allow this because his version of adjudication lies midway between Sidgwick-style appeal to a higher principle and the alternative metaphor of reflection, to be introduced shortly in the text.

court. In individual deliberation, sometimes only vague and shifting boundaries delimit the contesting commitments. Love for one's children can be hard to separate from the desire to pass on one's own ideals. The quest for achievement and the thirst for esteem can be inextricably entangled. Furthermore, all such desires and commitments are subject to change, both in themselves and in their relations. Accordingly, although the deliberator does not stand removed from the desires and commitments that are hers, neither is she simply saddled with them. There is room for her to revise them on reflection.

The idea of reflection provides a more appropriate metaphor for the deliberative resolution of conflicts. This may not seem like a metaphor, for "reflection" (or "practical reflection") may seem simply another term for "deliberation." But I do have something more definite and complex in mind, the core of which was introduced earlier under the label "Socratic reflection." Because to reflect is not to dissociate from oneself, in reflecting one meets oneself halfway (cf. Velleman 1989, 3). As I deliberate, I strive not only to adjudicate claims among my desires but also to understand those claims in terms that will make decision possible. For example: I want to go to hear an important lecture, but I am also hungry. "Well, if I go to the lecture, there is a nice café next door that serves great omelets." In such simple ways one's desires (and other sorts of commitments) meet one halfway. One need not postulate a special, higher-order desire that our desires accommodate our self-understanding and our deliberation in order to understand this phenomenon. It is enough to note that the desires and commitments are the decider's. That self-consciousness has these two sides is a commonplace, but one worth playing up in order to show how Mill's and Sidgwick's judicial imagery goes astray when applied to the individual deliberator. It is precisely because of this interaction of self-as-subject and self-as-object that the deliberator cannot sensibly take the stance of a disinterested judge with respect to her own desires and commitments.

In two different ways, therefore, I have tried to break down the correlation, built into the idea of superior validity, between generality and authority or overridingness. I have argued both that our ethical and practical convictions show no tendency to reflect this correlation and that utilizing the related judicial metaphor to understand deliberation bespeaks an oddly dissociated view of the self. We should conclude, to the contrary, that the principles used to settle a given conflict need not be more general in scope than either of the competing principles. Instead, we may look to how a given resolution of the conflict (or refusal to resolve the conflict)

140

fits with a host of more particular commitments. The way is cleared, in other words, for a holist approach to conflict resolution. The nature of this coherence ideal will be set out in the following two chapters. To anticipate its main lines in a formula, which I will immediately gloss: It will be bidirectional and holistic, seeking mutual support among all the practical norms to which one holds fast on reflection, but allowing that reflection may revise any norm. The arguments that lead us to reject the metaphor of an appeal to a higher authority also lend support to the sort of coherence ideal I will be defending.

Bidirectionality lies implicit in the breakdown of the association between authority and generality. By calling practical reasoning "bidirectional," I mean that in building justificatory connections it works both from the more general to the more specific and also in the other direction. "We work from both ends," as Rawls puts it (1971, 20). If even sometimes "the particulars are truer," this is the only reasonable way to proceed. Our general norms typically need the support of the more particular ones. Sidgwick saw the need to respect specific principles, but dreamt of arriving at a single self-evident principle of unlimited scope. The failure of that project leaves intact the importance of building upon particular convictions. Yet since some systematization is required if we are to deliberate rationally, there is every reason to expect that the relatively more general principles will take on some weight of their own. If so, that will enable us to build justificatory support in both directions.

The cure for segmentation of the psyche is holism. Whereas the judicial model encourages one to imagine an institutionalized hierarchy of courts of appeal, the idea of practical reflection works better without any fixed division of the soul into parts. (Here I am speaking of two alternatives within the theory of deliberation. Accounts aiming more broadly at psychological explanation, such as Freud's, may have use for a firm division of the soul at another level.) If, as Sidgwick emphasized, any two principles can come into practical conflict, then the effort to build mutual support should extend to building ties between any two principles. This rules out any strong partitioning of the rational agent's norms, such that coherence is to be pursued only within each part. Cross-cutting support, like cross-cutting conflict, is too important to allow any such segmentation much importance. Accordingly, some degree of holism, of building mutual support among all of one's norms, taken as a whole, is called for.

The opposite of dissociation – the third problem with the judicial metaphor – is identification. If one dissociates oneself from one's norms in imagining oneself as an impartial judge over them, one identifies with them to the extent one affirms them on reflection. One is sufficiently distinguishable from one's norms for this self-identification to be active and reflective, but sufficiently committed to them for an impartially judicial perspective to make no sense. This notion of reflective acceptance will be fully explored in §26.

It is clear that one's reflective self-identification is open to revision. Revisability is the final principal plank of the coherence ideal. If self-evident starting points are unavailable, even after a systematizing attempt such as Sidgwick's, then a deductive or "Cartesian" model of practical justification is not practicable (cf. Rawls 1971, §87). If every norm is in principle revisable, in the sense that none is a priori certain, then room for building mutual support or coherence is, by contrast, considerably enhanced, as subsequent chapters will amply demonstrate. To support the move to a coherence theory, I need not deny flat out that any norm is self-evident. Rather, I follow Sidgwick's lead with regard to his completeness requirement, and focus on those cases in which a conflict of norms has arisen. If two norms conflict, even contingently, then their claim to self-evidence is rebutted: If we retain them, we do so after deliberation or on due reflection, not simply as self-evident. If we add to this Sidgwick's further claim that any two practical principles are liable to conflict, and are more pessimistic than he about finding a single ultimate, commensurating principle, then we will do well to move to a coherence standard. When principles conflict, we have reason to revise them. How much reason, and under what sorts of conflict, are our next topics.

VII

Practical coherence

We have just arrived at the importance of building coherence among norms via considerations about how we may rationally settle conflicts among our norms. Yet the necessity of invoking some sort of coherence standard has been implicit in my argument ever since Chapter II, where I argued that practical reasoning should not be either reduced to deductive reasoning or assimilated to any pattern of necessary validity. These contrasting routes to a coherence account merge smoothly. The last section's argument suggests that our systems of norms are not and should not be pyramidally arrayed, with all value or warrant flowing from one or a few self-evident or self-presenting starting points at the peak. If there are starting points of this status, they are likely to be specific, scattered, and spread throughout our normative commitments. The question then arises how one can gather this dispersed warrant in support of a practical theory. Complementing this bidirectionality, Chapter II's argument implies that even if there were a few central starting points, practical reasoning could not flow of necessity from them alone. Instead, the nondeductive moves that are made from a norm to a conclusion can gain support from other norms in the system. To lay out this support is to build coherence among one's norms. This schematic answer about how to justify nondeductive moves, it will be noted, is also an answer to how to gather dispersed warrant, namely by connecting one's norms into a practical theory of sorts. In the present chapter, I will describe the many types of practical coherence (§21) and show that while there is no rational demand that coherence be maximized, there are strong pragmatic reasons to build coherence among one's norms (§22). Both coherence's complexity and its status as end rather than requirement will be important to showing that it does not become a covert commensurans (§26).

143

§21. GRADATIONS OF CONFLICT AND MUTUAL SUPPORT

Building coherence among one's norms and ends is a matter of finding or constructing intelligible positive connections or links or mutual support among them and of removing relations of opposition or conflict. Whereas we suppose ourselves readily to understand the sort of connections involved in deductive reasoning, the sorts of conflict and mutual support relevant to a coherence standard are harder to pin down. This is in part because they are so varied. As I proceed, I will examine the mutual support that comes from casting one pursuit as a means to another or one as sought for the sake of another; but I will also look at ways of connecting ends that more closely resemble the hypothesizing of explanatory theories in science. Mutual interference can show up in practical conflicts of the sort that troubled Sidgwick, but also in a persistent resistance to attempts at unification.

Regarding conflicts among norms, the first distinction to make is that between their occurrence and their strength. One may land by pure misfortune in a situation in which one is faced with norms whose joint satisfaction is impossible, under some very strong interpretation of "impossible." For instance, it can be your simple bad luck that you happen by the river in which someone is drowning just a few minutes before you are due to meet your intended at the altar. It is rare that obligations to drowning persons and to fiancés come into conflict (here, a scheduling conflict: the wedding can be postponed). It might be physically impossible for you (or: for anyone) to save two people who are drowning simultaneously at either end of a pond – or to rescue two sinking casks of coveted treasure – but such occurrences are even rarer, and are certainly not to be expected. Conversely, there are norms that may be expected to conflict, even if luck has it that they turn out not to. For example, even though the general ends "to remain a bachelor" and "to get married" conceptually cannot both remain satisfied, this clash might be buffered by fortune. Someone who never has any opportunity to make any decisions about how to deal with the opposite sex, never receives a proposal of marriage, and never faces alternatives significantly affecting matrimonial chances may never face a practical conflict between these ends. While this scenario is unlikely, its point is that although these ends "necessarily" conflict in some sense, they do not necessarily give rise to conflicting recommendations for action. To get norms that necessarily come into practical con-

144

flict, we need norms that are more global, such as "do everything with solemn dignity" and "do everything flippantly."

In assessing the rational import of conflicts whose occurrence is contingent, we should keep in mind an argument of Marcus (1980). One reason that it is important to recognize the logical possibility of moral dilemmas, she noted, is that sometimes what we ought to do is not to revise our moral views but change the world so that dilemmas of the sort we are facing do not arise. We can and should "stack the deck" in our own favor, as she put it. The same point holds of practical conflicts generally. For instance, we might encourage people to sign medical directives indicating their attitudes toward various medical means of resuscitation, so that we will less often face conflicts between (a) avoiding their unnecessary suffering and (b) avoiding one's paternalistic substitution of one's own judgment for theirs. The conflict will not arise if we know what they would have wanted.

So far in discussing the occurrence of practical conflicts between two norms, I have mainly contrasted conceptual necessity with luck; but of course there are a variety of other significant gradations in between these two extremes. Before I go into these, note that there are two other contexts in which these degrees matter for our purposes: in determining the strength of conflicts once they occur, and in the strength of positive connections among norms. Recall the structure of a moral or practical dilemma (§6), which includes the idea that it is impossible for the agent to satisfy both of two (or more) norms. In what sense, we now ask, is satisfying the two norms "impossible?" Gradations of necessity will become gradations in the strength of practical conflict.[1]

In order of increasing distance from true logical impossibility, and culminating in a form that is not strictly an impossibility at all, we may set out this aspect of the extrinsic scale as follows:

(a) Conceptual impossibility (e.g., being a married bachelor).
(b) Physical impossibility.
(c) Impossibility given human nature.
(d) Impossibility given the constraints of current technology.
(e) Improbability.

Also important to distinguish are:

---

1 These gradations may also be plugged into the sense in which a means is "necessary" to achieving an end (cf. §5), generating in that way gradations of instrumental support.

(f) Impossibility given time constraints;
(g) Conflict in principle;
(h) Conflict by tradition; and
(i) Conflict given current laws and institutions.

Each of the first five of these notions, as normally interpreted, embraces the cases higher on the list. For example, when we think about what is possible given human nature, we typically take as given all physical laws as well. Although hard to place in this progression, impossibility given time constraints deserves special mention. A scheduling conflict may rest on the physical impossibility of being in two places at the same time. For example, consider the diplomat who has scheduled nearly simultaneous meetings on June 15, in Manila in the evening and in Managua in the morning: There is no way he can make both of these meetings. Nonetheless, it is worth separating this variant out from other cases of physical impossibility because it is often so easy to reschedule. Postponing is an essential human activity, typically involving only a slight revision in one's goals (cf. Mabbott 1953, 114).

The practical implications of these different sorts of necessity or impossibility are quite different. In general, there is little point in trying to buck impossibilities of either of the first two kinds. If the occurrence of a practical conflict between two norms is physically necessary, there is nothing we can do to avert it. Once in a conflict where the two recommended courses are physically incompossible (cf. §6), there is no point in trying to have it both ways. For impossibilities of the remaining types, whether it is reasonable to take their limitations as givens in deliberation depends upon the practical question one is facing and the opportunities one has. Their significance also depends, I will now argue, on the ways in which they lean in a hidden way on other ends besides those that conflict.

Impossibilities involving human nature stand at an interesting crossroads. What is necessary because of human nature might at first glance appear to be a species of physical necessity; yet there is an evaluative significance to the notion of human nature that disturbs this assimilation. Physically possible changes, perhaps brought about by radical new technology, could conceivably create presumed members of the human species who departed from human nature. For example, in order to prevent the myriad conflicts between career aspiration and family obligations that arise as parents attempt to care for their children, some bright genetic engineer might team up with an in vitro fertilization clinic to invent a way in which humans could be born as adults, hard-wired with all they need to know to take care of themselves. This does not seem a physical impossibility. Yet to omit childhood is to overstep the bounds of human nature, it may seem; and this provides a special reason not to consider such farfetched possibilities. Notice, though, that this reason is at least partly normative. It is not that its departing from human nature makes it especially unlikely, but that it makes it especially undesirable. Having long childhoods is such a central feature of who we are, as human beings, that even if we recognize it as a vulnerability and a weakness that might conceivably be removed, we will not recognize as a gain what flows from that change in who we are (cf. Nussbaum 1986, 376, and Nussbaum 1990, essay 15). Necessities arising from human nature are special because they both reflect and help define our evaluative stances. To analyze such necessities, therefore, will likely require articulating some of one's most important ends.

For the diplomat of a few paragraphs back, speculations about proposed trans-Pacific rocket service, which could become available early in the next millennium, are idle. When seeking sufficient means to one's ends, and when assessing whether a proposed means is necessary, it seems appropriate to define *available means* relative to current technology (or, more precisely, relative to the technology that will be available at the projected time of action). Yet this is obviously a slippery notion. Sometimes we can say in absolute fashion that technology does not exist to do something: We do not now know how to produce controlled fusion at room temperatures, for instance. Although we have no reason to believe that doing so would violate the laws of physics, it has never been done and we do not know what it would take to do it. In the case of our diplomat, however, rocket technology exists to lift him into quasi-orbit and deposit him in Manila; it is just that no one wants to spend the millions of dollars needed to charter the Space Shuttle for him. Rocket technology is not available to him at a reasonable price. Yet as already noted in §9, the question, At what cost? is one that refers, implicitly or not, to the agent's other ends. The dollar price really reflects the importance of constraint by underlying background ends, most of which compete for those dollars. It is the omnipresence of this sort of constraint – represented less mercenarily! – that will form the basis of my own holistic proposals. The fact that ordinary thought about what is technologically possible builds in this background constraint gives my proposals an additional foothold in common sense.

Whereas these sorts of impossibility could generate a contradiction, by the sort of argument discussed in §6, the type (e), improbability, would generate only a "probabilistic inconsistency" of the form "*p*, but probably not-*p*" (cf. BonJour 1985, §5.3). What counts as improbable? If I wrote two IOU's at the same time, knowing that I would be unable to fulfill both promises of repayment unless I won the big lottery jackpot for which I hold one ticket at 1 : 3,000,000 odds, the fact that I had this hope would not count as much of an excuse. If, on the other hand, I had a "reasonable hope" that those who owed me money would ante up before my notes become due, then perhaps that would excuse my action.

Norms can conflict in principle in ways that can be understood wholly apart from whether they generate a conflict in any actual case. Think of the scorn that Nietzsche heaped upon those who value the cozy nooks of bourgeois domesticity, aiming to settle down and raise a family; and consider the contempt that the bourgeois might shower in return upon the self-indulgent, irresponsible, and asocial misfits attempting to live up to a Nietzschean ideal, aiming at self-expression and independence from the ways of the common herd. The ideal of each side is partially defined by its depreciation of the other. While it might be possible to live a life that united the Nietzschean and the bourgeois ideals, attempting to do so does not seem like a wise course. The mutual hostility of the two ideals, expressed on a principled basis, makes it likely or expectable that conflicts will arise in the attempt.

A somewhat different situation is presented by norms or ideals that conflict by tradition. An example might be the relation between sexual freedom or promiscuity (it is hard to find a neutral term, here) and successful marriage. On a theory of marriage that made mutual faithfulness an important plank of marital success, this would be a conflict in principle. Let us imagine, however, someone who faces this issue without being committed to any articulate theory of marriage. Since marriage is an institution that transcends or cuts across many different traditions that have varying attitudes toward marital fidelity, it is easy to suppose that the tension between successful marriage and the sexual promiscuity of one of the partners is merely the artifact of a particular tradition. "Marriages are no worse in Samoa or in France, or wherever it is that sexual relations are freer," it may be thought. Still, the traditional tension is worth paying attention to, for a number of reasons. First, in a culture such as that of the contemporary United States in which the tension is widely thought to exist, married couples have to adapt themselves to this tradition in countless subtle ways. Second, it may be that the tradition exists for forgotten reasons which, if articulated, could convert the mutual hostility into a principled one. Third, these implicit reasons might turn out to be correct or compelling.

We often are committed to norms that conflict, given current laws and institutions. Antigone's decision to bury her brother despite Creon's decree forbidding it is a dramatic and old example. In the United States today, to give a newer example, it remains impossible to pursue a military career and be fully open about one's homosexual activity. This layer of conflict needs separate note because while agents will often rationally assume that they must work within given legal and institutional constraints, working to change them is also often possible. Rationality does not rule out civil disobedience.

The nature of mutual support requires some examination independently of the nature of practical conflict. To be sure, each type of conflict suggests some kind of support. To the logically incompatible corresponds the logically inseparable, to the conceptually incompossible corresponds the conceptually wedded, to the physically impossible corresponds the physically necessary, and so on; however, some types of mutual support are not easily viewed as simple opposites of the kinds of conflict already catalogued. I wish to go over four of these: (i) orderings of finality, (ii) contingent synergy, (iii) explanatory support, and (iv) narrative unity.

(i) Orderings of finality. Ordering one's norms as means to end or as being sought one for the sake of another builds the most important sort of intelligible connection among them. Labeling something as a means to an end that one seeks provides an initial explanation why one seeks it. The full-blown relation of pursuit for the sake of an end carries further implications for how one would regulate one's norms (§7). The latter relation is the most important one for building systematic connections among one's norms. A system of ends so ordered will include resources for resolving conflicts reasonably.

(ii) Contingent synergy. Just as practical conflicts can arise by mischance, so practical support can be contingent or even fortuitous. By sheer luck, for example, one can sometimes kill two birds with one stone. It still does happen, for instance, that an academic gets a job offer in the same town that his or her spouse does, allowing a move to that town to serve both career and marriage. Aspirin regularly taken for headaches can turn out to prevent heart disease. Reusing plastic wrap can both cut down on one's contribution to the solid waste crisis and save money. And so on. In addition, ends can turn out to reinforce one another through their pursuit, the world being the way it is. For ex-

ample, pursuing opportunities for truly peaceful contemplation may, in our bustling world, lead one to religious retreats; and sincere participation in religious retreats may provide additional, doctrinal reasons to pursue peaceful contemplation.

(iii) Explanatory support. Explanatory relations typically figure centrally in the concept of coherence when it is applied to knowledge or scientific understanding. Insofar as an agent has reflected sufficiently upon his or her practical commitments for them to represent elements in an articulated self-understanding, they will begin to be unified in ways that importantly resemble the explanatory theories of the scientist (cf. Bittner 1989, 119, 130). Somewhat overgeneralizing this point, Hurley writes that "deliberation involves the search for a theory about our values as they actually are" (Hurley 1989, 238). To all of our theories, explanatory relations are central. Although the point is debated, it does not appear that explanatory relations can be reduced to independently well-understood logical relations. Efforts to produce a logic of induction, for instance, have long foundered on the difficulty of providing an account free of assumptions about what human interests explanations serve, what seems salient to us, and what concepts seem to us validly projectible into the future.[2] Ends, as just noted, are invoked to explain actions. Given what we are normally interested in, we take the fact that I needed a covering to explain why I made a cloak. To be sure, someone might be curious why I decided upon a cloak rather than a fur coat. Such a person will require a fuller explanation. Take a case, then, that forces such curiosity on us: "I needed some food to eat; caviar is an edible foodstuff; therefore, I got some caviar." Since we tend to doubt that anyone needs caviar, the simple need for food seems not sufficient to explain the action. The demand for a perspicuous explanation, in other words, is not satisfied by any old end–means connection. If we now transfer this result back to the prospective context of deliberation, we can see that the analogue of this demand will be useful in getting the agent to articulate her ends. This provides yet another route whereby the normative presuppositions of everyday life (e.g., that caviar is an extravagance) enter into the deliberative construction of practical coherence.

---

2 The philosophically famous example of a failure of projectibility is "grue" (Goodman 1979) which we would translate as "green if examined before the year 2000, and blue otherwise." Formal criteria of induction seem to indicate that "all emeralds are grue" is supported by the evidence, yet we balk. Accordingly, explanatory relations need to be identified separately (Harman 1986).

150

(iv) Narrative unity. Someone's ends can also cohere as elements in their intended life story. To begin to spur students to reflect about their value commitments, one of my philosophy colleagues has them write their own obituaries, as they would hope or predict they would be. Looking back upon our lives to date is a principal way in which we form our self-understandings. Projecting forward to looking back upon our entire lives is a good way to crystallize out of those self-understandings the hopes and aims we have for the long run. One relatively formal way to take these into account is to formulate a "life plan" that avoids conflicts, in particular scheduling conflicts, so as better to satisfy one's ends over a lifetime (cf. Rawls 1971, §63). A more qualitative approach would do so by trying to live a life that made sense as a story. To do so is to seek what has been called "narrative unity" (cf. MacIntyre 1984, esp. 173–4). Unfortunately, it is not particularly clear what narrative unity amounts to. A human life, but not all works of modernist fiction, has a beginning, middle, and end.[3] Although it seems fruitless to try to give general criteria for what counts as a story or a good story, human traditions clearly provide a rich stock of stories against which these questions can be answered case by case. There is some overlap between narrative unity and explanatory support. If we take the "caviar syllogism" of the last paragraph as the sketch of a story, the "reader" will clearly want to know why fish eggs suddenly took such a prominent position in the plot. But the notion of narrative unity also raises more purely aesthetic considerations, such as balance, proportion, and variety, which do seem to be relevant to human lives. Goethe, at least, wanted his life to be a beautiful one.

Practical coherence, then, can be built in many ways. In addition to the great variety of ways in which conflicts can be avoided, there are more purely positive ways of arriving at norms that are mutually supportive. The simplest exploit ways in which, by chance or because of human nature or circumstance, different courses of action support each other in their execution. Explanatory support goes beyond this, and provides the essential tool of any person's attempt at formulating a coherent *conception* of his or her ends. Narrative unity can also contribute to one's self-conception, but it can be sought after from a less theoretical perspective. The question now is what reason, in general, we have to promote any of these types of practical coherence.

---

3 Note, however, that nothing prevents an agent from unifying her commitments around a cause that will outlast her lifetime, such as preparing for the Second Coming or regaining independence for her people.

§22. PRACTICAL COHERENCE AS AN END

All of the last section's myriad distinctions about grades of conflict and mutual support are important to assessing the relative force of these various arguments as applied to different interpretations of coherence. For the sake of simplicity in exposition, however, I will largely rely upon the reader to consider how things would be different for different variants of conflict and mutual support, rather than explicitly overlaying the classification on my assessment of the arguments. Instead, I want to mention yet another distinction, which turns out to be crucial in assessing the force of the pragmatic arguments. This is the distinction between the coherence of someone's set of norms at a given time – which all of the last section's discussion was implicitly about – and the constancy of someone's commitments through time. The two notions are clearly independent: One may be resolutely, nay, stubbornly committed through one's whole life to conceptually incompatible aims; and one may shift adherence erratically from one neat system to another. I will use "coherence" to refer to the virtue of the system of norms at one time, and "constancy" to the virtue that applies to the system as it shifts through time.[4]

Coherence and constancy become interwoven as we attempt to plan our activities. Coordinating our activities with others and with ourselves over time is the crucial pragmatic benefit of coherence. Because many of our most important activities extend over a good period of time, however, this benefit will not be reaped without a modicum of constancy. Some coherence and some constancy are necessary for planning. In assessing the pragmatic benefit of coherence, however, we should separate out what is due to constancy.

In some contexts, however, constancy is the more important virtue for securing the pragmatic benefits of coordination. Consider Farmer Dan, who intends both to grow wheat and to grow vegetables this summer, knowing that he cannot succeed at both. The agricultural situation might be as follows: Unless Dan keeps steadily tending the wheat field, the wheat will wither and die; and unless Dan keeps steadily tending the vegetable plot, the vegetables will wither and die. It is possible for him to do the subsidiary actions of tending both plots fairly well; but if there is enough rain for the vegetables the wheat will rot, and if there is enough sun for the wheat the vegetables will be burned. A natural way for Dan to forge a coherent set of intentions would be as a contingency plan: He could

---

4 On constancy as a virtue, cf. MacIntyre 1984, 183, 242; Velleman 1989, ch. 8.

aim to have a crop no matter how the weather turns out (wheat if it's dry, vegetables if it's wet); but Dan is not so sophisticated, and subscribes to the simpler, conflicting intentions as stated above. This is a perfect case for "letting the world decide" a conflict; and since the conflict will be settled by the weather, the pragmatic benefits of expunging it are not so great. Despite having plans that cannot jointly be realized, Dan can perfectly well go about buying all the needed fertilizer, cultivating the soil, and doing whatever else he needs to do in pursuit of both plans (cf. Bratman 1987, 137). This is a humble example of rational decision making in the face of unresolved conflict. If Dan were to fail to be constant in his devotion to these two intentions, however, spending alternate weeks throwing his all into the wheat or into the vegetable patch, then, if the facts are as stated, he would end up with no crop at all. Yet some coherence among one's aims is crucial to coordinating one's actions with others and with themselves. Michael Bratman gives the following example: "If I plan both to leave my car at home for Susan and also to drive my car to Tanner Library, all the while knowing that I have only one car, I am unlikely to succeed in my effort at coordination" (Bratman 1987, 31). As a general matter, this point about the pragmatic benefits of coherence is undeniably significant.

If we turn from avoiding conflicts to positively building mutual support, the argument from coordination becomes weaker. Unifying one's system of ends does not always provide compelling benefits. Imagine the case of Ingrid, who is a passionate amateur astronomer, an avid gourmet cook, a devoted volunteer at a shelter for battered women, and a successful business executive. There may be nothing that binds together her varied vocational and professional interests: Indeed, their very diversity may appeal to her. (Of course there can be unity in diversity; but if it is claimed that the unity *is* diversity, then the notion of unity ceases to be useful.) These interests will compete for her time and energy. If astronomy keeps her up late at night, Ingrid will have to decide whether her effectiveness at work is being impaired by lack of sleep. If a crisis arises at the shelter when she's in the middle of folding together a mousse, she will have to decide what interest to sacrifice. Such scheduling conflicts are pervasive in our lives. Set the conflicts aside, though, and ask whether there is any further contribution to coordinating her actions that would come from unifying her various passions into some grand scheme. Will she be better able to plan her life for being able to say that her astronomy helps put momentary business setbacks in perspective, or that the praise she garners as a cook helps her appreciate the masochism of those battered women who cook for their cruel husbands? It is hard to see how. She may even find that up to a point the tension among them is a healthy and invigorating one. The conflicts between such disparate commitments might be energizing, each helping throw into relief what is valuable about the others – as, perhaps, in the life of Leon Botstein, who is both president of a prestigious liberal-arts college and a successful avant garde symphony conductor. Further, some people's lives are unified not by connections among their practical commitments at all, but by the unity of their personal styles. Many of history's and literature's most vivid characters – Cesare Borgia, Falstaff, Oscar Wilde – are defined more by the boldness or the humor or the piquancy of their styles than by the constancy or coherence of their commitments, and we may perhaps best understand them thus. In some cases, this style might define a person's character without even being endorsed by that person. Think of the self-deprecating and kvetchy characters often portrayed by Woody Allen. There is undeniably an intelligible unity to such characters that derives from their style, despite the fact that commitment to that style is not even a higher-order end they would avow. Unity of the person need not come from practical coherence.

Some degree of practical coherence is clearly generally important to both intrapersonal and interpersonal coordination. Resolving conflicts among one's intentions is typically of great help to one's planning, since it enables one to work with a relatively settled view of one's future. Since this benefit of firmness and decisiveness must be balanced against the benefits of flexibility and redundancy, it will be likely to support only a moderate degree of practical coherence. Although the argument from coordination is not likely to support a requirement for an extensive degree of systematization of one's practical commitments, it will provide much stronger reason to avoid conflicts involving conceptual or physical impossibilities. Let us also distinguish between systemic coherence and mere connectedness to a subsystem. The difference in question is between whether a person's practical commitments are *all* mutually supportive (or at least nonconflicting) in any of the ways distinguished in the last section, or only *some* (subsets) of them are. While it is true that the coordination of an individual's life or of society can survive a conflict, of any degree, between any two ends or commitments, neither can survive in a situation in which the various commitments of the individual or individuals are in no way mutually supportive or mutually connected.

Let me turn now to the second sort of argument for practical coherence, which turns on an end, happiness, that it might be presumed that all rational agents have. A traditional conception of happiness as a unified and necessary end of human action is thought by many to underwrite strong requirements of practical coherence. As we saw in Chapter VI, Sidgwick and Mill were drawn to happiness as potential systematizer of our aims, independently even of whether the agent's own or the general happiness is taken to be the object of morality. There our concern was with whether such a commensurating end was rationally required. Now we look more deeply at the content of happiness, addressing an argument that rests upon a particular, "totalistic" way of interpreting it.

Rüdiger Bittner has recently developed the connection between happiness and practical coherence along the following lines.[5] He suggests that we understand happiness as a higher-order end to be sought by every human being – higher-order, in that it represents the satisfaction of other aims. The view of happiness Bittner discusses departs from ordinary usage, which seems to allow that someone might be happy if just one or two of her dreams are realized. Instead, it makes reference to what one wants throughout an entire lifetime, defining a "maximum" condition that "leaves nothing to be desired" (Bittner 1989, 123). Accordingly, to adopt some plan without regard to how it fits in with the other things one wants is to flout the desire for happiness. To represent a good reason for action, Bittner argues, a plan must fit in sensibly with one's existing commitments, which at least implies that "nothing recommending a plan that possibly conflicts with the (previously?) projected happiness can be called a good reason" (121–2). In subsequent chapters, I will be arguing for a conception of rational deliberation of ends that resists the lure of maximization. Bittner's proposal raises an important general issue about practical coherence, however, which is best taken up in connection with the vague goal of the unity of the self.

The question is when the coherence allegedly involved in happiness is best understood ex ante and when it is best understood ex post.[6] Of course, since many of the relations of mutual support are symmetrical, it will not matter if one looks at them from the vantage point of one's present self or one's future self. Theoretical unification, however, and the explanatory coherence it entrains, may involve relations of inductive support

---

5 Bittner 1989, ch. VI. Bittner is expounding and elaborating a view of happiness he attributes to Kant.

6 This question also arises for attempts to analyze happiness in terms of the satisfaction of desires or preferences. Should the analysis, for purposes of deliberation at time t_0, of happiness at future time t_1 depend on the desires/preferences that the agent will have at t_1, or rather on those that the agent has at t_0 that refer to or are otherwise relevant to what will happen at t_1? See the debate between Hare 1989 and Brandt 1989.

or explanatory inference that are not temporally symmetrical. Once coherence has been crystallized in such a theoretical form, differences of perspective can arise. Bittner's conception of happiness provides a good example of how this can be. Happiness, as he conceives it, is simply a function of the satisfaction of other desires. At any one time, a person's desires "project" an image of happiness, involving their total satisfaction through a lifetime; however, desires change, implying a change in the content of the projected happiness. To demand that any intention or plan "fit in" with one's projected happiness is therefore ambiguous: Must it fit with what would produce happiness as that is currently projected by the agent? This ex ante version of the requirement would yield a very conservative stance toward changes in one's commitments. To expect only that an intention "fit in" with the happiness that would be projected once that intention were adopted, by contrast, is to demand only that this intention reflect a true want of the agent's. If it does, then the happiness that will be projected ex post will by definition reflect that intention, and so necessarily it will be "fit in" with this later conception of happiness.[7]

It might be thought that happiness, conceived along these lines as involving "total" satisfaction of one's wants, implies that one's wants must be jointly satisfiable – that is, that the achievement of one's aims is compossible. Bittner seems to think that it does, for he appears to infer from the fact that a proposed intention might *possibly* conflict with existing ones that it thereby conflicts with "the projected happiness" (121–2). But what if the existing intentions already conflict with each other? Is happiness then ill defined, according to Bittner? Whether this practical coherence is to be required as a normative matter is of course the issue that this chapter is addressing. The last section's discrimination of degrees of practical coherence helps clarify the issues involved in the totalistic conception of happiness. For instance, one natural interpretation of the degree of coherence that happiness, as total satisfaction of wants, requires is that the wants defining it be jointly satisfiable given the limitations of logic, conceptual impossibility, physical laws, and human nature. Their joint satisfaction should not be impossible, in these strong senses, else the happiness that is projected is projected vainly.

---

7 Bittner seems also to demand that intentions "fit in" with all previously existing longer-range plans, and to suggest that if they do not then they thereby conflict with projected happiness (121–2). This is either to adopt the excessively conservative ex ante interpretation of happiness or else to beg the question here at issue about the rational importance of coherence.

To go beyond this to require that it be impossible that the wants ever conflict – to require, in other words, that they be jointly satisfiable in all physically possible worlds – is to depart radically from the way most people conceive their happiness. Consider Clara, a youngish woman who has always longed – and still longs – for a career as a concert pianist, but in the meantime is miserable because forced to support herself in a grueling job as a waitress that leaves little time or energy for practicing. In her case, musical and material wants collide, yet the happiness she projects is a situation in which she is able to support herself (quite well, thank you) as a concert musician. Should she readjust her projection of happiness by dropping one of these wants just because they now conflict, and thereby declare herself happy after all? As Elster would remind us, that would be like the fox declaring that he hadn't wanted grapes, after all, once he learns that they are out of reach (Elster 1983). A formal way of setting out how much conflict to accept, consistently with one's aim for happiness, will not be forthcoming.

I conclude, then, that the demand for strong coherence is not built into our conception of happiness. Either strong coherence fails to follow from the ideal of happiness as a total satisfaction or else that ideal is not our conception of happiness: In proceeding by examples I have not tried to sort out which way the claim fails.

Nonetheless, although individuals who seek to be happy are not conceptually forced to bend their ideals and aspirations to accommodate the opportunities their life actually affords them, they are given some reason to adapt by this most general aim. The pursuit of happiness is greatly aided by *some* systematization of one's ends.

While neither of the two arguments I have canvassed shows practical coherence to be indispensable to some end or condition that is rationally necessary, each shows it important to a general end that is valuable. In the case of the pragmatic benefits of coordination, the value of practical coherence seems principally instrumental. Coherent planning is a means to avoiding mess-ups. In the case of the link to the ideals of happiness and the unity of the self, by contrast, the connection is a constitutive one. Some important degree of practical coherence among most of one's ends seems to be an essential element in each of these broader aims. These instrumental reasons for pursuing practical coherence are general and deep enough to lend intelligibility to coherence-enhancing moves in deliberation. In this prima facie way, practical coherence is typically rational to pursue. It cannot be demonstrated that any particular level of practical coherence is a means necessary no matter what end one pursues, but only that considerable practical coherence is an important means to most humans' living successfully and well.

These instrumental arguments for the rationality of pursuing practical coherence are best viewed as supplementing the argument to be developed in §26, to the effect that practical coherence is the central element of practical justification, valuable as a constitutive means of the reflective ordering of pursuit. While that argument will in some ways go deeper than those surveyed here, my argument for a coherence approach follows its own advice in seeking mutual support from whatever quarter it may be found. The more straightforward instrumental arguments provide reasons for respecting the ideal of practical coherence even to some of those who are initially skeptical of its regulative value.

VIII

Reflective sovereignty

Can a coherence approach meet Sidgwick's challenge? Can it truly ground an alternative way of systematizing practical commitments? In particular, can it do so without covertly constructing a commensurating standard? The task of the present chapter is to show in general how it can. More extended examples of coherentist system building will be given in Chapter X.

§23. DEWEY'S ANTITELEOLOGICAL HOLISM

Showing how a coherentist approach can systematize without commensurating will require spelling out more fully what that approach is. To begin with, this will mean learning from two views that depart in opposite ways from the sort of coherence standard I will be defending. The first, which I will discuss in detail in this section, exaggerates the implications of revisability. It is true that the coherence approach allows that any commitment is open to revision. Emphasizing this at the cost of overlooking the possibilities for system that remain, this first view sees little point in trying to build any theory, however provisionally stated. I will take Dewey's account of deliberation as exemplifying this antisystematizing position. The second, to be discussed in the following section, recaptures a place for theory at the cost of unduly restricting the scope for revisability. There, my example will be a recent model of case-based deliberation. Obviously, my own aim is to defend a truly holistic account, one that maintains strong system despite allowing an unrestricted scope for revising commitments. Section 25 will show how the notion of specifying ends helps reconcile these desiderata. Section 26 will then spell out how the coherence ideal for deliberation integrates them without becoming a commensurating standard. To reinforce this conclusion, §27 will explain how the reflective search for coherence lies embedded in the psychology of the deliberator.

159

This last point strongly echoes Dewey. In some respects, the very topic of deliberation of ends is a Deweyan one. Certainly Dewey insisted that the only ends that would be recognized by a sound approach to ethics and to practice are what he called "ends-in-view." These objectives arise only in, and are defined in the first instance for, some particular deliberative problem (Dewey 1988b: "Theory of Valuation" [hereafter *TOV*], 223–4). "In being ends of *deliberation*," Dewey writes, ends-in-view "are redirecting pivots *in* action" (1967: *Human Nature and Conduct* [hereafter *HNC*], 155).

Deliberation typically arises, in Dewey's view, when habitual or ongoing activity meets some obstacle (*HNC*, 127: cf. Velleman 1989, 15). The situation calling for deliberation is variously described by Dewey as being one of "disintegration" (*HNC*, 133), as one in which there is "some lack [which] prevents the immediate execution of an active tendency" (*TOV*, 205) or an "actual or threatened shock and disturbance" (*TOV*, 239). In addition to picturing a single tendency that gets blocked, Dewey also recognizes that deliberation will arise when impulses conflict: "[Deliberative] choice is not the emergence of preference out of indifference. It is the emergence of a unified preference out of competing preferences" (*HNC*, 134). Sometimes activity comes to a halt for the simple failure of a means, as when a flat tire interrupts my usual commute or when my chosen career path seems to lose the "meaning" it had (cf. Putnam and Putnam 1990). At other times, one must pause because alternatives to the habitual become more attractive, as when leaving at my usual commuting hour will cause me to miss my child's school play. It would be unfair to place too much weight upon Dewey's precise formulations, here. His wider point seems simply to be that deliberation occurs only when the habitual control of action breaks down, whether for want of a means, or because of a conflict, or because no habit obviously covers the situation at hand.

Unless we recognize that Dewey is not to be taken too literally or narrowly in his characterization of the occasions of deliberation, we may be tempted to read him as putting forward the "integration" of action or the restoration of activity as the single higher-order end to which deliberation is answerable.[1] Since Dewey's "instrumentalism," so crudely read,

---

1 Such was Bertrand Russell's tendency in his criticism of Dewey's wider pragmatism, which similarly invokes the contrast between "problematic situations" and "successful activity." Supposing that Dewey meant in these formulations to give criteria for knowledge, Russell found the view seriously deficient. Whatever belief leads me to fixing my tire is not thereby true; and the general notion of "successful action" is a matter needing

is easily and justly made the subject of ridicule, it is more charitable and perhaps also more correct to read him, as Richard Rorty has, as abstaining from putting forward generally specifiable criteria – of knowledge or of deliberation – at all (R. Rorty 1982). "The standard of valuation is formed in the process of practical judgment or valuation" (Dewey 1979 [1915], 39). This standard hence must be formulated anew for each situation of decision (Parodi 1989, 236). Thus, when Dewey writes that "an end is a device of intelligence in guiding action, instrumental to freeing and harmonizing troubled and divided tendencies" (*HNC*, 159), we must take this as a psychological remark about the function of ends and not as a normative one setting up a higher-order end of harmonizing.

That Dewey would refrain from putting forward any simple criterion for deliberation is seen in his firm rejection of any commensurating good. For instance, although Dewey found the utilitarians' emphasis on consequences salutary, he is emphatic in rejecting their unitary way of evaluating consequences. By introducing pressure toward ignoring qualitatively distinct reasons that may lurk, Dewey argued, commensurating approaches get things backward:

> Deliberation is not an attempt to do away with this opposition of quality by reducing it to one of amount. It is an attempt to *uncover* the conflict in its full scope and bearing. What we want to find out is what difference each impulse and habit imports, to reveal qualitative incompatibilities by detecting the different courses to which they commit us, the different dispositions they form and foster, the different situations into which they plunge us.
>
> In short, the thing actually at stake in any serious deliberation is not a difference of quantity, but what kind of person one is to become, what sort of self is in the making, what kind of a world is making (*HNC*, 150).

Dewey recognizes that where past deliberation has left one with an end-in-view that remains unquestioned for the moment, it may be appropriate to calculate means to that end in a merely quantitative way. But "to reduce all cases of judgment of action to this simplified and comparatively unimportant case of calculation of quantities, is to miss the whole point of deliberation" (*HNC*, 151). Dewey alludes to the argument that commensurability is a prerequisite of rational choice and answers it by repeating his repudiation of fixed criteria: "We find in this conception of a fixed antecedent standard another manifestation of the desire to escape the strain of the actual moral situation, its genuine uncertainty of possi-

ethical specification that may be true or false, rather than stating a standard that may be assumed in advance of all inquiry (Russell 1989).

bilities and consequences" (*HNC*, 166). Postulation of a commensurans is yet another symptom of the pervasive quest for certainty, which must be resisted.

Consonant with the ideas that deliberation arises from some particular problematic situation and that ends-in-view have no appropriate fixity is Dewey's suggestion that the interpretation and criticism of an end-in-view always takes account of the means available for achieving it. Since an end-in-view has an "organic" connection with the available ways of achieving it, it must not be understood "apart from the means by which it is to be attained [or] apart from its own further function as means" (*TOV*, 227; the latter restriction we have met above in the idea that ends are instrumental to resolving problematic situations). This famous "continuum of ends–means" allows for revisionary pressure on ends-in-view. If roasting a piece of pork requires burning down a house (to repeat an example Dewey uses), then the means with which that end-in-view is connected in the situation will provoke us to envision another menu.

Those aspects of Dewey's view laid out so far are quite consonant with my own. Some, like the notion that deliberation is in part an exercise in self-construction, is one that I have given prominence from the beginning. Further, in Dewey's talk of remaking oneself and the world one can see the very broad scope that he accords to deliberation. Above all, it extends to criticizing ends-in-view, whose fixity is never more than provisional:

Deliberation is irrational in the degree in which an end is so fixed, a passion or interest so absorbing, that the foresight of consequences is warped to include only what furthers execution of its predetermined bias. Deliberation is rational in the degree in which forethought flexibly remakes old aims and habits, institutes perception and love of new ends and acts (*HNC*, 138).

The broad scope for revision that this implies is an idea that I will continue to develop in the remainder of this chapter.

In addition to noting that ends-in-view are defined by their role in deliberation, and thus by their "organic" connections with the possibilities, however, Dewey also expressed considerable hostility to the idea of ultimate ends in general. Viewing most past moral philosophy as engaged in a futile and misguided quest for a summum bonum, Dewey rejected any attempt at giving a discursive and general account of the good: hence his rejection of criteria of deliberation. While I am no friend of "criteria" in a narrow sense, I want to suggest that this negative and antitheoretical side of Dewey is one that we should reject. We will see that Dewey's strictures against ultimate ends are exaggerated and set up a straw opponent.

The idea that there is a unique, fixed ultimate end is one that Dewey views as one that "was foisted by Aristotle upon western culture and endured for two thousand years" (*HNC*, 154–5). He sets himself to destroy it. This traditional notion of an ultimate end Dewey sees as combining four flaws: fixity, "finality," single-mindedness, and noninstrumentality. (1) *Fixity.* That ends should not be viewed as fixed we have already seen. Dewey takes the traditional view as holding that ends are "a priori absolute" (*TOV*, 241). (2) *"Finality."* In the traditional notion of "final" ends Dewey claims to hear the stipulation that they are supposed to be "things lying beyond activity at which the latter is directed." He protests that "nothing happens which is *final* in the sense that it is not part of an ongoing stream of events" (*TOV*, 229). (3) *Single-mindedness.* The traditional view is further faulted for its insistence on a unique ultimate end. According to Dewey, however, "there is no such thing as the single all-important end" (*HNC*, 158). Furthermore, the habit of thinking in terms of a unique ultimate end contributes to the sort of "fanaticism, inconsiderateness, arrogance and hypocrisy" that comes from pursuing one ideal no matter what the cost (*HNC*, 157). (4) *Noninstrumentality.* Single-minded fanaticism also arises, Dewey believes, from the belief in the notion of an end-in-itself: "This arbitrary selection of some one part of the attained consequences as *the* end and hence as the warrant of means used . . . is the fruit of holding that *it*, as *the* end, is an end-in-itself, and hence possessed of 'value' irrespective of all its existential relations." In any case, he takes "end-in-itself" to be "a self-contradictory term." That is because, on his view, it is absurd to set up "any 'end' " as standing apart from the continuum of ends–means (*TOV*, 227–8).

While we have much to learn from this critical side of Dewey on deliberation, the principal point to note in correction of it is that deliberation organized around an ultimate end need not involve any of these four flaws. To repeat, in case some of my readers share Dewey's prejudices about ultimate ends, *none* of these faults need be exemplified by a conception of the ultimate end. Section 7's gloss of "final end," for instance, makes it plain that final ends need not be understood as terminating action. On the interpretation there put forward, an end is a "limit" in a regulative and not a temporal sense (cf. Gewirth 1991, 69). Indeed, since Aristotle emphasizes that the highest good must be some form of activity (arguably including practical and even political activity), Dewey has done him an injustice in attributing to him a view of the ultimate end as something divorced from action. In the next chapter, we will see that recognizing even an ultimate end does not imply accepting a single-minded theory

163

allowing for only one kind of value, for it is compatible with allowing multiple, distinct final ends.

With regard to the sin of recognizing ends final in my sense, namely ends choiceworthy for their own sakes, I must confront Dewey more squarely. Contrary to his apparent supposition, a final end can be regarded as choiceworthy in itself while at the same time being employed as a means to further deliberation and being critically evaluated in light of the costs of achieving it. In terms of §7's analysis, the first of these possibilities is built into the notion of a final end, which is defined as appropriately regulating those activities pursued for its sake. The second possibility is also allowed for by the analysis, which holds that a final end would be sought even if no other goods result, not that it would be sought at all costs, no matter what bads result.

The final supposed flaw is fixity. If the ultimate end is fixed a priori, independently of circumstances, then it is bound to remain remote and abstract, having little chance to meet practice except via some form of Peripatetic syllogism (§5). But why must the ultimate end be seen as "fixed" in a sense that excludes further determination by reference to concrete situations? Here one feels that Dewey has confused Aristotle with Kant. Aristotle, in fact, repeatedly stresses that he has been able to give only an "outline sketch" of the good, which will require further determination later (most importantly in *N.E.* I.7). Furthermore, since Aristotle, unlike Kant, is quite willing to accept contingent empirical facts as a basis for filling in the content of the good, this further determination is responsive to particular circumstances of action (§27). If it is progressively specified in light of the agent's circumstances, then the ultimate end will clearly cease to be remote and abstract. The objects of deliberation, like the objects of all inquiry, are not propositions, but things and events (Dewey 1988a [1939], 57). But in his overwhelming emphasis on action and consequence, Dewey slights the activity of developing a conception of the good. The place he allows for principles is merely a heuristic one, parallel to Mill's "secondary principles" (cf. *HNC*, ch. 7). Despite all his talk about the agent deciding through deliberation "who to become," Dewey has a surprisingly shallow notion of who the agent is. The agent is not identified in terms of an articulated structure of ends or principles, but instead, in a more empiricist vein, with a set of tendencies, impulses, and habits. These are subject to rational criticism, of course; but once reformed, what matters is their causal influence and not their content. Even if most of our actions were habitual and unreflective, this view would still underplay the role of norms in an agent's deliberation about "who to become."

What we saw in Chapter VII, in fact, was that the very idea of practical coherence or harmony – what Dewey identifies as, as it were, the goal of deliberation – requires a sophisticated working out in terms of a range of different relations among norms. Just as an end (whether or not final) can be instrumental to effective planning, so too an articulated overall conception of the good, in which one's various ends are related, can be crucial in achieving a harmony among one's desires and aims. For this reason, if for no other, Dewey underplays the importance of an individual's practical theory. If Dewey is indeed uninterested in developing standards to guide deliberation, this silence in his view may not be a flaw from his perspective. Since *we* are interested in setting out how one might deliberate rationally about ends, however, we need a better understanding of how to develop and revise a noncommensurating practical theory. For one view of how to do this, we turn to a sophisticated recent version of case-based weighting.

§24. CASE-BASED WEIGHTING

Dewey was too hasty in rejecting the possibility of a systematizing practical theory, wrongly thinking that it would have to be built pyramidally from self-evident or a priori axioms – from fixed "ultimate ends." What, though, will a holist practical theory look like? To begin with, since it does not build from a single norm or end of greatest generality, it will importantly build from numerous more specific norms and ends. How, though, will it cope with the multiple ways in which these specific commitments clash in practice? Perhaps the readiest answer is that it will find ways of differentially weighting these commitments so as to generate an all-things-considered decision. Although this weighting may be regarded as preserving coherence, I will now argue that it fails fully to learn the lessons of Dewey's emphasis on revisability, stopping short of recognizing how any norm can be revised on the basis of other norms. The weighting idea wrongly suggests that the specific value categories themselves remain fixed, leaving only the weighting to shift. Since the specific value categories may be understood as the ends, the weighting approach appears not to leave any room for deliberation of ends.

There are many different ways in which this weighting idea might play out. In one version, the formal apparatus of preference-based decision theory is adapted to cope with the existence of more than one index (e.g., Keeney and Raiffa 1976). Such an approach tends to look like maximization manqué. A more informal weighting approach would instead emphasize the case-based nature of deliberation. If our deliberation importantly proceeds case by case, with the various specific considerations that count emerging out of the cases, then a multiattribute analysis will seem like a genuine theoretical achievement. Individual nonmoral deliberation does often proceed from cases. In the past, I may have been cheated by a car mechanic who charged me for unnecessary work, and I may have decided on the basis of that case that I would always insist on a second opinion before ordering repairs. Now comes a case, however, in which the mechanic is my brother-in-law. Is the governing case the earlier car mechanic case (in which the mechanic was a stranger), or rather all the other cases in which I have been willing to place trust in family members? Jonsen and Toulmin (1988), in arguing that moral reasoning must work from cases in such a way, have developed a model of case-based "casuistry" that emphasizes the search for cases analogous to the one at hand. Where the decision is difficult because equally strong analogies point to opposite conclusions, they lean heavily on the intuitive judgment of the person of practical wisdom.[2]

The version of a weighting approach on which I want to focus here, by contrast, combines the discursive explicitness of multiattribute decision theory with the emphasis on cases that characterizes the new casuistry. I have in mind the sophisticated account of case-based deliberation in ch. 11 of Hurley 1989.[3] Her discussion has two additional virtues that draw me to it. First, it provides a deep philosophical rationale for the claim that working with a list of "specific" values or ends, far from being merely a failure of systematizing nerve, is how in principle one ought to proceed. Second, it nicely complements Dewey's version of holism by emphasizing the role for theorizing in deliberation.

Like Dewey, Hurley regards deliberation as an arena for self-construction (which may involve self-discovery as well as self-invention). In deliberation, she writes, agents "are seeking their very identities as

2 One can understand the complaint (in Donagan 1977, 23) that to call this intuitive assessment "weighing" or "balancing" is "fraudulent"; but this metaphorical use of these terms is well entrenched in Western culture – embodied, as it is, in the figure of blind Justice – and is a convenient one for the comparative intuitive assessment of competing considerations.

3 Subsequent references to *Natural Reasons* within this section will give the page number only.

persons" (262). But Hurley's description of this self-construction differs markedly from Dewey's. Working in terms of a contrast between deliberate and habitual action, Dewey sees deliberation's fashioning of the self in terms of its effect upon the constellation of impulses that will activate the individual. What matters is what the person will do. Hurley, by contrast, proffers an "account of deliberation conceived as a kind of self-interpretation" (36). This emphasis upon the Socratic aspect of deliberation, upon the way in which the agent understands her commitments and their interrelation, is a salutary corrective to the thinly causal or behaviorist cast that Dewey tends to give to the deliberative search for harmony.

Hurley is quite explicit that deliberative self-interpretation is a matter of building a theory of one's own commitments. She introduces her chapter on deliberation by saying that she will "examine in detail examples of the kind of theoretical activity, or deliberation, that aims at coherence" (203). On her view, "when we say that a particular alternative would be right, it is part of what we mean that there is some theory which is the best theory about the specific values that apply to the alternatives at hand and that this theory favours a particular alternative" (12). In other words, the notion of rightness, or of what ought to be done, all things considered, builds in a reference to the best theory about our specific values, whatever that theory might be (cf. 194).

Pursuing the notion of practical theory in a way antithetical to Dewey's insistence that only the single problematic case at hand matters, Hurley's model of deliberation gives central importance to comparison cases. Her model has the following structure: First, we describe the problem at hand and the alternatives available. Second, we analyze the alternatives to uncover the specific values at stake. Third, we collect comparison cases in which these same specific values are involved and on which we hold settled judgments. Fourth, we construct a function that tells us how much weight to give each of the specific values in various circumstances; this weighting function accounts for the information represented by the settled comparison cases. If one specific value wins out over another in a case analogous to the one at hand, add weight to the former value, unless there are important differences of circumstance that allow us to distinguish the cases. By a combination of weights and circumstantial distinctions, we should be able to construct a function that matches our considered judgments in the settled cases and determines what to do in the case at hand. (Hurley does not assume either that the best such theory is available to us or that such a function necessarily exists.) If no such weighting emerges clearly we may need to consider a wider range of comparison cases (211–17). Hurley's model is more sophisticated and articulate than this brief summary can convey, and does an admirable job of suggesting how an appeal to cases works in practical reasoning.

A weighting model such as Hurley's offers a mode of theorizing that partially respects the force of Dewey's attack on deductive hierarchy. It suggests how deliberative theory can proceed without succumbing to the chimera of a single, fixed, ultimate end which so attracted Sidgwick and so infuriated Dewey. Yet there remains an important layer that – on the story told so far – remains beyond deliberative revision, namely the list of specific values being weighted.

Insofar as the list of specific values is held fixed across different contexts of deliberation, as a case-based weighting model of seems to require, it suffers from a kind of abstraction to which Dewey rightly objected. By holding the delineation of the specific value categories apart from deliberation, a case-based weighting account departs radically from the Deweyan "continuum of ends–means." Furthermore, nothing in such an account tells us how we might compare the recommendations of two coherence functions, each working from a different set of specific values. On a case-based weighting account, therefore, ends are not truly subject to deliberation; or if they are, we are not told how their revision might be rational. If deliberation stopped there, the self-construction it involves would be shallow for opposite reasons than in Dewey. In Dewey's picture, self-construction is shallow because there is insufficient structure to the self's commitments; on the cased-based weighting model, self-construction is shallow because the list of specific values is not directly subject to deliberation.[4] For this reason, although elements of Hurley's rhetoric point to a more thorough holism, her account of deliberation is insufficiently holistic. Further, there is no way, within this model, to assess the relative coherence of two theories that involve different lists of specific

4 In Hurley's case, it should be noted that her explicit model of case-based weighting does not exhaust the possibilities she sees for practical reasoning. In general, she rejects any account of rationality that erects certain principles to the status of fixed sufficient conditions, endorsing Putnam's refutation of conventionalism (189–90). She allows that reflection may lead one to revise the list of specific values (218), but insists that while they "have discrete and elastic identities, they are not indefinitely malleable" (244). There is a presumption against doing so by drawing arbitrary lines, but it is "rebuttable." We can draw them to avoid attributing too many inconsistencies or anomalies in our pattern of judgments (247). Yet insofar as Hurley has given us a hint of what a "theory of the cases" would look like, it is tied to the weighting model.

values. Hurley's emphasis on the importance of theory in deliberation is helpful; but to arrive at a workable account of deliberation of ends we need to wed this emphasis on theorizing with Dewey's emphasis on revision. In doing so, a natural question will be: What else can one do besides weighting the various specific values that compete in a given situation? As I will now suggest, one can specify the values in question to build a case-based theory.

§25. SPECIFICATION AND THEORETICAL CONTINUITY

Is there a way to allow that ends are revisable without going to Dewey's extreme of rejecting a role for discursive systematization, and hence for ultimate ends, altogether? Is there a way for ends to function as guiding principles except via a deductivist schema? If we accept the need for discursive systematization but reject the necessity of a central, commensurating ultimate end, what alternative is there to an approach such as the case-based weighting of specific values? If we seek discursively to reconcile and systematize the conflicting claims of our many ends, how can we do this except by varying the weighting structure whereby we assess their joint impact on what we ought to do, all things considered? To construct a workable alternative to antidiscursive pragmatism, on the one hand, and case-based weighting of specific values, on the other, we need to define a discursive relation more flexible than deductive implication, as exemplified by the Peripatetic syllogism. This relation must allow for systematic practical theory to develop without arrogating to itself the role of generating all decisions by subsumption. Further, it should allow us to display how a single theory gets progressively refined through revision. There are two challenges, here: to show how ends can be brought to bear in practice discursively but not deductively, and to show how revision of ends is compatible with continuity in practical commitment.

When two norms conflict, straightforward deductive application of the norms is blocked by the impossibility of acting on both of their dictates.[5] Revision of one or both of the norms may then seem called for; but the question arises whether in being "revised" they are really being overthrown or put to one side, rather than guiding action in any way. How can they guide action, though, if they cannot be applied deductively?

5 The remainder of this section adapts a portion of Richardson 1990c.

According to Dewey, deliberation in the face of conflicts will be reasonable if[6] it can devise a "*way* to act," or light upon a conception of the object of action, "in which all [competing tendencies] are fulfilled, not indeed in their original form, but in a 'sublimated fashion,' that is, in a way which modifies the original direction of each by reducing it to a component along with others in an action of transformed quality" (*HNC*, 135). Since Dewey's focus on actions rather than norms reflects his excessive hostility to deliberative theory, and since an explanation of the way in which the action reflects the "original" norms would be facilitated if the principle of the action were explicitly stated rather than simply left to the observer to infer from the action's features, we might think the following reformulation of Dewey's idea by James Wallace to be an advance: "[When moral considerations conflict,] the aim [of deliberation] must be to modify one or more considerations so that it applies, so that its original point is to some degree preserved, and so that one can live with the way [of proceeding] so modified" (Wallace 1988, 86). The key unanswered question, however, for both Dewey's and Wallace's versions of this pragmatist account is, what licenses us to call a modification or sublimation of an original norm still in some significant sense the *same* norm that we started out with? Why is it not a self-contradiction to speak of modifying a consideration so that *it* applies? Is not what "applies," in the end, just a different norm or consideration? Again, we need an account of the sort of nondeductive discursive relation that makes sense of the continuity persisting through revisions. Without it, it would seem that we might just as well rest content with Dewey's antitheoretical pragmatism.

While there are many nondeductive relations that might serve here, one that fits the bill perfectly is that of specification, defined in §10. This is the one for us to focus on, given the importance it has for deliberation about ends (§13). The idea of specification complements the general pragmatic approach by laying down conditions on the relation between the initial norm or norms and their modifications that explain how the original norms are being respected (in a "sublimated fashion"). By integrating a role for revisions in the basic list of ends, pragmatism as filled out by specification yields a more truly holistic and untrammeled coherentism than what we saw in the case-based weighting model. Typically, at least, the revisions sanctioned by the holistic standard of rationality (to be set out in the next section) will trace a path of progressive specification that

6 Because it can be reasonable to recognize conflicts as unresolvable, we should not say "if and only if" here.

responds to the contexts of deliberation. In this way, the specification relation will enable us to explain how deliberation of ends can be discursive and yet avoid fixed abstractions of the sort Dewey vilified. As I argued in §11, specification marks out a paradigm of the transmission of practical commitment. In addition, by giving us a way to articulate how a specific norm is meaningfully related back to a more abstract one, the notion of specification helps secure a role for a stable practical theory that seems as elusive on the general conception of a change in view as it is unattainable conceived as a deductive hierarchy. System is more attainable by specification because the norms need not be taken as fixed or as formally absolute, and so will conflict less readily and adjust more easily than the sort of norms postulated by a pure model of application. Nonetheless, the connection back to an initial norm afforded by the notion of an instance of a general norm's absolute counterpart enables one to set out clearly what has remained the same in the course of specification. By making clear what remains constant despite modifications, the specification relation allows one to distinguish the progressive refinement of a theory that remains the same in essentials from the mere shifting from one holistic equilibrium to another.

The advantages of regarding ends as progressively specifiable over a case-based weighting model that treats them as fixed and qualifies them only by numerical weights may be brought out by means of an extended example. Let us consider a choice that is the personal counterpart of what is now a major policy question. It is a choice faced by a committed environmentalist – one convinced that he should, within reason, live his life so as to minimize his adverse impact on the ecosystem. And now the momentous question is: Should he use disposable diapers for his baby or cloth ones? He is enough of an environmentalist that we may ignore questions of convenience and the baby's well-being (allergies, dryness, and so on), and focus solely on the relevant environmental values.[7]

Here is one approach our environmentalist might take: He might make a list of all of the kinds of environmental damage relevant to this choice. Using paper-and-plastic disposables causes tree loss, topsoil erosion and

---

7 For simplicity of presentation, I ignore some options, such as washing cloth diapers – or emptying disposables – at home. Since the following paragraphs were first written, a number of prominent environmental organizations have declared that, even taking account of the environmental effects of cleaning and transporting cloth diapers, disposables are environmentally worse. Although I have not seen their detailed analyses, we may suppose that they must have followed something like the course of reasoning set out in the text in order to have come to their unequivocal recommendation.

disturbance of animals at the logging site, air pollution from logging vehicles, water pollution from the pulp plant, oil consumption and air pollution during plastics manufacture, energy consumption in disposable diaper production, and strain on available landfill space and biological hazards in disposing of the soiled diapers. In using cloth diapers there are pesticides used in growing cotton, air pollution from the farming vehicles, energy consumption in manufacturing cotton diapers, energy consumption in transporting and washing cotton diapers, incremental strain on the sewage system of emptying the cloth diapers into the public sewers, and water pollution from the detergent and bleach used in cleaning the cloth diapers. Being compulsive enough to develop such a list, our deliberator is certainly not going to rest content with an intuitive balancing of this complex set of pros and cons. In order to be more systematic, he instead may try to develop an "environmental impact index" that (1) develops a measure of each of these different types of effect and (2) assigns that measure a weight. But how is such a weighting, more simple-minded than the sort discussed in the last section, to be rationally defended? The task seems hopeless, and its value merely heuristic. If this factoring into pros and cons is just a more complicated version of intuitive balancing, it might be easier just to go by his gut reaction to the overall choice.

This abortive effort at weighting these different types of environmental harm, however, will not be in vain if it leads our deliberator to reflect on the way he would specify his guiding norm. We started by supposing that his single overriding relevant principle was to protect and preserve the environment: But what shall he mean by this? Preserve it in what state, from what dangers? Reflection on the various pros and cons can be of heuristic value in helping him further specify his central principle. Thus, while many of the harms on either side seem to cancel out, in a rough way, there remains a salient difference between the two options – one that might be captured by the notions of material flow versus energy expenditure. Disposable diapers come from the forests and the oil reserves and end up in landfills. Cloth diapers stick around, but require a lot of pollution-generating energy consumption to do so. This overall contrast suggests that it will be important, for the purposes of making this choice, whether our environmentalist specifies his leading norm in one of two broadly familiar ways. First, there is the more old-fashioned conception of the conservationist: the supporter of wilderness areas, hiker (or perhaps NRA member), and reader of John Muir, whose notion of preserving the environment centers on the idea of keeping those parts of nature not yet touched by humankind from becoming disrupted. Second, there is the newer, more urban-oriented and liberal environmentalist who focuses on those parts of the earth where man's influence is already noticeable, is concerned largely with human health, and seeks to minimize the pollution of populated areas. The first specification would lend differential support to the use of cloth diapers, the second to the use of disposables (at least if the biohazard can be contained). How will our deliberator decide which specification of his guiding norm to adopt (supposing he is initially unsure)? Here is where his effort at ranking the particular harms involved, though incomplete and insufficient to yield a single-valued index, will nonetheless help, for it is likely that his pattern of ranking reflects one of these specifications more than the other. This differential could draw his attention to the way he would specify his guiding norm. Once he focuses on this question, it is likely that this more finely specified version of his environmental end will fit with and will help make sense of a broad range of his policy positions. It is here that a case-based way of setting out this sort of fit between a practical theory and a set of case judgments is very helpful. This fit would justify or explain his adopting that specification. If he can specify his guiding norm more finely in one of these two ways, then which diaper option he should choose will become relatively obvious.

In narrating this course of deliberation, I have cast the appeal to settled views in analogous cases as a way of confirming the agent's specification of his environmental end. That this specification guides his practical theorizing, however, is a crucial addition to the case-based weighting method. Rather than taking the dimensions of value as fixed, this example proceeded by way of revising the principal end with which it began. Without this attempt to refine his specification of his environmental end, this deliberator's analysis of his case judgments would be mired in the myriad details of sulfur dioxide dispersal rates, landfill shortages, and so on. It is such guidance that the idea of specification insists upon in its combination of extensional narrowing and intensionally relevant qualification. Progressive specification must work substantively from an initial norm by adding predicates that are not irrelevant to it. By allowing for the construction only of a mathematical function to weight a set of factors, the case-based weighting model of deliberation leaves out the aspect of theory that builds intelligibility and explains the pattern of regulation that the case judgments reflect. If self-interpretation is really the goal, simply developing a weighting function is a peculiarly obtuse way to pursue it. Only if this weighting is subordinated to a broader effort to specify and revise one's ends will the patterns of weights that emerge from examining cases contribute significantly to self-understanding. By bringing out the broader meaning of patterns of case judgments and incorporating it into refined conceptions of the ends, specification builds on and enhances the case-based approach. If the ends are seen as given in a fixed list in advance, this possibility for forging perspicuous practical theory is foreclosed.

Once the central role for specifying ends is recognized, it becomes clear that the delineation of more specific goods or values is also subject to revision that responds to this specification. For instance, the biohazard represented by disposable diapers residing in landfills might in turn be specified in different ways, depending on how the guiding environmental end is specified (in the actual path of deliberation, of course, revision and insight might move in the opposite direction). "Biohazard" might be understood in a way that focused on the potential effects on human health, concentrating especially on transmissible disease. Alternatively, it might be understood in terms of the interference by diaper-borne bacteria (themselves a form of life) with the ecosystem surrounding the landfill. As this example indicates, the set of specific goods cannot usefully be taken as fixed, for they need to be refined, along with more general ends, in the course of deliberation. Furthermore, it is seriously to be doubted that there is any such thing as a final factoring of specific goods or values (down to the level, say, of the effects of *E. coli* on snail darters living within a mile of landfills). Dewey was right that the contexts of deliberation face us with ever-new constellations of value and disvalue, opportunity and cost. On this account, he even recognized an important role for heuristic principles (*HNC*, ch. 7). Where he erred was in thinking that ends could not play this guiding role. The notion of specifying ends explains how they can.

§26. MUTUAL SUPPORT AS THE BASIS OF RATIONALITY IN SPECIFYING ENDS

When the parent of the last section resolves his diapering problem by specifying his governing environmental aim more finely, he has deliberated in a way that meets minimal conditions of rationality. The specification relation helps make explicit the guiding discursive link between his general underlying commitment and his decision. The specification, as we imagined it, maintained and indeed enhanced the relations of mutual support between his stance on this issue and a wide range of related environmental commitments. Further, in specifying his general environmental end in part by reference to which interpretation would make the most sense of his detailed positions on timberlands, biohazards, and so on, his deliberation has respected the subordinate reasons to which he is committed. His thinking, in other words, satisfies Sidgwick's first three postulates of practical rationality: discursiveness, respect for subordinate reasons, and practical consistency. Accordingly, this example of deliberative specification of an end, which Chapter IV argued could be a case of truly practical thinking, seems also to be a case of reasoning.

While the notion of specifying ends does help show how practical system can be built nonhierarchically, this conclusion may not much impress those who saw a commensurating form of system as a prerequisite of rational deliberation. "It is one thing to systematize one's practical norms," they will say, "and another to do so rationally!" This objector does not deny the sorts of claims I have made on behalf of my proposal so far. For the sake of argument, at least, he is willing to grant that one might well specify an end or norm in a discursively explicable way. What he denies is that this is enough to establish that the specification has been rationally generated. The problem is that there are all too many possible paths of specification that might be taken. For instance, our parent could instead have specified his environmental end with emphasis on avoiding waste, perhaps by focusing on the mutual support between this interpretation and his general aversion to waste in nonenvironmental contexts. What justifies specifying the environmental end in one way rather than another? (I should note that I am using "justification" in a fairly broad sense, here. I do not mean to imply that there is necessarily any call upon the agent to justify his or her specification *to* anyone, either on account of the good or the right or on account of truth. "To justify," in this context, will be roughly the same as "to give good reasons for.") What kinds of reason can be given for specifying an end one way rather than another? The objector will urge that there are only two ways in which the choice between alternative paths can be made: either by looking to see which one maximizes coherence or else intuitively. Either way, he concludes, my attempt to make out a method of deliberating rationally without appeal to commensurability fails: If the choice between paths is made by maximizing coherence, then rationality is achieved by treating coherence as the commensurating end. If the choice is made by a situation-specific intuition, then it is not made rationally. Is there a rational basis for determining which specification should be adopted?

If my view were a straightforward version of a coherence theory of justification, it would be simpler just to say so; however, I allow for the possibility that some practical judgment or judgments could turn out to be self-evident, and hence not depend upon connections of mutual support for their justification (on parallel issues in epistemology, cf. Davis and Bender 1989). In allowing for this possibility, I depart from most recent forms of coherence theory in epistemology. Perhaps the end of self-preservation is self-evidently choiceworthy, or the end of basking in the sun. For the purposes of the present study, I am content to remain agnostic on this question, in part because the practical importance of this concession is quite limited. While there may be ends of self-evident appeal, the status of any given end as self-evident is subject to rebuttal by the contingent conflicts that will arise between it and other ends (cf. §20). To admit that there can be ends whose justification does not depend upon mutual support is not yet to admit that there are ends whose justification is secure in the absence of mutual support even when they conflict with other ends. The latter I would deny: The absence of practical conflict must be regarded as a necessary background condition for claims to self-evidence. Here we generalize an idea of Sidgwick's: It is not simply that the self-evident ends must be mutually consistent in their practical implications, but also that their claim to self-evident justification must be seen to depend on the absence of practical conflict with other ends, including some not self-evident ones, to which the agent is committed. For example, if the self-evident end of self-preservation (if such it be) conflicts with the demands of the more contestable end of acting courageously on the battlefield, the justification of the former is thrown open to question, however secure it may have seemed before conflict arose. Since practical conflicts are pervasive, and since mutual support is the inverse of the multiple tiers of practical conflict, practical justification will, indeed, typically depend upon mutual support, whether or not there are severally self-evident ends.

Mutual support, holistically addressed, among the commitments that stand firm on reflection, is the main positive basis of practical justification. As we saw in the last chapter, since mutual support is not simply a matter of the absence of practical conflicts, it crucially depends upon building argumentative and explanatory connections among the various relevant norms and beliefs. As I argued in the last section, a particularly important form of supporting connection is traced out by the relation of specification. This leading idea of mutual support may now be filled out by linking it to the theme of Socratic reflection first introduced in §4 and fleshed out by the four characteristics of the reflective search for coherence first identified at the end of §20.

First, we note that mutual support may be built *bidirectionally*. Sidgwick being wrong to suppose a necessary association between generality and authority, justification need not descend from a single ultimate end (or even from a few). The possibility of inductive argument – of supporting a general end by showing how it sums up or organizes a commitment to a number of more particular ends – indicates that the lines of support can travel in different directions. It may proceed from the specific to the general or in the other direction. My focus on the relation of specification in no way undercuts bidirectionality, for the relation itself is defined without reference to the direction in which the link is forged.

Second, this strategy of justification must allow that *revisions* that aim to build mutual support may similarly occur in any direction and of any norm. Although the possibility of self-evident norms is allowed for, it is not assumed. Justification does not demand a self-evident basis in every case. Instead, any norm is viewed as in principle open to revision, in that justification does not take for granted that any stands firm a priori.

Third, justification is *holistic* in two related senses, each building on the resistance to segmentation flagged in §20. (a) It is assumed that any practical commitment is potentially relevant to the specification or revision of any other. It is not assumed that there is any stable way of partitioning one's practical commitments into mutually irrelevant sets, as between, say, one's moral commitments and one's nonmoral commitments, or one's work-related commitments and one's domestic commitments. The relevance that matters, here, is a practical sort: For the obvious reasons of temporal and budgetary limitations, any practical norm is apt to bump up against any other in practice. This being so, the justification of the way one is specified may need to take account of any other it may bump up against. Further, (b), the assessment of mutual support is assumed to require, in the ideal, a survey of the whole system of norms. For reasons related to the collapse of fundamental "independence" assumptions, as discussed in §15, one cannot assume that the overall mutual support exhibited by a system of norms can be adequately assessed by adding up (as it were) the degree of mutual support between every pair of norms in the system.

Fourth, what is being assessed for its mutual support is what stands firm for the agent on reflection. Practical commitments all being viewed as, in principle, revisable, this idea of justification looks to no authority other than the deliberating agent. (Nussbaum, forthcoming, shows this aspect of reflective sovereignty to have been prominent among the ancient Stoics.) In this way, this idea expresses and deepens the ideal of first-person reflection rather than recurring to the ideal of an appeal to a higher authority. The agent, of course, may in turn defer to whichever authorities she thinks deserving of trust. The point is simply that the question of what does and does not remain fixed is ultimately a matter of what seems acceptable to the agent, on reflection. I will refer to this feature of the idea of justification as *reflective sovereignty*.

It may help to clarify and make vivid the contours of this general idea about justification in the absence of ultimate criteria to show how it is exemplified by Rawls's notion of wide reflective equilibrium (Rawls 1975). Although this is an idea introduced in the context of moral and political theory, it can easily be adapted to the context of individual deliberation – with some necessary modification, to be discussed in the following section. Rawls's idea is that normative reflection begins with some "considered judgments," or judgments made in favorable conditions. These may be at any level of generality, and hence may represent either initial theoretical commitments or initial judgments about what ought to be done in particular types of situation. Then, working "from both ends," the systematizer proceeds to build relations of mutual support among these judgments, recognizing revisability in so doing by "pruning" and "adjusting" them (Rawls 1971, 20). As I interpret and develop the ideal of reflective equilibrium, no fixed division between a body of "data" and a theory "retrodicting" it can be maintained. This is for two reasons. First, any element of the "theory" being constructed might, in principle, licitly induce further revisions and adjustments in one's more concrete considered judgments. Second, and by the same token, once the relevant range of judgments is in reflective equilibrium there is no further need for a theory. A wide reflective equilibrium already takes into account the available considerations pertaining to the relevant alternative theories and includes the adoption of one of them. These two features – thorough revisability and the embrace of theory – together account for reflective equilibrium's holism.

The reflective sovereignty exemplified by Rawls's notion thus goes beyond the "consideredness" of the judgments involved, and the fact that the relevant ones are the ones that remain firm on reflection. Deliberation (like the construction of moral theories, according to Rawls) is thus an exercise in "self-examination." As the idea of Socratic reflection indicates, deliberation essentially occurs in psychologically definite human "selves" with distinct characters and emotions.[8] It thus cannot be reduced to a

---

8 Moody-Adams 1990, 232, rightly emphasizes that this "Socratic" feature of ethical and practical reflection is central to Rawls's ideal of reflective equilibrium, but would instead

relationship of any kind among propositions or conceptions. Even our ideals for practical deliberation reflect the ways our thinking is embodied in the flesh. This said, I am now able to show why deliberation of ends that proceeds by building practical coherence need not in the process commensurate the ends it addresses.

As an initial matter, it is important to note that the notion of coherence is not without power to guide the deliberator down one path of specification rather than another. Comparisons of systemic coherence are often possible, and require no precise or quantitative measure. Consider the following pedestrian case. If at 11:58 I want to eat lunch right away but also want to get a letter in the mailbox before the noon pickup, the improvement in coherence that comes from postponing lunch by five minutes is readily understandable. To be sure, I might have followed a different deliberative path and instead postponed mailing the letter by two hours, but then my letter might arrive a whole day later – a significant epistolary difference – whereas "by 12:05" is an easily acceptable specification of "right away" (Mabbott 1953, 114). My point is not that we can simply intuit comparative degrees of coherence. Rather, I mean to have suggested the skeleton of the complicated contextual rationale that would explain why it yields a better fit to postpone lunch than to postpone mailing the letter. In spelling out that rationale, one would find that instead of converging around a commensurans it "fans out into a whole arborescence of concerns" (Wiggins 1987, 101).

In arguing that we can often compare alternative paths of specification in terms of their comparative contribution to practical coherence, I expose myself to that horn of the dilemma which charges me with covert commensurability. My first line of defense against this imputation is that nothing in my account commits me to the idea of *maximizing* coherence, and some elements pull against it. Given reflective sovereignty, the deliberator, and not any one criterion, is to settle the acceptable limits of the effort at systematization. Contrary to Sidgwick's strict insistence on the completeness of rationality when conflicts arise, it is sometimes reasonable to recognize a tragic conflict as such. Since nothing in the idea that the rationality of a specification may be set out in terms of enhancement of coherence implies that coherence is to be maximized, this proposal is

explain it in terms of all-encompassing "self-conceptions" that are in some sense the objects of ethical inquiry and agreement. On her account, the "Socratic" features of ethical and practical inquiry are explained in terms of reflection being *about* a conception that the self has of itself and its world. See also Korsgaard, forthcoming, Lect. III.

179

compatible with allowing for the recognition of unresolvable conflicts (cf. Hurley 1989, 261).

My objector will not be impressed with this move, however. He will claim that I am employing an old dodge, that of characterizing the ideals I defend as holding merely prima facie. Coherence binds the rational agent unless it comes up against some other, competing requirement of rationality. To give a name to the consideration that blocks systematization in the name of recognizing conflicts, we might call it "integrity." A certain kind of integrity demands that we stick by our commitments, even if doing so sometimes lands us in unresolvable conflicts (cf. McFall 1987). (If "integrity" is not a good name for the counterweight to coherence, perhaps simply a form of constancy or conservatism would do: cf. Gärdenfors 1990, 29.) As my objector (not I) now interprets my view, it puts forward at least two prima facie principles of practical rationality, coherence maximization and integrity. When coherence guides us, he claims, it does so by commensurating the considerations that come under its umbrella. When the push for coherence conflicts with integrity, however, its direct guidance is suspended and the only way to decide is by balancing these two ideals against each other intuitively.

To illustrate this stage of the objection, I propose the following example. Suppose that Samantha has two main aims: to promote social justice by reforming the legal system in favor of the poor and oppressed and to earn a large income to support her family in the style to which they have become accustomed. Unfortunately, she finds it impossible to pursue both of these ends in her actual situation. Coherence would be enhanced by revising her reformist aim as follows: Instead of working specifically for justice for the poor and oppressed, she could simply work for justice as an active member of the adversary system – that is, as a litigator. Yet integrity, which typically favors ideals over more mundane aims, here asks that she stick by her reformist efforts even at the cost of some material sacrifice. How can she settle this higher-level conflict between coherence and integrity, except in terms of whether she can "stomach" becoming a lawyer? Since I recognize no principle higher than coherence, but nonetheless allow that it can yield in favor of integrity, it seems that rationality necessarily gives out at that point.

In answer, I assert that this appearance is mistaken. An intuitive balancing of coherence with integrity will indeed seem the only alternative to maximizing coherence so long as we stick with the idea that rationality depends upon an appeal to a higher authority. But §22's defense of coherence did not cast it as an ultimate end; instead it assumed that there are other ends more final than coherence, for the sake of which coherence is pursued. And in any event, the ideal of coherence cannot properly adjudicate in Samantha's case, for it would be biased in its own favor. But of course I vehemently resist this metaphor of an appeal to a higher authority. It is the reflectively sovereign deliberator, I want to insist, in whom the only relevant sort of authority is invested – the only sort, that is, recognizable from within relative rationality.[9] The ideal of the reflective search for coherence thus clashes deeply with the notion that the deliberator is looking for some ultimate criterion of choice. Yet as my previous examples have already implicitly indicated, this ideal is not therefore silent about how to deliberate. Deliberators may approach higher-level conflicts, conflicts such as that between coherence and integrity, in the same way that they approach more concrete ones, namely by reconsidering the specification of the norms involved.

The complexity of coherence and integrity makes it easier to specify them. Let me illustrate this for coherence. In Samantha's clash between a reformist ideal and the real world, she must ask why she cannot fully attain both of her goals. It is obviously not physically impossible to earn a good income as a social reformer; however, a fairly permanent social regularity frustrates her, since entrenched economic powers are not likely to reward the crusader for the poor and oppressed with a high salary. In specifying the coherence standard that guides her practical reasoning, should Samantha take for granted the constraint of such social regularities? To the contrary, her reformist zeal argues for continued struggle in the face of the obstacles they pose. Let us suppose that Samantha is too materialistic to want to sacrifice her luxuries, and hence becomes a litigator. (We will have occasion to consider cases involving more unrelievedly virtuous deliberators in Chapter X.) Even as a litigator, however, she might reasonably retain her political ideals as nagging reminders that will spur her to seek justice for the poor should the opportunity unexpectedly arise. For this reason, then, she might resist the strong systematizing interpretation of coherence developed by Sidgwick in favor of one that made a sharper distinction between conceptual and physical impossibilities, on the one hand, and impossibilities arising from contingent even if foreseeably permanent features of human life, on the other. The mutual support among the norms she retains on reflection would thus be enhanced.

In specifying coherence, part of what the deliberator does is to look

9 This, I believe, is also the message of Frankfurt 1971 as clarified by Frankfurt 1988, 159–76.

through this general norm to the various more concrete norms it helps order. This approach, which is licensed by bidirectionality, also makes sense substantively, and supplements the simpler instrumental arguments for coherence put forward in §22. We value practical coherence largely for the sake of how it helps us live our lives in pursuing the various other aims we have; but the regulative force of these other ends is rightly filtered through the layer of maintaining practical coherence. Similarly, we do not value integrity only in the abstract, but primarily as an alternative way of summing up attachment to certain aims we think of as virtuous or as worth our constancy. I do not rule out the possibility that we may also value coherence and integrity for their own sakes. Still, part of their importance derives from more concrete ends; and when these more abstract, systemic ends clash, it makes sense to look back to the way they build mutual support among more concrete commitments to see how coherence and integrity might be revised or specified anew.

There is no paradox in supposing that the coherence standard might be itself subject to revision so as to enhance the coherence of the deliberator's set of commitments. This would be nonsensical if coherence had to serve as the principle of highest appeal. Since, on my view, it is the deliberator who is sovereign, she may easily abstract from the way she has specified coherence if it comes into conflict with another end, such as integrity, and she may revise her specification of the more skeletal version of coherence that remains. If justification could flow only from the top down, this plurality of interpretations of coherence might well block any attempt to compare the degree of mutual support offered by each of them. Each might well be self-endorsing in the circumstances. Yet since justification can also flow from the bottom up, as from Samantha's reformism, it may be possible to build a case for one interpretation of coherence over another without begging the question. What I am defending in this book is a way of deliberating, not a single ultimate principle to guide all deliberation. In Samantha's case, deliberation that holistically builds coherence or mutual support among those of her norms that remain firm on reflection could nonetheless limit her specific understanding of coherence in such a way that integrity prevails.

All arguments must come to an end somewhere, Wittgenstein remarked. One way to put my present point, however, is that on the model I propose there is never any one particular place at which deliberative argument – or discursive practical reasoning – must come to an end. It is the sovereign deliberator who declares closure, as it were, not some ultimate principle. While the rational deliberator's decisions will respond to reasons in ways we have explored, there is no ultimate, deciding reason. Nonetheless, rational systematization is developed by building mutual support. The continuities traced by the specification relation allow this effort at systematization to continue through refinements and revisions, even ones that reform the deliberator's working understanding of coherence. Therefore, even though the ideal of practical coherence guides this process of deliberation, that ideal does not serve as a commensurating end. There being no commensurating scale in terms of which to maximize, rational choice along these lines does not maximize anything.

The interplay between revision and the construction of mutual support, as mediated by the sovereign deliberator, is a theme that enables me to fill out my remark in §4 to the effect that reflection has a constitutive role in determining what an agent ought to do. Certainly within relative rationality, to which I have been strategically confining myself, what an agent ought to do depends to some extent on what he or she would affirm on due reflection. For example, within relative rationality, it is plausible to suppose that whether Samantha ought to go into the practice of law does depend upon whether she can find a way, acceptable to her on reflection, of reconciling that plan with her commitment to justice. This dependence may arise, for example, from norms of justice that build in latitude for the reflective conscience – that let what counts as a just action depend, to some extent, on what the agent finds on reflection to be just. On this basis, of course, what she should do will depend only on *conscientious* reflection. If what her reflective acceptance ratifies is a sincere effort at building mutual support, her decision can be justified by setting out discursively the support it garners from her various commitments. In the decision with which I supplied Samantha, this is allowed by abstracting and then respecifying her commitment to justice. What the ideal of reflective coherence then rules out is her (a) getting as far in the deliberation as thus revising her conception of justice but (b) deciding to remain a political activist nonetheless for no further articulated reason. Her ends, as respecified, do not support that decision, and would support the alternative.

§27. PERCEPTION, EMOTION, AND THE PARTICULARS

I now want to argue that the idea of a search for reflective equilibrium can be broadened to embrace the particulars that are so prominent for the deliberator, creating what I will call an "extended reflective equilibrium."[10] Doing so will require recognizing the place for emotion and perception within reflective equilibrium. It will also deepen our understanding of the way in which deliberation involves reflective sovereignty, making more concrete the claim that deliberation is within a self and concerned with self-awareness and self-construction.

Starting with W. D. Ross's pluralist intuitionism in ethics, an astonishing number of attempts to articulate the ways in which practical reasoning responds to the particulars have resorted to evoking the *phronimos*, Aristotle's "person of practical wisdom (*phronēsis*)" (e.g., Gadamer 1975; Larmore 1987; Jonsen and Toulmin 1988; Dunne 1993). Sensitivity to the particulars is a hallmark of the *phronimos*, a result, somehow, of a well-trained perception. The perceptiveness of the *phronimos* is presumably supposed to be a reflection of his virtue and a product of his moral education (cf. Sherman 1989). It also depends upon experience, which acquaints the agent both with the "starting points" with which ethics and practice are concerned (1142a11–23) and with a host of particular empirical facts that must be known to assess proposed actions (1141b14–22). The experienced and well-trained – and virtuous – deliberator, the *phronimos*, must bring his sensitive discernment to bear on the particulars of the case at hand. In deciding, for instance, to what extent a given departure from the mean is blameworthy, Aristotle suggests that "the discernment rests with perception" (1109b23; cf. 1126b5). This is the phrase quoted by Ross to describe what must be done when two prima facie (or possum) principles conflict, except that on his translation the *decision* rests with perception (Ross 1930, 42).

This difference of nuance is important: If all that Aristotle's characterization of practical wisdom comes down to is that, in the end, one must *decide* as "perception" (that is, intuition) dictates, then the possibilities of discursive reasoning are cut short and what had looked like a promising historical reference falls flat. To be sure, Aristotle's insistence that the *phronimos* must be a person of trained and experienced virtue may be thought to bolster a more modern – and more suspect – restriction such as Ross's on the group of people whose intuitions are trustworthy, namely "the best people" (Ross 1930, 41). This leaves us in the dark, however, as to the nature and operation of this supposed "perception" of what is

---

10 I first put forward the idea of an "extended reflective equilibrium" in Richardson 1986. Nussbaum (1990, 69) briefly comments on this proposal. I believe that the account of self-perception to be offered in this section fits reasonably well with Aristotle's view of the role of perception in practical wisdom, as set out in *N.E.* VI; I made a textual case for this claim in Richardson 1986.

to be done. It is not that one cannot perceive what ought to be done in a given situation. Indeed, in distinguishing specification from application in §10, I embraced the Aristotelian idea that deliberation normally concludes with the perception of "what is to be done." In cases where deliberation is not needed, this perception may be sufficient, and not irrational to follow; where deliberation is needed, however, it should be rational, and its rationality requires discursively statable grounds (§19). Saying only that one must perceive what ought to be done, therefore, short-circuits the stage of deliberation. On my own proposal, the specification relation provides a way of explaining how norms can guide us in deciding what we ought to do even while they conflict. Instead of simply trying to figure out which of the norms will override, we can specify them in a way that enhances mutual support, revising them when necessary and when doing so is acceptable to us upon reflection. This process may seem so entirely discursive that there is no essential place for perception. I now want to suggest that this impression is false, and that "discernment" well captures the role for perception in the deliberative specification of ends.

The main ideas, here, are quite simple. There are two sorts of things to be discerned: features of the agent's situation and "starting points." Regarding the first of these, sensitive perception will be required to see what values are at stake in any choice. Recently, Murdoch (1980), Blum (1980), and Nussbaum (1990) have reminded us that we cannot even properly speak of "the choice" without assuming that the agent has perceived some opportunities for good or ill that compete practically in a way requiring immediate resolution. Emphasizing this brings onto the table a whole layer of psychology that the decision-theoretic literature hides by starting with well-defined alternatives. While my own talk of "available options" in §5 flirted with this danger, I seek now to correct for any distortions it introduced. Often, in actual deliberation, the emotions crucially focus our attention on certain aspects of a situation. Even apart from any assumption about the virtuousness of the deliberator, we must allow that the influence of emotion on our perception is often salutary. To take a dramatic sort of example, consider that fear can concentrate the mind, making us alive to avenues of escape, possibilities of rescue (cf. A. Rorty 1982). Although someone who is afraid will tend to exaggerate the danger he faces, his heightened perception of ways of avoiding it may outweigh any tendency to entertain false hopes, and this net gain in tactical judgment might be thought more important than the loss in accuracy of assessment. This is one instance of the familiar and well-documented phenomenon that emotion often heightens our attention at the same time as it directs it.[11] We can expect, then, that similar trade-offs will be involved in any specific instance of being "upset." While the responsible, responsive, and emotionally informed discernment of the possibilities and problems for action are obviously of cardinal importance in deliberation, I have little to add to what has been said by the writers already mentioned in this paragraph. I refer the reader to their discussions.

Regarding the second role for perception, that concerning the "starting points," my suggestion is the following: Consistently with a general emphasis on first-person reflection, one may take the perception of starting points to be a discernment of one's own commitment to certain ends. The reason to speak of this as "perception" rather than simply as "awareness" of an "ordinary" introspective sort is that it is an awareness that arises only in the course of deliberation about a concrete situation. The reflective self is not self-transparent (as Korsgaard, forthcoming, Lect. III, stresses). While dialogue is one route to self-knowledge, self-perception is another. One's attempt to think through what to do causes one to perceive aspects of one's commitments that would not have come to the fore otherwise. These ends, of course, are the "starting points" of further deliberation.

The medium of this concrete reflective self-awareness of ends, often, is emotion. Our emotions generally express our normative commitments. This is a cardinal point of Aristotle's ethics, which regards virtue as residing in a complex pattern of emotional response that leads to action. For this reason, the emotions elicited by some ethical or practical problem are sources of revealing self-perception. Because some judgments cannot adequately be expressed except when accompanied by the appropriate emotion, this emotional layer is essential to full self-awareness. We can be left groping for words adequate to express our judgments, and forced consequently to rely upon tone of voice to add the difference. "It was horrible!" for example, is said in many ways. If one finds oneself judging that the tax policies of one's country, say, are wholly unjust, but detects in oneself no traces of righteous indignation, one must begin to wonder whether one is deceiving oneself, or is cowardly about acting on these convictions and hence repressing the emotion that would be appropriate

---

11 For a summary of some of the experimental evidence for heightened attention and selectively improved learning due to emotional arousal, see Gilligan and Bower 1984. Philosophers who have recently stressed the role of emotion in heightening and directing our attention include A. Rorty (1980b); de Sousa (1987, ch. 7); Roberts (1988); and Nussbaum (1990, Essays 6 and 11).

to feel in conjunction with the judgment. In such ways, emotion, or the lack of it, can be a centrally important clue leading to self-awareness of ends.

Given this informative role for perception and emotion, what can we say in general about the favorable emotional conditions for the responsible and responsive discernment of one's situation and oneself? Rawls's notion of "considered judgment" is meant to capture what can be said at a general level about the constraints on the inputs of reflective equilibrium – on the set of items among which reflective coherence is sought. Rawls defines the sort of "considered judgments" relevant to a theory of justice quite unobjectionably as "simply those rendered under conditions favorable to the exercise of the sense of justice, and therefore in circumstances where the more common excuses and explanations for making a mistake do not obtain" (Rawls 1971, 47–8). More controversial, however, is his characterization of the circumstances of likely error about justice. Claiming that they resemble the circumstances for error in general, Rawls suggests that "we can discard those judgments made with hesitation, or in which we have little confidence. Similarly, those given when we are upset or frightened, or when we stand to gain one way or the other can be left aside" (1971, 47). Although Rawls says no more than this about how to identify a considered judgment, he might be thought to be suggesting that the influence of any powerful emotion must be set aside if one is to have a judgment that is appropriately "considered."

Nussbaum (1990, 175), who does understand Rawls's characterization of "considered judgment" this way, asks whether we should "automatically mistrust the information given us by our fear, or grief, or love (for being in love would surely count as a case of 'being upset')." We have just seen some reasons why we should not; and Nussbaum eloquently defends the claim that many of our ethically valuable relations to others – above all, love – cannot be described or evaluated properly without strong emotion. To be sure, it must be admitted that some emotional states are so violent that they entirely disrupt the process of judgment. Extreme fear can be paralyzing. In a fit of rage, someone who is violently upset may say or think all sorts of rash things that they regret later and never fully endorsed. We are all rightly warned by the example of Othello, who let his aggravated emotions cloud his perception of the facts. It may be such cases of violent emotions that Rawls had in mind in excluding judgments made when frightened or upset; yet the attempt to rid oneself of strong emotion can result in creating unconscious roadblocks and hidden sources of self-deception. For instance, many of us try so hard to maintain at least a superficial equanimity and a surface calm that holding strong passions at bay ends up being more self-deceptive than enlightening.

Furthermore, if emotions are sometimes essential to fully expressing our normative commitments and if these commitments are worth expressing, then we must allow that sometimes the proper expression of our considered judgments must be accompanied by strong and violent passions. For example, a proper and "reliable" judgment about the Holocaust or the Bhopal disaster – one appropriate as a starting point for further deliberation – will naturally include horror at the enormity of these wrongs. Indeed, it is plausible that we will not see the true enormity of the wrong unless we become upset by the basic facts of these horrors. This incorporation of violent emotion within considered judgment is compatible with reflection.[12] In cases as extreme as these, there is reason to think (1) that one's initial reaction might be a numbed shock; (2) that the outrage and the horror would thus intensify, to a point, on reflection; (3) that this heightened emotion on reflection would be appropriate; and (4) that this heightened emotion on reflection would at least help one grasp more clearly aspects of the horrible situation that one had perceived but whose significance has taken one some time to digest. It seems, therefore, that the general claim that optimal ethical judgment is made in a condition free from strong emotion is at best an exaggeration.

For deliberation of ends in general, then, the least we can say is that the emotions are often crucially important, both as inputs in their own right (helping articulate considered judgments when words fail us), as clues to one's commitments (which often find emotional expression), and as means to the sensitive perception of particulars, argued above to be needed. Far from being incompatible with the ideal of reflective equilibrium, emotional and perceptual particularity is essential to working out the Socratic ideal of first-person reflection. That Rawls's work has not led others to see this earlier can only be because Rawls developed this idea for a relatively impersonal subject matter. For questions of individual deliberation, however, the relevant ideal is that of extended reflective equilibrium, which incorporates emotionally informed perceptions of the particulars of the situation of action and emotionally guided awareness of one's commitments as elicited in response to the situation.

These roles for perception and emotion in situational discernment, self-

---

12 Contrary to Nussbaum (1990, 175), who writes as if reflection (on Rawls's view) necessarily precluded powerful feeling, I am suggesting that the two can be combined.

awareness, and the characterization of considered judgment help make concrete the sense in which deliberation guided by the search for reflective coherence is within a self. The deliberating self is recognized to be fully embodied, with passions that influence and integrally express thinking and with perceptual abilities that reflect both trained patterns of thought and commitments to action. On the view I am defending, these features of embodied thought are not viewed as limitations that should be abstracted away from in characterizing the ideal practical thinker. Rather, following Aristotle, we recognize that our ideals of practical thinking necessarily reflect, accept, and endorse these implications of embodiment (cf. Nussbaum 1990, Essay 15). Rational deliberation is essentially embodied in a sovereign deliberator, not abstractable into a set of relations among propositions.

Since it puts forward no further standards by which the agent is to determine what is acceptable on reflection, there is necessarily a nondiscursive layer to this view. Practical justification will not turn out to be discursive "all the way down." Since the justificational view is holistic and bidirectional, however, it is always open to the agent to keep pursuing the question why, if doing so proves fruitful. The existence of this ineliminable element of intuition in the account of justification does not imply that it traces justification back to self-certifying intuitions (cf. Rawls 1971, 44). Instead, the rational support – for example, for specifying an end in a certain way – that derives from providing an improvement in mutual support among the norms found acceptable on reflection may always be viewed as rebuttable by further considerations. Specifically, it is always open to being surpassed by a competing specification that provides even greater mutual support.

I am now in a position to sum up the claim to rationality of reflectively specifying ends in a way that enhances mutual support. This ideal of reflective coherence can support the most important of Sidgwick's postulates of practical rationality, understood as marks of what makes a process of thinking rational. (Completeness with respect to conflicts and superior validity of the grounds of adjudication we have seen reason to reject.) First, the requirement of discursiveness is satisfied, for all reasons recognized are ones that may be articulated on reflection. Emotion and perception are taken as providing clues potentially pointing toward articulable commitments, not in themselves as reasons. Justification, on this account of reflective coherence, rests on statable principles. Second, the bidirectional search for coherence helps ensure that reasons that are subordinate according to the working theory are nonetheless respected by its systematizing. Finally, this account incorporates a respect for the demands of practical coherence, albeit in a different form than supposed by Sidgwick's postulate. Presuming a hierarchical form of justification, in which warrant would flow from one or a few self-evident first principles, Sidgwick held that these first principles must never give conflicting advice. Subordinate principles are expected to conflict; first principles must not. On the bidirectional and holistic ideal I have been developing, by contrast, there is no supposition that such first principles must exist. Accordingly, respect for practical coherence is diffused more broadly among the system of norms, and conflicting advice is recognized as but one way among many in which mutual support will fall short of its theoretical maximum. Deliberation that specified or revised norms, including end-norms, in a way that both enhanced mutual support among the norms that remained acceptable on reflection and responded to the discursively articulable pleadings of other norms (including "subordinate" ones), would have a strong claim to rationality. Yet because this rationality resides in the sovereign deliberator and not in some supreme systematizing principle, no commensurability has been created. Rational systematization is possible without commensurability. Without leaning on a commensurating standard, covert or overt, ends may be reflectively and rationally specified. Since, as §13 showed, specifying ends can amount to adopting new ones, new ends may be rationally adopted without depending on or establishing deliberative commensurability.

Part Four

Source

IX

Sources and limits

I have argued that one can deliberate about ends (§8), that ends can be deliberatively specified (Chapter IV), and that deliberative specifications of ends can be subject to rational support and criticism in terms of their overall fit within a system of mutually supporting norms found acceptable upon reflection (Chapter VIII). One may accept these points, however, and remain skeptical about the possibility of deliberating about the (or an) *ultimate* end. Regarding an ultimate end as a source of value is here the principal obstacle.

§28. REMAINING GROUNDS OF SKEPTICISM

We may distinguish four sorts of principled consideration supporting this residual doubt about extending rational deliberation to ultimate ends.

First, there may remain some commitment to what might be called "normative foundationalism" regarding practical reasoning (cf. Audi 1989, 35–6). This is the view that while we may deliberate about ends, if our deliberation is to have any normative force then this must be obtained from an ultimate end that is not subject to deliberation. On this view, even if an ultimate end is not by definition a "source of value," it must be regarded as such if practical reasoning is to have normative force. To overcome whatever resistance to deliberation about the ultimate end resides in those who think that normative force must flow from it, my approach will be to describe in the following chapter a number of examples, as realistically as I can, in which deliberation with a claim to normative force concerns an ultimate end.

A second source of doubt about whether we can deliberate rationally about ultimate ends hangs upon the positive features of my own account rather than anything more general about normativity or practice. My argument for rational deliberation of ends has focused on the possibility of specifying ends in a justifiable way. This very characterization seems to imply that there is some end to be specified. At the limit, therefore, it seems there must be some ultimately abstract end – happiness, perhaps, or perhaps the very idea of the ultimate end – that is otherwise merely formal and that is to be specified. Otherwise, how can deliberation that specifies it get going? Now since, as I have all along emphasized, the specification relation involves no temporal priority, it supports abstracting as well as specifying moves in deliberation. Accordingly, one way to counter this ground for doubt would be to emphasize the flexibility of bidirectional systematization, which could set up an ultimate end as a way of making sense of diverse intermediate ends. Another, however, is to show how far deliberation that specifies can go in transforming a supposedly "formal" account of an ultimate end. My examples in the following chapter will take both tacks. The Aristotelian example of §32 will show how deliberation can lead to a new conception of the ultimate end by respecifying the elements of its "formal" definition. The Rawlsian example of §33 will pursue the alternative strategy by showing how deliberation focused on two competing final ends can arrive at a united practical ideal that serves as an ultimate end.

Third, some have argued that an ultimate end is too large and abstract an entity even to figure in individual deliberation. For instance, Broadie (1991, 198) ridicules the suggestion that Aristotle thinks of the person of practical wisdom as deliberating from a "Grand End," an explicit, definite, and fixed conception of an ultimate end:

Few of us would claim to know either at first or second hand what it is like to deliberate with a view to realizing a Grand End. We can hardly imagine this except schematically, whereas we can easily reproduce in our heads quite possible versions or imitations of deliberations pertaining to various crafts, as well as nonspecialist deliberations concerning familiar describable ends such as buying a house, helping a friend out of difficulties, or obtaining a diploma.

If we cannot meaningfully deliberate concerning an ultimate end, then a fortiori we cannot meaningfully deliberate to adopt one. Now, contrary to Broadie's particular form of this skepticism, the content of the ultimate end need not be fully definite at the outset (cf. Richardson 1992c). Rather, it is a crucial task of deliberation to specify the ultimate end. Again, in my account the ultimate end does not serve as the final criterion. So there are abstract reasons to think that the kind of deliberation about ultimate ends that I defend is less implausible than the deliberation by reference to a Grand End that Broadie dismisses. Yet the only really convincing way to rebuff this sort of skepticism is to present plausible examples, as the next chapter will do.

Finally, it may be suspected that these accounts of deliberation about supposedly ultimate ends work only because they take for granted a more or less pragmatist theory according to which the *real* ultimate end is practical coherence. Yet my argument in §22 about the reasonableness of allowing that some practical dilemmas are unresolvable already indicated that I do not regard practical coherence as of overriding importance in any obvious sense. Further, that practical coherence does not function as a commensurans in the view I am proposing (§26) reinforces the fact that it does not serve as the ultimate end. The central place of reflective sovereignty within the coherence ideal implies that this is not a correct description of my view. We there saw, in the example of Samantha, how rational deliberation can respecify the coherence ideal itself.

It remains, then, to address the grounds for the source obstacle that suggest a purported need for an ultimate foundation or starting point for practical reason. Since I aim to reject this suggestion while at the same time defending the possibility of deliberating about ultimate ends, I must indicate what an ultimate end is, if not an ultimate foundation or source of practical reasoning. To do so, the following section will set out an account of the notion of an ultimate end that emphasizes its character as limit rather than as source. Then in preparation for showing that deliberation can embrace the deliberative resolution of an ultimate end's content, §30 will indicate the place of dialectic within deliberation.

§29. THREE CONCEPTIONS OF AN ULTIMATE END

In this section I criticize two interpretations of the concept of an ultimate end and put forward a third alternative.[1] In particular, I mean to examine the relation – central in some philosophical traditions – between multiple final ends and the one ultimate end. This terminology is not terribly felicitous, in that an "end" already connotes finality, and "final" and "ultimate" seem synonyms. I stick with it, nonetheless, because of its fit with traditional translations of Aristotle, who uses comparative and superlative forms of the adjective *teleios* in qualifying ends. I will be following the Aristotelian tradition in its essentials (as I understand them: cf. Richardson 1992a). My aim is to develop an interpretation that, while remaining true to traditional understandings of what is meant by "ultimate

1 This section has benefited from the critical comments of Alisa Carse, Jorge Garcia, Judith Lichtenberg, David Luban, Terry Pinkard, Georges Rey, Geoffrey Sayre-McCord, Nancy Sherman, Michael Slote, Alan Strudler, and David Wasserman. I am grateful for their help.

end," nonetheless makes room for deliberation to resolve upon an ultimate end's content. This interpretation, which I call the *regulatory conception* of the ultimate end, will also be seen to support the possibility of deliberation of ends more generally. In proceeding in this way, I do not mean to answer by definition my question about the possibility of deliberating about ends. Rather, my aim is to show how philosophical interpretations of the idea of an ultimate end wrongly hinder this possibility. The two conceptions that I will undercut, the *source* and *indirect* conceptions, have unduly influenced our thinking, preventing us from recognizing the degree to which we may reason about ends and criticize desires. Even if we adopt the regulatory conception in their place, however, constructive work will remain to be done to show how the possibility of deliberating about ends might be realized. Further, it is my hope that the interpretation of the idea of an ultimate end that I defend will recommend itself on grounds independent of its allowing for the possibility of rational deliberation extending to ends. In particular, I believe that it better fits the phenomena of deliberation and better provides for a unified theory of practical reasoning.

It really is the *notion* of an ultimate end that I am concerned with in this section. We must not assume that we know without explication what the phrase "ultimate end" means. As will be seen, none of the three rival interpretations I will consider places much constraint on the *content* of the ultimate end. Once one fixes upon one of these three interpretations, it will remain a further question what the ultimate end is. Indeed, it will remain a further question, for each individual, whether he or she pursues an ultimate end. None of my discussion in this section will presume the existence of an ultimate end, even for a single deliberator.

The three conceptions of the notion of an ultimate end may be separated by two questions. First, are ends sources of practical justification? If so, then the conception of the ultimate end will be what I will call "direct"; if not, it is "indirect." Second, if ends are sources of practical justification, does all justification originate in or derive from the ultimate end? An affirmative answer to this second question yields the source conception; while a negative answer yields a regulatory conception. As we will see, the source conception, which answers both questions affirmatively, has the disadvantage of making it difficult to see how the ultimate end itself can be subject to deliberation or rational criticism. Since the two questions are independent, it would be possible to have an indirectly regulatory conception that answers both questions negatively, seeing all ends as heuristic structures for deliberation, to be justified otherwise. Perhaps inculcating the entire hierarchy of ends is in some other sense optimific. Yet since this possibility is little defended, I mention it only to set it aside. The indirect conception that I will discuss instead answers the first question negatively and the second one positively, casting the ultimate end as that end through which all justification flows even though it does not originate there. Finally, the regulatory conception that I favor answers the first question positively but the second one negatively.

The thought that motivates the source conception is that the end justifies the means, a thought that it extends to the level of the ultimate end. Justifying the means is, at any rate, what a final end is supposed to do, on this reading. To be sure, sometimes being necessary to some end is insufficient justification for an action; but perhaps these breakdowns can always be explained by the existence of some conflicting end and appeal made to a higher end to settle the conflict. Anticipating this possibility, the source conception casts the ultimate end as the highest court of justificatory appeal and the unimpeachable source of all justification. This understanding of the ultimate end as source of value descends from Platonic and neo-Platonic origins. Sidgwick's account of the ultimate end as an ultimate court of appeal, laid out in Chapter VI, also builds in the idea that the ultimate end is the source of value.

A nonmetaphysical route into the source conception proceeds via the idea of a justificatory regress, as Korsgaard explains (1986a, 488):

An end provides the justification of the means; the means are good if the end is good. If the end is only conditionally good, it in turn must be justified. Justification, like explanation, seems to give rise to an indefinite regress: for any reason offered, we can always ask why. If complete justification of an end is to be possible, something must bring this regress to a stop; there must be something about which it is impossible or unnecessary to ask why. This will be something unconditionally good.

Korsgaard calls the unconditionally good pinnacle of this pyramid the "source of value," and identifies it with the ultimate end.[2] In the Aristotelian tradition, similar arguments from the regress of reasons to the necessary existence of an ultimate end have long drawn accusations of fallacy. The imputed error – recently dubbed "Anscombe's fallacy" – is that of illicitly shifting from the claim that each action must be justified by reference to some good to the claim that there is a single good that

---

2 This identification of the source of value with the ultimate end is apparently relaxed in Korsgaard's forthcoming *Tanner Lectures*. If so, the resulting account becomes much closer to my own.

justifies all actions (MacDonald 1991; cf. Anscombe 1976, 34). If the regress argument were supplemented with the Sidgwickian argument about the need for an ultimate court of appeal when ends conflict, however, that might restore the picture of a justificatory pyramid in which the reasons all flow from a single source at the apex. Further, to vary the metaphor, once having found an ultimate end that puts a stop to the regress, one has located the root of value, and can reverse direction to trace the justification that flows from it out into the diverse branchings of subordinate ends.

The source conception allows that we can and do argue about what is unconditionally valuable; but this is only because what is ultimate in the practical justification of an action or plan is not necessarily ultimate in the philosophical justification of a particular view of the ultimate end's content. What is unfortunate about this picture is its presumption of a need for Sidgwickian system and the degree to which it puts the content of the ultimate end beyond the scope of deliberation or practical reasoning. If the ultimate end is to be the source of all practical justification and the basis for resolving all of the practical conflicts we face day to day, then what we learn as we attempt reasonably to resolve those conflicts cannot be put to use to refine our view of what the ultimate end is. At best, coming up against a rationally unresolvable conflict will merely indicate, in negative Sidgwickian fashion, that we have not yet found the true ultimate end. The philosophical "metajustification" of the whole practical edifice is required to rest on abstract and metaphysical – not to say shaky – arguments, such as the (Aristotelian?) argument that only a process without end can serve as the ultimate end, or the (Kantian?) argument that beings capable of regarding themselves as supremely valuable are therefore supremely valuable. Reliance on highly abstract philosophical arguments of this kind is the fate of the source conception because since all practical justification must flow from the ultimate end, the justification of the ultimate end itself can in no way be practical. The whole justificatory picture, therefore, balances a philosophical pyramid on the point of the practical one, yielding a sort of hourglass in which philosophical justification flows through the bottleneck of the ultimate end, to fall out below as so many grains of practical wisdom. This is yet another cost of trying to live within Sidgwickian ideals for ethical science, an aim criticized in Part Three.

A rather extreme reaction to these difficulties with the idea of a "source of value" would be to conclude that instead of looking to ends to justify actions at all, we should look to more particular sources, such as the desires of the agent. This is the tack taken by the indirect conception. As indirect, it looks to some other source besides ends for reasons for action. Despite this, however, it allocates to the ultimate end a special role in transmitting this justification to action. According to this view, it is overly simple to see reasons for action as having a basis in belief and desire. More must be said, for desires conflict pervasively. Here, this conception, too, can invoke Sidgwickian considerations of system. Reason, as Sidgwick insisted, must speak with one voice. Accordingly, true reasons for action must refer, not simply to the agent's desires, but to "rational desires," desires that would persist after correction so as to avoid incompatibilities and other irrationalities. These two kinds of desire – actual and corrected – are mirrored, on the indirect conception, by a division of labor between intermediate final ends and the ultimate end. While intermediate final ends reflect intrinsic actual desires, the ultimate end is properly the portal through which justification passes, for the ultimate end is that state or condition – whatever it might be – that would represent for the agent the total satisfaction of rational desire.

By this reasoning we arrive at the indirect conception of an ultimate end.[3] What makes this version of the ultimate end a representative of indirect justification is that instead of simply identifying the ultimate end as "to completely satisfy all of one's rational desires," it takes the satisfaction of rational desire to be the source of justification and puts forward complete satisfaction as a criterion that any proposed ultimate end must meet. A considerable amount of calculation would have to go into figuring out what sort of balance and combination among one's various intrinsic desires or final ends made for a feasible and compatible – and hence rational and completely satisfiable – set. This sort of ultimate end will be a certain set of activities and pursuits ordered in a certain way – namely whatever set it is that would yield complete satisfaction of rational desire.

This indirect way of referring to rational and compatible desires seems to raise the possibility of rational criticism. But the question is: On what does the notion of rational intrinsic desire stand? How, to begin with, does this view discriminate, as it must, between intrinsic and instrumental desires – between, say, wanting a tool just to have it and wanting a tool just in order to accomplish some task? To allow a well-formed interpre-

---

3 An instance of the indirect approach that explicitly distinguishes roles for final versus ultimate ends in this way is elaborated by MacDonald 1991. Where MacDonald says "weak ultimate end," I say "final end": see his n. 28; his gloss of "ultimate end" I take to be given by what he calls a "strong ultimate end."

tation of "complete satisfaction," the constraints on rational desire must be strong enough to cope with conflicts, even contingent ones. Otherwise, the projection of a "complete" satisfaction will prove a vain one. As we have seen (§6), contingent conflicts cannot be excluded by indubitable logical principles. Moreover, while there is some reason to think that real duties cannot conflict, real desires do so continually. To avoid the vanity threatening the push for *complete* satisfaction, the indirect theorist might sacrifice some simplicity for realism and shift to *optimal* satisfaction; but here, trade-offs such as the one between coherence and integrity faced by Samantha (§26) will pose continual problems. What determines what level of conflict is optimal, on this view? There is no ready answer.[4]

Accordingly, this indirect conception of the ultimate end has twin defects. First, insofar as it is simply built up from the connection between final ends and desires, so as to yield an aggregate notion of complete satisfaction, it necessarily remains too inarticulate about the basis for criticizing desires. The ultimate end is not selected for *its* fit with other commitments. Instead, it stands in for a coherent set of desires, forged one knows not how. Rather than serving as the ultimate guide to practical reasoning, the ultimate end of the indirect conception must wait on the main work of practical reasoning, which must take place before the ultimate end can take determinate content, and which proceeds on principles independent of the ultimate end. Second, if this background practical reasoning is limited to making desires coherent, it may lack adequate critical bite. As I mentioned in §1, it certainly seems possible to imagine agents – such as Rawls's monomaniacal grass-blade counter or the person who won't work with Henrys – whose desires, while not conflicting, nonetheless are irrational. The indirect conception overly insulates desires from the regulative potential of the hierarchy of ends.

On the regulatory interpretation of the idea of an ultimate end, ends are the basis of justification and the ultimate end regulates. In other words, every end is a source of justification, and the function of the hierarchy of more final ends is not directly to provide a better or less conditional

---

4 In addressing Anscombe's fallacy, MacDonald argues that practical reasoning directed toward generating a "coherent overall plan" that will include only compatible desires will allow the agent "to maximize satisfaction of her desires" (56). That this argument for the existence of a single ultimate end begs the question against those who doubt it can be seen in the fact that, as MacDonald admits, the claim is trivial: What is maximized is the satisfaction of "rational" desire, *by which is meant* desire that coheres in an overall life plan (58). What should a coherent life plan look like? What form of coherence need be involved?

justification but to assure an appropriate qualitative regulation of pursuit. How this works may be brought out by building on and extending the unified account of what it is for x to be sought "for the sake" of y (where x and y need not even be distinct) developed in §7. As has been noted in the Aristotle literature, even a final end may be subordinate to another end as a constituent, specification, or causal contributor. Listing these types of "for the sake of x" relations, however, does not provide any account of what they have in common.[5] This §7 aimed to provide. On my analysis, it will be recalled, "S pursues x for the sake of y" means, first, that S would pursue x even if the only value realized in so doing would be (that described by) y; and, second, that S reflectively accepts y as appropriately regulating x and not vice versa. The condition of reflective acceptance already builds in an element of regulative structure that adds to the more motivational counterfactual condition. What I will now show is how this same basic analysis easily extends to the notion of an ultimate end.

The regulatory antisymmetry that this analysis entails is enough to model a hierarchy of ends, given an agent whose pursuits are appropriately complex. An ultimate end will exist if the hierarchy converges on a single end. Since this analysis is part of a direct interpretation of the ultimate end, there is no need to look outside ends for justification of a proposed ultimate end. Rather, the ultimate end may be seen as emerging from the agent's structure of pursuit, wherein some ends are sought for the sake of others. As is most obvious in the case of Aristotle's hierarchy of crafts at the outset of the *Nicomachean Ethics*, views about what appropriately regulates what are taken as data upon which a conception of the ultimate end may build (cf. Broadie 1991, 12). In developing his interpretation of "ultimate end," he defines an "unqualifiedly final" end is one sought *only* for its own sake. Since Aristotle recognizes the existence of multiple final ends, one cannot get an unqualifiedly final end simply by finding the unique final end. Further, since Aristotle realistically assumes that the achievement of any final end will also yield pleasure, itself a final end, and argues that pleasure itself must be regulated by reference to virtue, it will prove impossible to find an unqualifiedly final end simply by locating one that makes no contribution – as causal support, constituent, or specifica-

5 On constituent means, cf. Greenwood 1973, 46–7; Ackrill 1980, 18–20; Wiggins 1980a, 224. On specifying, cf. Wiggins 1980a, 228. MacDonald 1991 provides a comprehensive and realistic catalogue of the many different kinds of relations that can hold between one end (one object of pursuit) and another to which it is subordinate by this relation, but gives no general account of the relation of pursuit for the sake of an end.

tion – to any other final end. If we would in general seek virtue for its own sake, would we not still pursue happiness even if the only value thereby realized were virtue (cf. Korsgaard 1986a, 490)? On the regulatory conception, if there is any unqualifiedly final end, it must be one that attains this status because it is not appropriately regulated by reference to any other end. We would choose it for its own sake, and the degree and manner in which we pursue it requires no modulation or determination by reference to any other end. While a final end in general qualitatively limits the appropriate pursuit of those things sought for its sake, an un-qualifiedly final end is self-limiting. To be sure, it is still possible that there could be several such. In my view, the reason that Aristotle avoids Ans-combe's fallacy is that he does not try to prove that there must be exactly one unqualifiedly final end; rather, he locates one such end, happiness or eudaimonia, and provides grounds for doubting that there is any other such end. The ultimate end, then, is the unqualifiedly final end that is uniquely suited for the regulation of human life.

A practically coherent and mutually supportive relationship among one's ends, I have been suggesting, makes for a well-regulated human life. Although the regulatory conception resembles the indirect conception in building in an appeal to coherence, it focuses on the coherence or mutual support among ends, thereby keeping the relevant relations of "pursuit for the sake of x" center stage in any deliberation concerning ends. The search for coherence can make good use of the regulatory structure that the hierarchy of ends allows. Even if the hierarchy is not rigid, its regu-latory structure will offer more possibilities for criticizing desires than will coherence merely among desires themselves. The regulatory conception specifies that the agent must accept the higher end as appropriately reg-ulating the lower. This constraint provides a check at least against the sort of irrationality involved in having children for the sake of collecting more four-leaf clovers (§1) or helping the homeless solely in order to get elected (§13). My point is not that the idea of a regulatory ultimate end guarantees that such misspecifications are ruled out. Rather, it is that the regulatory aspect of this analysis (even in relative rationality) rules them out on a basis that the alternative accounts lack, and that is deepened when ex-tended to the level of the ultimate end. To exhibit this potential more fully will require the examples of the following chapter. There we will see how well the regulatory conception leaves the door open to objective content and criticism. I should note, however, that the regulatory con-ception does leave open the material possibility that the ultimate end might turn out to be the complete satisfaction of rational desire.

This regulatory interpretation of the idea of an ultimate end has a number of additional theoretical advantages. To begin with, it avoids the difficulties that the two justification conceptions have with providing practical justification for a version of the ultimate end. Far from accepting the hourglass constriction imposed by both the source and the indirect conceptions, the regulatory conception can accept quite a decentralized justification. Any end that stands firm on reflection can be accepted as a ground of justification. Furthermore, in resting the notion of the ultimate end in the hands of the reflective agent, the regulatory conception accepts what is valid in the idea that "we must be the source of value" (Korsgaard 1986a, 505) without having to adopt the dubious and sententious neo-Kantian explanation that this is because we are so valuable. Reflective sovereignty is better preserved if reflection is not conceived as having necessarily to look to some particular source of value. We are the source of value just in the sense that, as Rawls puts it, "there is no way to get beyond deliberative rationality" (Rawls 1971, 560). Nothing follows from this about what is valuable. As Wittgenstein wrote, "To say: in the end we can only adduce such grounds as *we* hold to be grounds, is to say nothing at all" (Wittgenstein 1969, §599). In particular, it is not to say that since they are our grounds, and we hold them to be important, we must take ourselves to be important.[6]

Because it rejects the hourglass constriction, the regulatory conception also allows for an account of practical reason that is more unified than can its rivals. It is more unified than the indirect account because the work of justifying a substantive version of the ultimate end is not left offstage. Rather, it is incorporated into the effort to set out the structure of pursuit, which its definition of an ultimate end incorporates by reference. Whereas the indirect interpretation leaves one needing a separate account of rational desire, the regulatory account stands on its own. A candidate ultimate end is practically justified if it regulates subordinate pursuits in a way that is acceptable on reflection, though this does not rule out asking philosophical questions about whether it is the appropriate sort of thing to take as regulating all of one's pursuits. In comparison to the source conception, the regulatory conception's greater unity stems from its allowing for deliberation about the ultimate end. This central practical commitment is seen as subject to practical, and not merely theoretical, reasoning.

6 I intend these provocative remarks as merely suggesting a possible line of response to the powerful and profoundly worked out position Korsgaard develops in her forthcoming *Tanner Lectures*, which became available too recently for me to digest fully. These remarks will at least serve to help differentiate my position from hers.

The regulatory conception also best captures what an ultimate end is supposed to be. Each of the other conceptions tends to undermine itself, in that each defines an ultimate end by reference to a certain presumptively desirable state of affairs that would obtain were the end achieved. On the source view, an end is ultimate just in case it is capable of fully justifying human pursuit. Perhaps it could make a life worth choosing as a human life. On the indirect view, an end is ultimate just in case it is capable of yielding complete satisfaction of rational desire. In so interpreting the idea of an ultimate end by reference to these states of affairs that result from or come along with its attainment, each of these conceptions inevitably draws the question, "But what is so good about those consequences? Why should we want or pursue that?" The question whether or not to have lived a human life does not seem practically relevant, and the demand for justification can be rebuffed (cf. Anscombe 1976, 34). The satisfaction of rational desire, for its part, may be thought to pale in comparison with mystical union with God, or to be too egoistic to justify. While the perspectives from which these doubts can be raised are multiple, the present point is simply that by identifying the achievement of a certain presumptively valuable state of affairs as the mark of the ultimate end, these conceptions prompt them. Furthermore, the attempt to answer them sounds like a further search for some still more ultimate end. By contrast, the regulatory conception identifies the ultimate end using counterfactuals about what the agent would choose, and specifically would choose as appropriately regulative of the subordinate ends. This not being a consequence, the question "why?" does not arise in the same way. The regulatory conception's hierarchy of ends is built by asking "in what circumstances?" and "in what way?" – not by asking "why?" It does not reject the need for practical justification, but seeks it through coherence. Its ultimate end – the only end sought only for its own sake – is supremely regulatory, not uniquely justifying.

The regulatory conception of the ultimate end, therefore, allows for a fuller scope to deliberation of ends than do its rivals. It provides no intrinsic encouragement to a desire-satisfaction standard of practical rationality, and hence affords greater possibilities for criticizing desire than do the alternative views. Finally, the regulatory conception, in building more directly upon a more general account of what it is to pursue something for the sake of an end, comes closer to capturing what we *mean* by an "ultimate end" than do its alternatives. If we would escape the dead end of desire-satisfaction theories of practical rationality, we would do well to revive the Aristotelian interpretation of the ultimate end as the target by reference to which to regulate our strivings. It serves not to generate value but qualitatively to regulate or delimit one's pursuits.

§30. DELIBERATIVE THEORY AND DIALECTIC

While the last section argued that the regulatory conception of an ultimate end allows for more avenues for practical justification than do its rivals, this possibility will still seem rather abstract. Can this justification really be practical? Can the bidirectional and holist justification that the regulatory conception will allow really be a matter of deliberation? Can anything as remote as an ultimate end's content be at play in deliberation? These questions are particular versions of more general worries about the role of theory in deliberation.

Deliberative theorizing, if any there be, must respect the fact that many of one's particular practical commitments remain tacit and inexplicit. Partly for this reason, I insisted in §27 that the reflective equilibrium relevant in individual deliberation must be extended to embrace the perceptions and emotions that arise in the situation of action. The particular commitments that come to light in these ways help one decide whether one can accept that certain ends regulate certain others. Thus, in §8's example of the politician who ends up refusing to see helping the homeless solely as a means to getting elected, it was the situationally induced perception of the crassness of so doing that provided the crucial reason for his change in view. Avoiding being crass in this very particular way emerged as an end that he hadn't until then considered relevant. In good holist fashion, this end could be subordinate in hierarchical terms and still provide reason for the revision.

While the tacitness of such particular commitments – many of them inculcated in early youth – tends to inhibit deliberative theorizing, their sources facilitate it. Many of these particular value commitments and ends result from culturally informed upbringing and education. This normative education typically both includes some explicit theory (of democracy, of truthfulness, and so on) and praises some exemplary individuals whose value theories might be explored. These culturally complex and theoretically sophisticated views become part of us. For better or worse, they go a long way toward shaping our starting points when we deliberate. Ever since the Enlightenment, of course, it has been popular for those of rationalist temperament to revolt against this cultural determination of value commitments; but I am one rationalist who does not join this revolt. To take an unpalatably extreme recent example of this rationalist tendency,

R. B. Brandt has suggested that these cultural influences necessarily distort our appreciation of the true "facts" that are relevant to rational choice. These "facts" are those pertaining to the pleasure that we actually obtain by engaging in an activity, where "pleasure" refers to something like the tendency to want to keep doing the activity (Brandt 1979, ch. 6). Like Epicurus before him, Brandt argues that cultural influences interfere with our appreciation of this bottom-line layer of "facts," ever attempting to channel and sublimate our urges in ways that our individual rationality would not and should not endorse if we underwent "cognitive psychotherapy" designed to make us optimally aware of the "facts." Now, it is not my present purpose to argue against this proposal, which is frankly built upon a persuasive redefinition of "rational" and which seems to me absurd. Rather, I simply aim to bring out the fact that this proposal about setting aside the influences of culture and tradition itself depends upon a radical and sweeping theoretical systematization of our normative commitments. Like Bentham's, in fact, Brandt's rejection of tradition rests on a hedonistic value theory (though their definitions of pleasure differ). Furthermore, Brandt is probably right that undoing the effects of culture (insofar as that may be possible) would require an extremely thorough and highly cognitive course of psychotherapy. This would bring to consciousness the place of traditional commitments within one's life and provide one with strategies for neutralizing them. The lesson is that whether one welcomes or shuns cultural and traditional influences on individuals, one must recognize that individuals' attempts to grapple with their internalized legacy must confront the theories that inform this influence, whether to overthrow them or to build upon them. For example, Augustine waged a polemic against the Manichaeism of his youth, yet also incorporated into his theology a similar focus on the problem of evil. Rational deliberation will often require becoming self-conscious about the cultural origins and interpretation of one's commitments, therefore; but this awareness need not erode commitment to traditional views. Sometimes reflection erodes them (cf. Williams 1985, 148, 167–9), but sometimes it reinforces them.

In addition to providing a natural route into theory, this need to confront one's tradition shows how a single person may be led to hold the views of others relevant to his or her deliberation. Consider the case of a draft-eligible youth deciding whether to petition for exemption from military service as a conscientious objector. A patriot who wants his country to survive, he also finds war barbaric and inhumane and at odds with the commandment not to kill. In determining whether he really does conscientiously object to war on religious grounds, he would do well to consult some of the leading texts of his tradition. To these he can turn not only as authorities governing any member of his faith, but also as aids to interpreting and understanding a creed he has already internalized. His religious upbringing will have left him with views relating to respect for life, adherence to divine commandments, and service to country. Although he may not until now have studied his tradition's views on war, these presumably build upon and reflect in a somewhat coherent way the more general themes that survive within him as traces of his religious upbringing. He can turn to these writings and theories on the morality of war, therefore, not merely with the curiosity of seeing how other people have dealt with the tension between patriotism and nonviolence, but also in the hope that they will have managed to arrive at a coherent accommodation of these ends understood roughly as he interprets them. Since these writings build upon and develop the theory that has informed his education, they have a special relevance to him as he seeks to arrive at a coherent way of reconciling the different commitments with which this upbringing has left him.

As this case reminds us, although deliberation essentially occurs within a self, it also often leads one to consider the views of others. The practical need to find ways to build mutual support among our many ends leads us toward a theory of what we take to be good – not inexorably, but in ways that have strong rational support. There are at least three reasons why one should pay attention to the views of others as one deliberates – reasons that would apply even apart from joint action and claims made on one by others. The first, which we have just seen, is that their views may just be the explicit versions of the ones that tacitly inform one's strivings.

The second reason to pay attention to the practical arguments of others is simply that they may have some good ideas. One may admire how some have managed to combine aesthetic and political interests in their lives, for instance, and seek to understand how they managed to do so. One will want to know how they interpreted the ideals of beauty and of politics, and whether their harmonious integration was a matter of luck, inimitable personal style, or reproducible principled accommodation. In addition to thus analyzing the life of someone who met a similar challenge in an exemplary way, one would also profit from reading Kierkegaard on the general subject, to help prevent oneself from arriving at an overly facile view of how to combine these apparently opposed ideals.

The third sort of reason to take account of the views of others in deliberation is that they may have been dealing with the same problems in a more literal sense. Especially if one takes a realist and objectivist stance about values – a matter on which I have remained largely agnostic – then one may take it that the agent's attempts to weave together beauty and political participation are referring to the same objects as her predecessors' parallel attempts. Both are about the same goods; both are engaged in the same effort at understanding the same set of relationships between them. In this vein, Aristotle writes, "Some of these views have been held by many men and men of old, others by a few persons; and it is not probable that either of these should be entirely mistaken, but rather that they should be right in at least some one respect or even in most respects" (*N.E.* 1098b26–9). The search for practical coherence leads the deliberator into theory, therefore, and for the three reasons given the theories of others are relevant and potentially helpful to the deliberator.

X

Ultimate ends

The task of this chapter is to show via examples how rational deliberation can embrace the dialectical specification and adoption of an ultimate end. Such realism as I can provide will be important, for an additional source of skepticism about deliberation extending to ultimate ends, beyond those mentioned in §28, is pragmatic rather than principled. It holds, not that the normative force of practical reasoning depends upon taking the ultimate end to be nondeliberable, but that people do not bother to extend their deliberation to the level of the ultimate end, which it views as a philosopher's abstract invention rather than a feature of ordinary deliberations. While philosophers may reason about ultimate ends, and while their reasoning may be subject to holistic checks, this does not mean that we can *deliberate* about ultimate ends. To counter this debunking form of doubt, I need to show how specification of an ultimate end can indeed enter into an individual's deliberation about what to do. Although this effort leads me into some fairly lengthy exercises at writing fiction, in some respects they remain not nearly detailed enough. In neither of my examples will I be able to do more than merely suggest the groping search for equilibrium that would characterize actual deliberations. By and large, all I can do is to trace out a realistic trajectory of deliberation's conclusions.

§31. VIRTUOUS DELIBERATORS

Since my examples of deliberation that extends to ultimate ends involve deliberators who begin with roughly Aristotelian or liberal commitments, I must confront the suspicion of circularity that this raises. Circularity might be a problem from two quite distinct points of view: that of my overall project of showing that rational deliberation can extend to ultimate ends, and that of holding open the potential objectivity of this deliberation. Since I will want to claim that the regulatory conception of the ultimate end, holistically specified, is well suited to objective development, I seek to address both of these aspects. I will discuss it with special reference to Aristotle, where it centers on the notion of practical wisdom (*phronēsis*).

In Aristotle's texts, the problem of circularity arises above all from the fact that he defines virtue as lying in a mean state as determined by the person of practical wisdom (the *phronimos*: N.E. 1107a1–2; cf. N.E. VI.1), while also holding that *phronēsis* requires virtue. Critical attention has focused on the question: How can the *phronimos* be identified independently of an antecedent conception of virtue? Do we have any neutral or ethically noncontroversial way of locating the virtuous so that we may learn from the deliverances of their perception? It has been doubted that we do (though in offering the example of Pericles, Aristotle invokes a then-common view about who has *phronēsis*). Posing the questions in this way places the emphasis on whether or not one can isolate a group whose faculties of perception are superior. Yet the reading of the importance of trained practical perception offered in §27 suggests a different way of seeing the circularity. The only reason to pay attention to the perceptions of the *phronimos*, on this alternative view, is that they are perceptions of ends that are virtuous. This shifts our worry to whether there is any way to identify virtue independently of the perceptions of the *phronimos*. The answer is yes: We can start with the *endoxa*, the considered judgments of the many and the wise, as to the content of virtue.

From the perspective of my own positive account of deliberative rationality, this is as far as I need to go with this question of circularity. In my Aristotelian example of the next section, I will be imagining a deliberator with what Aristotle would call virtuous commitments; but I have no need to assume that these represent true virtue. Indeed, the sort of relative rationality that this book extends to ultimate ends does not suffice to imply or require true virtue, much as true virtue may require reasoning about ends.

From the perspective of maintaining the possibility of objective rationality, however, it is important to push a little farther. The idea of a progressive specification of ends may help out with the further questions of ethical epistemology involved. It is true that in a certain sense Aristotle's definitions of virtue and *phronēsis*, so interpreted, are "logically defective" (Broadie 1991, 193) in that each is definitionally dependent on the other. Allowing for a bidirectional strategy of theory construction that works from the *endoxa*, however, it is easy enough to see how one might get initial fixes on virtue and on *phronēsis*, and that each could be progressively specified in tandem with the other. In particular, the content of virtue that is "as specified by" the person of practical wisdom would not, on this reading, be regarded as fixed. Rather, it would be seen as open to further specification as called for when new practical problems arise. The continuity preserved by the specification relation can help explain how it is that it is *virtue* that is being determined. In this way, as Aristotle contemplates, the "outline sketch" can be filled in.

§32. DELIBERATIVE REVISION OF AN ARISTOTELIAN HIGHEST GOOD

In this section I will develop an example portraying deliberation that revises the core elements of the ultimate end, as understood in a more or less Aristotelian way. The idea will be that this deliberation, which will parallel some of Aristotle's own arguments, will result in a view of the ultimate end that more nearly resembles Aristotle's own interpretation of the highest good than the one with which the deliberator, whom I will call Euboulos, started. Before I present the example, therefore, it will be useful for me to say a bit about Aristotle's interpretation of the highest good. Doing so will reinforce the fact that this deliberation concerns a paradigmatic ultimate end and will help make plausible §30's claim that dialectical argument can contribute to the deliberative specification thereof.

The core Aristotelian understanding of the highest good I take to have two principal elements, each of which is described in *N.E.* I.7.[1] The first of these is that the highest good must be an ultimate end, in just the sense analyzed above (with inspiration from Aristotle) in §29. That is, it must be the "most final" end, the only end sought only for its own sake, a notion that in turn may be understood in part in terms of its appropriate self-regulation. In addition, Aristotle characterizes the good as implying a special sort of "self-sufficiency" that makes a life choiceworthy and lacking in nothing (*N.E.* 1097b9–17). So the highest good is a self-sufficient ultimate end. Although other interpreters might wish to claim that additional features should be added to the list of formal characteristics of the highest good, these are the two I will focus upon. In fact I believe they are the principal defining marks of Aristotle's highest good. A prime example of further dialectical specification of the content of the highest good, focusing on these formal marks, may be found in Aristotle's dis-

---

1 I defend this interpretation of Aristotle's notion of the highest good in Richardson 1992a.

cussion of the place of friendship within the eudaimonic life in *N.E.* IX.9. My example centers on this issue.

To make it plausible that deliberation can get some purchase even on the formal marks of eudaimonia, I will describe at length a hypothetical case in which the content of the requirement or ideal of self-sufficiency is at issue. I will show that both this abstract ideal of self-sufficiency and its precise interpretation make a difference to the outcome of this case. I will illustrate how this formal aspect of eudaimonia can be at stake in deliberation and can be rationally specified according to the general conception of deliberation of ends. In turn, this will indirectly indicate how the overarching hypothesis of the end of eudaimonia (formally described) could be deliberatively set up or revised by a broader and more complicated deliberation than I can recapitulate here. The order of this hypothetical deliberation will be the opposite of Aristotle's argument, in that it will start with a refined conception of friendship and proceed to specify self-sufficiency and finality.

Imagine, then, the choice of Euboulos of Karystos, a fictional but virtuous young man of fourth-century Greece. Partly in reaction to seeing the ups and downs of his father's political career, Euboulos early became attached to the traditional ideal of self-sufficiency celebrated by the poets and philosophers. For the nonce, Euboulos understands self-sufficiency as independence from others. He wants to be like the great men of legend, whom he sees as self-sufficient. In addition to holding self-sufficiency valuable for its own sake, Euboulos believes that it will help ensure that one's life is pleasant. He is convinced that whatever else one might say about the happy life it must be pleasant, but also that happiness goes beyond pleasure. Another legacy from his father that Euboulos affirms on reflection is the view that one must live up to one's human potential. This will mean engaging in virtuous or excellent activity that both fulfills one's nature and is pleasant. Euboulos's departure from his father is to consider that another set of virtues besides the political virtues are the most important, at least for him. Perhaps idealistically, Euboulos also wants to aim for happiness in his own life. Further, let us suppose that he initially thinks of happiness as the one final end, the one end worth seeking for its own sake, all other ends being sought for its sake. Self-sufficiency and proper virtue will lead one to happiness, which in turn will comprise pleasure.

The combination of his enjoyment of philosophy and his commitment to self-sufficiency has led Euboulos to consider becoming a philosopher. Now a concrete option has come up that he is seriously weighing. Another young man from Karystos, also of a political family, had gone to Athens a few years earlier to study with Diogenes the Cynic. The youth has written home several times praising this idiosyncratic teacher as not only preaching a strict ideal of self-sufficiency but also living up to it. While Euboulos's father had strongly opposed his son's previous proposals for going to study in Athens, this recommendation by a fellow citizen of the same class has induced the older man to soften his opposition. Euboulos can go to Athens to study with Diogenes the Cynic if he wants. However, Euboulos is torn because he deeply values his friendship with Ariston, a youth of his same age and class with whom he had grown up in Karystos and in whom he had always confided his hopes and ideals. Euboulos fears that his going to Athens would spell the end of this friendship, which he values both as an instance of friendship in general and in its particularity. Being a sober and cultivated young man, Euboulos understands the value of this friendship as being grounded upon a shared commitment to living well and excellently, rather than upon a mere commercial sort of utility or the paltry and fleeting pleasures of social amusement. Unfortunately, unlike Euboulos, Ariston is committed to remaining in Karystos and becoming politically active there.

Faced with this particular conflict between friendship and self-sufficiency, Euboulos will naturally ask himself whether he is indeed committed to these two ends for their own sake. Would he pursue each even if nothing else – not even happiness – were to result from them? The answer is yes. When he pursues either of them – for instance friendship – are his decisions appropriately regulated solely by seeing the subordinate value merely as a means to happiness? In this conflict, would it be acceptable simply to determine which course provides the best means to happiness? He decides not, for he sees that these two other ends, though subordinate, each has claims of its own to regulating his choices, claims that would be washed out by seeing happiness as the only end with regulatory import. Being a brooding young man, he takes the two conflicting ends here very seriously indeed. He cannot abide the idea of simply "doing whatever will make him happy," as a carefree uncle advises. To reason in that way would be to fail to respect the true importance of his tie to Ariston and his commitment to the ideal of self-sufficiency. He concedes happiness a preeminent role in resolving the conflict, but a role necessarily compatible with describing the conflict as one between final ends. Since this is the first time he has consciously faced a conflict of final ends, this reflection will lead to a new specification of happiness's finality. He had held that all other ends are sought only for the sake of happiness. Now he realizes that other ends besides happiness are sought for their own sakes. Accordingly, he concludes that happiness must be, not the only final end, but the most final, or ultimate, end, in the sense of being the only end sought only for its own sake. While this specification better fits the structure of ends to which he is committed, there is no clear sense in which he is merely discovering that happiness is an ultimate end in this sense. Rather, this novel practical conflict elicits a specification that coheres with his other ends.

This conclusion does leave him somewhat puzzled, however, about what he means by "happiness." If happiness can regulate the other final ends, he decides, this is not because it is some supremely valuable state or activity wholly distinct from them to which they must bow, but instead because it somehow incorporates or makes reference to at least some of these final ends, structured in a certain way. This hypothesis is supported by the examples of the self-sufficient heroes he admires, whose lives seem to have been governed by quite complex ideals. In addition, Euboulos rejects the more single-minded interpretations of various of his contemporaries – those who seek their happiness solely in sybaritic pleasures, those who devote themselves fully to pursuing political honors, and even those ascetics who devote themselves so uncompromisingly to philosophy that they have let all friendships fall by the wayside. These men deprive themselves of a truly happy life, he feels, because they each fail to realize – or realize only badly – some important aspect of their human potential. If "happiness" is to name the ultimate end that would correct for these failings, then it must name an excellent or virtuous way of living that accommodates within it multiple final ends corresponding to different facets of human nature. This specification of his conception of happiness is thus supported by his particular commitments to self-sufficiency and self-realization.

With this revision in his "priorities" to guide him, Euboulos now must confront the conflict between self-sufficiency and friendship itself. Are these final ends really at odds, here, or can he reconcile their demands? He needs to examine more closely how he would specify these aims. To begin with, he asks himself, does self-sufficiency logically exclude friendship? Thinking of the past heroes he had considered self-sufficient, Euboulos realizes that most of them provided for the needs of the household without depending on outside aid. Since he takes friendship in general to be a final end, Euboulos has reason to specify self-sufficiency in a way that logically allows for friendship. Further, he believes that human nature, of which happiness expresses the flourishing, is sociable. Both these reasons give him grounds to specify self-sufficiency as a kind of independence that does not imply a solitary existence and potentially applies to a person who lives together with his parents, children, and wife, and more generally with his friends (cf. *N.E.* I.7, 1097b9–12). Euboulos notes that even Diogenes, while in many ways antisocial, does not live as a hermit, but instead lectures in Athens and takes on students. Furthermore, Euboulos understands that his friendship with Ariston does not imply that he stands in need of something – a useful item of commerce, say, or light amusement – for the sake of which the friendship is pursued. A friendship such as his with Ariston is pursued for its own sake. This discrimination suggests to Euboulos a related distinction in the kind of independence built into the ideal of self-sufficiency. He had initially thought of this independence negatively, as an almost literal cutting off from society, a lack of interaction with others. Now he has reached the thought that one's self-sufficiency means that one has no need of interacting with others, in the sense that there is nothing he needs to get from others. A self-sufficient life, as it is, contains all that one needs. If so, then virtue-friendship, which does not imply any literal neediness, seems logically compatible with the self-sufficiency of a life lived with others.

Fine. But Euboulos will want to figure out more concretely how friendship fits into this self-sufficient life. What are the goods that the self-sufficient life must contain? Since Euboulos's end of self-sufficiency is part of his overall conception of happiness, he can look to this more general guiding idea for an answer to this question. Since happiness (he holds) is a life of pleasant self-sufficiency, the self-sufficiency he is most concerned with is pleasant. On reflection it seems right to him that the self-sufficiency he aims at is not a life of miserable insularity. And since happiness is both an ultimate end and self-sufficient, it will enhance the coherence of his ends to understand the self-sufficient life in a way that is compatible with it being an ultimate end. This observation initially suggests to Euboulos that the self-sufficient life must contain all final goods; but soon he realizes that he cannot live his life by that ideal. There are too many things he values for their own sake: friendship and self-sufficiency, but also excellence in music and oratory and other aims as well. Further, he knows he could be perfectly happy (could live a perfectly good life) without realizing all of these aims. Accordingly, he decides he must specify more narrowly the set of goods that a self-sufficient life must include. His conception of happiness already contains a principled ground for doing so. He thinks of happiness as a self-sufficient life that expresses the completion or fulfillment of shared human nature. Again taking the happy self-sufficient life as the paradigm of self-sufficiency, he can say that the final goods that must be included in a self-sufficient life are the goods that are final for all men by nature. This degree of inclusion does not seem absurd to Euboulos. It fits with his concentration on friendship and self-sufficiency, which all men do seek – music and oratory being more particular interests. This specification finally yields a workable version of his ideal of self-sufficiency.

Now he must determine whether friendship of the sort he has with Ariston is a good final by nature. I have already said that he values his friendship with Ariston for its own sake. He also finds being with Ariston and benefiting him intrinsically pleasant. He wonders whether this is an accident of his particular constitution – if it were, it would not be supported by his newly specified conception of happiness. On the basis of the following dialectical argument, picked up from his fellow intellectuals, he decides that it is no personal quirk: Pleasure, he began by thinking, is a kind of activity. Taking this idea seriously, he decides that pleasure decomposes into various kinds of pleasant activity. Consistently with the role of the notion of human nature in his notion of happiness, which he views in part as a life of pleasant activity, Euboulos specifies the naturally pleasant as activity that expresses a completed or developed human nature and that is one's own. Now since Euboulos and Ariston are both virtuous, he rather smugly concludes, their actions generally reflect a shared aspect of human nature. Further, Euboulos considers even the actions of Ariston that he merely hears about or observes as in some sense "his own."[2] He is ashamed when his friend acts badly and proud when he acts well. These considerations give him grounds for believing that the pleasure that he gets from his friendship with Ariston is pleasant by nature. If it is pleasant by nature, then it is choiceworthy by nature, and hence one of the goods that the self-sufficient man must have. Once self-sufficiency and friendship are respecified in these ways, therefore, there is not even a contingent conflict between these two ends. Self-sufficiency demands that such friendships as Euboulos has with Ariston be a part of one's life.[3] It does

---

2 I do not believe that Aristotle's statement that the friend is "another oneself" (*heteros autos*: 1170b7) requires any other construal than the relatively unexciting and metaphorical one I have adopted here.

3 Aristotle concludes the argument in *N.E.* IX.9 in exactly these terms. To make this plain, I will quote the passage with explanatory glosses inserted between square brackets: "If, then, existence is desirable in itself for the blessed man (since it is by its nature good and pleasant), and that of his friend is very much the same, a friend will be one of the things that are desirable [in itself by nature]. Now that which is desirable [in itself] for him [and if for him then by nature: 1170a14–15] he must have, or he will be deficient [or "lacking":

not require the sort of withdrawal from the active life characteristic of the philosopher. Since this resolution helps build mutual support among his ends as specified, Euboulos has reason to accept it.

Does this mean that Euboulos should stay in Karystos? One cannot conclude that so fast. Having revised his conception of self-sufficiency, and accordingly his conception of happiness, he has far less reason to go study with Diogenes the Cynic than he had thought. But his deliberations have suggested a lot of other considerations that he must weigh before he makes his final decision. We can anticipate one difficulty he may face. It may turn out that philosophical contemplation, too, is a naturally final end. If so, Euboulos will have escaped one conflict of ends only to fall into another. How he might deal with the second conflict is a topic for another day.

I have presented this story of Euboulos's deliberation so exhaustively for a reason. I wanted to illustrate in a fairly realistic way how deliberative specification of ends could productively use the full range of arguments that Aristotle deploys in the *Nicomachean Ethics*. For instance, it arrives at the specifications of self-sufficiency and finality Aristotle offers in I.7 and reproduces his dialectical argument about the value of friendship in IX.9. I would like the reader to be convinced by this example that deliberative specification of ends could follow the course of the whole of the *Nicomachean Ethics*. In addition, although I purposefully cast it as working toward an Aristotelian interpretation of the highest good, I hope that it shows how that notion may be of use in an individual's deliberations about practical problems. Broadie has argued that the Aristotelian highest good cannot have this function, and is instead a goal only for the politician who aims to foster the conditions necessary for citizens' happiness (Broadie 1991, 45–7; cf. Richardson 1992c). Her argument, however, is addressed against the view that all practical problems are to be solved by deducing answers from a fixed interpretation of the ultimate end. On the sort of account I have been developing, by contrast, the ultimate end aids deliberation as a sketch that may be progressively specified in the course of deliberation. Euboulos's deliberative specification of happiness, finality, and self-sufficiency is an example of how this process might work at the most abstract reaches, yet remain a course of deliberation addressed to a particular practical decision. Euboulos's specifications are everywhere guided by arguments laying out the mutual support to be attained by

the same adjective as in the definition of the self-sufficiency requirement] in this respect. The man who is to be happy [*eudaimon*] will therefore need virtuous friends."

specifying in the suggested ways. This is not to say that these arguments are unassailable. My thesis is simply that they are responsible to common standards of rational criticism.

The example of Euboulos illustrates my claim that no aspect of an ultimate end is immune in principle from deliberative revision. He initially pursued a highest good, "happiness," interpreted positively only in terms of finality and negatively only as being distinct from pleasure. In the course of his deliberation, this conception gets significantly revised and specified. Simple finality becomes unique, unqualified finality. Happiness becomes interpreted in terms of multifold human excellence and self-sufficiency. Solitary self-sufficiency becomes social self-sufficiency inclusive of natural final ends. Each of these specifications and revisions is occasioned by a particular practical conflict and resolves that conflict in an unexpected way. In short, there is nothing about this ultimate end which is not subject to deliberation. Furthermore, since happiness, as Euboulos interprets it, is an ultimate end that embraces the virtues and the natural goods and organizes a conception of a good life, to specify happiness is to be able to specify all of one's ends.

Nonetheless, since Euboulos began with a conception of an ultimate or uniquely final end, albeit not yet defined in precisely Aristotelian fashion, one may suspect that there remains a still more abstract core of the idea of an ultimate end that stands immune from deliberation. To counter this remaining possibility, I will turn to an example in which rational deliberation sets up an ultimate end where there had been none.

§33. RAWLSIAN SPECIFICATION OF POLITICAL IDEALS

As a second example of deliberation involving an ultimate end, it will be useful to move to a philosophical context sharply divergent from Aristotle's theory of the human good. Since the theory of deliberation that I have been developing is broadly Aristotelian, one may suspect that while it serves well to explain Aristotle's own elaboration of the ultimate end, it may not be as useful outside Aristotle's system. More generally, I seek to show that holistic deliberation of ends can proceed from any of a broad variety of starting points. It remains a form of relative rationality (§3). Like the models of instrumental rationality that it seeks to supplement, my model of deliberation of ends is meant to accept a broad range of possible initial inputs. A particularly striking way of showing that the model is not tied to an Aristotelian content would be to show that it can proceed within a Kantian view, in which individuals' pursuit of happiness is sharply constrained by the requirements of morality and claims about natural teleology do not play a central role in determining the content of what is to be sought.

John Rawls's development of a liberal theory of political justice fits this bill, for two reasons. First, Rawls's subject matter – the justice of the "basic structure of society," or of its "constitutional essentials" – does not significantly overlap with that of the *Nicomachean Ethics*. In Rawls's case, unlike Aristotle's, we are dealing from the outset with political ideals to which individuals subscribe, but which are potentially distinct from their personal aims. Second, Rawls self-consciously develops his theory for conditions of pluralism, marked above all by the prevalence of multiple, incommensurable conceptions of the good in society (Rawls 1971, 127). Whereas Aristotle proceeds in the confidence that there is a human good to be understood, Rawls prefers to remain relatively noncommittal about the human good, and instead limits his value claims to the presuppositions appropriate for a theory of justice for the basic structure. Rawls, like Kant, takes the diversity of human conceptions of the good as a principal reason for refraining from developing a philosophical account of the good as the basis for a political conception of justice. Instead, Rawls's theory starts out directly from considered judgments about justice rather than from individuals' pursuits, and builds a theory of justice that exhibits how those considered judgments, once systematized, constrain the basic structure of society rather than forming the ultimate end for all our striving.

In *A Theory of Justice*, Rawls set out to give "a consistent rendering" to a number of political ideals that had been thought by many to be at least potentially at odds. If seen as capital-letter abstractions maximally realized in libertarian and welfare-state systems, respectively, Liberty and Equality obviously pull us in incompatible directions. Rawls aimed to build a consistent view importantly incorporating each of these ideals, partly by interpreting them and partly by imposing a priority ordering among three principles (Rawls 1971, 106, 204; Rawls 1982, 41). Liberty comes first in order of priority. The first principle of Rawls's "justice as fairness" requires that the basic structure afford each person an equal right to a fully adequate scheme of equal basic liberties compatible with a similar scheme of liberties for all (Rawls 1982, 5). By specifying that he is speaking of liberties rather than liberty, Rawls helps to move the discussion off Liberty as a capital-letter abstraction. If we think of Liberty as an abstraction, it seems conceivable to go about maximizing it, and hence to sacrifice all in its name. By insisting that the liberties be thought of as a concrete plurality, Rawls fends off such a quantitative interpretation of liberty (Rawls 1982, 47–9). Further qualifying the first principle by requiring that the relevant liberties be "basic" to the constitutional tradition of Western liberal democracies is another important step toward reconciling the three Revolutionary ideals. Equality, in its turn, is not treated as a simple pattern to be approximated. Instead, Rawls suggests, it is already represented in the insistence upon equal liberties noted above and in the principle next in order of priority, which requires that basic social institutions ensure a fair equality of opportunity. Finally, the remaining principle – the famous "difference principle" – which holds that inequalities in life chances that are allowed by the other principles must also redound to the benefit of the least advantaged, expresses not only an aspect of equality but also a commitment to the fraternity of citizens. In thus beginning essentially with a project of reconciliation, Rawls's project takes a very different shape from Aristotle's of giving content to the bare notion of eudaimonia. Rawls's issue more resembles the problems of conflicts of value discussed in §§6 and 22. Like Aristotle, however, Rawls quite self-consciously arranges his theory as a progressive specification of some highly vague ideals. Rawls's theory specifies ends so as to enhance the mutual support among them. In recent writings, Rawls expresses his aim to reconcile the values of freedom and equality by referring to an "overarching fundamental intuitive idea," which can be regarded as a second stage and as the *expository* starting point of his theory. This is the idea "of society as a fair system of cooperation between free and equal persons."[4] For my Rawlsian example, I draw on arguments made by Rawls himself about the special importance of assuring the equal worth to all citizens – the "fair-value" – of the political liberties (cf. Rawls 1971, 224–8, 233–4, 277–9; 1982, 42–6). Of course, if Rawls himself were appointed to the Supreme Court, there would be no surprise in seeing his ideals have practical impact. To show how ideals of this sort can play a role in deliberation without the direct interference of philosophers, however, my example balances the basic virtue of its deliberator with the seaminess of her surroundings.

She is a Democratic candidate for the U.S. Congress in the initial stages

4 Rawls 1985, 231. Although Rawls there uses the term "ideal-based" to describe his own theory (236n.), the revision of this essay in Rawls 1993 drops the term and reaffirms his commitment to bidirectionality and holism (8n., 45, 242n.). Accordingly, I think that it avoids misunderstandings to think of the "fundamental intuitive ideas" as "fundamental" only in the expository sense of serving as a beginning and the deliberative sense of serving as an abstract ideal to specify, and not in any justificatory or foundational sense.

of her campaign. A central theme of her candidacy is her argument that the Republican administrations of the preceding decades have been too blind to what has been called "the fairness issue." That is, they have been too insensitive to the importance of distributive fairness and equality across a whole range of issues, from tax reform to trade policy. Yet the Candidate is adamant that she does not simply wish to revert to the old confidence in the strongly centralized welfare state. The vast regulatory missions of earlier decades not only wasted taxpayers' money, she feels, but also affronted individual liberty in various ways. Accordingly, she would prefer to address issues of fairness by making the income tax structure more progressive. To sum up her position in a slogan, she adheres to liberty *and* equality: neither without the other. We may further assume that this is not merely a slogan for her. She is deeply committed to these ideals, and views her political vocation as directed toward their realization. A former law professor (though not a philosopher), she is also quite reflective in her approach.

Given her criticism of previous Democratic programs that attempted to promote fairness or equality, she obviously knows that these two ideals are in tension. In particular, she has been sensitive to criticism from her friends farther to the left, who argue that her focus on fairness through tax reform neglects the position of the truly poor, who cannot benefit from a reduction in income tax rates since they pay none in any case. The poor, these friends argue, lose out on both counts, for the liberties that they are assured by the Constitution are vitiated in practice because they lack the means to exercise them. Their liberty to work, to buy a home, and to pursue happiness are merely "parchment guarantees," meaningless in practice. These liberties lack practical worth for them. In response to these criticisms, the Candidate has developed the following defense of her dual commitment to liberty and equality. One prong of it mirrors Rawls's emphasis on basic constitutional liberties. These most important liberties, she holds, reside more in the Bill of Rights than in the Declaration of Independence and aim more at preserving procedural fairness than at promoting happiness. A second prong of the Candidate's Rawlsian reconciliation of liberty and equality is a distinction between basic liberties and their practical worth to those that have them (cf. Rawls 1971, 204–5; 1982, 40–1). Third, by accepting a rough partition of basic social institutions into two fundamentally different kinds of institutions – those (especially the courts) establishing basic rights and liberties and those (especially the administrative bureaucracy) effecting the distribution of advantages – she further has decided to treat poverty and relative deprivation as affecting the worth of liberty rather than as (by definition) show-ing that these liberties do not exist. This distinction is basic to her working reconciliation of liberty and equality, for equal liberties are to be assured by the constitutional scheme of rights, to which any more strongly redis-tributive efforts aimed at shoring up the practical worth of these liberties should be held subordinate. In this way, appropriate provision for material equality or fairness for the poorest will be prevented from overwhelming the scheme of equal basic liberties, yet will not be neglected. In concrete political terms, again, this means that the Candidate is a stronger supporter of the American Civil Liberties Union than of the welfare state.

Now, however, the Candidate faces a challenge from a different direc-tion. Initially, she had decided that her campaign would accept donations from so-called political action committees (PACs) – entities that are set up, usually by powerful industrial or lobbying organizations and associa-tions, so as to funnel money to favored candidates. Contributions from PACs tend to be quite sizable, for they are not subject to the same legal limitations as are contributions from individuals. The Candidate's oppo-nent – who happens to be wealthy enough to finance his campaign with his own money – has decided to attack her on the basis of her acceptance of PAC contributions. The negative advertisements picking up this theme have a double message. First, they cast doubt on the sincerity of her com-mitment to equality: "This candidate professes to be a friend of the dis-advantaged, yet accepts huge contributions from powerful corporations." Second, they ridicule her "liberty plus equality" theme as inconsistent: "Is she for the liberty to make political contributions unfettered by gov-ernment restrictions, or for the equal influence on the political process assured by one-person–one-vote? Which is it? She will not say. Vote for the candidate who will tell it to you straight!" She must decide how to respond to these ads, and in particular whether to stop accepting PAC money. Although there are of course many strategic considerations per-taining to this decision, these ads have caused her to wonder, as she oth-erwise might not have, whether her dual ideal is truly coherent. Being a conscientious person, she wants to work this out.

Trying to be helpful, her advertising consultant suggests a new slogan that would embrace freedom and equality while sounding less dualistic. Echoing the Great Society platform of Lyndon Johnson, it trumpets a Well-Ordered Society, in which is achieved "a system of fair cooperation between free and equal persons." (While she could have picked up this idea from reading Rawls, I seek to emphasize that it could enter merely as a verbal formula, without any central practical commitment to it that would suggest top-down reasoning.) The Candidate likes this new turn of phrase, and will try to work it into her speeches; but is it just an empty verbal formula, or does it really suggest a way of reconciling her twin political ideals? She decides that it does, in fact, have a number of important substantive virtues. To begin with, it reflects her commitment to the strong form of practical coherence implied by her insistence upon looking to her ideals of freedom and equality as a basis for her concrete political platform. If these ideals are to guide her through policy decisions here and now, then they must be coherent not merely in principle but also in light of the contingent facts. Further, this formula explicitly connects freedom and equality to another broad ideal that she had had in mind, but had not seen as having particular political implications, namely that of society as a system of fair cooperation, characterized by the rule of law and above all by a stable constitutional system. Although recognizing that this general ideal is not a subject of controversy in most American politics, she decides that articulating it is important, for it sets out that freedom and equality are not to be pursued in the abstract, but within the context of a workable constitutional scheme. In addition, by casting freedom and equality as features of this scheme, it builds into those ideals the sort of subordination to constitutional order that she thinks appropriate. Accordingly, she decides that this new slogan, which represents her political ideals in a newly unitary way, is one that she would endorse on reflection as enhancing the mutual support among them.

Yet this general ideal will be of no help in her present predicament unless she can put it to use in working out a position on accepting PAC money. Her opponent's attack has raised doubts in her mind about the validity of her separation between the basic liberties and their equal worth. PACs epitomize how economic power can undercut the practical value of an ordinary citizen's political liberties. In an election in which PAC money flows freely, she fears, the voice of the individual citizen who is not affiliated with one of these associations gets drowned out, and the value of this citizen's political liberty gets effectively nullified. Now, this is a consideration that threatens to undermine altogether her roughly Rawlsian compromise between liberty and equality, for the way it is worked out depends crucially upon the distinction between the liberties and their worth. (For a full development of such a criticism, see Pogge 1989, §§11–12.) Simply assuring everyone – actual persons and legal persons alike – the legal liberty to participate in political campaigns will fall far short of guaranteeing each citizen equal influence over the political process. Yet a direct commitment to the equal worth of liberty seems too utopian and too costly, from a practical point of view.

I imagine her meeting this difficulty by revising the reconciliation between liberty and equality that has been sketched out so far. She will do so by means of a distinction, used to specify further the scope of the liberties to which a strong requirement of equal worth applies. This distinction is suggested and supported by her new unitary slogan with its implicit focus on the constitutional system. It is the distinction between the political liberties (what Rawls, following Constant, calls the "liberties of the ancients"), especially the freedom of equal political participation, and the civil liberties ("the liberties of the moderns": cf. Rawls 1971, 201, 222; 1982, 13), including the freedoms of expression and movement. Rather than applying a first-priority requirement of equal worth to all of the liberties, the Candidate (like Rawls) decides that only the political liberties must be subject to equalization. The reasoning behind this differential is simple: Although the liberties of the person may have an intrinsic value even greater than the liberties of political participation, the latter control the procedural fairness of the legislative process. If this procedure is perverted, then the rich and powerful will not merely enjoy liberties of de facto greater worth; they will also be able to pass laws that tailor the liberties and other social rules to their own advantage. In this way, the disparity in the practical worth of the basic liberties could be magnified over time. In part because the Candidate's personal ideal is to contribute, by participating in the legislature, to an instance of "quasi-pure procedural justice," in which a fair procedure adequately continues specifying the general ideals of justice (cf. Rawls 1971, 362), protecting the integrity and fairness of this procedure is of central importance to her. For these reasons, then, she decides that the equal practical worth, or "fair value," of the basic political liberties must be guaranteed.

Having arrived at this respecification of her initial ideals of freedom and equality in light of her new unified ideal of fair cooperation, the Candidate will have strong reason to rule out accepting contributions from PACs. The very existence of PACs, she will naturally conclude, represents an affront to the requirement of the fair value of political liberties, resulting in tremendous inequalities in influence upon the electoral process. Whether this new specification of her political ideals actually leads her to refuse to accept PAC money may depend, of course, on other factors (as at the parallel point in the example of Euboulos), such as how she deals with the tension between them and her desire to get elected. For our purposes, however, the important point is that she has arrived at a new conception of the political ideal by which she aims to regulate her conduct.

I have cast this example as a case in which someone moves toward a unified conception of their ideal of political justice. The Candidate being a professional politician sincerely committed to justice, this ideal is for her an end. Whether it is an *ultimate* end depends on whether it requires regulation by any other end, or rather is seen as appropriately self-limiting. This in turn depends upon the strength of her sense of justice, and in particular on whether she accepts the Rawlsian claim that the requirements of justice or "the reasonable" should "frame" or delimit any other aspect of one's conception of the good. Rawls, of course, argues that the citizens of the well-ordered society corresponding to justice as fairness will see the requirements of political justice as delimiting their pursuit of all other goods, and that the social institutions of this society will tend to support the formation of this strong commitment. Certainly, such people seem possible. For them, political justice can be an ultimate end – not a "dominant end" in Rawls's sense, as something simply to be maximized, but as an ultimate end as I have defined it, namely an end sought for its own sake and only for its own sake, not needing to be regulated by reference to any further end for the sake of which it is sought. In fact, Rawls's talk of the right "framing" the good suggests this status for justice, for it allows that individuals' other ends will enter into the progressive specification of their overall commitments, so long as this remains compatible with the fundamental requirements of justice. Lest I be misunderstood, let me repeat that I do not mean that Rawls puts forward justice as the ultimate end, nor that his theory implicitly depends upon such a claim. Rather, for the citizen of the well-ordered society with an effective sense of justice, I am suggesting, justice would have the status of an ultimate end.

To make realistic the claim that the Candidate may set up justice as an ultimate end by the sort of reasoning sketched above, we need only add that she had taken the claims of political equality and political liberty to be peremptory. Suppose, in other words, that at the outset she had thought of each of these ideals to which she and others ought to conform and adapt their pursuit of other goods. She viewed each, in other words, as ends more final than personal advantage or happiness. None of her other ends, furthermore, have any appropriate claim to regulating the demands of these political ideals. Yet neither equality nor liberty was an ultimate end, for each had to bow to the demands of the other. By integrating them into one coherent ideal, and therein retaining and indeed strengthening their claim to frame or delimit subordinate goods, she adopts through deliberation an ultimate end where she had had none. Because of the way this "larger plan" respects the force of these subordinate considerations, however, this ultimate end is not what Rawls calls a "dominant end" (1971, 528): it is not a commensurans. Some of the rational support of this deliberation was set out in my story, while for the rest I lean on Rawls's fuller argument. The conclusion is that rational deliberation can set up an ultimate end.

To conclude this part of my argument, let me briefly pull together the various results already reached. Allowing for deliberation of ends in general depends upon seeing the qualitatively regulatory role that ends have (§7). Once this is recognized, the fact that deliberation can specify initial commitments can be shown to imply that it can promote them to the status of final ends (§13). Defending the rationality of this sort of move depends importantly on seeing that systematization may be built bidirectionally and holistically (Chapter VIII). The Candidate's reasoning also followed a promoting path: Equality and liberty each being final ends, the conception of justice accommodating them in a coherent way might easily be regarded as not needing further regulation by anything else. Yes, liberty and equality each needed regulation in terms of the other; but the combined ideal of political justice does not. It is adjusted so that it need not be further regulated by any other end. This way of arriving at an ultimate end through rational deliberation is conceptually possible so long as an ultimate end is not seen as a source of value, but instead as a supremely regulatory aim (§29).

In addition to promoting an end to ultimate status, we can deliberate about any aspect of an ultimate end's content. This was the point of the last section's example, which focused on the two central defining elements in Aristotle's conception of the highest good, finality and self-sufficiency. These were shown to be revisable in deliberation. If two such defining elements can be rationally revised, then any aspect of an ultimate end may be specified and revised in deliberation. This process can be rational because it can appeal to practical coherence for its justification.

In sum, an ultimate end may be set up or adopted by rational deliberation and revised by rational deliberation. In every important sense, therefore, we may rationally deliberate concerning ends, including ultimate ends. While the Aristotelian and Rawlsian structures of argument do afford considerable potential for objective criticism of initial ends, whether deliberation about ends can be objective is a question I postpone until after we have faced the challenges involved in deep cultural disagreement.

Part Five

Disagreement

XI

Interpersonal deliberation

There are both defensive and constructive reasons to try to extend my account of deliberation of ends to explicitly interpersonal contexts. To begin with the obvious positive reasons, the nature of interpersonal deliberation is of interest in its own right, both philosophically and practically. Much actual deliberation is interpersonal. Even when a single individual is deciding what to do with his or her life, he or she may seek advice from others and deliberate with them about some personal choice. More strictly interpersonal are the discussions within groups and institutions of various kinds about what that body will do. As a practical matter, we would like to know to what extent the theory of individual deliberation developed in the last chapters can apply to the setting of ends in these interpersonal settings. Whether the general account of rational deliberation of ends I have developed can extend to interpersonal settings is not the same question as whether it can be objective. Philosophically, however, interpersonal deliberation is of interest not only because of the structural problems posed by interpersonal settings, but also because as we try to extend the theory of individual deliberation to the interpersonal setting, additional scope for objectivity will enter. I do not mean to imply that intersubjectivity is equivalent to objectivity; but if there is some correlation between the two, then the attempt to work out an intersubjectively acceptable understanding of final ends would require attaining a greater degree of objectivity than does an individual's deliberation of ends. The very least one can say is that the issue of interpersonal deliberation of ends raises issues of objectivity in interesting ways not yet treated by my account of individual deliberation. Although I will continue to work out the possibilities of a rationality relative to individuals' initial commitments, I will also be concerned to show what room there is for objectivity in their shared deliberations about final ends.

§34. THE NEED TO TAKE UP INTERPERSONAL DELIBERATION

The defensive reason that I must consider interpersonal deliberation at this point – a reason that exists wholly independently from any attempt at objectivity – is that otherwise there would remain an important weakness in my argument that individuals can deliberate rationally about ends. This danger may be brought out in terms of the following objection. My account of rational deliberation hinges on likening an individual's revision of her ends to working out a theory of her practical commitments. The guiding idea is for her to work out a theory that exhibits strong mutual support among the various ends to which she is committed. In the last chapter I presented a pair of examples designed to show how this effort at self-understanding could extend to ultimate ends. Yet the implications of these examples are severely limited, the objection now goes, for in each case I simply assumed the existence of a deliberator with a fairly coherent and culturally homogeneous set of initial commitments. What assurance is there that deliberators whose initial commitments are not so homogeneous – who are not "rigged" so as to come out with Aristotelian or Rawlsian conclusions – will be able to deliberate rationally about ends? The "possibility" of deliberation of ends is not so interesting if it simply refers to the fact that one can coherently imagine certain deliberators whose initial commitments are such that minor revisions in them will lead to a unified view of an ultimate end. We wanted to know more generally whether it is possible for *us* to deliberate rationally about ends!

This objection can be given still more bite by reference to the common situation of modern societies. In ways that I will examine in detail in §36, many societies, including our own, are marked by a plurality of radically different conceptions of the good. Especially in fairly mobile and socially somewhat fluid societies such as the contemporary United States, this means that the sort of deliberator imagined in the last chapter, who has a set of initial commitments that are potentially coherent because they have a unitary cultural source, will be comparatively rare. Indeed, if Alasdair MacIntyre (1984) is to be believed, moral discourse has broken down in modern societies in large part because of the Babel of contrasting cultural and philosophical influences that are jumbled together in our upbringing. In the meantime, however, it is obvious enough that the phenomena of cultural pluralism from which he begins do make it unsatisfying to rest the case for deliberation of ends on the supposition that one starts with Aristotelian or Rawlsian deliberators, each brought up within a single

232

tradition. In our current cultural circumstances, we want to know whether rational deliberation can bridge the kinds of divergence that cultural pluralism creates.

Insofar as my discussion is confined to responding to this objection, it will enter into interpersonal deliberation only in an ersatz way. The objection threatens to undercut Part Four's results regarding an individual's deliberation. As such, it can be tested by reference to a single deliberator whose initial commitments, rather than being more or less from a single tradition, are instead themselves deeply split. This is the individual from a divided background – someone with a mother from one culture and a father from another, someone who spent childhood in one society and adolescence in another, someone whose country underwent revolutionary changes during his or her lifetime, or someone whose personal conversions and varied attachments has left him or her with a confusion of divergent values. If MacIntyre is right, all of us in modern society are in this boat; but it helps focus the objection to imagine a single deliberator who fully embodies the splits of cultural diversity. In pursuing this hypothesis, I will ignore constraints of psychological realism. The divided individuals I discuss are less integrated than perhaps anyone could really be and still remain rational; yet as individuals they each have all the reasons to seek practical coherence set out in §22. From this point of view, the question is: Can such people deliberate rationally about ends, and if so how? If such people could overcome the barriers to rational deliberation of ends, then the objection from cultural incommensurability fails. In thus nominally reinserting the problems of diversity within the bounds of an individual psyche to deal with this objection, I will be treating the distinct problems of interpersonal deliberation only indirectly rather than head on.

Even when I touch more constructively on interpersonal deliberation, I will abstract from two important features of political deliberation, the division of deliberative responsibility and the authority of process. The first of these features correlates with the division of labor, and tends to characterize all human institutions, political and otherwise. In any complex organization, even the most democratic, not all members deliberate about everything the organization does; and even in the most autocratic there is no one person who makes all decisions. That this is so becomes particularly obvious if one thinks in terms of the progressive specification of norms; for example, while there may be one person who has general oversight of production and marketing, say, there is no one person who thinks both about the quality-control mechanism of the widget assembly line and the precise placement of magazine advertisements for widgets.

The second feature, reliance upon a process of interpersonal deliberation invested with some authority of its own, is again a typical way in which the division of deliberative responsibility is realized institutionally (cf. Hurley 1989, 339–48). Yet as a historical matter, things might well develop the other way around, division of substantive concern following upon the establishment of a legitimate process. As this highly schematic outline of these common features of human groups already indicates, a thorough look at interpersonal deliberation would confront some important philosophical issues not involved in an individual's deliberation. These include questions about how a division of deliberative responsibility can be justified or explained; whether it is compatible with the sort of holism that I have been defending; how one can characterize the "thinking" of the organization that relies upon it to carry out its functions; also what would make a process of interpersonal deliberation legitimate; in what circumstances, if any, individual deliberators ought rationally to defer to the process; and how such a process might best be structured to promote the rationality of collective deliberation. In abstracting from these issues, I acknowledge, I will be leaving the distinctive problems of political deliberation to one side.

The more abstract approach to interpersonal deliberation that I will be taking is better captured by the idea of negotiation. This is interpersonal, yet requires no set structure of issues nor any presumed authority. Even deeply divided parties may negotiate. And while the dictionary suggests that in negotiations there is some matter to settle, what this is may initially be quite vague and variously understood. There is some difference or dispute, and practical concerns on either side prompt an effort at a deliberated resolution. Insofar as the idea of negotiation suggests that individuals are on either one predefined side or another, however, I will sometimes abstract from this idea, too. My real concern is with how differences in culture and values impede rational deliberation.

§35. THE DIFFICULTY OF EXTENDING THE VIEW

The protean nature of the ideal of coherence may encourage the thought that the account of deliberation developed in Part Three may simply be generalized to cover interpersonal deliberation. After all, Rawls puts forward the idea of reflective equilibrium in the hope that one day all citizens may *share* one. Cannot *we* together seek mutually supporting specifications of *our* ends? Surely it would be an objectionable form of individualism, bordering upon solipsism, to suppose that individuals formed their norms in isolation from social and cultural influences! Why not then take the next step, and acknowledge that deliberation of ends is intrinsically part of a broader social dialogue? Unquestionably, it is. I would not want to underrate the importance of the "social construction" of individuals. What I do want to do in this section, however, is to set out why, despite this, it will not do simply to suppose that the account of deliberation so far offered may be transferred to the social stage simply by being writ larger.

The difficulty of so extending my view centers on the essential role it accords to embodied reflection. Recall that my proposals about deliberation of ends hinge on reflectiveness in two ways. The first, which is important to showing what alternative there is to appealing to a single norm of the highest authority, and hence to relying upon a commensurans, is the idea of reflective sovereignty (§26). Rather than investing final authority in some norm or other, as it were, the deliberator retains the authority to accept or reject a given specification of his or her norms. The second, which further elaborates the sense in which practical deliberation is a "Socratic" subject, marked by self-examination, is the emphasis on the importance of self-perception (§27). Emotionally guided perception of oneself and of one's circumstances, I argued, is crucial to bringing forward aspects of the agent's commitments that would otherwise remain submerged. Each of these roles for reflection highlights that deliberation occurs within an embodied psyche. Reflective acceptance is intrinsically a psychological act, not abstractable in the form of a set of rules or propositions. If it were, then those would become the hidden, ultimately authoritative norms of fixed characterization; but I have argued that there are none such. Accordingly, it is the deliberator him- or herself – as a self – that remains sovereign in deliberation. The emotionally aided forms of self-perception, in particular, bring to the fore the embodied aspects of the self. Queasiness in the stomach and palpitations of the heart, in addition to the more cognitive aspects of emotions, can be clues as important in deliberation as anything seen or heard. Human deliberation essentially relies upon such bodily signs to remind us of our practical commitments. While one might imagine an agent constructed so that all of its normative commitments are explicitly present to it, as in a set of instructions in a computer program, it is not clear what relevance this idea would have for the possibilities of our deliberation about ends.

Neither of these reflective features of deliberation transfers easily to an interpersonal context. No group of people is a "self" in the relevant sense. While a group may together reflect about some question, there are no

235

general grounds to expect that there will be a locus of reflective sovereignty within the group. Perhaps some locus or framework of reflective sovereignty could arise or even be deliberately constructed, as through a social compact or constitutional convention. This possibility branches off toward topics in political theory that I leave aside for now. Even granting the existence of a legitimate, sovereign decision-making body or structure within a polity, however, it will not be easy to extend the idea of reflective sovereignty to this level. If "sovereignty" is retained in "the people," as is sometimes said about the United States, for instance, then the mere existence of a legitimate political sovereign will do nothing to explain how that sovereign can reflect upon its various commitments in such a way as to resolve conflicts aptly and authoritatively. To do so in a way truly analogous to the account of individual deliberation would seem to require thinking of all of the citizens as forming a supraindividual self capable of reflection; and such an idea is a fiction more extreme even than any concocted by Rousseau. If, by contrast, political sovereignty is located in a more limited body then the question will arise how the deliberation involved is really interpersonal. Consider for simplicity an absolute monarch who literally is the sovereign. Being an actual, embodied self, he or she may well reflect about what is good for the nation. There is nothing especially interpersonal, however, about such deliberation. Hybrid cases, such as constitutional monarchies, sovereign legislatures, and systems of divided sovereignty, would present mixtures of these two sorts of problem. If the sovereign body is a group, then questions remain: How can its members reflect and deliberate together, and how can its deliberations relate to the commitments of the other persons for whom it acts?

For similar reasons, the second aspect of reflectiveness does not transfer straightforwardly to the interpersonal level. It is not that indirect clues about people's commitments are not needed or available in groups. They certainly are, in the form of demonstrations, opinion surveys, changes in group morale, and so on. Rather, the problem concerns *whose* commitments are thus revealed. If one could assume that collective deliberation was proceeding within a structure designed to ensure that "our" commitments were best fulfilled, and these clues were looked to as evidence about what "our" commitments were, then the analogy would work better. The mere availability of such clues, however, does nothing to create such a structure. Moreover, within the general area of interpersonal deliberation there are many contexts – such as the negotiations between deeply divided opponents that will be my central concern – in which instead of a "we" there is from each point of view an "us" and a "them."

236

In such cases, structures of deliberation are themselves apt to be contested. Accordingly, in this respect my coherentist proposal would need an account of the structure of dialogue that would play a role parallel to the utilitarian's symmetrical aggregating function. It would have to explain how the information thus indirectly gathered about the commitments of individuals will be made relevant to the collective choice.

Therefore, because my account of deliberation of ends builds in important roles for the reflective self, it cannot be transferred without further work to the interpersonal level. This is not because I accord some sort of ultimate ontological or explanatory primacy to the individual self over society. To the contrary, I would be quite dubious of such a philosophical individualism. My theory's limitation is more prosaic and less deep, and results simply from the facts (1) that human individuals on the one hand and societies or groups on the other are quite different in kind, and (2) that I have made use of the former but not directly the latter in explaining the nature and possibility of deliberation of ends. To extend the account to interpersonal deliberation, therefore, would require further attention to the distinct nature of groups and societies. In what follows, I will begin very modestly, as I indicated, by focusing on the nature of cultural difference and interpersonal negotiation or dialogue – partly, again, because I want to bring my results back to the single person of divided commitments.

§36. PHENOMENA OF DEEP DISAGREEMENT

Fundamental divergences among individuals' conceptions of the good present the distinctive problems of modern politics, going beyond simple conflicts of values. There are three levels of conflict to distinguish here. The first and most basic occurs when values are similar but incompatible. The relative simplicity of the problem of competing similar interests is expressed by the wit of Francis I, who complained of Charles V, "What my brother wants, that I want too," namely Milan (quoted in Kant 1956, Ak. 28). Grant and Lee may both want sole possession of Richmond (cf. Rawls 1971, 526), and neither New England nor Canada may want acid rain; but while these disputes are hard to settle, the problems they pose may be understood in the same way as those of the boxing ring and the bazaar. In part because politics aims to reconcile the competing interests of citizens in a justified and not merely ad hoc fashion, it must recognize that ends are not sufficiently settled in advance. This becomes obvious if one attempts to specify the ends involved: "That acid rain be reduced"

237

may be agreed upon, for example, but "that acid rain be evenly reduced across New England and Canada," unfortunately, is not. The second level of conflict, then, involves explicit disagreement over the final ends that should be sought. There are two aspects to it: the divergence in the content of the ends put forward and the impossibility of realizing these ends jointly. (Without this incompossibility, one would not necessarily have any conflict at all, but rather the sort of variety that helpfully greases our countless daily skirmishes in the marketplace, where a variety of preference facilitates exchange.) Another example of a conflict of this second sort would be the issue of Québec's possible separation from Canada, where some put forward the end of an independent francophone state and others maintain the aim of a unified Canada that includes Québec.

Yet this second sort of conflict still falls short of capturing the distinctive problems of modern politics. It is a form of conflict among final ends routinely faced by a single individual, even one of undivided loyalties. The third, characteristically political, level of conflict involves clashes between entire conceptions of value. The following chapter will explore exactly what this means; we can understand it easily enough by reference to the wars of religious toleration of seventeenth-century Europe. These involved not merely clashes between the partisans of incompossible ends, but between adherents of different religions. While their religions directed them to different final ends, they also provided them with contrasting models of reasoning, dissimilar concrete exemplars of virtue, and differing sets of propositions regarded as unquestionable. They subscribed to considerably different comprehensive conceptions of the good and contrasting theories of the world and how to live in it. Pluralism – the wide diversity and deep conflict among different conceptions of ends prevalent in modern societies and different patterns of life and of institutions that go with them – poses the distinct problem of modern politics.[1] It is the seeming incommensurability of the many conceptions of the good prevalent in modern societies that gives rise to what I have elsewhere called "the depth of pluralism" (Richardson 1990b).

While the nature of this third level of disagreement is not yet clear, the first prerequisite to understanding it is to avoid assimilating it to the second sort of conflict, that between incompossible final ends. A common habit of historical exposition and revolutionary abstraction threatens to efface the distinction between these two levels, and must be resisted. I am referring to the habit of describing politics primarily in terms of a clash

1 I shall speak of pluralism as a description of society, not as a doctrine.

238

among what Isaiah Berlin has called "the Great Goods," such as Freedom, Equality, Justice, or Salvation, leaving the concrete individuals involved in the background. When the historian proceeds in this way, perhaps no great harm is done; but when ambitious political activists succumb to such a vision, Berlin warns us, they become willing to "sacrifice . . . living human beings on the altar of abstractions" (Berlin 1988, 15–16). In addition to posing real practical dangers, the habit of thinking of political conflicts in terms of such capital-letter Values neglects three aspects of pluralism's complexity. First, as Berlin's own work in the history of ideas has vividly shown, most memorably with regard to freedom, the values influential in politics are not best thought of as rigid, capital-letter abstractions – the understanding of values undercut in Chapter IV – but rather as complex bundles that evolve in subtly different ways in different contexts. Only if we are sensitive to these concrete variations in the specification of values, and only if we remember the concrete, flesh-and-blood human beings whose values they are, will we understand the normative basis of such conflicts as those between Protestants and Catholics in seventeenth-century England. In a case such as that, what divided people included certain relatively concrete aspects of the interpretation of a Christian ideal of salvation that was shared in the abstract. Since (as the notorious limitations of Locke's advocacy of toleration make vivid) the influential combatants all accepted the abstract ideals of Christian Redemption and Salvation, attention restricted to these capital-letter abstractions would shed no light on the controversy. Second, it is not likely that the banner of a single Value will adequately represent the commitments of any one citizen. Rather, we may expect that most (if not all) people are committed to an irreducible plurality of final ends. What will matter in defining the difficult conflicts of political pluralism will not simply be which values they accept, but how they order and arrange them in a normative theory. Third, an important additional aspect of deep pluralism lies in the divergence between people's entire understandings of the world and their place in it, matters that cannot be reduced to their structure of ends at all. The Anglicans, Catholics, and Dissenters of Stuart England differed in their beliefs about such matters as whether the Host undergoes transubstantiation during Mass and the way in which good works contribute to salvation. To understand the conflicts among persons that make for deep political pluralism, we shall have to recognize how their conceptions of ends are embedded within broader structures of belief.

To reinforce this abstract description of deep disagreement among people and to provide a case with which my subsequent constructive suggestions may grapple, let me now describe a concrete issue in some detail. It is the case of a hypothetical disagreement between a liberal, pragmatic Westerner and a traditionalist Sunni Muslim jurist in Pakistan over the treatment of women who bring rape complaints in Pakistan. Alternatively, it is the case of a single person divided between such backgrounds and commitments. Having referred to the nature of political pluralism to help indicate the contours of deep disagreement, I now abstract, as I said I would, from any specific political context. Accordingly, I will describe this disagreement without paying much attention to the institutional and practical setting within which it arises. I will not try to say what business it is of the Westerner how female victims of rape are treated in Pakistan, nor in what political forum he might try to meet his Pakistani interlocutor to discuss what to do about the matter; or again, I will not describe the concrete circumstances requiring the divided individual to deliberate about these matters.[2] These aspects of the practical setting would of course be crucially important once one got to the stage of trying to resolve such a disagreement. At the moment, however, I confine my attention to trying to lay out its depth. I assume that the reader is familiar with the Western, liberal side of this disagreement.

In 1979, under the military dictatorship of General Zia ul-Haq, the Parliament of Pakistan enacted ordinances designed to enforce the traditional Islamic prohibition (*hadd*, plural *hudud*) of *zina*, sex outside marriage. Both the offense and the punishment are based directly in the Qur'an, the word of God as revealed to the Prophet Muhammad, and the Sunnah, the well-attested and authoritative reports of the actions and words of the Prophet. In codifying the divine law, these ordinances resolved a famous ambiguity that resides in the fact that the Qur'anic punishment for *zina* is 100 lashes, whereas the Sunnah prescribes stoning the culprits to death. The statutes adopted the harsher punishment of the Sunnah for adult married Muslims, designating the Qur'anic lashing as the punishment for all others. As Muslims defending these provisions to Westerners often point out, few adulterers are ever stoned to death, for while the tradition prescribes stoning, it also sets out evidentiary requirements so strict that they are rarely met. To impose the penalty of stoning, either the act of adultery must be testified to by four witnesses of integrity (that is, four male Muslims) or the culprit must four times confess without

---

2 One might think of the deliberations of Benazir Bhutto, raised in Pakistan and educated at Oxford and Harvard, reelected as prime minister of Pakistan in 1993 and, as this book goes to press, aiming to reverse the legal provisions described in the following paragraph.

recanting. If four upright male eyewitnesses are not available, the testimony of eight Muslim women eyewitnesses may be substituted, according to Islamic law as enacted in Pakistan. In this same version of these principles, however, the lesser penalty of whipping may be imposed on the basis of "ordinary" – that is, residual British – standards of evidence.

This treatment of adultery is harsh by Western standards, but an even more dramatic gulf exists between the attitudes common in Western liberal democracies and those prevailing in Pakistan concerning the treatment of women who allege that they have been raped. In one notorious case of the 1980s, Jehan Mina, thirteen years old and unmarried at the time, lodged a formal complaint alleging that she had been gang-raped. The alleged rapists were acquitted. Yet the medical records that the girl had submitted to the court in a vain attempt to prove that she had been raped did convince the judge that she had had sex multiple times. Accordingly, she was charged with *zina*, convicted, and sentenced to be whipped and then imprisoned for five years. Although not many women have actually been punished for adultery in this way as a result of bringing rape charges, it appears to be quite common that they are countercharged with adultery.[3]

Further depth to this particular cultural disagreement may be brought out by reference to the Qur'anic tradition of which this law is a codification and to the tribal customs within which it is also enmeshed. In the Sunni branch of Islamic jurisprudence, which is the one dominant in Pakistan, it is held that there is no longer any room for the interpretation (*ijtihad*) of the divine law. The gates of *ijtihad* closed, as it is poetically put, within three centuries after the Prophet's death – that is, in the tenth century of the Christian Era – when the four great schools of jurisprudence had allegedly completed their interpretive work. Whereas Shi'ite Muslims accept as authoritative a more rationalist style of interpretive reasoning in which the imam attempts to draw results from certain highly general principles, the traditionalist Sunni insists that reasoning to new results is neither necessary nor allowed (see Noori and Amin 1987, ch. 1). The law has been promulgated and sufficiently interpreted already; the task now is simply to live up to it and enforce it. Given this attitude that the immutable divine law has been revealed and in theory requires no reinterpretation, it appears unlikely that the traditionalist Sunni would be willing to pay much heed to an argument that the provisions of the code should

---

3 See *The Herald Annual* [Karachi, Jan. 1992], cover story, "The Politics of Rape," pp. 37–54. The quotations later in this section are drawn from this source.

be revised to reflect the changing position of women in a modernizing society. It is the modernization that must accommodate the law and not vice versa.

Pakistani legal practice in this context is thus bolstered by an explicit and elaborate theological jurisprudence, but it also has roots in tribal customs that antedate Islam. These are reflected in the Pakistani term for the rape of a woman, *uss ki izzat lut gai*, literally "she has been robbed of her honor." Actually the honor in question is not really the woman's own. It is her paternal family's honor that is at stake. The woman's honor – in ways not so different from European traditions – is wrapped up with her virginity and chastity. What is more distinct about the Pakistani custom, shared by most of its various subcultures, is both the allocation of responsibility for the safeguarding of this honor and the response to its violation. The woman is to be protected by her family, both from the physical threat of sexual aggression and from the lures of prostitution and illicit sex. If of her own free will she succumbs to the latter, it becomes her father's or brother's duty to kill her in order to preserve the family honor.[4] If she is raped, the injury to family honor is similar; but in this case, it is traditional to "suggest" that she commit suicide. To bring a legal action against the rapist is to drag the family's dishonor further before the public. The blot on the family's honor is indelible, and is certainly not cleansed by a judicial proceeding. Restoration of the victim's psychological and physical well-being is not a central goal. Personally carried-out revenge against the rapist might be another matter. According to a report in a Pakistani magazine, "When a four-year-old Baloch girl was recently raped by a baker in Lyari, her father, in keeping with tribal customs, wanted to kill both his child and the culprit. It took a good deal of persuasion on the part of [a women's group working on behalf of rape victims] to make the father accept the legal recourse."

To some extent this sort of customary view of family honor, which preexisted the Prophet, has become incorporated in Islamic law. It is often pointed out that Islam makes no sharp separation between adultery and rape, treating both as branches of *zina*. In Pakistan's Zina Ordinances, rape is legally defined as

"sexual intercourse with a woman or man, as the case may be, to whom the offender is not legally married," and where the act is committed against the will

---

4 Cachia 1989 preserves and translates some blood-curdling oral ballads of contemporary Egypt that celebrate the heroism of the brother who has the courage to maintain the family honor by cutting his prostitute sister limb from limb.

of the victim, without the consent of the victim, or with the consent of the victim obtained under duress, or where the victim has consented in the false belief of being legally married to the offender, who has misled the victim into believing so.

This legal definition reproduces the Islamic category of *zina-bil-jabr*, or unconsented *zina*. It is noteworthy here that the salient line is between whether or not the sex outside marriage was knowingly consented to, and not whether it was forced. In the background here one seems to see, again, a concern with whether the woman's honor was sullied, rather than with whether she was done some injury by an aggressor.

The disagreement between a traditionalist Sunni Muslim from Pakistan who would defend these provisions and a liberal Westerner who would deplore them seems quite deep, therefore, in various ways. The disagreement is dramatic on its face. It is connected, furthermore, with wildly different views about how positions on such matters are to be justified. And it is rooted in strikingly contrasting ways of life, in concrete customs that contrast markedly. Such a disagreement certainly seems deeper than a simple territorial squabble. Philosophical work must be done, however, to defend this intuitive sense of depth. This work will be undertaken in the next chapter, affording a more perspicuous account of the conceptual incommensurability that seems involved in such a case. The question of the possibility of reasonable dialogue between a liberal Westerner and a traditionalist Sunni will not be forgotten; I will return to it in Chapter XIII.

§37. INTERPERSONAL REFLECTION

There are two distinct challenges posed to my account, then, by problems of interpersonal deliberation that do not occur in the ordinary case of a single individual. The first, arising from the separateness of persons and laid out in §35, concerns the dependence of Part Three's model of deliberation upon the sovereignty of reflection and the need for input from emotionally guided perception. The second, arising from the differences among people and initially characterized in §36, concerns the depth of disagreement that arises when disputants hold contrasting and even incommensurable conceptions of the good. To cope with these challenges, I will need to develop an interpersonal counterpart to the ideal of individual reflection. Accommodating the separateness of persons, it must intrinsically allow for a plurality of participants. Respecting the depth of possible disagreement among them, it must involve a holism that to the extent possible avoids begging questions against one or the other of the competing views. As the example of the Pakistani law on rape suggests, it will be difficult to find any perspective that is entirely neutral between deeply clashing points of view. Any proposal such as my own that works out broadly pragmatist and liberal ideals is unlikely to appeal greatly to a traditional Sunni jurist. Yet we should not take such limitations as fatal at the outset. For now, I would like you, the reader, to decide whether you find these proposals attractive. This section will provide a preview of my constructive suggestions about interpersonal deliberation, completing the initial picture of the problems and prospects for extending the sort of account developed in Part Three. It will do so by characterizing the sort of dialectic that can stand to interpersonal deliberation as holistic reflection stands to an individual's deliberation. The following three chapters then work out this proposal in more detail.

My proposals build on Aristotle's conception of philosophical dialectic. Lacking a Hegelian allegation of necessity and formal uniformity – or even a Platonic connection to the theory of ideas – Aristotle's dialectic fits well with the ideal of reflective coherence that I have developed. Philosophical dialectic began as stylized dialogue. On account of their author's literary genius, Plato's dialogues come the closest of any representations of philosophical dialectic to reproducing the interpersonal character of dialogue. Already by the time of Aristotle's *Topics*, the question-and-answer form of Socratic dialectic seems to have been institutionalized enough to serve as a means of training students in the Academy (cf. Stump 1989). According to the *Topics* (100a30–1), Aristotle's work wholly concerned with dialectic, that reasoning is dialectical which proceeds from *endoxa*, from the reputable views of the many and the wise. One feature of deep disagreement is that what looks like a narrow practical dispute can ramify into a global divergence on religion, standards of evidence, and ways of seeing the world. Aristotle's philosophical dialectic, holistically pursued, is at home with such connections. There is no a priori limit to how abstract or seemingly "central" an issue dialectical reflection may take up. This feature of dialectic is illustrated by one of Aristotle's most prominent uses of dialectic, namely his argument for the principle of noncontradiction in *Metaphysics* IV.4. As this argument indicates, Aristotle holds that dialectic represents the route to first principles or starting points (*Topics* I.2).[5] Holist dialectic is similarly not bound to work within a single theory.

---

5 The dialectical nature of Aristotle's arguments for the principle of noncontradiction is well brought out by Irwin 1988, §§97–101. In 549 n. 13, Irwin quotes Ross's view that

If it were, it could hardly address deep disagreement. Although my examples of holistic deliberation in Chapter X were cast as efforts at theory construction, as if from pretheoretical or prototheoretical materials, nothing prevents a holist approach from reconciling opposed theories. In fact, some of the more interesting quandaries faced by individuals, such as Aristotle's about the value of friendship, or Rawls's about the relative place of freedom and equality in a theory of justice, can be described without strain as instances in which a single person is pulled in different directions by opposed theories. As long as there is some initial agreement, at some level, from which to start, holist reflection will have some leverage for bringing opposed theories into line, just as it can bring conflicting ends into line. The deliberation that achieves this, like the more far-reaching cases of an individual's deliberation of ends, will amount to theory construction.

What are the theory-building tools of this flexible dialectic? While specification will remain a crucial one, there are three other cognitive operations that are at least as important: abstraction, distinction, and analogy. Informally, we can think of these operations as pertaining to two distinct variables, specificity and relevance. Specification and abstraction can be regarded as "vertically" following a single norm as it becomes more specific or more abstract. Distinction and analogy "horizontally" vary the degree of relevance recognized between one norm and another.

Specification was defined and treated at length in Chapter IV. The most important feature of it for present purposes is that it is a relation between two norms that allows one to trace the significant continuities in a path of revision, as shown in §25. In making an initial norm more specific, it also is so constrained as to give its product a credible claim to represent or respect that initial norm.

By "abstraction" I just mean the inverse of the specification relation (cf. O'Neill 1989, 208–13 on the importance of abstraction). If norm p specifies norm q, then q abstracts from p, and conversely. To arrive at a specification of a norm is to make it less abstract, whereas to produce an abstraction of a norm is to make it less specific. Abstraction can help with locating areas of initial agreement. We "abstract from our differences."[6]

the argument in *Metaphysics* IV.4 is "the best specimen of an establishment of first principles by dialectic," as contemplated by *Topics* I.2.

6 "Abstraction," as I will use the term, however, does not include the approach to political dialogue recommended by Larmore in his "neutral defense of liberal neutrality." Although he writes that "the strategy is to *abstract from* what is in dispute" (1987, 50), he simply means that we should set aside those premises on which we do not agree.

Often, the effort to abstract from disagreement requires creativity, as the philosophical dialectician – that's you or me – seeks simultaneously to abstract from a pair of clashing norms so as to locate convergence. Sometimes, it will be relatively obvious how to do so, as in the case of rape in Pakistan. As I suggested in the last section, we can agree with the Pakistani establishment that rape is wrong, even though we and they specify this norm quite differently. What I now want to emphasize is that even this simple location of a point of agreement is already the product of a dual abstraction. In other cases, jointly abstracting toward an agreement point will require considerably more discernment. Complete success requires that the norm at which one arrives by abstraction is not only one upon which the disputants can agree, but also one that each can acknowledge as capturing much of the force in (not necessarily "behind") the initial norms that it abstracts. "Rape is wrong" does so quite handily, for the disagreement is largely located in disparate contextual features (religion, the law of evidence) in this case. Whether an abstract principle marks a significant point of agreement obviously depends on the controversy. For instance, although the bare formula that "all persons are to be treated as equals" may not seem to say very much, jointly arriving at it by abstraction might be crucial in a dispute among South African factions.

Distinction is the time-honored tool of philosophical dialecticians, including many analytic philosophers of our own day. Whereas specification narrows a single norm, distinction separates the domains of two competing norms. Alternatively, it partitions the domain of a single norm, allowing it to be specified differently for each context. Distinction allows answering the disputed question, not by "yes" or "no," but by "it depends." Since Aristotle aims in dialectical inquiry to explain the element of truth in each of the contesting positions, he often relies upon making distinctions. A prime example of this is his discussion of the value of friendship in *N.E.* IX.9, which lay behind the example in §32. The dispute over whether the happy man must have friends was answered with a distinction: Those who say no are correct insofar as they are thinking of friendships based on pleasure or utility, but wrong insofar as they have in mind friendships based on virtue, which is the highest form of friendship.

Analogy too has been a favorite tool of philosophical dialectic since Socrates. By finding relevant similarity where it had not previously been seen, dialectic represents the inverse of distinction. By helping throw the structure of an argument into relief, analogy can make an essential step toward reaching a more abstract and general version of a position. For instance, Aristotle's analogy between friendship and proper self-love in

N.E. IX.8 sheds light on each, and reinforces the fact that the underlying view centers on goodness, as embodied in virtuous activity, rather than interest. In the case of a deep disagreement, analogy will be vital to extending mutual understanding; empathetically projecting the right analogies is necessary to an adequate translation of the interlocutor (Do their views about *aretē* correspond to – do they play a role analogous to – our views about virtue, or to our views about excellence?).

Although these tools of dialectic, familiar above all from dialectic's philosophical employment, are indispensable to addressing deep disagreement, philosophical dialectic itself is not up to this task. In *Topics* VIII, Aristotle lays out rules for a dialectical "questioner" and "answerer," and distinguishes competitive, "gymnastic" (training), and philosophical roles for dialectic. The former two forms of dialectic have an essentially interpersonal form, but do not involve a search for the truth. Competitive dialectic involves opponents who seek either to pin their adversary in a contradiction or to avoid being so trapped. Sincerity in answering is not expected of dialectical competitors, to whom Aristotle gives interesting advice about how to throw one's adversary off the scent. Gymnastic dialectic is similarly interpersonal, in that it involves a relation between student and teacher. Here, sincerity is expected, "for a learner should always state what he thinks (for no one tries to teach what is false)" (159a29–30). Since the teacher addresses what is believed by the learner, and strives to communicate on the basis of her greater knowledge, the interpersonal element of gymnastic dialectic is irreducible. The philosophical use of dialectic differs from the other two forms in large part because whereas in the other two "another party is involved," whose anticipation of the paradoxical implications of some thesis one is attempting to impede for the moment, this is not the case with "the philosopher, and the man who is investigating by himself" (155b7–11).[7] For the philosopher, the anticipation of these implications is welcomed, as it helps in framing principles that will fit with and make sense of the reputable views. In doing so, however, the philosopher may work alone in the sense that she aims to arrive at a reasonable reconciliation of the views of others that is satisfactory to herself on reflection, not at any form of actual agreement among these other people. She aims at her own reflective equilibrium, not necessarily at an equilibrium shared with others. In the true interpersonal case, however, those who disagree may not even want to find a way to agree. Further, there

---

7 The *kai* may well be epexegetic: "the philosopher, that is, the man who is investigating by himself."

is a big difference between addressing the views or "reputed opinions" of others and actually confronting other people with whom one disagrees, who may not strike one as reputable. Accordingly, we must plumb the depths of conceptual incommensurability before we can say how deliberation might be adapted to deal with the interpersonal case.

We may remark now, though, that truly opening deliberation to other persons cuts two ways. On the daunting side, the embodiment of reflective sovereignty in a flesh-and-blood person means that one cannot learn how that person would or should revise her views simply by reviewing a list of her opinions. Even if this list includes priority rules and higher-order rules for the revision of commitments, it will fall short of dictating or implying what she will find acceptable on reflection. Yet there is also a more positive lesson to draw from the unsuitability of philosophical dialectic as an answer to deep disagreement. Although a theory may be stronger taken as a whole than considered bit by bit because of the holistic connections among its elements, this same holism may make the holder of the theory more capable of bending. Suppose that the deliberative task were the impersonal one that it is conceived to be in philosophical dialectic, namely to reconcile two *theories* that deeply disagree. Where the disagreement is deep, the theories may be built around contradictory axioms. Since the philosopher is approaching the problem as a single disinterested individual, and thus impersonally, she faces opposed views rather than opposed persons. As I will argue in §42, what function as rules or a priori axioms for individuals do so, as Wittgenstein suggests, in an "as if" fashion. A theory, by contrast, can be articulated in a tightly deductive axiomatic hierarchy. If two such theories are built around contradictory axioms, there seems little room for the philosophical dialectician to come in and split the difference. That Euclidean geometry is in a sense intermediate between the Reimannian and Lobachevskian geometries – recognizing that one parallel may be drawn through each point, not none or two – does not soften the irreconcilability of these axiom systems. (There may be external, pragmatic grounds for preferring to employ one of these geometries over the others; but in returning to a pragmatic context we have shifted from the axiomatic context back to the truly interpersonal plane.) If deep disagreements are to be rationally resolved, it must be possible to represent the competing views faithfully in some way other than as hierarchically organized axiom systems. Although the personal (i.e., interpersonal) nature of deep disagreements impedes their philosophical representation, it also makes it unlikely that an axiomatic presentation

248

will capture the competing views. My concern is with the sorts of deep disagreement that actually occur, not with what is philosophically imaginable; and deep disagreements importantly occur between groups of people. What makes them deep we must now strive to understand better.

XII

Disagreement in concept and in practice

One way to try to make sense of deep disagreement would be to analyze it as resting (also) upon conceptual incommensurability of some kind. Yet as one presses toward complete conceptual incommensurability, it is difficult to hold on to the depth of disagreement that one was trying to explain in the first place. While some will not be surprised that after trying to plumb the murky depths one comes up empty-handed, we will all learn from understanding more explicitly why this is so and how it may be squared with the apparent phenomena of deep disagreement. Accordingly, in the next section I will describe how one gets lost in the alleged depths of disagreement. Section 39 will turn to underlying difficulties with "the very idea" of a framework or "conceptual scheme," in terms of which conceptual incommensurability is defined. This will pave the way for a less conceptually ambitious but more enduring recasting of the notion of conceptual distance, which will be set out in §40.

§38. THE ELUSIVENESS OF DEPTH

In elaborating the idea of conceptual incommensurability, I cannot pretend simply to be uncovering the idea that unites all of the diverse cases of deep disagreement. Instead, let me simply put forward an initial definition of it intended to capture those aspects of the phenomena that particularly pose a problem for my theory of rational deliberation of ends. To ease comparison between the levels involved, this definition is parallel to the definition of deliberative value commensurability in §16. Thus:

Two conceptions A and B are commensurable with respect to a given question if and only if it is possible to pose the question within each conception and – prior to choosing between these conceptions' answer to the question (for purposes of deliberation as to that question) – to identify some single theory or standpoint in terms of which considerations for accepting A's answer to the question over B's, and for accepting B's over A's, can be adequately arrayed and understood.

As in my definition of value incommensurability, it is ex ante incommensurability that interests me, as this is the form important in deliberation.[1] Note, further, that the definition leaves open whether or not the commensurating theory or standpoint, in terms of which the considerations are to be arrayed, is one of the two theories in contention or rather some third theory (cf. Williams 1981b, 77–9).

We should not assume that the theory or standpoint that serves as a basis for comparing the two conceptions in question must be as general or as large-scale as Christianity or scientific method. All that is needed is some framework, some constellation of concepts, however humble, in terms of which the two conceptions can be brought into contact. This commensurating "theory" might be a skeletal core set of notions that the two conceptions can be found to have in common. It provides something like what Bernard Williams (1981b, 135) has called a "*locus* of exclusivity," explaining in what sense two conceptions are rivals. When two conceptions are to some degree commensurable, the locus of exclusivity is the question or the questions to which they both provide answers. Two commensurable conceptions are rivals if they provide divergent answers to at least one question. Mendelian genetics and the big bang theory are presumably not rivals in this sense, since they are not directed to any common questions. Similarly with the conception underlying Loyola's *Spiritual Exercises* and that underlying Bocuse's *Cuisine Minceur*, however much they differ in their animating spirits. One can connect the spiritual with the gastronomic, as did the film *Babette's Feast*. *Cuisine Minceur*, however, is not a good candidate for this linkage.

What is paradoxical then about the idea of deep disagreement is that as one presses toward depth, the possibility of disagreement begins to evaporate. Unless there is some question on which two conceptions yield divergent answers, it is difficult to see how they disagree; but if they do diverge on a single question, then they are not totally incomparable. While totally incommensurable theories may appear to contradict each other,

---

1 Lukes (1991, 38) brushes off conceptual incommensurability in science largely on the ground that "ex post . . . the problem dissolves: subsequent developments sooner or later select out which criterion or criteria turn out to have been the best indicator(s) of progress." While this blank check for writers of Whig history is disturbing in itself, my main objection is that arguments against conceptual incommensurability that rely in this way on an ex post perspective neglect how conceptual incommensurability can affect deliberation.

they cannot do so in fact. To be sure, since comparability is just the first condition of conceptual commensurability, as I have defined it, comparability does not suffice for commensurability. For instance, two religions might yield different prescriptions about how to pray without there being any way to construct a framework for adequately assessing their contrary recommendations. Further, comparability on a single question does not necessarily go very far in mitigating depth of disagreement. Thus, the Phalangist Christians and Shi'ite Muslims of Beirut disagree on one question that they can both formulate: Who should control Beirut? Yet this degree of comparability does little to reassure us of their positions' further commensurability or rational tractability. In fact, the names by which they call Beirut in their own languages may reveal that their understandings of the city are embedded in such different cultural histories and conceptions that they only barely are referring to the same place. (Such is the case, as MacIntyre has argued, with the names "Londonderry" and "Doire Colmcille" in the similarly fraught circumstances of Northern Ireland: MacIntyre 1985, 7.) Still, there may be a third description of the city – "the city at 33° 53' N, 35° 30' E" – in terms of which a question can be posed to which the Phalangists and Shi'ites give obviously opposed answers.[2]

But is the disagreement thus secured meaningfully deep? It is less this question posed in geographic terms than the city, Beirut, itself that serves as the locus of disagreement in this case. There is no mystery about this disagreement. Things seem to have boiled back down to the same sort of simple conflict of interests mentioned in §36. Just as Grant and Lee wanted Richmond, or Charles V and his brother wanted Milan, the Phalangists and the Shi'ites want Beirut. When things come to blows, is it just that there is no time, and no context for discussion, to allow the disagreement to manifest its depth? Grant and Lee, at least, surely also were the champions of widely different forms of life. Or should we say that the conceptual depth of the disagreement has succumbed to the pressure of events?

Plainly there are widely different ways of understanding the notion of a locus of disagreement. At one extreme is the literal rendering, in which the locus is an ancient city, a coveted spring, a playground swing, or an oil-rich seabed. Disagreement over such as these can resemble the relatively (though not wholly) inarticulate territorial disputes of hyenas or

2 Thus, as Williams stresses (1981b, 134) all that is required for comparability is that there be *some* formulation of a question with regard to which the two conceptions disagree. This description need not be perfectly neutral. In the Londonderry case, for instance, while the IRA might object to using the Greenwich Meridian, they can still apply it without any trouble.

wolves. In these cases, what allows for disagreement is the simple physical integrity – which need not mean indivisibility – of the domain being fought over. At the other extreme is conceptual commensurability, providing not only comparability as a basis of posing common questions but also a common way of arraying arguments pro and con, perhaps even an agreed system of alternating statements and rebuttals. In between these poles lies a whole spectrum of cases, in which what allows for disagreement is a varying mix of conceptual and practical factors. Williams, who rightly held that there can be a locus of disagreement (or "exclusivity") even in the absence of significant conceptual comparability, described this possibility as occurring when "it is impossible to live within both" of the competing conceptions (1981b, 135). This formulation seems to have the advantage of holding on to depth as long as possible. Thus, it appears to explain the difference we sense between the dispute over Milan and the dispute over Beirut. Whereas the Hapsburg brothers shared not only parents but an imperial worldview, and hence would have no trouble "living within" each other's outlooks, it would be disorienting to be both a Phalangist and a Shi'ite.

Yet there are three problems with Williams's attempt to hold together depth and disagreement. First, we have no good way of assessing counterfactuals about the psychological state someone would be in were she to come to inhabit a second worldview. Second, actual cases have also shown us that people manage to live with apparently quite contradictory conceptions without difficulty. One can be a rentier capitalist in the morning, a radical reformer in the afternoon, an ascetic in the evening, and a sybarite after dinner. Third, there are impossibilities and impossibilities. Although mention of the difficulty of "living within" a conception initially invites us to think of difficulties involving cognitive dissonance, bad faith, and strained synthesis – difficulties with maintaining one's "hold on reality," as Williams puts it – far more mundane impossibilities might also obtrude. Someone attempting to lead a double life might get ostracized or shot. We are again back to the point at which the intuition of depth is crushed.

We do need something like the notion of conceptual incommensurability to explain how deep disagreement differs from simple value incommensurability. Yet the difficulties of keeping the intuition of depth alive while pressing for conceptual incommensurability indicate that the bare definition of this notion is not enough to do the needed work. We need a better understanding of the structure of conceptual incommensurability – and of the "standpoints" or conceptual schemes that go into it – in order to shield our understanding of differences as we plunge for the depths. I intend to sketch such an account. Before doing so, however, I must face a powerful argument according to which such submarine structures of the soul are sheer fictions.

§39. THE VERY IDEA OF TOTAL CONCEPTUAL INCOMMENSURABILITY

As Donald Davidson noted at the outset of his influential essay, "On the Very Idea of a Conceptual Scheme" (1986c, 183), "the trouble is, as so often in philosophy, it is hard to improve intelligibility while retaining the excitement." He recognized, in other words, the difficulty of retaining both philosophical clarity and the intuition of depth. As was perhaps appropriate in a Presidential Address to the Eastern Division of the American Philosophical Association, Davidson opted for clarity over the unsettling excitement of depth. For many, Davidson's arguments killed the excitement contained in the talk of conceptual incommensurability, which originated in the philosophy of science of Thomas Kuhn and others. I will argue that this obituary was premature; but first we must examine the powerful reasons that led Davidson to opt for clarity, arguments that rule out making sense of conceptual schemes in terms of some relation to the unorganized "content" of experience. One lesson we may learn from Davidson is that if we are to make sense of the notion at all, we will have to do so in some other way. Another is that the idea of "total" conceptual incommensurability does not make sense. In an attempt to undermine the intelligibility of the idea of conceptual schemes, Davidson first urges that it involves a dualism of scheme and content (or point of view and what is viewed, etc.), which he labels the "third dogma" of empiricism. He then canvasses various ways one might try to make sense of this dualism. Although his arguments are organized around a rather informal survey of the metaphors used to express the role of conceptual schemes, they embed profound philosophical insights. The metaphors, he suggests, are of two basic types: Either conceptual schemes *organize* experience or reality or else they *fit* experience or reality. Quite different considerations pertain to whether either can give sense to the idea in question.

Davidson's argument makes crucial use of the idea that charity is an unavoidable principle of interpretation, constitutive of our attributions of meaning. This is a view that Davidson absorbed from his teacher W. V. O. Quine, modifying it in detail in ways we will examine. Like Quine, Davidson holds that no strict dichotomy can be drawn between what is

254

true by virtue of the facts ("synthetic truth") and what is true by virtue of the meanings of terms ("analytic truth"). He also follows Quine in emphasizing the justificatory or epistemic holism of individuals' commitments. For Quine, who has importantly remained an empiricist, this epistemic holism is expressed in what has come to be known as the "Quine-Duhem thesis." As Quine puts it, "our statements about the external world face the tribunal of sense experience not individually but only as a corporate body."[3] Davidson's attack on conceptual schemes is one side of his attempt to undermine what he regards as the residual dualism of scheme and content, which he finds lurking in this notion of the "tribunal of experience."[4] Retaining a central place for sense experience (however reductively characterized) and replacing the sharp analytic–synthetic dichotomy with a gradation of directness of contact with that experience, Quine remained able to ask about the importance of conceptual schemes. As he metaphorically put it in *Word and Object*, our language is like an arch with its feet set in the clay of experience but with loftier conceptual tracery buttressed by intermediate stones that indeed rest the whole on experience but are not determined by it as directly (Quine 1960, 11). Quine's most famous way of figuring the relative importance of conceptual structure within a language, however, is his thought experiment involving "radical translation" in *Word and Object*, ch. 2.

The radical translator seeks to interpret linguistic behavior – commonsensically identified on the basis of an antecedent knowledge of human behavior – without relying upon any prior cultural links as clues. Thus, the radical translator begins (somehow!) just with the informant's assent and dissent to utterances offered under varying empirical stimuli. Empathy, or the translator's views about what she would be saying if she were the interlocutor, is necessarily the main source of translational hypotheses (Quine 1987, 7). Yet there is also, according to Quine, a still deeper role for something like empathy, for even all possible empirical data leaves radical translation underdetermined. Justificatory holism and the Quine-Duhem thesis provide the two basic reasons for this. First, radical translation is like solving a set of simultaneous equations that leave too many

---

3 Quine 1980, 41. Quine there cites Pierre Duhem, *La Théorie Physique: son objet et sa structure* (Paris, 1906), 303–28. See now Quine 1991, 268.
4 Davidson 1986c takes up one half of this attack. For the complementary criticism of the role of the notion of sense experience (albeit in a form more traditional than Quine's), see Davidson 1989. For a general statement of Davidson's antifoundationalist holism, see his 1986a.

degrees of freedom. One can make sense of the informant's linguistic behavior by varying the translation of his terms or by varying the theory attributed to him (this is the side of indeterminacy of translation most stressed and developed by Davidson: see his 1986b). At an extreme, one can face a choice between attributing inconsistency or attributing a nonstandard logic. These are ways in which the justificatory holism of the *translational* theory yields indeterminacy. Second, as Quine has emphasized, the fact that the informant's own theories are underdetermined by experience in turn affects their translation. Insofar as there may be conceptual "slack" or idiosyncratic conceptual "vaulting" in the informant's view, these components will not respond easily or at all to the kinds of empirical tests available to the radical translator. In this way, as Quine says, the underdetermination of theory by fact shows up "in second intension," within the linguistic behavior that is the radical translator's data, to reinforce the indeterminacy of translation.[5] The indeterminacy of radical translation – this is not a thesis about ordinary, historically informed translation – is an idea that looks Janus-faced upon the notion of conceptual schemes. For Quine, the degree of indeterminacy is a measure of the degree of variation in conceptual scheme that is compatible with the facts. For Davidson, however, the indeterminacy of translation becomes the key to attacking the idea of a conceptual scheme.

Given indeterminacy, the radical translator must often choose between two alternative translations, one of which makes the informant out as being more daft than does the other. At this point, Quine says, the translator will need more than the empathy to generate hypotheses: She will need charity to decide between them. "One's interlocutor's silliness, beyond a certain point, is less likely than bad translation – or, in the domestic case, linguistic divergence" (Quine 1960, 59). This idea, that at some point it is worth accepting a more complicated translational hypothesis rather than attributing too much inconsistency or craziness to the interlocutor, has become known as the principle of charity. Quine sees charity as reducing the scope for indeterminacy, but not as eliminating it. Davidson places a lot more weight on charity:

Since charity is not an option, but a condition of having a workable theory, it is meaningless to suggest that we might fall into massive error by endorsing it. . . . Charity is forced on us; whether we like it or not, if we want to understand others, we must count them right in most matters (Davidson 1986c, 197).

5 Quine 1970, 179. The two layers of Quine's argument are well set out and insightfully criticized in Solomon 1989.

Davidson argues that charity squeezes out conceptual schemes, whether these are explained in terms of the metaphor of organizing experience or the metaphor of fitting experience. He observes that those who have claimed to find conceptual incommensurability in the history of science, including Thomas Kuhn and Paul Feyerabend, have always bolstered their claims by *describing* just how different are, for example, two scientists' conceptions of an "electron." Yet describing an alleged conceptual incommensurability presupposes a common language for description. Total incommensurability would be ineffable; but the comforting embrace of charity smothers the ineffable. Davidson constantly stresses that we work "from within," using *our* conception of language and *our* conception of truth. We should use someone else's?[6]

Continuing Quine's thought experiment about radical translation, Davidson suggests that (1) one test of total conceptual incommensurability would be total untranslatability of a system that nonetheless "fit" reality. Yet, (2) given holism and the Quine-Duhem thesis, the relevant notion is that of fitting reality as a whole, or fitting the totality of possible experience. (3) But to fit the totality of possible experience would be, as far as we could ever tell, to be *true*. However, (4) the notion of a set of linguistic utterances at once largely true but untranslatable is incoherent because we cannot "divorce the notion of truth from that of translation" (Davidson 1986c, 195).

Quine agreed with Davidson that one cannot make sense of the idea of totally incommensurable conceptual schemes, but defended the very idea of them. Our methods of translation – and especially the imagined procedures of radical translation – can translate any language:

We are already accustomed, after all, to cutting corners and tolerating rough approximations even in neighborly translation. Translatability is a flimsy notion, unfit to bear the weight of the theories of cultural incommensurability that Davidson effectively and justly criticizes (Quine 1981, 42).

The flimsiness of the notion of translation, however, also translates into flimsiness in Davidson's argument against "the very idea."

The reason that translation is such a limp notion is that we are of two minds about it. On the one hand, we are prone to seeing "impossibilities"

6 Compare Lewis 1983, 112: The one we interpret "should be represented as believing what he ought to believe, and desiring what he ought to desire. And what is that? In our opinion, he ought to believe what *we* believe, or perhaps what we would have believed in his place; and he ought to desire what we desire, or perhaps what we would have desired in his place. (But that's only our opinion! Yes. Better we should go by an opinion we *don't* hold?)"

of translation whenever a translation fails perfectly to mimic the attributes of what is translated. Poetry is thus often said to be untranslatable on this account, as there is no way for a translation to reproduce the original's exact effect upon the reader. This point may be extended to less consciously metaphorical texts, for the understandings these produce in their readers or hearers are a function of the entire context. As Wittgenstein puts it, "Whether a word of the language of [a strange] tribe is rightly translated into a word of the English language depends upon the role the word plays in the whole life of the tribe; the occasions on which it is used, the expressions of emotion by which it is generally accompanied, the ideas which it generally awakens or which prompt its saying, etc. etc." (Wittgenstein 1960, 103). Accordingly, one would have to re-create a suitably adjusted simulacrum of the alien context in order to produce a translation that yielded the same effect. But this is obviously impossible, not only as between distant languages, but also as between two closely related languages or two times in a given speaker's life. On the other hand, we pride ourselves on our ability to translate any language, even with the minimum of transmitted cultural clues, as in the cases of the decipherment of Linear B or of the Mayan hieroglyphs. Similarly we can translate the indigenous sign language of the deaf, even though it is not based on the syntax of any spoken language. To succeed in translating, by these radically different standards, is to have a systematic way of making sense of language.

It is not just that there are degrees of translatability. The vagueness of this notion makes it hard even to formulate a well-defined range. The more demanding pole is not satisfied by any actual trial, while the laxer pole is satisfied by anything that would count as language (and even, in the case of understanding, at least, by objects that would not count as language). Accordingly, if we try to get a handle on either of these notions by trying to separate two "senses" of translation, we will not make any progress toward defining degrees of satisfaction of translatability. The notions of "total translatability" and "complete nontranslatability" are ill formed. The ideal of total transparency and the hell of total opacity elude our imagination. Where the word "translation" is rightly usable, neither total success nor total failure is an outcome that makes sense.

Thus it is with agreement, as well. Philosophers influenced by Wittgenstein and Davidson have developed the idea that "there is no substantive disagreement without conceptual agreement" (Hurley 1989, ch. 3; Seabright 1987). For good Wittgensteinian and Quinean reasons, however, the line between the two types of agreement or disagreement will be neither sharp nor fixed. Accordingly, the slogan will, in practice, reduce to the idea that "there is no disagreement without agreement." This is the point that our discussion has reached. Neither total agreement nor total disagreement are ideas that make any sense. This is simply what Wittgenstein would call a "grammatical" point, a point about our use of the terms "agreement" and "disagreement." If this is correct, then since total conceptual incommensurability is a special kind of total disagreement, presumably it is not an idea that makes sense, either. That is, we cannot make any sense of it. As Davidson himself says, "There are extreme suppositions that founder on paradox or contradiction; there are modest examples we have no trouble understanding" (Davidson 1986c, 184). Furthermore, if the idea of total incommensurability fails to make sense, then so too does the reciprocal idea of total commensurability.

Unlike Davidson, however, I begin with taking deep disagreement to be a phenomenon with which we live and with which politics must cope. *Total* incommensurability of conceptual schemes may indeed not be a helpful idea in attempting to understand this phenomenon. Insofar as Davidson's argument is directed against the intelligibility of a total incommensurability of conceptual schemes rather than against the very idea of conceptual schemes, it is fairly convincing. But the *very idea* of conceptual schemes and their (nontotal) incommensurability may yet be what is wanted to make sense of deep disagreement. To make sense of the phenomenon of deep disagreement, therefore, we need to look for something less exciting than total incommensurability, while avoiding the excessive modesty (not to say prudery) of Davidson's abandonment of the very idea of conceptual schemes. We need some alternative way to assess degrees of depth of disagreement, degrees of conceptual distance. Quine thinks we can readily construct such a measure. All we need do is to compute the ratios of the lengths of pairs of sentences that are the shortest acceptable translations of each other. In effect, the more gloss and the more awkward circumvention required for translating back and forth between the two languages, the greater will be the conceptual distance between them. While this proposal has the reductive virtues of Quine's stolid empiricism, and seems intended to crush any remaining excitement clinging to the idea of conceptual distance, it flattens the notion to uselessness. In the following section, I will try to reconstruct the idea of conceptual schemes in another way, responding to what is valid in Davidson's critique and providing a more perspicuous (and exciting) assessment of conceptual distance.

§40. ASSESSING CONCEPTUAL DISTANCE

Instead of looking to the outcome of an attempt at translation or under-standing – to its degree of success or failure – to assess conceptual distance, we may look instead to the barriers that lie in the way of mutual under-standing. Doing so will have the advantage that even if we cannot con-struct an overall measure of the depth of disagreement, at least we will be in a better position to understand what it is.

Some of the most obvious barriers do not seem relevant here. I am thinking of stupidity and ignorance; obstinacy and arrogance; racism and bigotry. Of course rational deliberation among people who are seriously deficient in these respects will be mightily difficult. In addressing the philosophical challenge posed by deep disagreement to an ideal concep-tion of rational deliberation of ends, however, it makes sense to abstract from such defects – without, of course, presupposing in our deliberators a clairvoyant grasp of every human culture. To do so, I will simply pass over such obvious barriers in silence, and turn to ones that would face even the best-intentioned and most sensitive of normal individuals.

There are at least three kinds of barrier to mutual understanding that deserve our attention. Each is fully brought out in Thomas Kuhn's phi-losophy of science, especially in his conception of a "disciplinary matrix" (Kuhn 1977). They arise from the facts that (1) much learning is tacit, (2) much of what is learned is seemingly a priori or definitional, and (3) inculcation of a form of life or a set of specialized practices typically takes for granted a rough characterization of the ends that are treated as final within that endeavor. To the first of these corresponds the notion of a "paradigm" in the narrow sense: a salient example. To the second cor-responds the idea of a criterion, for what is seen as a priori or definitional will serve as a criterion of correctness for the elaboration of other parts of one's view. Finally, to the third correspond cognitive ends, including those of the scientist – simplicity and elegance, fruitfulness in engendering hypotheses, and explanatory value.

The correspondence of the second barrier with the philosopher's no-tion of a criterion is suggestive but also potentially misleading. To avoid resurrecting a scheme–content dichotomy or something like it, we should take pains to explain this notion of a criterion in a way that avoids running into the difficulties raised, for example, by Wittgenstein's later philosophy. In fact, the later Wittgenstein illuminates both the importance of prop-ositions that are hardened "as if" into rigid rules and the incoherence of the notion of a rigid rule taken literally. Accordingly, we will do well to try and couch our understanding of criteria in ways that respect both strains of his thinking.[7] To begin with, then, the fact that some proposition is treated as unrevisable does not imply that it is thought capable of serving as a rigid rule to guide behavior – linguistic or nonlinguistic – in the way that rails stretching out toward infinity would guide a train (cf. Wittgenstein 1958, pt. I, §218). The proposition might be recognized to be vague in various ways, or it might fail to be a universal generalization. It might, in other words, be understood as requiring specification, even though our practice grounds strong resistance to revising its core import. Furthermore, although to regard a proposition as a priori in this way is, in some sense, to *regard* it as criterial, this does not imply that it *is* a criterion either in any more objective sense or in a sense corresponding to the idea of a rigid rule. For instance, the law of the conservation of mass-energy may in some contexts be treated as "criterial" in the sense that if any line of reasoning yields a conflict with that law, one will seek some error in the reasoning or in the premises it invokes rather than revise the law. The principles that torture is almost never excusable and that chattel slavery is generally wrong (and plain wrong in all circumstances we expect ever to face) may be, for us, similarly resistant to revision in the moral sphere. Rather than serving as rules for how to apply some concept, however, criterial propositions in this sense serve rather as checks that catch one up short in a process of reasoning otherwise generated. Although bumping up against one of them occasions further reflection, they do not directly provide grounds or by themselves imply what is to be done.

In so understanding criteria, we can take seriously the "as if" in the following Wittgensteinian passage, which occurs in the middle of a discussion of whether the laws of arithmetic could be said to have an empirical basis:

It is as if we had hardened the empirical proposition into a rule. And now we have, not an hypothesis that gets tested by experience, but a paradigm with which experience is compared and judged. And so a new kind of judgment (Wittgenstein 1978, VI.22, p. 324).

The "rule" that Wittgenstein here has in mind is not a rule for applying a concept. It is not, for instance, a rule about how to apply the concept

---

7 Kripke 1982 brilliantly magnifies the strain of "meaning skepticism" in Wittgenstein which tends to undermine all fixed meanings. Although it was fashionable for a time to focus solely on the side of Wittgenstein's philosophy of language that seemed to make positive use of the notion of criteria, the pendulum has swung the other way. On the shift, see Wright 1984.

"add 2" in generating an infinite series. Rather, it is a "rule" such as "25 × 25 = 625." If anyone made the calculation and came out with the answer 615, we would discount the results of that empirical trial. "25 × 25 = 625" is a proposition shielded against assault.

Such hardened propositions can be barriers to mutual understanding when they are not concurred in by others. An example of this sort of barrier arose when Western reporter Daniel Zwerdling interviewed Pakistani Parliamentary leader Muhammad Ali Khan about the plight of female victims of rape in that country, as described in §36. Zwerdling arrived at an implication of the position apparently taken by Pakistani law – namely that women who bring rape complaints deserve a jail sentence for their adulterous, though probably involuntary, sexual involvement – that he took to be an obvious *reductio* of the position; yet Ali Khan not only embraced this implication but said that they deserve worse (Zwerdling 1990). Propositions that have hardened to the point of unquestionability for most liberal Westerners, such as that those who are raped are victims and that coerced participation even in otherwise criminal activity is not culpable, are here being questioned by the interlocutor. As in Wittgenstein's imagined case of the person who cannot find his feet with his interlocutor, the problem here is not one of knowing what the other is saying. Both were speaking English. The problem is being sure what the interlocutor is *really* saying (here again the dualism of "understanding" crops up). If there were some hidden problem of translation – if for instance "rape," in Pakistani English, did not necessarily connote coerciveness – then the disagreement here would not be as deep as it actually is. We cannot find our feet with this moral position because it is so hard to know how to begin to work towards agreement. Once our firmest propositions have been questioned, we throw up our hands in frustration. We may then be tempted to withdraw from contact or to try cruder behavior modification.

The hardened propositions that are like axioms for us are neither criteria for the application of concepts nor irrelevant to our concepts. If the above propositions about rape were directly criterial for the application of concepts of blameworthiness, then this disagreement would show that the Pakistani Parliamentary leader did not share our concept of blameworthiness, and he and the reporter would have been talking past each other. This would not be a disagreement so much as a misunderstanding avoidable by an appropriate translation. But the connection between these hardened propositions and our concepts, if one must speak this way, is not so simple. To be sure, if enough instances piled up in which we and our interlocutor diverged on questions of blameworthiness, we might begin to suspect that an adjustment of translation was in order. A few cases of divergence, however, are not enough to warrant this expedient. Nonetheless, divergence over a principle we find unquestionable indicates that our interlocutor has a very different working theory than we do. Since his working theory interconnects with all else that is said or thought in his culture on these topics, it could be said to form a distinctive feature of his conceptual scheme. Here I am not attempting to say anything new about radical disagreement, and certainly not to deny the grammatical proposition that disagreement depends on a background of agreement; what I am trying to do is to articulate the elements of a conceptual scheme, divergence with regard to which can make disagreements deep.

Although hardened propositions and tacit learning both give rise to what might be called paradigms, the way they pose barriers to understanding is quite different. Hardened propositions represent paradigms in the sense Wittgenstein mentions: that "with which experience is compared and judged." Since we consciously test our experience by them, we are relatively aware of what they are, or can articulate them fairly easily if brought up short by a conversation such as that between Zwerdling and Ali Khan. They impose barriers because we ordinarily rely upon them, and lose our footing when we can no longer do so. Tacit learning, by contrast, involves paradigms that are more particular, paradigms in the sense of the exemplars that help give meaning to our terms and principles. These are regularly lost to consciousness. While some extraordinary experience may remind us of them, they generally affect our thought and speech more by their residual causal traces than by their conscious presence. Accordingly, the paradigms involved in tacit learning can impose barriers to mutual understanding because we are unaware of how they have shaped one's thinking. Suppose, for instance, that one had been brought up to think of Frederick II of Prussia as an ideal monarch, a model of enlightenment and beneficence, even though he relied heavily upon his censors. This fact about one's formation would presumably have had important effects upon one's views about censorship; yet since the connection between Frederick and the theory of censorship is accidental, it could well remain hidden. Here, again, we have an exemplar that is hardly criterial of the concept or principle in question (acceptable censorship), but that nonetheless has an important effect upon how that concept or principle became formed. It is part of the web of belief surrounding that concept or principle and giving it life. Therefore, this sort of barrier to mutual understanding is indicative of a troublesome divergence of conceptual scheme. Or take another example, which is temporally closer to home. A newspaper story of a few years ago reported the trauma of a young child who had been mistreated and finally abandoned by its parents and family, most of whom were addicted to crack cocaine. Placement with loving foster parents could not undo all the harm of this child's horrible first years. "Even with the security of a permanent home," the article reported, "the child still has bitter memories. When his adoptive father's mother asked him to call her 'grandma,' the request unleashed an old pain. 'If I call you grandma,' the child responded, 'does that mean you can burn me?'" (*The Washington Post*, Sept. 10, 1989, A23). While everyone's grandmother is different, it is fair to say that this poor child's exemplar of that role diverged radically from that experienced by me and most of my readers. Yet the child will identify as its grandmother the same relative that we would: This is not a simple problem of translation.

The final sort of barrier to mutual understanding concerns the cognitive ends that implicitly define theoretical or intellectual success.[8] To take a familiar if oversimplified case, seventeenth-century scientists differed over the relative importance of two desiderata in judging the success of an astronomical theory: simplicity and compatibility with Roman Catholic theology. Such cognitive values – values that go into defining what is taken as theoretical success – may either be stated as explicit principles or be buried within certain exemplary solutions that were praised in the theorist's training. Sometimes it is a bit of both, as with the contemporary analytic philosopher's attachment to the value of "clarity" – an intellectual virtue that is more optional than charity. While there is no doubt that recent anglophone philosophers have indeed prominently used this value to judge the success or worth of philosophical writing, it is nonetheless quite hard to give any general definition of what is meant by clarity (and don't say, "of course *Richardson* has no idea what clarity is"!). Instead, one points to exemplars; and at this point one finds surprising divergence. For instance, some "analytic" philosophers would declare Wittgenstein's *Tractatus Logico-Philosophicus* to be a model of philosophical clarity. To others within the same broad tradition, it is a piece of mysticism bordering on the incomprehensible. Sometimes clarity seems to be a matter mostly of *how* arguments are set out, in which case David Lewis's writings might

8 See Kuhn 1970, 149; Newton Smith 1981. Lukes 1991 exaggerates in holding that Kuhn's case for conceptual incommensurability boils down entirely to an assertion of the non-objectivity and incommensurability of cognitive ends. Part of my purpose in going over all three barriers that Kuhn identifies is to preserve the distinctness between the two forms of incommensurability.

serve as exemplary; but sometimes clarity can also be a function of *what* is being said, in which case Lewis's penchant for speaking of possible worlds and otherwise multiplying metaphysical entities leads others to see nonsense: an argument cannot be clear, on this latter view, if we cannot know what it is about. In political argument, even the modicum of consensus upon cognitive values exemplified by certain academic disciplines is likely to be lacking, for there is no institutional support for it. Nonetheless, such cognitive values still influence our judgments of whether a political dispute has been resolved by satisfactory cognitive means. Appeal to or compatibility with sacred texts is an obvious case of this. In divergence pertaining to such cognitive values we have another sort of barrier to mutual understanding, one that can help explain deep disagreement.

We can therefore rehabilitate the notion of the conceptual scheme by reverting to these three sorts of barrier to mutual understanding: hardened propositions, tacit exemplars, and incommensurable cognitive ends. While all three were present in Kuhn's discussion from the beginning, his occasionally more radical rhetoric seemed to put forward a target vulnerable to Davidson's attack on the intelligibility of a total conceptual incommensurability. Having seen in the last section that this attack did not in fact touch the "very idea" of conceptual schemes, we may be confident that this tripartite structure may be useful in explaining the depth of disagreement in terms of divergence of conceptual schemes.

If all three sorts of barrier to mutual understanding are strongly present in a given case of disagreement, then it will make sense to say that this is a case of conceptual incommensurability. The challenge thus posed to reasonable dialogue is deep, for each of these barriers goes to the heart of what it is to justify or to set out considerations for or against a claim. Propositions hardened as if into rules, in serving as standards by which to test experience, thereby stand as the strongest sorts of premise available within a given conception. These are the first principles or the axioms upon which justification is taken to rest. Throw these in question, and one no longer knows how to array justificatory considerations. Paradigms in the stricter, tacit sense play a less central role in justification, but nonetheless importantly determine what counts as a consideration or as an effective argument for someone. This is particularly so in politics, in which anecdote and experience are likely to have a stronger influence on what gets counted as a good approach than does any axiom system. Finally, the cognitive values appealed to in any intellectual domain play an obvious role in determining or summing up what is understood by an "effective justification" by those working in that field. To array considerations in a way that wholly lacked simplicity or unification might not matter within some contexts, yet be a fatal flaw in others. Accordingly, where all three barriers are strongly present, it will be highly difficult to array the considerations taken to support one conception in the terms of another. The principles, the exemplary models, and the cognitive values will not be sufficiently shared to allow it. Or perhaps this conclusion should be put in a more qualified way, since it is so difficult to give a nonarbitrary specification of what it is for considerations to be "adequately" arrayed in the terms of another conception. What we can see is that these barriers to mutual understanding create something like an incommensurability of conceptual schemes by making it difficult to appreciate the justification of each conception from the point of view of the other.

§41. SPECIFYING COGNITIVE ENDS

Divergence regarding cognitive ends, those values employed in justified and adjudicating between theories, has emerged as one of three sources of conceptual incommensurability. If all conceptual incommensurability could be traced to this source, then my arguments would have already shown that rational deliberation would not be disturbed by conceptual incommensurability. At least in the internalized case, for the single deliberator who is of two minds, deliberation could proceed in the ways already described. Since conceptual incommensurability also has two other independent sources, however, we are not yet done. We must deal with the barriers imposed by divergence over hardened propositions (in the next chapter) and tacit exemplars (in Chapter XIV). Before I proceed to this new work, however, I would like to consolidate the conclusion about the applicability of specifying rationality to divergence of cognitive ends. For it may be thought that cognitive ends lie so deeply embedded in one's modes of thinking and become so criterial of what one takes to be reasonable or justified that they would not be susceptible of deliberative specification. To the contrary, I will argue that there is room for deliberative specification even in higher-order cognitive ends.

Truth is the first virtue of systems of thought, as justice is of social institutions. Yet just as justice falls short of being a sufficient virtue for political arrangements, so too truth should not be regarded as the only virtue of theories. To say this is not yet to lapse into any form of antirealism in metaphysics. Suppose one thought of theories simply as propositions concatenated in certain ways, and held that every one of these propositions were determinately true or false on account of their corre-

266

spondence or lack thereof with an independent reality. Still, it would be of interest to us how the theory concatenates these propositions. Are they arranged so as to generate additional true propositions to interpret continuously unfolding experience? If so, we might say that the theory exhibits *fruitfulness*. And while fruitfulness might be cashed out in terms of the long-run promotion of true beliefs, there are other cognitive virtues not reducible to truth. For instance, are the true propositions organized in a way that enables us easily to grasp their combined import? This would be one of the ways the virtue of *simplicity* would manifest itself. Are they structured so as to make apparent their continuity with theories adhered to in the past? In that case, we might say that this theory has the virtue of *continuity*. And so on. Of two theories with the same number (or proportion, or . . .) of true propositions, we would find the one better that better exhibited these further cognitive virtues. This suggests that these additional cognitive virtues are not merely instrumental to attaining truth.[9] They represent, or are taken to represent, independent intrinsic goods. These virtues of theories are also values of ours with regard to theories, naming what we aim for in a theory. They exemplify what I mean by *cognitive ends*. However hardheaded a metaphysical realist one is, one will still have reason not to neglect these other ends besides (correspondence with the) truth. As Hilary Putnam has put it (1981, 134), they form "part of our idea of human cognitive flourishing."

The principle of charity in interpretation (§39) offers a fascinating window on the role of incommensurable cognitive ends in deep disagreement. Although the principle of charity is often invoked to deny the existence of conceptual incommensurability, difficulties with interpreting the principle itself undercut this strategy. Charity requires specification and, as I will argue, may be pulled in different directions by the incommensurable cognitive ends to which it is responsible. Still, understanding the relation between them and charity will further underline the importance and possibility of specifying cognitive ends.

There have been many attempts to set out the principle of charity in canonical form. Its introduction into the context of radical translation by Quine was quite informal: "The maxim of translation underlying all this is that assertions startlingly false on the face of them are likely to turn on

---

9 Although Putnam 1981 vigorously argues for the importance of additional cognitive values besides truth, he concedes on p. 128 that *if* metaphysical realism were correct, then these additional values might well be shown to be merely instrumental to the attainment of truth. I am here suggesting that this would not be the case, even given a metaphysical realist's conception of truth.

hidden differences of language. . . . The common sense behind the maxim is that one's interlocutor's silliness, beyond a certain point, is less likely than bad translation – or, in the domestic case, linguistic divergence" (Quine 1960, 59). Yet in a footnote appended to this rather noncommittal version of the principle, Quine quotes N. L. Wilson's principle of charity (whence, apparently, its name): "We select as designatum that individual which will make the largest possible number of . . . statements true." Davidson's formulations of the principle of charity typically split the difference between Quine's and Wilson's. Like Wilson's, Davidson's is peremptory; like Quine's, Davidson's falls within the general rubric of providing the best explanation.

To pursue the scope and need for specifying the principle of charity, let us focus our attention on the appeal to charity in interpreting philosophical texts. For example, in what way is it appropriate to invoke charity to settle questions of interpretation that a philosophical text otherwise leaves open? Suppose the undisputed part of a text makes an argument that, as we understand it, is invalid, and suppose that another, quite obscure and ambiguous passage could be interpreted as supplying a missing premise so as to make the argument come out valid. Does charity dictate resolving the ambiguities in the latter passage this way? Interpreters of philosophical texts vary widely in their willingness to do so. At one extreme are those who use logical distinctions that could not have been formulated before Frege to determine whether, say, an Aristotelian argument is valid. If it is not valid by those lights, these interpreters feel free to divine the missing premises in patched-together fragments and throwaway lines. After all, what could be more uncharitable than to attribute to a philosopher an invalid argument? At another extreme are those who insist on collecting all the potentially relevant ancillary information before even attributing a structure of argument. Postponing or resisting the invocation of charity until the last moment does help reveal what is deeply different in the text or the culture being interpreted: but there is no hope of making this trade-off by looking to see which approach best reveals "the real meaning" of the text. What we mean by "the meaning" of a text is something we cannot prize apart from our practices of interpretation, contested though they be. Accordingly, to arrive at a reasoned methodological position which locates itself along the dimension of contrast just noted, the interpreter must specify the end of charity that guides his or her efforts.

Interpreting charitably, one naturally takes account of the cognitive aims the authors (if any) had in writing what they did. Consider, for example, the aim of challenging and provoking the readers, of awakening them from their dogmatic slumbers. Is the translator of Machiavelli's *Prince* to be charitable by resolving ambiguities and seeking to maximize the agreement between Machiavelli and ourselves? Or is it more charitable to Machiavelli to set him out as intentionally provocative and deliberately, teasingly cryptic? Should a translator of Nietzsche's *Thus Spake Zarathustra* aim above all to make it "make sense"? Is the beauty of Boethius's *Consolation of Philosophy* incidental to its message, such that its beauty may be sacrificed in a translation that aims above all to exhibit the validity of its arguments?

The complexity of the aims of philosophical writings, their irreducibility to the simple idea of speaking the truth, holds also of other forms of discourse. The poverty of literal truth-saying as a sole aim of speech is nicely set out by Harry Frankfurt, by means of an anecdote about Wittgenstein (Frankfurt 1988, 123). It seems that Wittgenstein spoke on the telephone with a friend who had recently been severely ill. When Wittgenstein asked her how she felt, she allowed as how she felt "like a dog that has been run over." Wittgenstein's indignant rejoinder: "You don't know what a dog that has been run over feels like." This little story indicates what a radical revision of our linguistic practices would be required to purge them of everything but attempts to state the literal truth. Charity to Wittgenstein makes one wonder whether he wasn't making a joke to cheer up his friend.

Because of the internal complexity of charity, which must be specified by reference to other, variously conflicting cognitive ends, we must give up any idea that the principle of charity stands proxy for some single, simple value such as intelligibility or truth. To "make sense" of some utterances or some text is manifestly an end begging for further specification, like the philosopher's "clarity"; and other ends are relevant to how the principle of charity gets specified. The same points will hold, *mutatis mutandis*, for the idea of a "best explanation."

It follows from this that far from holding conceptual incommensurability at bay, the necessity of charity illustrates one of the principal causes of conceptual incommensurability, namely the clash of incommensurable cognitive ends. If the incommensurability of these ends precluded rational deliberation about how to resolve tensions between them, then the necessity of charity, far from reassuring us about the possibilities of rational cross-cultural dialogue, would doom us to a situation in which even the very notion of cross-cultural understanding was subject to controversies falling beyond the ken of rational discussion.

As I argued in Part Three, however, even incommensurable ends are subject to rational deliberation and specification. It follows that the sorts of conflicts set out in this section do not, by themselves, pose a new challenge to the account of deliberation that I have developed. The possibility of specifying the end of coherence, which was defended in §26, indicates that the mere fact that the ends involved are cognitive ones of broad relevance to inquiry and interpretation does not mean that they cannot be reasonably specified. While I have not paused to develop a sample path of specifying charity, I have tried to say enough about the connections to other ends to suggest to the reader how this might go. Accordingly, in assessing the distinct challenges posed to rational deliberation by deep disagreement, we should focus on the remaining two barriers, divergence on hardened propositions and in tacit exemplars.

XIII

Dialectical softening

Where people differ radically over what they take to be axiomatic, it is likely that they also arrived at these beliefs through strikingly different tacit exemplars. The example of disagreement concerning the treatment of rape victims in Pakistan presented in §37 illustrated how both of these aspects of deep disagreement arise together. Their coincidence might be thought to exacerbate the difficulties of a rational bridge across deep disagreement. To the contrary, I will argue in this chapter: The dependence of hardened propositions upon tacit exemplars actually provides a way to soften the former. In other words, the importance of tacit learning undercuts the supposed rigidity of hardened propositions. In thus playing one barrier off against the other, I will leave tacit exemplars as the last remaining one to be reckoned with. Their importance will be assessed in the final chapter. While my imperative, defensive purpose for discussing interpersonal deliberation requires only that I deal with the case of the single person of mixed upbringing, it is simpler for purposes of exposition to stick with an interpersonal example. Although a single person of mixed upbringing can have absorbed radically divergent hardened propositions and cognitive ends from concrete experiences offering contrasting tacit exemplars, it is difficult to keep the tacit aspect of his or her internal division in view. In the case of different people from different cultures, by contrast, it is quite obvious. Accordingly, I will revert regularly to the case of rape in Pakistan to illustrate and test the abstract possibilities for which I will argue.

§42. THE TACIT GROUND OF RULES

As a first step toward addressing the barrier posed by hardened propositions, I will bring out how they depend upon tacit exemplars. In the case of learning, for instance, it has long been obvious that particular exemplars serve as vehicles that carry the pupil toward the general proposition. Philosophers have debated in what sense they are the vehicles, and how the general proposition can possibly be learned from (more) particular instances, given that they do not logically contain it. How does one move from five fingers plus five fingers making ten fingers and five toes plus five toes making ten toes to five plus five making ten? What allows for the leap of abstraction apparently required? Here philosophers have offered a variety of answers, ranging from the Platonic theory of "recollection" to empirical conditioning to the existence of innate structures of mind that facilitate the move. But set aside these different answers to this question, for a moment, and focus on what the question itself implies, namely the importance of a move that abstracts from the exemplars. In highlighting this implication, I am not endorsing a radically empiricist or particularist theory of learning according to which all data is initially innocent of general concepts and commitments. The point is a more modest one, namely that from whatever sort of basis, abstraction is required in learning most general propositions. Some may be self-evident, and some may be theorems derivable from other general propositions already learned; but most, again, will be learned in a way that involves abstracting from more particular instances or exemplars.

Whereas the Western philosophical tradition has focused attention largely upon the precise nature of this move and what licenses it, I want instead to stress that abstracting does not mean leaving the particular exemplars behind. If we were concerned solely with the general proposition and how it can be learned and justified – as we might be in the philosophy of mathematics, for instance – then we might be able to afford ignoring the particular exemplars once the general proposition had been secured. In deliberation, however, it is essential to see how they may be specified; and the way one specifies a general norm will inevitably depend somewhat upon the particular exemplars whereby one learned it. Normal human psychology accounts for part of this dependence. For instance, the lies we were punished for telling as children, thereby learning that lying is wrong, are likely not to have included "white lies" told to avoid hurting someone's feelings or fictional accounts of visits by Santa Claus. Despite these fairly systematic particular omissions, normal adults in our society are likely to have internalized a commitment (of some degree of seriousness) to the quite general norm, "lying is wrong." In these omissions we see an additional reason for recognizing that our norms are at least implicitly qualified by a "generally speaking" (cf. §10). Even so, the general norm will acquire some psychological force of its own, and will be accepted by the agent as having some normative importance. When it comes to the question of how further to specify it, however, it is both psychologically natural and rationally defensible that the agent should be guided by reference to the exemplars (now perhaps tacit and submerged) whereby it was learned. In saying that it is psychologically natural, I do not mean that we do not ever overgeneralize from our experiences in ways that we have difficulty reversing. But if someone who learned the wrongness of lying through this sort of exemplars later specified the prohibition on lying so as to allow benevolently lying to the seriously ill about their diagnosis, we would readily understand why. If the exemplars have become submerged, it will take work to recover them so as to reverse a possibly rash generalization; but this work is often worthwhile. By searching in this way for the particular roots of one's norms, one need not give the last word to the tradition into which one was raised. Rather, one simply shows an appropriate sort of humility about one's general positions, recognizing that for the most part they do not stand on their own and accepting guidance in specifying them from the more particular grounds whereby one learned them.

What of the possibility of a general norm that is self-evident and self-presenting, requiring no basis in particular examples either to make it known or to support it? I do not mean to rule out this possibility; but there are two reasons that it does not disturb my present point. First, I am concentrating upon how the agent will go on to specify the general norm. For instance, suppose that it were a self-evident and self-presenting truth that knowledge is a good to be pursued in this life. For this norm to guide action, it needs to be specified. In this process, the particular exemplars of learning that one admires will naturally be relevant. For the orthodox Sunni, the learned know the Qur'an (the word of God as revealed to Muhammad) and the *hadith* (the well-attested words and deeds of the Prophet), and their knowledge consists in part of their memorization of a vast body of text and in part in their ability to bring that memory to bear. For secularized Westerners, knowledge might be instead exemplified by an awareness and understanding of certain principles of natural science. The Sunni and the Westerner may agree that knowledge is good, but their different specifications of what count as important cases of knowledge will lead them to different specifications of this highly general end. Even if the general principle is self-evident and self-presenting, in other words, particular exemplars are important to its interpretation.

The context of my present argument also limits the relevance of the possibility of self-evident and self-presenting general norms. We are considering hardened propositions insofar as they make disagreement deep.

273

Accordingly, the general propositions relevant to our discussion are necessarily not ones that are self-evident to all. If they were, then divergence with regard to them could not form a basis of disagreement. To be sure, someone might *say*, without sounding silly, that it is "self-evident to the orthodox Sunni" that the injunctions of the Qur'an are to be followed, for they are the literal word of God, or that it is "self-evident to the secularized Westerner" that propositions not consistent with natural science must be rejected. What these expressions really indicate, however, is that these general principles are, after all, dependent upon the different concrete experiences, ways of life, and particular norms of these two individuals, which are referred to in shorthand fashion by calling them an "orthodox Sunni" and a "secularized Westerner."

The pervasive role for exemplars in learning led Wittgenstein to balk at saying flat out that "hardened propositions" such as arithmetical truths are "rules" independent of any empirical basis. In differentiating hardened propositions from criteria in §40, we saw that he says only that "it is *as if* we had hardened the empirical proposition into a rule" (Wittgenstein 1978, VI.22, p. 324, emphasis added). Part VI of his *Remarks on the Foundations of Mathematics* meditates on the fact that statements that function for us as paradigms of reality, or as analytic truths, nonetheless have an empirical basis of a sort in the training by which they are inculcated. Although Wittgenstein's thoughts on such matters arise from observations about learning, they nonetheless provide an additional argument against the idea that hardened propositions could govern independently of tacit exemplars. In a nutshell, the argument is that general rules by themselves cannot settle their own application. That is why we cannot rightly say that experience has in actuality hardened into a rule.

It is true that for many years it was popular to think that Wittgenstein was principally concerned with exploring the criteria for the application of concepts. It is now increasingly recognized, however, that Wittgenstein unsettles this notion, too.[1] The easiest, although not necessarily the most trustworthy way to approach this aspect of Wittgenstein's thought is to do so via the interpretation of Kripke 1982, which finds a kind of "meaning skepticism" in the texts. On Kripke's beguiling reading, one of Wittgenstein's main aims is to show that there is no fact about the speaker that

---

1 See, e.g., the postscript to Albritton 1966 and Wright 1984. Thus, although Wittgenstein often uses the term in his later writings, he far more often does so to raise a question about whether there are any criteria for the application of a concept than to suggest a criterion for doing so. For example, he asks: "What is the criterion of the visual experience? – The criterion? What do you suppose?" (Wittgenstein 1958, p. 198).

indicates what he means by a given concept. This is the point of the "private language argument," on Kripke's reading; but the alleged inner states in question are but one possibility for the sort of individual facts that might be invoked to fix meanings. The more general point is encapsulated by Wittgenstein's refrain that it is useless to invoke a rule to interpret a rule (e.g., 1958, §§84–6). At some point, "interpretation comes to an end" (1978, VI.38, p. 342). To consolidate the argument that there is no individual fact that settles meaning, Kripke asks us to imagine an individual carrying on Wittgenstein's favorite series: 2, 4, 6, ... The rule is "add 2," it seems. Adapting a device of Nelson Goodman's, however (and still undertaking to represent Wittgenstein's view), Kripke argues that there could not possibly be any individual fact that determined that someone meant to continue this series by "addition" as we typically understand it, as opposed to by "quaddition," which is just like ordinary addition except that in continuing this series beyond a certain finite number greater than any yet encountered in the individual's experience, one adds 4. Given the futility of postulating a further rule to govern the interpretation of the one in question, the lesson of this Wittgensteinian argument is twofold. First, it indicates that rules are not what some might have thought they were – self-sufficient guides for how to "go on" in the world. Second, it suggests that in those domains in which we do seem able to follow rules – as, say, in mathematics – our ability to do so, if it is to be explained at all, cannot be explained simply by reference to the rules being followed. This Wittgensteinian argument, then, shows that hardened propositions cannot stand on their own. They require constraint from some other source to guide their interpretation.

My suggestion, of course, is that tacit exemplars are necessarily involved in this further guidance required in following a rule. This general conclusion may be maintained quite independently of the precise account one gives of how this extra guidance works. For instance, it will hold whether the emphasis is put upon the social practices, the "form of life," wherein the rules are applied, or instead upon the idea "that there is a way of grasping a rule which is *not* an *interpretation*" (Wittgenstein 1958, Pt. I, §201). Practices are concrete entities replete with exemplary instances that tacitly inform how people go on. The noninterpretive grasp of a rule, if it is to be explicable at all, needs to be related back to the training within concrete practices, tacit reference to which makes it possible. The reader will recall that in §27 I emphasized the importance of a self-awareness of one's tacit commitments in supplementing the more explicit elements of one's deliberation. In the person of practical wisdom,

275

a trained grasp reflects concretely inculcated virtue.[2] Either way, then, it looks as if tacit exemplars must play an important role in giving a full account of how hardened propositions function as norms.

The recent history of the philosophy of science confirms that hardened propositions depend on tacit exemplars because of the nature of learning and the rules' lack of self-sufficiency. Thomas Kuhn, from whom I have taken the idea of the three conceptual barriers to mutual understanding, was in his detailed historical work well aware of the interdependence of hardened propositions and tacit exemplars. Yet in his early presentation of the "incommensurability" of radically different views, Kuhn seems to have been still (via Sir Karl Popper) under the sway of the positivist conception of rules Wittgenstein was attacking. Take the first of these points about Kuhn first. Largely because the work of science is never completed, he held, the principles that define "normal science" remain open to further specification and revision (Kuhn 1970, 23–4). Recalcitrant facts will remain within the field that the science marks out for itself, and other unexplained phenomena will remain outside that field. Room for further articulation and revision will persist. The student's training in normal science, Kuhn emphasizes, depends throughout on an appeal to exemplars. Accordingly, accepting certain propositions as if they were axiomatic comes together with a context of learning that also prepares the way for questioning those propositions. Of course, to use the vocabulary that Kuhn made notorious, to question (rather than merely to specify) a very central proposition will require a "revolution" and may result in a "paradigm shift." Since revolutionary periods in science are analogous to deep disagreements, this vocabulary should not scare us. What we are looking for is the kind of rationality available in defense of revolutionary moves.

Rational ways of coping with deep disagreement will elude us, however, so long as we see its dependence on tacit exemplars simply as exacerbating the problem. If we cling to the idea that rationality *must* proceed from "hard" rules (whether of scientific method or of good practice), radical divergence among rules that furthermore depend upon divergent concrete exemplars will seem to confirm that rationality cannot address radical disagreement. Kuhn himself, however, quickly saw that a better view of scientific practice would result from dropping this prejudice

---

2 McDowell 1984 goes too far in casting the needed "grasp" as an inexplicable intuition of which way to "go on." I suggest that the account of self-perception put forward in §27 offers a better way for McDowell to combine his emphasis upon the idea of the "way of grasping a rule which is *not* an *interpretation*" with his insistence that this grasp is like the trained perception of the *phronimos*.

about rationality, thereby allowing for a more flexible account of the grounds of theory choice. It was left to Paul Feyerabend to champion the idea that conceptual incommensurability implies the impossibility of rational resolution of difference. If one examines Feyerabend's writings (especially Feyerabend 1978), the persistence of the (neo-)positivist idea that rationality depends upon "hard" rules leaps to the fore. By contrast, for the context of practical deliberation, I have been defending an account of rationality that does not depend upon general norms being either deductively applicable, unrevisable, or the source of value.

§43. HOLISM'S OPENING

Given the pervasive dependence of hardened propositions upon tacit exemplars, as set out in the last section, we may now see in outline how rational deliberation will be able to make headway despite deep disagreement. (1) Even if hardened propositions diverge, their dependence upon tacit exemplars for their working specification means that there may be room to work from agreement on more specific matters toward a consensus at the level of general principle. (2) As we saw in §39, the idea of *total* disagreement or *total* conceptual incommensurability is incoherent. This implies that there must be some agreement, at some level, with which deliberation may work. (3) Since the holistic conception of practical reflection developed in Part Three allows that deliberation may work from the more specific to the more general or vice versa, revising in either direction, it may accept an agreed starting point at any level of generality. This entrée for reasonable discussion I will call "holism's opening."

Let me elaborate on the third of these points. It is crucial to this strategy that the account of rational deliberation that I am defending will accept an agreed starting point of any sort. Since rationality in deliberation is largely a matter of the mutual fit among commitments, it is not necessary at first to find norms that both disputants can embrace as a priori principles or self-evident axioms. Accordingly, it may proceed in the face of divergence over hardened propositions. Agreement can begin with obvious, mundane details, or with the practical "nitty-gritty," in Richard Rorty's phrase (1987, n. 20), and later seek a more generalized expression. Jonsen and Toulmin have claimed that their experience on a U.S. national commission on medical ethics showed it was generally easier to get the panel to agree on the rightness or wrongness of a given, relatively specific class of cases – for example, the sort of consent required for medical research involving competent adult subjects – than it was to articulate general principles (Jonsen and Toulmin 1988, 16–18). While the lesson that they draw is that general theory is not a necessity, my argument in Chapter VIII, extended to the interpersonal case, implies rather that this basis of relatively particular agreement can be used to generate shared theory, which one might need to address further cases not yet the subject of agreement.

Alternatively or by alternation, of course, agreement can begin very vague, abstract, and tentative, and reach for greater specification and firmness. In the Pakistani rape example, both a liberal Westerner and a traditionalist Sunni will agree that rape is wrong. Even though they differ sharply about the nature of this crime, the place of women in society, the relative reliability of male and female witnesses, and the relevant religious background, this abstract point of agreement provides a place for reasonable dialogue to begin. The holist point, for the present, is just that it does not matter that the initial agreement does not comprise well-specified first principles. Holist reasoning can begin from a contingent agreement at any level of abstraction or firmness.

It will be objected that I am here illicitly strengthening the conclusion of the Davidsonian argument against total disagreement. That argument showed that it is incoherent to imagine two people who disagree about *everything*, not that it is incoherent to imagine two people who disagree about all propositions *relevant to a given topic*. Yet I am implicitly assuming the latter, far stronger conclusion in supposing that this argument shows that, say, there must necessarily be some agreed proposition relevant to the treatment of rape victims on which Western liberals and Sunni Muslims agree. Yet this does not follow from Davidson's conceptual arguments! In response, while I must admit that it does not, strictly speaking, follow, we may nonetheless see that something of the sort may be generated by reapplying the sort of argument that Davidson deployed against total disagreement. If the liberal Westerner and the traditionalist Sunni really do disagree about the treatment of rape victims, then there must be some propositions about rape (and about victims) on which they agree. For instance, I mentioned in first setting out that example that the legal definition of "rape" in Pakistan embraces categories of fraud and mistake that American usage would leave out. That is no great problem. But now suppose that the Pakistani definition covered those cases but omitted from its purview cases of physically forced intercourse. We would then readily conclude that these two interlocutors were not talking about the same thing, and rightly doubt whether the homophonic translation from Pakistani English was correct. This conclusion might appear paradoxical, es-

278

pecially if thought to imply that by beginning from the bare necessity of some agreement somewhere one could proceed in stepwise fashion to demonstrate that everyone agrees about everything. This does not follow, however, for there is a crucial difference between the general and the specific applications of the argument. Davidson intended the argument as revealing a necessary fact about the relations between different people's views. The more specific extensions of the argument, by contrast, are contingent. *If* two people disagree meaningfully about some question, then there must be some propositions relevant to that question on which they agree. It is, of course, possible that they do not disagree meaningfully on some question. For instance, although modern physicists can disagree with Aristotle about motion, they cannot disagree with him about quarks. A traditionalist Sunni may have no view on whether the fate of Pakistani women who bring rape complaints violates a right against self-incrimination, for he may recognize no such right. Accordingly, the narrower question of whether women's right against self-incrimination should be protected by sheltering them from prosecutions based on their rape complaints is not one from which our interlocutors may productively begin in dealing with their wider disagreement about the treatment of rape victims. Nonetheless, our abstract arguments show that there must be some relevant agreed proposition from which they may begin. Holism will always have an opening.

§44. SURMOUNTING DISAGREEMENT ON HARDENED PROPOSITIONS

This is an appropriate point to remind the reader that I am testing and extending an account of deliberation. The reasoning with which I am concerned, therefore, is reasonably focused on some question about what to do. I am not addressing global attempts to reconcile entire worldviews or conceptual schemes. This ability to take matters piecemeal is important. It allows me to employ a generalized version of Rawls's idea of an "overlapping consensus" (Rawls 1987, 1989). The notion defines the sort of agreement required for interpersonal deliberation of ends to proceed.

To be sure, in the interpersonal context even less demanding notions of deliberative success are available. For instance, one might count a joint deliberation a success just in case the parties agree about what to do, and recognize it as an instance of deliberation of ends just in case the ends of at least one of the disputants are reformulated on the way to this agreement. On this lax criterion of agreement, the ends of the disputants need

279

not come to coincide. For instance, imagine two factions deeply disagreeing about the regulation of abortion. One decides to accept a certain degree of regulation because it is what their moral precepts require. The other faction goes along with this because its members realize that the political party that most of them support (on the basis of other values besides those directly relevant to abortion) will lose heavily in the upcoming elections unless they do so. Mere agreement about what to do, when it has such a contingent instrumental basis, is what is called in political theory a *modus vivendi* (cf. Rawls 1987). It is a result that allows the disputants to live peaceably with one another. Although it thus averts the use of force, it need not be endorsed as morally acceptable or as supported by the relevant cognitive ends or hardened propositions of either side.[3]

One way to get beyond a bare *modus vivendi*, and at the same time to try to reach for some objective content in what is agreed, is to imagine that the interpersonal bargaining is governed or constrained by some such values as mutual respect, respect for individual autonomy, or civility. The last of these imposes a relatively minimal constraint. Richard Rorty invokes it in describing his ideal of philosophy as continuing an interdisciplinary "conversation," which he distinguishes from an "inquiry," in that only the latter must begin from shared ends – especially, I suppose, shared cognitive ends (Rorty 1979, 318). Although a civil conversation is certainly more polite, and probably more responsive to substantive ideas, than much of *modus vivendi* politics, Rorty deliberately casts it as not amounting to much of an agreement. Other theorists, particularly liberal theorists, have thought conversational constraints to have stronger implications (e.g., Habermas 1990). Both Ackerman's and Larmore's neutralist liberalisms (Ackerman 1980; Larmore 1987) develop the norm of respect for individual autonomy as a constitutive constraint on hypothetical political dialogues, and thereby aim to support liberal conclusions. Whatever interest these strategies may have as political theories – as, in effect, dramatic ways of using the value of autonomy to support a certain set of political principles – their central reliance on principles that are not, in fact, accepted by all the parties makes them of little interest in addressing the problem of deep disagreement. Those for whom respect for autonomy, say, is not a centrally important commitment would not accept this constraint on their deliberations, unless it followed from some previous deliberation. Those who do rally around respect for autonomy will accept

3 In this and the succeeding few paragraphs, I make use of a set of distinctions developed in Richardson 1990b.

its dictates without having been told to do so by the political philosopher. Yet the idea of a constrained *modus vivendi* has been attractive not only as a way of yielding liberal conclusions, but also as a way of making intelligible how significant agreement on political principles might coexist with a continuing cultural pluralism.

There is, however, another important way of modeling this possibility, namely in terms of Rawls's idea of an "overlapping consensus." In this approach, the conversation is limited, not by being constrained to respect a given value, but by taking up only one topic at a time (in Rawls's case, the issue is to determine in outline the essentials of a just constitutional scheme). An overlapping consensus will exist if (1) the disputants can agree on normative principles to govern the limited domain selected, and (2) not merely for tactical reasons, as in the abortion example of two paragraphs back, but on the basis of their most fundamental moral beliefs or their conception of the ultimate good. Since there is no requirement that these more fundamental principles coincide, the idea of an overlapping consensus explains how a true normative agreement on political principles – one forged on the basis of the disputants' distinct conceptions of the good and not simply as a product of bargaining and compromise – can coexist with a healthy pluralism.

Overlapping consensus is a more appropriate ideal for the case of internalized deep disagreement than either of its competitors. A single person of divided background will not be doing well if she is forced to come to a *modus vivendi* with herself, ceding ground to half of her commitments only so as to avoid externally threatened disaster. An intriguing case of a *modus vivendi* compromise between deeply divergent views within a single person is that of Solomon Perel, the subject of the movie *Europa, Europa*. A Jew born in Germany between the wars, he survived World War II by passing himself off as Aryan, attending an elite Hitler Youth school for four years. To manage this feat of survival and deception, he now says, he had to reach a point at which he actually believed (in some sense) that the Jews were vile conspirators and actually felt (at some level) loyalty to Hitler. As is typically the case with *modus vivendi* accommodation, however, there was no sense in which either aspect of his persona could find acceptable the views of the other. Although a way of continuing to act is worked out, there is no agreement on principle. While Perel could probably not have done better than he did, his internal division must have taken a terrible psychological toll. We would not have been surprised had it issued in myriad irrationalities, from weakness of the will to destructive psychosis. Civil conversation with oneself sounds more pleasant, but still

281

will not do as an ideal. Although there can be sound political reasons to restrain dialogue between people to ensure its civility, these reasons do not transfer to the single-person case. There are times when we positively need to be rude to ourselves, at least in the privacy of our own thoughts. Self-respect is an important value, and even perhaps a virtue, but it is not achieved by deliberately refraining to reflect about certain issues. Different reasons, pertaining to the need for selective denial and self-repression so as to maintain sanity, may operate in the person of divided background; but by their nature these are reasons that she cannot reflectively endorse while maintaining them – at least not across all deliberative issues. For example, take the common case of someone raised in one tradition of religious orthodoxy who has married someone of another. She may do perfectly well with the various compromises involved in meshing their religious commitments so long as she represses disquieting thoughts about how they will raise their children. The constrained *modus vivendi* built by keeping this potentially disruptive issue off the agenda will unravel if and when this practical question of child rearing ever arises. Furthermore, when it does, if she feels that she has betrayed her ancestral religion in accommodating her husband, there is no use in her trying to refrain from thinking such self-condemnatory thoughts on the ground that doing so is uncivil. In an account of deliberation in general – as opposed, for instance, to an account of legislative deliberation in a constitutional democracy – it will not do to build in the sort of restrictions that the model of civil conversation supposes.

So far, my arguments about the possibility of deliberation in the face of deep disagreement have been the following. First, underlying incommensurability of cognitive ends is in itself no bar to rational deliberation because value commensurability is not a prerequisite of rational choice. Second, since total disagreement is impossible, there will always be an opening for holistic deliberation. Third, as just noted, this deliberation need not aim at comprehensive agreement, effacing all divergence over exemplars, cognitive ends, and hardened propositions; rather, it simply needs to arrive at an overlapping consensus on the practical issue at hand. It remains, finally, to sketch how an interpersonal dialectic, of the sort set out in §37, can exploit holism's opening so as to build the required overlapping consensus, despite an initial divergence over hardened propositions. To do so, I will return to the example of rape victims in Pakistan first described in §36. For concreteness, let us suppose that the interlocutors are a Western liberal who takes as axiomatic certain norms of human equality, and a traditionalist Sunni judge (a *qadi*), learned in the *hadith* – the accepted sayings of the Prophet – and in Islamic jurisprudence, who takes as axiomatic the content of the Qur'an.

One opening for holistic deliberation in this case was already noted in the last section, namely the proposition that *rape is wrong*. If this is not immediately realized, it may take a mutual effort at abstraction – from different legal definitions of "rape" and from different concrete patterns of treating rape victims and those they accuse – to bring it to the fore. This will be an initial exercise in dialectic. It provides a principle useful for organizing subsequent discussion. Even across the deep divide between them, our Western liberal and orthodox Sunni may without strain jointly specify it further as the principle that *rape is a crime*. To be sure, our two interlocutors disagree in detail about what a crime is. The *qadi* will understand this idea in relation to the fivefold classification of actions under the comprehensive divine law – as commanded, recommended, indifferent, disliked, or prohibited (cf. Ziadeh 1990, 75). The liberal Westerner will likely understand the notion of a "crime" somewhat more positivistically, in terms of what is forbidden by the state. Nonetheless, there is no serious obstacle to their abstracting to a more neutral understanding of a crime as a serious wrong for which one deserves to be punished (cf. Doi 1984, 222).

If these two agree that rapists deserve to be punished, whence the disagreement about how to treat rape victims? In working toward consensus here, there is an important dialectical role for the distinction between "women who bring rape complaints" and "women who have been raped." Those who publicly defend the flogging of female rape complainants generally do so on the assumption that they are speaking about women who have committed adultery (*zina*), not about women who have suffered from rape or unconsented intercourse at the hands of someone not their husband (*zina-bil-jabr*). It is the purported omniscience of a liberal, Westernized press that presents the cases of women such as Jehan Mina as cases in which the woman was raped. These defenders of the law presumably doubt that they have been. Although I am inclined to think otherwise, we will not see how progress can be made in the face of this deep disagreement unless we abstract for a moment from different views on this factual question. On the stipulation that a woman has been raped, a traditionalist *qadi* will impose no punishment upon her, for as the Prophet apparently said, "my ummah [my believers] will be forgiven for crimes it commits under duress, in error, or as a result of forgetfulness" (quoted in Doi 1984, 227–8). Thus the crucial question becomes, Has she been raped or not? In turn, this focuses our attention on the law of evidence.

At this level, too, you will recall that the disagreement is deep. Even accepting traditional Islamic views about evidence, however, it seems that convicting a woman of *zina* solely on the basis of admitted intercourse outside of marriage fails to take seriously the possibility that she has been raped. If, as suggested above, the orthodox will require that culpable cases of *zina* be consenting, then even after intercourse outside marriage is proven a further question should remain as to whether or not the woman consented, or indeed was coerced. It is fully consonant with Western law for the burden of proof to fall upon those who would prosecute someone for a crime. Applying this idea consistently, however, should shift the burden once the woman is herself charged with *zina*. Accordingly, failure to meet the standards of evidence necessary to prove the intercourse was coercive so as to convict the rapist should not mean that one thereby has proven, by standards of evidence necessary to convict the woman, that the intercourse was consenting. In other words, it seems that the relevant standards of evidence, whatever they are, are not being consistently applied. This should be possible to show within the assumptions of the *qadi*, for Islamic law lays down strict standards of evidence for prosecuting all *zina* charges. Bearing false witness in adultery cases is itself a *hudud* crime punishable by flogging, for the Prophet himself was concerned about the danger of false convictions for adultery. This being the case, the strict standards of evidence applied for *zina* cases in general should be applied to the question whether the intercourse in question was coerced or not.

Why is a double standard being applied? It seems fairly clear that the answer has more to do with tribal or ethnic traditions concerning honor (*izzat*) than it does with Islamic law and culture. It is in the former context, rather than in the context of the Islamic law of *zina*, where there is really little difference between adultery and rape. Either way, the woman who lies with a man outside marriage has put a blot upon her family's honor. So far as I know, there is nothing in the Qur'an that licenses the idea of the father or the brother either killing the woman so sullied or recommending that she commit suicide. The Islamic law of adultery makes explicit that punishment is to be imposed by the *qadi*, who is to attend to the strict standards of evidence set out above. In tribal practice, by contrast, an accusation seems to be deemed enough to go upon. This has a certain logic to it, in that the family's honor is already stained as soon as an accusation of adultery is made. For many in Pakistan, it appears, these tribal practices provide a rich source of exemplars that become integrated with the conservative Muslim male's understanding of the Qur-'an. Yet this is a good example of the way in which hardened propositions can be played off against tacit exemplars; for since our *qadi* by hypothesis accepts the Qur'an and Sunnah as axiomatic, and since these tribal practices clash with the divine law by undercutting the latter's standards of evidence for *zina* cases, the tribal ideas must be resisted.

Even so, there will still arise cases in which two men of presumptive integrity will be willing to testify as eyewitnesses on behalf of a rapist, saying that he did not coerce his victim. Their testimony would satisfy the lesser standards of evidence required for condemning the woman to a second-tier Qur'anic punishment of a mere few dozen lashes and a mere few years in prison. At this point we broach the second layer of this deep disagreement, namely the view (alluded to in §36) that the testimony of women is worth half that of men. Accordingly, it would require the testimony of four female eyewitnesses to defend the complainant. Can there be any argument over this 2 : 1 ratio, which is allegedly based in the Qur'an? In fact, there can be and has been; and this argument again illustrates the usefulness of dialectical distinctions. The verse of the Qur'an that supports this differential is quite explicit: "Call in two male witnesses from among you, but if two men cannot be found, then one man and two women whom you judge fit to act as witnesses; so that if either of them commit an error, the other will remember" (Sura Al-Baqara, Ayat 282; trans. N. J. Dawood). Opponents of the application of this differential to *zina* cases have argued, however, that this passage should be understood in context. It occurs in a paragraph that begins, "Believers, when you contract a debt for a fixed period. . . . " In essence, these critics urge that the differential norm of evidence be specified so as to apply solely to commercial transactions (Khan 1985, 147; Weiss 1986, 102; Jalal 1991, 106).

Following up this possibility through two further layers will exhibit ways holistic dialectic can soften hardened propositions. The *qadi* might resist this specification by invoking more general texts about the intellectual inferiority of women – for there are *hadith* to this effect. Before sketching how debate on this question might go, note that at this point the *qadi* has admitted that the Qur'anic provision requires specification in terms of its fit with other (perhaps more general) elements of the text. Feminist opponents of the 2 : 1 ratio and its application to *zina* cases have taken two different and complementary tacks in arguing within the Islamic texts. The first is to collect opposed texts, which tend to show that the testimony of women is accepted as equally trustworthy as that of men or more generally that women are not intellectually inferior to men. It is noted, for instance, that the Muslim law of evidence developed first and foremost as a set of views governing which purported sayings of the Prophet would be accepted as genuine, and that hundreds of *hadith* have been accepted on the sole basis of the testimony of the Prophet's last wife, 'Aisha (Weiss 1986, 102). The second is to attempt to undercut the various misogynistic *hadith*. One way to do this within the Islamic law is to put the Islamic elaboration of the notion of a trustworthy witness to work in its home context. For instance, Fatima Mernissi (1991, 61) attacks the integrity of Abu Bakra, a freed slave and the source of many of the most misogynistic sayings attributed to the Prophet, on the grounds that since he was flogged for false testimony in a *zina* case he does not count as the sort of person whose testimony can be accepted, let alone relied upon. In other words, in addition to counterposing one set of canonical texts against another, revisionists may also question, on a basis internal to the tradition, which texts should be accepted as canonical.

Even if the general position that women are in some way intellectually inferior to men could be rebutted from within the Qur'an, there would remain an important layer of principled resistance to revising the traditional law of evidence on this basis. This is the orthodox Sunni view, mentioned in §36, that there is no longer any room for interpretation (*ijtihad*). The content of the law is fixed, and it is not licensed for anyone to reinterpret it. Under the traditional interpretation of the Hanafi school of jurisprudence, the leading one in Pakistan, the testimony of women is not accepted in *zina* cases. End of argument – or so it seems.

One might try to take the tack of the Islamic modernist Mohammad Iqbal, and argue that the idea that the "gates of *ijtihad*" have closed is a "pure fiction [that] turns great thinkers into idols" (quoted in Irfani 1985, 42). However, since my hypothetical *qadi* is described first and foremost as a traditionalist Sunni, let me instead describe a possible dialectical clarification of the question whether novel interpretation of the law is permissible. Three distinctions are needed. The first is that between revising and elaborating (cf. Masud 1977, 21). The second is that between the Qur'an, on the one hand, and the interpretations thereof by great thinkers such as Abu Hanifa, the founder of the Hanafi school, on the other. The third concerns the breadth of the term *ijtihad*. For some, its meaning seems confined to the analogical extension of the law (cf. Hasan 1986, 7). For others, *ijtihad* simply means the "best possible attempt at seeking the truth by any means of reasoning" (Hasan 1986, 18). Clearly, the Qur'an and the actual sayings of the Prophet are texts that must not be revised; and clearly, *ijtihad* in the sense of a reasoned application of these principles, or these principles as interpreted by one of the four schools, is necessary. What seems above all at stake in the divisions among the Islamic political parties in contemporary Pakistan is whether the content of the law may be *revised* in reaction to new and changed circumstances. Yet the arguments canvassed above for confining the 2 : 1 ratio to commercial cases do not go so far; rather, they claim that a true interpretation of the divine law would have concluded, at any time since its revelation, that this was its meaning. What is revised is not the Qur'an, but rather the interpretation of the Hanafi school.

This clarification may not mollify our traditionalist *qadi*. Unquestioning adherence to the Hanafi school may, in fact, constitute the central commitment of his professional role. Even so, the opportunity for reasonable argument does not end here. The Hanafi school itself could be combed for provisions that could be shown to conflict with the broad application of the 2 : 1 rule. Another, more interesting approach would be to question this hardened proposition directly. *Why* must the gates of *ijtihad* be thought closed in this sense? In particular, is there any basis in the Qur'an itself for saying that by the end of the ninth century A.D. the opportunity for interpreting the divine law had come to an end? Surely neither the divine word nor its messenger will be found to lay down any such specific and future-oriented dictate about how they are to be interpreted. Rather, the textual basis for the doctrine of the closure of *ijtihad* will presumably lie, instead, in quite general views about the fallibility of human reason (cf. Noori and Amin 1987, 21–2). But now a tension within the traditionalist view, thus supported, opens a chink for holist dialectic to wedge in the second of the three distinctions noted above. If human reason is badly fallible, then only the Qur'an and the actual sayings and practices of the Prophet are trustworthy; but in that case, there is no basis for placing ultimate trust in the reasoning of Abu Hanifa and his disciples. Thus, if our *qadi* finds a strong fallibilism in the Qur'an, then he undercuts his own professional stance. What the *qadi* might say in response to this argument I do not know. A study of the eleventh-century traditionalist Ibn Hazm might uncover some sophisticated answers. I think I have done enough, however, to indicate that despite the acceptance by our *qadi* of hardened propositions quite at odds with those accepted by the Western liberal who has been guiding this rather Socratic dialogue behind the scenes, reasoning can go on. Divergence in hardened propositions does not prevent rational deliberation from moving toward agreement.

Since my presentation of this hypothetical argument has come to an end for now, let me just remind you of its point. The question that guided it was whether divergence on hardened propositions represents an insurmountable bar to reasonable deliberation. In particular, it was whether the internalization thereof by an individual would prevent him or her from resolving rationally any practical conflicts that might arise between them. This background concern with the internalized case licensed the otherwise unnaturally restrained and patient character of the hypothetical course of dialectic that I described. Having to inhabit a single mind will give adherents even of incommensurable views a strong motivation to come to some sort of consensus. (Not necessarily a dominant motivation, however, as the case of Solomon Perel shows.) Obviously, distinct persons may lack comparable motivation for consensus; but motivation to seek a reasonable consensus can also easily be lacking where the disagreement involved is not deep at all. My intention, again, was to focus on the sorts of barrier that the depth of disagreement poses to reasonable deliberation, and in particular upon the problem of divergence in hardened propositions. My claim is that this barrier is not necessarily insurmountable.

Nothing in my argument proves, however, that *all* barriers posed by divergence in hardened propositions are reasonably resolvable. My example, which was narrowly focused, is connected with broader issues on which it might well be harder to reach agreement. For instance, should adultery be the subject of criminal punishment at all? Should Pakistan become a signatory of the United Nations Convention on the Elimination of Discrimination Against Women? Should the 2 : 1 evidentiary ratio apply to commercial transactions? And so on. We would have to take these cases one by one to see how the dialectical argument might go on. In general, however, I am content with the more modest conclusion that some deep disagreements involving divergence in hardened propositions can be resolved. After all, this modesty involves no difference in kind with the position I have taken regarding conflicts that are not deep. As I stressed in Chapter VII, there can be irresolvable clashes between the values and norms *within a single conception*. Therefore, deep disagreement does not introduce the element of irresolvability. My positive claim is simply that holistic deliberation can sometimes rationally resolve conflicts of ends or values stemming from divergent hardened propositions, whether within a single normative conception or between incommensurably different ones.

§45. WHO WE ARE

Who can participate in holistic dialectic, understood as directed toward genuinely interpersonal deliberation? I will suggest that this ideal is relatively open as to who "we" are. Maintaining this openness goes hand in hand with keeping a place for truth.

Identifying rationality with a set of a priori criteria is a kind of conventionalism, and one that courts relativism. If our criteria dictate one answer, and yours dictate another, that is that; it is then difficult to make room for a fact of the matter. Because holistic dialectic refuses to rest with criteria, in this sense, it insists that inquiry may continue, even after any given standard's answer has been given (see §26 on revising the coherence standard). In this, holistic dialectic is guided by something at least functionally similar to a commitment to transcendent truth. It allows for revisions where there is reason to make them. Explicit attachment to some conception of transcendent truth (e.g., Kant's) does not guide practice except insofar as it is specified by reference to additional cognitive ends (e.g., respecting the sway of the moral law by limiting the pretensions of reason to make room for faith). Building a conception of reasoning around a specified understanding of truth will thus foreclose important substantive possibilities. Holistic dialectic, by contrast, allows its commitment to truth to emerge *implicitly* from its openness to whatever considerations arise.

This openness of holistic dialectic helps extend the potential scope of interpersonal dialogue. Parochially declaring a particular conceptual scheme criterial of truth, by contrast, has the obvious consequence of writing off the views of others who do not share it. A more subtle but equally insidious dismissal of others is involved in giving up on objective truth entirely, for it leads to what one philosopher has described as a kind of "cognitive apartheid" (Sperber 1982, 179–80; cf. Gibbard 1990, 207). Relaxing their concern with the truth, many contemporary cultural relativists have come to accept, in a disturbingly complacent fashion, a narrow "we." This limitation on the scope of reasoning with others has also been accepted by some who are not explicitly relativists, such as Richard Rorty in one of his moods. He has written of the need to accept, for some purposes, at least, a "lonely provincialism":

We – the liberal Rawlsian searchers for consensus, the heirs of Socrates, the people who wish to link their days dialectically each to each – cannot [simply abandon all of our initial commitments]. Our community – the community of the liberal intellectuals of the secular modern West – wants to be able to give a *post factum* account of any change of view (Rorty 1989, 44).

One gets the impression that these liberal searchers for consensus will have little to say to traditionalist Sunnis. Yet Rorty moves too quickly from the fact that dialectic will not appeal to absolutely everyone to the conclusion that its "we" is limited by its initial appeal. The reason that he makes this leap seems to be connected to his claim that the "pragmatist" approach that he favors can do without a "theory" of truth. A pragmatist, in Rorty's definition, is someone who views "truth as . . . what is good for *us* to believe" (1989, 37). Yet even if this characterization of truth escaped being a "theory" of truth (as Rorty suggests) because it leans on no form of "metaphysical comfort," still it insidiously limits the scope for interpersonal dialogue by building in a reference to "us." Rorty claims that the reason his narrow "we" does not lead him into an "offensively parochial" position is that he accepts a Quinean holism, in which the "we" is continually rewoven (1989, 40). Yet the tinge of parochialism will remain so long as Rorty describes his current "we" as narrowly as he does and so long as he holds to a conception of truth that already builds in a reference to an "us" that can reflect this narrowness.

By remaining silent, in general, about the nature of truth, holistic dialectic remains relatively open to reaching an overlapping consensus with anyone. What goes wrong in Rorty's appropriation of Rawls's justificatory strategy is that he generalizes this strategy to all of discourse, proposing *überhaupt* to work within the fundamental ideas about justice prevalent within the Western liberal tradition and to avoid, so far as possible, metaphysical presuppositions. While Rawls's effort is a sensible and even masterful response to a relatively deep disagreement within the Western liberal tradition, it makes no sense to use his same boundaries in approaching every possible controversy. Our dialectical approach will remain offensively parochial unless we recognize that there are no preset limits to the "we." I, too, propose a way of extending Rawls's justificatory strategy to other domains; but my suggestion centers on the idea of overlapping consensus, for which the substantive basis may be expected to vary from issue to issue. Far from defining a "we" in advance by setting down some substantive commitments to which all interlocutors must be committed, it simply seeks whatever partial basis of principled agreement may be reached with each set of interlocutors on the practical question at hand. For example, while Rawls's suggestion that political theory eschew metaphysical debates about the ultimate nature of persons may make sense as a strategy for reaching overlapping consensus on the constitutional essentials of society, there are other issues – such as the morality of abortion – for which this strategy will make no sense. The fundamental idea that I adopt from Rawls here is not his particular suggestion about how to bound the inquiry he pursues – for this will vary from topic to topic – but rather the very idea of seeking partial, overlapping consensus rather than supposing that all is lost if comprehensive agreement on foundations cannot be reached. As I have argued, depth of disagreement resulting from divergence in hardened propositions need not prevent holistic dialectic from forging a new "us." To speak as if the "we" of dialectical discussion had a boundary fixed in general is deeply at odds with the spirit of holism.

XIV

Realizing rationality

Of the three main barriers to mutual understanding that make for deep disagreement, that of tacit exemplars is the one that remains. Chapter XII argued that the incommensurability of cognitive ends can be dealt with rationally in the same way that conflicts of incommensurable ends may be in general, while the last chapter argued that a clash of hardened propositions does not create an insuperable barrier to interpersonal deliberation. Divergence in tacit exemplars, however, poses the hardest problem of all. Addressing it will require at least imagining some needed institutional support.

§46. INSTITUTING DELIBERATIVE FREEDOM

Tacit exemplars resist rational deliberation because it is difficult to become fully aware of them. Their influence in giving life to the terms we use and the views we hold is so pervasive that it is very difficult to bring them all to consciousness, let alone to obtain a critical perspective on them. This problem also crops up outside situations of deep disagreement: The tacit commitments that shape every individual's practical thinking may, at times, interfere with reasoning, causing distortion or myopia. Yet in §27 I argued, in effect, that these tacit commitments could aid rational deliberation. They can provide highly nuanced sources of guidance, and can underwrite an important kind of practical perception. Via the sort of self-awareness spurred by the demands of deliberative choice, tacit commitments can become explicit. Still, this reliance on tacit commitments even in the case of a single individual of undivided background heightens the worry we now face, namely that these structures of commitment, although sometimes partially revealed, are nonetheless mostly hidden and mostly beyond the purview of rational thought. Relying upon tacit exemplars as a source of input for deliberation, as I did in §27, highlights the possibility that these inputs themselves are not all subject to rational

292

discussion. In the case of the virtuous Aristotelian or Rawlsian deliberators of Chapter X, this means, further, that there is a problem of epistemological circularity. For a well-brought-up Aristotelian, say, to have the wide range of nuanced commitments needed in order to resolve practical questions of virtuous action in the appropriate way, he must have been educated according to what amounts to a highly complex pattern. Yet to establish the content of this pattern would seem to require the sort of nuanced Aristotelian understanding that it presupposes. Hence, to know what one must know in order to establish an Aristotelian system of education seems to presuppose that one has been raised as an Aristotelian. It becomes difficult to imagine how this pattern of education could be deliberately instituted in the first place.

In §31, I addressed this problem of circularity in establishing particular content by pointing out that progressive, deliberate specification of a given tradition can take place intergenerationally. Any deliberator who starts with recognizably Aristotelian commitments, for instance, must have had an upbringing that passed along certain tacit commitments; but he need not be able to reproduce all of the nuances and distinctions that the person of practical wisdom would want to insist upon. A principal purpose of Aristotle's general discussion of the virtues was to guide the lawgiver's design of education. In a first "Aristotelian" generation, it might not prove possible to write or think anything as detailed as the *Nicomachean Ethics*. The sketch of the human good and the human virtues by which the lawgiver is to direct his aim might then be even less unified and even more vague. In this respect, a work such as Aristotle's is a product of a relatively stable and flourishing culture. If it were to have happened that political leaders after Aristotle had followed his advice and had used his ethics to shape education (even that of the elite), we would have had reason to expect that the Aristotelian account of virtue and the good could have been refined still further. If we thus extend our perspective beyond that of an individual's lifetime, and consider how educational policy might evolve through deliberate refinement, we can see how reasoning may be brought to bear in shaping these tacit commitments.

Whether the effort to specify a tradition can extend rational endorsement to its particularities depends upon the content of that tradition. By supporting deliberative freedom, some traditions encourage individuals' efforts at becoming critically self-conscious of their tacit commitments. In addition to questioning authority, in other words, one is taught to question oneself – not simply to do what one's habituated instinct directs but to reflect self-critically upon one's gut reactions. Family and school promote this reflective habit in a host of particular contexts. The parent asks the child *why* he wants to be excused from chores, or tells him to work out with his sister a fair basis for sharing a toy. "Use your words" is a refrain for primitive induction into interpersonal dialectic. Being rude to parents or teachers is punished, but not all forms of arguing with them is discouraged. Although a child who cites the Constitution in defending her privilege of wearing a tank top may seem obnoxious, parents in a democracy will do well to encourage such forms of civil questioning of authority. In a host of such ways, the particular influences of upbringing can inculcate tacit commitments to a form of life that gives a central place to reasoning about the good and the right. As the child reaches maturity, this reasoning will sometimes take the form of appeals to increasingly universal principles, ones that in turn enable her to step back, deliberatively, from the particular institutions that gave her the capacity to reason in this way.

For education into deliberative freedom to be successful, families and schools clearly must embody some form of commitment to rational deliberation. Since I am speaking of a form of rationalism shared at least across the Aristotelian and Kantian traditions, I do not want to be too specific about the content of this commitment. We may at least recognize that some forms of family organization – involving, for instance, a complete submission to apparently arbitrary paternal power – do not seem compatible with fostering the child's confidence in being able to criticize authority or her ability to deliberate in dialogue with others. Undoubtedly other aspects of family life common even in contemporary Western liberal democracies fail to promote these ideals as well as they might. In the schools, as well, there is a difference between an emphasis on the rote learning of authoritatively presented knowledge and the critical engagement of the individual reasoner with the material. For an extreme version of this sort of contrast, one might take the girls' Qur'anic schools of the traditional Islamic world, in which the emphasis is upon the correct enunciation of passages that the young women need not trouble themselves to understand, on the one hand; and an American college seminar in liberal political theory (or civics) that encourages student input, on the other hand. To foster deliberative freedom, educational institutions need to recognize the value of individual autonomy, or somehow accord importance to the reflective convictions of each individual. In viewing each individual as a potential reasoner in some way, these institutions of family and school would embody an important aspect of the Enlightenment ideal of universal human equality.

Such institutions do not sprout like mushrooms simply manifesting some common genetic imperative. To foster families and schools that educate reflective citizens in these ways requires the explicit support of the laws. Historically, the law has been an important implement in rolling back the sort of authoritarian control over child and student inimical to the growth of deliberative freedom. In the schools, at least in the United States, the more important issue in this connection is not so much authority (which, arguably, has been too far undermined already) but freedom. Given the racial and ethnic diversity of many schools and adolescent pressures for conformity, policies are needed to promote reasonable dialogue over gang fights, to foster a willingness to listen to others while being critical of one's own perspective rather than adhering belligerently to the habits and trappings of one's own clique. In formulating these policies, the maturely deliberative legislator or administrator needs to find ways of promoting the ideals of universal respect and rational equality in his or her particular context. Thus, while the aim will be to produce good citizens for a liberal democracy in which their views may freely develop (within some bounds) and are consulted in the running of the government, this abstract aim cannot directly dictate child-rearing and educational policy. It must be considerably specified in terms of its fit with other goals and in light of the policy maker's particular context.[1]

To realize thoroughly the possibilities of rational deliberation, then, there must be critically reflective individuals oriented by ideals of some universal content and appropriately supported by particular social institutions. We may now bring these three layers together. The point is that if individuals are inculcated with a whole set of tacit commitments embodying the ideals of reflective rationality because their family and school give these ideals pride of place, and if this embodiment in turn results from a previous generation's reflective deliberation about how best to educate citizens of a liberal democracy, then the loop is closed. Society would then have interpersonally pursued a path of deliberation about its ends that had overcome the barrier to explicitness embodied in tacit exemplars. Tacit exemplars would have become the subject of deliberation and reform. At least a generation must pass before the reform can have

---

1 To say more about what sort of institutional realization might best support holist dialectic would require a far more detailed study of democracy and administration than I am prepared to undertake at present. While my account supports, in an abstract way, what has been a growing chorus of voices calling for a richer public dialogue about ends (e.g., Reich 1988; Gutmann and Thompson 1990; Sullivan 1990; Galston 1991), it does not yet add any concrete suggestion about how this is to be achieved.

an effect: That is why a lone individual cannot generally take this route around the influence of tacit exemplars. A society, however, may do so. For this to work, it will depend (in ways that I am not prepared to specify) upon that society being a liberal or democratic one. If the deliberation-promoting education is imposed by an archangel or a Platonic guardian who hides his reasoning for doing so, then the loop is not closed in the same way. On the picture I am after, by revising its ends over time, a society can prevent tacit exemplars from providing an insuperable barrier to deliberation.[2]

For the single individual of deeply divided commitments, this inter-generational solution is not available. Such a person, however, is apt to be more aware of tacit commitments than in the general case. The reason for this stems precisely from the clashes among the tacit commitments into which that person was raised. For instance, take the person who is com-mitted both to orthodox Sunni Islam as practiced in Pakistan and to ways of the liberal West prevailing in the United States. To have become at-tached to each of these sets of commitments, this person will have to have been exposed to contrasting exemplars, many of which will pertain to roughly the same topic. Islamic ideals of the chaste woman, praised by ballad and by cleric, will coexist with the glossy and alluring ideal woman of Western advertisement. In being pulled back and forth between such contrasting concrete images, this complex person is bound to become more aware of them than is someone of simple, undivided loyalty who can just take for granted that (e.g.) on the tennis court women must wear short white skirts. Habits and institutions supporting reflection will also help the person who internalizes a cultural conflict – especially in coming to some resolution. As regards tacit exemplars, however, this person less needs such help than do the parties to a truly interpersonal cultural clash. The emotional layer of self-perception is one reason for this (§27); for although tacit exemplars are difficult to articulate, this person's emotions will bring them to the fore in ways not easily reproduced on the inter-personal level. Therefore, while the institutional support for deliberative freedom needed to get interpersonal deliberation about clashing tacit ex-

2 This ideal has been presented in a way that arrives at the structure of Hegel's concept of Ethical Life, or *Sittlichkeit* (Hegel 1967, Pt. III), as reconstructed in Richardson 1989. Hegel, of course, presented *Sittlichkeit* not as an ideal possibility but as a necessary working out of reason. For an example of a philosopher who has both confronted the problem of the depth of pluralism and developed a nonnecessitárian version of the Hegelian ideal of social integration, we can do no better than to look to Rawls's *Theory of Justice* (compare Pinkard 1987, 38–51 with Pinkard 1988, 135–42).

emplars going would assist the individual of divided loyalties, this help is not, strictly speaking, necessary.

§47. THE VALUE OF COHERENT AGREEMENT

Holistic dialectic, as I have described it, cannot claim to be neutral with respect to cognitive ends. "Holistic dialectic" is the name of a normative theory of cognitive operations. It is not put forward simply as a description of "what we do," although in some contexts we do already do it (speaking dialectical prose without knowing it). It is normative both externally in its intent (I put it forward as a recommendation about how to cope with deep disagreements) and internally or constitutively with respect to the disputants (for a process of holistic dialectic confers a rebuttable claim to rationality upon the revisions it endorses). Furthermore, holistic dialectic wears its central commitment to the value of coherent, reasonable agreement on its sleeve. This is the regulative, complex cognitive end to which it appeals, albeit not to the exclusion of competing ends such as integrity. My proposed approach to deep disagreement is openly committed to the former cognitive value, and hence renounces any claim to total neutrality among competing conceptions. In disavowing the ambition to show that holistic dialectic can or should fairly resolve *every* deep disagreement, I have already to a considerable extent dulled the sting of an accusation of nonneutrality. That means that we can take up the attacks upon this value commitment on their merits.

The principal attacks on this central value commitment of holistic dialectic will come from two opposite directions. One sort of criticism comes from those who feel that reasonable agreement is too modest a cognitive aim, and who insist on respecting only the objective truth, which they hold to be independent of agreement. This objectivist complains against dialectic that even if there are incommensurable conceptions, the effort to reconcile them is irrelevant to the search for the objective truth. The matching sort of criticism from the other direction holds that seeking reasonable agreement already imposes too restrictive a cognitive goal: One should welcome the Dionysian revelry of the spirit, the unrestrained play of the conversation, or the revolutionary succession of paradigms. Since §45 explained the openness of holistic dialectic to objective truth, I will here concentrate more on the latter class of objectors. These are quite various. The Nietzschean genealogist seems to recommend a celebration of the multiplicity of incommensurable perspectives because they dissolve the idea of a unitary truth. Others put forward this celebratory value, not as the sole alternative to truth, which is declared a chimera, but rather as a supplement to it. The latter, I take it, is the stance of many neo-Nietzscheans influenced also by Foucault as well as of certain French "postmodernists." A greater value than consensus, they imply, is unsettling received views so as to stir things up and so as to break the repressive hold of power upon our minds and our actions (see, e.g., Lyotard 1984; Connolly 1989). Whereas dialectic aims at forging agreements, the neo-Nietzschean gadfly aims at breaking them up. Agreements, especially at the political level, are seen as the shackles of individuality-suppressing power. Although such views do not always recognize the cognitive end of truth, they could do so but subordinate it to a kind of individual autonomy or cultural openness.[3]

The reason that I cast the objectors as putting forward competing cognitive ends is that insofar as they might want, instead, to be making philosophical claims about the kinds of objectivity that are *possible*, I have already answered them. In §36 I argued that deep disagreement, extending to conceptual incommensurability, is not only possible but prevalent. Accordingly, conceptual incommensurability is not to be avoided simply by invoking truth as a talisman. The relativist or Nietzschean side is addressed by the bulk of my argument in favor of the possibility of rational deliberation even in the face of deep disagreement. If I am right, then the mere multiplicity of incommensurable conceptions does not mean that Dionysian revelry is all that one is left with: A more objective approach, extending to collective rationality if not indeed to objective truth, is possible. (As I have repeatedly indicated, I leave the establishment of interculturally objective truths about final ends to others.) Since, therefore, the degree of objectivity embodied in reasonable agreement is, at least in principle, available, and since there is no obvious path toward truth apart from holistic dialectic, the remaining objections concern whether my proposal strikes an appropriate and defensible balance among the values of truth, agreement, and the celebration of difference.

The force of these objections depends crucially on whether they are assessed as against the problem of deep disagreement in the internalized form that I am forced to confront in defending my theory of reasoning or rather as against a true interpersonal extension of that theory. In the first context, the question is what an individual's attitude should be to the

3 Accordingly, while I will imitate the strategy of MacIntyre 1990 in seizing the middle ground between two such positions, I want to be clear that the opponents I intend to address are not to be construed as narrowly as are his "encyclopedist" and genealogist.

sharply divergent commitments that divide him or her. In this internalized version, coherent agreement becomes simply a version of practical coherence, the value of which was defended in §§22 and 26. As I there argued, holistic reflection remains open to truth or objective reasons. Revelry in deeply antagonistic practical commitments, by contrast, is far less attractive a strategy for a single individual than it is for a society or group. One can take conflicts among one's values to be a sign of one's vitality and still see reason to weave them together coherently. Accordingly, the route taken by holistic dialectic in resolving a clash within a single individual's deeply divergent views is not seriously objectionable in these ways. In the second, truly interpersonal context, these objections to the ideal of holistic dialectic become more weighty. I pursue this further layer to the argument because I want to explore the potential objectivity of reasoning about ends.

Within the regulative commitment to reasonable agreement, holistic dialectic is perfectly well able to take up the proposals about cognitive ends put forward by the objectors. In the case of the objection from truth, there is no general conflict between seeking reasonable agreement and seeking the truth. I do not claim that reasonable agreement is intrinsically evidentiary of truth. Any such claim would have to be underwritten by some special assumptions, such as ones asserting a teleological tendency of human reason to find the truth (cf. Barnes 1980). Rather, I claim only that the cooperative use of dialectic can include a search for objective truth, though it need not. Although this conception of dialectic is built around the value of coherence, there is nothing in it that commits it to a coherence *theory* of truth or knowledge. Accordingly, the disputants might each insist on pursuing the objective truth in their dialectical discussion, either according to a shared interpretation of truth or according to idiosyncratic interpretations. To be sure, there are some interpretations of objective truth that are downright hostile to the ideal of reasonable agreement. Plato, with his sharp separation of knowledge from opinion, is the grandfather of many of these. A mystic's understanding of truth as essentially esoteric, and accessible only to the initiated, will have little respect for the idea of reasonable agreement. So be it. I cannot argue against such approaches here, but only record my dissent. Anything I could say would, in any case, be of little interest to such an objector, since I am not one of the initiate. Yet in general there seems to be no inherent conflict between the value of objective truth and the value of reasonable agreement.

The celebration of difference or change stands in more direct conflict with the attainment of agreement. Two facts mitigate this conflict, however. First, as I argued in §44, holistic dialectic can proceed by building an "overlapping consensus" limited as to subject matter, allowing the agreement attained to remain compatible with a considerable degree of pluralism. In criticizing Rawls's development of the idea of overlapping consensus, Stuart Hampshire (1993, 46) portentously asks

how a choice is made between . . . two pictures of human nature . . . and between the resulting two pictures of the structure of politics: first, the traditional and Rawlsian picture of a dominant practical reason finding an overlapping consensus in the embedding of liberal values of freedom and equality in basic institutions. Second, the Heraclitean picture of the unavoidable and life-giving clash and friction of competing moral ideals and contrary visions of life founded on memory and passions, a clash that is precariously controlled and regulated by imperfect institutions of adversarial argument and arbitration.

The answer to this disingenuous question, which embeds a sharp contrast between reason and passion that I have resisted, is simply that there is no need to choose. Seeking coherence does not come close to crushing the diversity and conflict among human commitments; and promoting a just constitutional structure will not remove adversarial elements from society. Holistic dialectic allows a balance to be struck between the pursuit of diversity and the pursuit of reasonable agreement. In fact, Rawls's particular working out of the idea of overlapping consensus suggests how we might draw a dialectical distinction with respect to the value of diversity: Diversity with respect to conceptions of the good is to be valued, but only within the limits of justice with regard to the basic structure of society (cf. Kant 1974). As this distinction tends to imply, collective agreement with respect to each individual's religious beliefs or vocational ends, for instance, is not to be expected. By specifying or qualifying the scope for the values of diversity and agreement in some such way, we can employ the generalized notion of overlapping consensus in the way set out in §44.

The second feature of holistic dialectic that mitigates the conflict is that insofar as the neo-Nietzschean has any arguments in favor of celebrating diversity, these may be heard within holistic dialectic. Since, as I have just admitted, there is at least some prima facie conflict between the values of agreement and celebrating diversity, there is no pretense that the hearing that the Dionysian gets will be neutral. Nonetheless, his case can be heard, and if the reasoning is sound it may well move the disputants. That holistic argument will always find a useful foothold somewhere in the views of the others, even if only in relatively specific aspects of their view (§43), explains how the reasoning might move them despite not being neutral. It builds from something that they do, in fact, accept.

What I have just said will strike some as ignoring how much holistic dialectic tilts against the neo-Nietzschean or postmodernist, by forcing everything into an argumentative mode. Narrative, or history as a "curative science" as Foucault conceived it, for instance, might be the preferred mode of expression for these opponents of systematization. To see how a focus on argument might be thought relevantly limiting, consider how, according to Foucault, "the historical sense gives rise to three uses that oppose and correspond to the three Platonic modalities of history" (Foucault 1977, 160):

The first is parodic, directed against reality, and opposes the theme of history as reminiscence or recognition; the second is dissociative, directed against identity, and opposes history given as continuity or representative of a tradition; the third is sacrificial, directed against truth, and opposes history as knowledge.

Furthermore, Foucault explicitly attacks the idea of transforming difference "into that which must be specified within a concept, without overstepping its bounds." Treating difference as a problem to be dealt with by specification is, according to Foucault, "the first form of subjection" (1977, 182). Here, I must admit, the ideal of holistic dialectic does, in fact, come up in front of a limitation of sorts. Foucault and his followers will not be happy with this ideal. Although my response is necessarily partisan, it also is pacific. In my view, this sort of celebration of difference provides a needed corrective to the everpresent danger that systematization will overreach. To do without concepts under which to range diverse particulars, however, would be disastrous. Certain understandings of reality do need parody, certain conceptions of identity do need dissociating from, and certain understandings of truth should be sacrificed. To totalize these responses to systematization, however, is to fall into the same sort of dominative vice that these neo-Nietzscheans are so good at identifying in others, and in any case leads one into babbling incoherence. Accordingly, insofar as curative history helps celebrate important differences, it will remain open for the systematizing and constructive dialecticians to be edified by its work. My own systematization, or that of any effort at holistic dialectic, will rightly draw fresh satire particularly appropriate to it. In fact, the recovery of difference via parody and dissociation is always dependent upon working from and against some particular historical effort at systematization, some particular disease that needs a cure. Since this antisystemic mood in philosophy is thus time-bound, the Nietzschean and even neo-Nietzschean unmaskings cannot be appropriately taken to threaten my account of holistic dialectic, for they are directed against opponents (positivist and neo-Kantian, largely) that have now exited the stage. The mockingbird of Sils-Maria spreads its wings only with the falling of the dusk.

Yet to say that coherent agreement, as a cognitive end, is not necessarily inimical either to objective truth, on the one hand, or to unsettlement, on the other, is not yet to say why coherent agreement should be the guiding star for interpersonal dialogue or negotiation.

To defend the value of coherent agreement, I resort – as I did in defending the value of practical coherence in §§22 and 26 – to showing how it contributes to certain other ends. There is no inconsistency in this mode of defense: This cognitive end can guide interpersonal deliberation without being a final end (though I suspect that for many it is). Coherent agreement is instrumental to two kinds of value: It is a prerequisite of effective action and a basis for justification or legitimation. The first of these connections emerges from the arguments of §19, where I argued that reducing practical conflicts is important to an individual to act effectively, with guidance from his or her general commitments. Reflective and theory-guided action is crucial not only to individuals' success in achieving their general ends, but also to their unifying their lives – whether around a narrative structure or a static one. (Notice that since the mutual support can be expressed in terms of narrative, the ideal of coherence that I affirm does not endorse "argument" to the exclusion of "narrativity.") This argument pertaining to individuals may be extended to a group of people in disagreement whenever there is a call for undertaking collective action or forging a collective identity. For instance, a nation that cannot reconcile its commitments to the ideal of democracy and to its own economic prosperity by specifying them appropriately is in danger of undercutting its effectiveness as an actor on the world stage. Its conflicting aims will lead it to take steps that appear contradictory and hypocritical – now supporting a dictatorial emir who makes available a source of cheap oil, now attacking as dictatorial some less well endowed regime. An approach to foreign policy that treats such apparent conflicts simply as occasions for "pragmatic," logrolling compromise will lack the coherent commitment to ideals that is essential to leadership both at home and abroad.

In this way, the contribution of coherent agreement to effective action is intimately bound up with its role as a basis for legitimation. On the frankly liberal ideal I am now invoking, it is important to be able to legitimate social actions and institutions by justifying them on the basis of principles that all can accept. On Scanlon's variant of this idea, the guiding ideal of moral theory is to seek principles that no one who is sincerely motivated to come to agreement can reasonably reject (Scanlon 1982). In this way he interprets the liberal ideal of impartiality in a contractualist fashion. (While Scanlon treats this idea as constitutive of moral truth, I again forswear this mode of defending the value of coherent agreement.) A certain conception of reasonableness is here joining with an ideal of publicity to form what Rawls has called the ideal of "free public reason" (Rawls 1985, 230). Pursuing coherent agreement in free public dialogue does help legitimize institutions thereby endorsed.

Both of these instrumental arguments are attacked by the neo-Nietzscheans and postmodernists. They complain that too much emphasis on effective action by the collectivity enforces conformity at the expense of individuality and encourages the effective movement of a monolith at the cost of suppressing potentially valuable but disruptive movements within it. The ideal of free public reason, in its turn, is derided as a hang-over from the old and dangerous Enlightenment yearning for transparency, for the total and open "justification of the social world" (Waldron 1987, 135). This latter ideal reaches its apotheosis in Habermas's depiction of an ideal speech situation in which the mutual conditions of discourse can be mutually and openly endorsed by all (Habermas 1990). This ideal of universal agreement is attacked by Lyotard as "terrorist" in its suppression of the "heteromorphous" character of human discourse (Lyotard 1984, 63, 65).

Since there is something valid in these attacks, I want to respond to them by filling out the dialectical distinction made above with the help of Rawls's idea of an overlapping consensus. Above, the point was simply that the consensus that is sought may be quite limited in subject matter. Now I can explain the significance of this fact more fully. To begin with, while consensus is important to effective collective action, not all domains of life are appropriate arenas for collective action. Further, since there are many collectivities of varied sizes, it makes sense to leave freedom for authority and action available at many different levels. Federalism is at least a possibility, and one compatible with the claim that effective collective action requires coherent agreement. Only if the need for collective action were completely denied would this argument for the value of coherent agreement wholly lose its force. Accordingly, merely making the connection between coherent agreement and effective collective action should not run afoul of those who complain of *excessive* collectivization. But what of the demand for justification? Here, too, the universal ambition apparent in Habermas is not a necessary feature of the argument that connects coherent agreement with public justification. Within the Western liberal tradition, at least, most choices that an individual makes in deciding how to live are not regarded as requiring *public* justification. They are that individual's own business. Again, it is only a view that completely denies the need for public justification of any action or institution that will negate the value of coherent agreement in supporting such justification. Accordingly, the liberal tradition has resources within itself for preventing the ideal of consensus from becoming uncomfortably "totalizing"; and if it is pursued more moderately the value of consensus is real.

§48. POSSIBLE OBJECTIVITY

I conclude that deep disagreement, even extending to conceptual incommensurability, does not preclude an individual's rational deliberation of ends. Each of its three main causes may be neutralized by an appropriately holist dialectic in the ways we have canvassed. The divergence that arises from differently weighting incommensurable cognitive ends may be addressed by deliberation that specifies the ends in terms of their mutual fit rather than by looking in vain for a supervalue in terms of which to commensurate them all (§41). Hardened propositions may be softened by exploiting the opportunities for respecification inherent in their tacit dependence on the concrete exemplars and practices that give them life (§42). These tacit commitments, in turn, may be the subject of deliberative revision as long as they include a sufficiently concrete commitment to reflective criticism. Accordingly, by making use of holist dialectic, an individual of divided upbringing may deliberate rationally about his or her ends even when they conflict across the lines of the disparate traditions to which he or she holds allegiance. (That one may, of course, does not imply that one should, as noted in §1.) These conclusions apply in attenuated form to the genuinely interpersonal case, where there is less compelling reason to pursue coherent agreement and deliberative freedom depends more on institutional support both to encourage commitment to this goal and to help bring tacit exemplars to light. That the truly interpersonal solution thus depends upon substantive normative preconditions is not itself a flaw, but does raise the question of objectivity.

The whole of my argument in Part Five has maintained an openness to objectivity while not trying to establish it. Although I have not tried directly to counter the moral or evaluative skeptic who denies the possibility of objective evaluative knowledge, or even the non-cognitivist who claims that evaluative statements lack truth-values altogether, I have pursued a more constructive strategy of laying out the sort of reasoning that takes the content of normative commitments seriously. The conception of holistic dialectic that I have developed may be taken as receptive to the truth *if* that be the appropriate standard. I want to close, then, by revisiting the potential for objectivity of my account of rational deliberation of ends.

Allowing for thoroughgoing criticism of starting points is crucial to remaining open to objectivity. Most contemporary theories of practical rationality attempt to proceed on a solely analytic or a priori basis. This restriction results in a curious bifurcation between instrumental theories unabashedly relative to initial commitments and noninstrumental theories that wholly reject such relativity, instead affirming "agent-neutral" and universal requirements (e.g., Nagel 1970, qualified in Nagel 1986, 159). These contemporary theories either accept contingent initial commitments quite uncritically, or else they attempt to ignore them altogether. By embracing a holistic view, I have attempted to steer between these extremes so as to provide a theory of critically relative rationality. The conception of deliberation of ends that I have defended is significantly less "relative" than the end–means conceptions that have often been equated with relative rationality. Whereas both conceptions define rational moves that are relative to an initial set of ends, the one I have been defending allows for the rational criticism and revision of these ends. A principal burden of this study has been to show just how deep and powerful this revision can be. Because holistic deliberation of ends can incorporate arguments justifying a moral theory in wide reflective equilibrium, this theory of deliberation supports the "conception of the agent or person as an integral being who has the capacity to consider whether his preferences can be supported by reasons and to revise them accordingly" (Darwall 1983, 101).

The potential critical force of the reflective search for practical coherence gives rise to a kind of objectivity. How it does so may be explained by reference to the Aristotelian and Rawlsian illustrations of deliberation about ultimate ends in Chapter X. The kind of objectivity involved might be called "internal objectivity." Internal objectivity is not an objectivity *sub specie aeternitatis*, nor a Kantian objectivity understood in terms of the idea of a transcendental necessity according to rules. Instead, it is simply the objectivity of critical distance, of a point of view that allows for some correction for unreflective personal bias and for some intersubjective validity (cf. Rawls 1971, 516–17; Nagel 1986, 4–5). Achieving this kind of qualifiedly objective point of view need not involve a suppression of relevant particular facts and perceptions: As I argued in §27, these will have their place in an extended reflective equilibrium. Rather, what is needed is that an appropriate point of view be defined *within* the structure of arguments that produce the extended reflective equilibrium and justify what is held therein. It is for this reason that I term this kind of objectivity "internal." The internal objectivity of the Aristotelian and Rawlsian paths of deliberation hinges on their respective appeals to the human function and to the fundamental intuitive idea of society as a system of fair cooperation among free and equal citizens. Within the Aristotelian structure, the internally objective point of view, to which he turns in *N.E.* I.7 to specify his sketch of the ultimate end, is that of the distinctive human function that differentiates us from other animals. Or better, it is the point of view of the effort to specify in ethical terms what this distinctive human function is. Understood in this way, the notion of human function poses a question that facilitates the reflective detachment from initial commitments without precluding a reflective reaffirmation of any of them. Although the point of view is not ethically contentless, it does seem suited to the reflective suppression of prejudice. A similar reflective detachment and qualified neutrality characterizes the (substantively different) Rawlsian focus on the above social ideal. Since Aristotle and Rawls each work within a holistic method, neither of their views is wholly independent of initial commitments, for each must reflect considered convictions; but each point of view provides a convenient and relatively stable fulcrum. By resting on this fulcrum, arguments grounded in some commitments can bring to bear leverage on the rest of the system of commitments. The fulcrum can be moved to avoid letting the lever snap: The metaphor should not be taken to suggest that the fulcrum is unrevisable in principle. In fact, we have seen examples in which the focal points of view of each theory both play a rational role in revising more specific judgments *and* in turn get respecified themselves. It is the effort to organize one's deliberations around such a focal point that brings the critical distance necessary to the rational adoption of ultimate ends. This kind of internal objectivity goes some way toward erasing the limitations that are thought to be inherent in relative rationality.

Of course, if Aristotle were correct about the metaphysical basis of his account of the function of man, or Kant were correct that the sort of theory of moral personality that Rawls finds politically reasonable to endorse in fact has an a priori basis, then the claim to objective rationality of deliberation organized around such starting points would be a lot stronger. For reasons influentially capsulized by MacIntyre 1984, how-ever, many doubt that ethical objectivity of this strong kind is attainable. In this book, I have done nothing to justify or criticize Aristotle's or Kant's claims that their moral theories express the true nature of practical reason and enjoy a necessary or a priori grounding. Yet I would suggest that by establishing that we can deliberate rationally about ends and with internal objectivity, the argument of this book has provided an important footing on which those aiming to defend an objective account of the human good may build. As I have been at pains to show, the ideal of holistic reflection is hospitable to this further objectivity. Far from excluding the possibility that some judgments are necessary or a priori, my theory of deliberation would welcome the event that a reflective equilibrium be shared on such a basis. While a complete assessment of the opportunity for rational de-liberation of ends must therefore await ethical answers, the theory of de-liberation developed in this book, which keeps a place open for the ethical results that would fully realize that possibility, has shown how rational deliberation can extend to an ultimate end.

References

Ackerman, Bruce A. 1980. *Social justice in the liberal state*. New Haven: Yale University Press.

Ackrill, J. L. 1980. Aristotle on eudaimonia. In *Essays on Aristotle's ethics*. See A. Rorty 1980a.

Aizpurua, Jose Maria, Jorge Nieto, and Jose Ramon Uriarte. 1990. Choice procedure consistent with similarity relations. *Theory and Decision* 29:235–54.

Albritton, Rogers. 1966. On Wittgenstein's use of the term 'criterion.' In *Wittgenstein: The Philosophical Investigations*, ed. George Pitcher, 231–50. New York: Doubleday.

Allais, Maurice. 1979 [1953]. The foundations of a positive theory of choice involving risk and a criticism of the postulates and axioms of the American school. In *Expected utility hypotheses and the Allais paradox*, ed. Maurice Allais and Ole Hagen, 27–145. Dordrecht: D. Reidel.

Allan, D. J. 1955. The practical syllogism. In *Autour d'Aristote*, ed. S. Mansion, 325–40. Louvain: Publications Universitaires de Louvain.

Anscombe, G. E. M. 1976. *Intention*. 2d ed. Ithaca: Cornell University Press.

——— 1989. Von Wright on practical inference. In *The philosophy of Georg Henrik von Wright*, ed. Paul Arthur Schilpp and Lewis Edwin Hahn, 377–403. La Salle, Ill.: Open Court.

Aquinas, Thomas. 1981. *Summa theologica*, trans. Fathers of the English Dominican Province. 5 vols. Westminister, Md.: Christian Classics.

Aqvist, Lennart. 1967. Good Samaritans, contrary-to-duty imperatives, and epistemic obligations. *Nous* 1:361-79.

Aristotle. 1984. *The complete works of Aristotle*. The Revised Oxford Translations, 2 vols., ed. Jonathan Barnes. Princeton: Princeton University Press.

Arrow, Kenneth J. 1984. Utilities, attitudes, choices: A review note. In *Individual choice under certainty and uncertainty*, 55-84. Cambridge, Mass.: Harvard University Press.

Audi, Robert. 1973. Intending. *Journal of Philosophy* 70:387–403.

——— 1989. *Practical reasoning*. London: Routledge.

Bain, Alexander. 1865. *The emotions and the will*. 2d ed. London: Longmans, Green.

Barnes, Jonathan. 1980. Aristotle and the methods of ethics. *Revue Internationale de Philosophie* (No. 133–4):490–511.

Berlin, Isaiah. 1988. On the pursuit of the ideal. *New York Review of Books*. March 17, pp. 11–18.

Bittner, Rüdiger. 1989. *What reason demands*, trans. Theodore Talbot. Cambridge University Press.

Black, Max. 1989. Some remarks about 'practical reasoning.' In *The philosophy of Georg Henrik von Wright*, ed. Paul Arthur Schilpp and Lewis Edwin Hahn, 405–15. La Salle, Ill.: Open Court.

Blum, Lawrence. 1980. *Friendship, altruism, and morality*. London: Routlege & Kegan Paul.

BonJour, Laurence. 1985. *The structure of empirical knowledge*. Cambridge, Mass.: Harvard University Press.

Brandt, R. B. 1979. *A theory of the good and the right*. Oxford: Oxford University Press.

1989. Fairness to happiness. *Social Theory and Practice* 15:33–58.

Bratman, Michael E. 1987. *Intention, plans, and practical reason*. Cambridge, Mass.: Harvard University Press.

Broadie, Sarah W. 1987. Necessity and deliberation: An argument from *De Interpretatione* 9. *Canadian Journal of Philosophy* 17:289–306.

1991. *Ethics with Aristotle*. New York: Oxford University Press.

Broome, John. 1991. *Weighing goods: Equality, uncertainty, and time*. Oxford: Basil Blackwell.

Cachia, Pierre. 1989. *Popular narrative ballads of modern Egypt*. Oxford: Oxford University Press.

Campbell, Richmond, and Lanning Sowden, eds. 1985. *Paradoxes of rationality and cooperation: Prisoner's dilemma and Newcomb's problem*. Vancouver: University of British Columbia Press.

Charles, David. 1984. *Aristotle's philosophy of action*. Ithaca, N.Y.: Cornell University Press.

Connolly, William. 1989. Identity and difference in liberalism. In *Liberalism and the good*, 59–85. See Douglass et al. 1990.

Cooper, John M. 1975. *Reason and human good in Aristotle*. Cambridge, Mass.: Harvard University Press.

Darwall, Stephen L. 1983. *Impartial reason*. Ithaca, N.Y.: Cornell University Press.

Davidson, Donald. 1980. *Essays on actions and events*. Oxford: Oxford University Press.

1986a. A coherence theory of truth and knowledge. In *Truth and interpretation: Perspectives on the philosophy of Donald Davidson*, ed. Ernest LePore, 307–19. Oxford: Basil Blackwell.

1986b. *Inquiries into truth and interpretation*. Corrected ed. Oxford: Oxford University Press.

1986c. On the very idea of a conceptual scheme. In Davidson 1986b, 5–20.

1989. The myth of the subjective. In *Relativism: Interpretation and confrontation*, 159–72. See Krausz 1989.

Davis, Wayne A., and John W. Bender. 1989. Fundamental troubles with the coherence theory. In *The current state of the coherence theory*, ed. John W. Bender, 52–68. Dordrecht: Kluwer Academic Publishers.

de Sousa, Ronald. 1987. *The rationality of emotion*. Cambridge, Mass.: MIT Press.

Dewey, John. 1967 [1922]. *Human nature and conduct* (cited as *HNC*). In *The middle works, 1899–1924*, ed. Jo Ann Boydston, vol. 14. Carbondale: Southern Illinois University Press.

1979 [1915]. The logic of judgments of practice. In *The middle works, 1899–1924*, ed. Jo Ann Boydston, vol. 8, 14–82. Carbondale: Southern Illinois University Press.

1988a [1939]. Experience, knowledge and value: A rejoinder. In *The later works, 1925–1953*, ed. Jo Ann Boydston, vol. 14, 3–90. Carbondale: Southern Illinois University Press.

1988b [1939]. Theory of valuation (cited as *TOV*). In *The later works, 1925–1953*, ed. Jo Ann Boydston, vol. 13, 189–251. Carbondale: Southern Illinois University Press.

Doi, 'Abdur Rahmān I. 1984. *Sharī'ah : The Islamic Law*. London: Ta Ha Publishers.

Donagan, Alan. 1977. *The theory of morality*. Chicago: University of Chicago Press.

Douglass, R. Bruce, Gerald M. Mara, and Henry S. Richardson, eds. 1990. *Liberalism and the good*. New York: Routledge.

Dunne, Joseph. 1993. *Back to the rough ground*. Notre Dame, Ind.: University of Notre Dame Press.

Elster, Jon. 1983. *Sour grapes: Studies in the subversion of rationality*. Cambridge University Press.

Euripides. 1960. *Iphigenia in Tauris*. In *Greek Tragedies*, ed. David Grene and Richmond Lattimore, vol. 2. Chicago: University of Chicago Press.

Feyerabend, Paul K. 1978. *Against method*. London: Verso.

Fodor, Jerry, and Ernest Lepore. 1992. *Holism: A shopper's guide*. Oxford: Basil Blackwell.

Foot, Philippa. 1983. Moral realism and moral dilemma. *Journal of Philosophy* 80: 379–98.

Foucault, Michel. 1977. *Language, counter-memory, practice*. Ithaca: Cornell University Press.

Frankfurt, Harry G. 1971. Freedom of the will and the concept of a person. *Journal of Philosophy* 68:5–20.

1988. *The importance of what we care about: Philosophical essays*. Cambridge University Press.

Gadamer, Hans-Georg. 1975. *Truth and method*. New York: Continuum.

Galston, William A. 1991. *Liberal purposes: Goods, virtues, and diversity in the liberal state*. Cambridge University Press.

Garcia, J. L. A. 1987. Why Sidgwick's project had to fail. *History of Philosophy Quarterly* 4:79–91.

Gärdenfors, Peter. 1990. The dynamics of belief systems: Foundations vs. coherence theories. *Revue Internationale de Philosophie* (No. 172):24–46.

Gärdenfors, Peter, and Nils-Eric Sahlin. 1988. Introduction: Bayesian decision theory – foundations and problems. In *Decision, probability, and utility: Selected readings*, ed. P. Gärdenfors and N.-E. Sahlin, 1–15. Cambridge University Press.

Gauthier, David. 1990 [1975]. Reason and maximization. In *Moral dealing: Contract, ethics, and reason*, 209–33. Ithaca, N.Y.: Cornell University Press.

Gewirth, Alan. 1991. Can any final ends be rational? *Ethics* 102:66–95.

Gibbard, Allan. 1990. *Wise choices, apt feelings: A theory of normative judgment*. Cambridge, Mass.: Harvard University Press.

Gilligan, Stephen G., and Gordon H. Bower. 1984. Cognitive consequences of emotional arousal. In *Emotions, cognition, and behaviour*, ed. Carroll E. Izard, Jerome Kagan, and Robert B. Zajonc, 547–88. Cambridge University Press.

Goodman, Nelson. 1979. *Fact, fiction, and forecast*. 3d ed. Indianapolis: Hackett.

Gowans, Christopher W. 1987. Introduction: The debate on moral dilemmas. In *Moral dilemmas*, ed. Christopher W. Gowans. New York: Oxford University Press.

Greenspan, Patricia S. 1983. Moral dilemmas and guilt. *Philosophical Studies* 43: 117–25.

Greenwood, L. H. G. 1973. *Aristotle: Nicomachean Ethics book six*. New York: Arno. First published by Cambridge University Press, 1909.

Griffin, James. 1986. *Well-being: Its meaning, measurement, and moral importance*. Oxford: Oxford University Press.

1991. Mixing values. *Proceedings of the Aristotelian Society* Suppl. Vol. 65:101–18.

Gutmann, Amy, and Dennis Thompson. 1990. Moral conflict and political consensus. *Ethics* 101:64–88.

Habermas, Jürgen. 1984. *The theory of communicative action*. Vol. I, *Reason and the rationalization of society*. Boston: Beacon Press.

1990. *Moral consciousness and communicative action*, trans. Christian Lenhardt and Shierry Weber Nicholsen. Cambridge, Mass.: MIT Press.

Hampshire, Stuart. 1993. Liberalism: The new twist. *New York Review of Books*. August 12, 43–7.

Hampton, Jean. Forthcoming. The failure of expected utility theory as a theory of reason. *Economics and Philosophy*.

Hansson, Bengt. 1981. The decision game: The conceptualisation of risk and utility. In *Ethics: Foundations, problems, and applications* (*Proceedings of the Fifth International Wittgenstein Symposium*), ed. Edgar Morscher and Rudolf Stranzinger, 187–93. Vienna: Hölder-Pichler-Tempsky.

Hardin, Russell. 1988. *Morality within the limits of reason*. Chicago: University of Chicago Press.

Hare, R. M. 1981. *Moral thinking: Its levels, method, and point*. Oxford: Oxford University Press.

1989. Brandt on fairness to happiness. *Social Theory and Practice* 15:59–65.

Harman, Gilbert. 1986. *Change in view: Principles of reasoning*. Cambridge, Mass.: MIT Press.

Harsanyi, John. 1977. On the rationale of the Bayesian approach. In *Foundational problems in the special sciences*, ed. R. E. Butts and J. Hintikka. Dordrecht: Reidel.

Hasan, Ahmad. 1986. *Analogical reasoning in Islamic jurisprudence*. Islamabad, Pakistan: Islamic Research Institute.

Hegel, G. W. F. 1967. *Philosophy of right*, trans. T. M. Knox. London: Oxford University Press.

Herman, Barbara. 1984. Rules, motives, and helping actions. *Philosophical Studies* 45:369–77.

Hume, David. 1986. *A treatise of human nature*, 2d ed., ed. L. A. Selby-Bigge, rev. P. Nidditch. Oxford: Oxford University Press.

Hurley, S. L. 1989. *Natural reasons: Personality and polity*. New York: Oxford University Press.

Irfani, Suroosh. 1985. The progressive Islamic movement. In *Islam, politics and the state: The Pakistan experience*, ed. Mohammad Ashgar Khan, 31–68. London: Zed Books.

Irwin, Terence. 1988. *Aristotle's first principles*. Oxford: Oxford University Press.

Jalal, Ayesha. 1991. The convenience of subservience: Women and the state in Pakistan. In *Women, Islam, and the state*, ed. Deniz Kandiyoti. Philadelphia: Temple University Press.

Jeffrey, Richard C. 1983. *The logic of decision*. 2d ed. Chicago: University of Chicago Press.

Jonsen, Albert R., and Stephen Toulmin. 1988. *The abuse of casuistry: A history of moral reasoning*. Berkeley: University of California Press.

Kant, Immanuel. 1956. *Critique of practical reason*, trans. Lewis White Beck. Indianapolis: Bobbs-Merrill. Citations will refer to the pages in the relevant volume of the Prussian Academy Edition (here Vol. V), using the abbreviation "Ak."

    1964a. *Groundwork of the metaphysics of morals*, trans. H. J. Paton. New York: Harper & Row. [Ak. Vol. IV.]

    1964b. *Metaphysical principles of virtue*, trans. James Ellington. Indianapolis: Bobbs-Merrill. [Ak. Vol. VI.]

    1974. *On the old saw: That may be right in theory but it won't work in practice*, trans. E. B. Ashton. Philadelphia: University of Pennsylvania Press. [Ak. Vol. VIII.]

Kavka, Gregory. 1983. The toxin puzzle. *Analysis* 43:33–6.

Keeney, Ralph L., and Howard Raiffa. 1976. *Decisions with multiple objectives: Preferences and value tradeoffs*. New York: John Wiley & Sons.

Khan, Mohammad Ashgar. 1985. Political and economic aspects of Islamisation. In *Islam, politics and the state: The Pakistan experience*, ed. Mohammad Ashgar Khan, 127–63. London: Zed Books.

Kirwan, Christopher. 1967. Logic and the good in Aristotle. *Philosophical Quarterly* 17:97–114.

Kolnai, Aurel. 1978. *Ethics, value, and reality*. Indianapolis: Hackett.

Korsgaard, Christine M. 1986a. Aristotle and Kant on the source of value. *Ethics* 96:486–505.

    1986b. Skepticism about practical reason. *Journal of Philosophy* 83:5–25.

    Forthcoming. The sources of normativity. In *The Tanner Lectures on Human Values*, vol. 15, ed. Grethe B. Peterson. Salt Lake City: University of Utah Press.

Krausz, Michael, ed. 1989. *Relativism: Interpretation and confrontation*. Notre Dame: University of Notre Dame Press.

Kripke, Saul A. 1982. *Wittgenstein: On rules and private language*. Cambridge, Mass.: Harvard University Press.

Kuhn, T. S. 1970. *The structure of scientific revolutions*. 2d ed. Chicago: University of Chicago Press.

    1977. Second thoughts on paradigms. In *The essential tension: Selected studies in scientific tradition and change*, 293–319. Chicago: University of Chicago Press.

Lance, Mark. Forthcoming. Subjective probability and acceptance. *Philosophical Studies*.

Larmore, Charles E. 1987. *Patterns of moral complexity*. Cambridge University Press.

Levi, Isaac. 1986. *Hard choices: Decision making under unresolved conflict.* Cambridge University Press.

Lewis, David. 1981. Causal decision theory. *Australasian Journal of Philosophy* 59: 5–30.

——— 1983. *Philosophical papers*, vol. 1. New York: Oxford University Press.

Łukasiewicz, Jan. 1951. *Aristotle's syllogistic from the standpoint of modern formal logic.* Oxford: Oxford University Press.

Lukes, Steven. 1991. Incommensurability in science and in ethics. In *Moral conflict and politics*, 33–49. Oxford: Oxford University Press.

Lyotard, Jean-François. 1984. *The postmodern condition: A report on knowledge*, trans. Geoff Bennington and Brian Massumi. Minneapolis: University of Minnesota Press.

Mabbott, J. D. 1953. Reason and desire. *Philosophy* 28:113–23.

MacDonald, Scott. 1991. Ultimate ends in practical reasoning: Aquinas's Aristotelian moral psychology and Anscombe's fallacy. *Philosophical Review* 100:31–66.

McDowell, John. 1984. Wittgenstein on following a rule. *Synthese* 58:325–63.

McFall, Lynne. 1987. Integrity. *Ethics* 98:5–20.

MacIntyre, Alasdair. 1984. *After virtue.* 2d ed. Notre Dame, Ind.: University of Notre Dame Press.

——— 1985. Relativism, power, and philosophy. *Proceedings and Addresses of the American Philosophical Association* 59 (September):5–22.

——— 1990. *Three rival versions of moral enquiry: Encyclopedia, genealogy, and tradition.* Notre Dame, Ind.: University of Notre Dame Press.

Marcus, Ruth Barcan. 1980. Moral dilemmas and consistency. *Journal of Philosophy* 77:121–36.

Masud, Muhammad Khalid. 1977. *Islamic legal philosophy: A study of Abū Ishāq al-Shātibī's life and thought.* Islamabad, Pakistan: Islamic Research Institute.

Mele, Alfred R. 1984. Intending and the balance of motivation. *Pacific Philosophical Quarterly* 65:370–6.

Mernissi, Fatima. 1991. *Women and Islam: An historical and theological enquiry.* Trans. Mary Jo Lakeland. Oxford: Basil Blackwell.

Mill, John Stuart. 1911 [1881]. *A system of logic, ratiocinative and inductive.* 8th ed. London: Longmans, Green.

——— 1979 [1861]. *Utilitarianism*, ed. George Sher. Indianapolis: Hackett.

Millgram, Elijah. Forthcoming. Pleasure in practical reasoning. *Monist.*

Moody-Adams, Michele M. 1990. On the alleged methodological infirmity of ethics. *American Philosophical Quarterly* 27:225–35.

Moore, G. E. 1902. *Principia ethica.* Cambridge University Press.

Murdoch, Iris. 1980. *The sovereignty of good.* London: Routledge & Kegan Paul.

Nagel, Thomas. 1970. *The possibility of altruism.* Princeton: Princeton University Press.

——— 1979. The fragmentation of value. In *Mortal Questions*, 128–41. Cambridge University Press.

——— 1986. *The view from nowhere.* New York: Oxford University Press.

Newton Smith, W. 1981. *The rationality of science.* London: Routledge & Kegan Paul.

314

Noori, Ayatollah Yahya, and Sayed Hassan Amin. 1987. *Legal and political structure of an Islamic state: The implications for Iran and Pakistan.* Glasgow: Royston.

Nozick, Robert. 1970. Newcomb's problem and two principles of choice. In *Essays in Honor of C. G. Hempel*, ed. Nicholas Rescher, 114–46. Dordrecht: D. Reidel.

Nussbaum, Martha C. 1978. *Aristotle's "De Motu Animalium": Text with translation, commentary, and interpretive essays.* Princeton: Princeton University Press.

1986. *The fragility of goodness: Luck and ethics in Greek tragedy and philosophy.* Cambridge University Press.

1990. *Love's knowledge: Essays on philosophy and literature.* New York: Oxford University Press.

1991. The literary imagination in public life. *New Literary History* 22:877–910.

Forthcoming. *The therapy of desire: Theory and practice in Hellenistic ethics.* Princeton: Princeton University Press.

O'Neill, Onora. 1989. *Constructions of reason.* Cambridge University Press.

Parfit, Derek. 1984. *Reasons and persons.* Oxford: Oxford University Press.

Parodi, Dominique. 1989. Knowledge and action in Dewey's philosophy. In *The philosophy of John Dewey*, ed. Paul Arthur Schilpp and Lewis Edwin Hahn, 229–42. La Salle, Ill.: Open Court.

Pinkard, Terry. 1987. *Democratic liberalism and social union.* Philadelphia: Temple University Press.

1988. *Hegel's dialectic: The explanation of possibility.* Philadelphia: Temple University Press.

Piper, Adrian M. S. 1988–9. Hume on rational final ends. *Philosophy Research Archives* 14:193–228.

Pogge, Thomas W. 1989. *Realizing Rawls.* Ithaca, N.Y.: Cornell University Press.

Prior, A. N. 1954. The paradoxes of derived obligation. *Mind* 63:64–5.

Putnam, Hilary. 1981. *Reason, truth and history.* Cambridge University Press.

Putnam, Hilary, and Ruth Anna Putnam. 1990. Epistemology as hypothesis. *Transactions of the Charles S. Peirce Society* 26:407–33.

Quine, W. V. O. 1960. *Word and object.* Cambridge, Mass.: MIT Press.

1970. On the reasons for indeterminacy of translation. *Journal of Philosophy* 67:178–83.

1980. Two dogmas of empiricism. In *From a logical point of view: 9 logico-philosophical essays*, 2d ed., 20–46. Cambridge, Mass.: Harvard University Press.

1981. On the very idea of a third dogma. In *Theories and things*, 38–42. Cambridge, Mass.: Harvard University Press.

1987. Indeterminacy of translation again. *Journal of Philosophy* 84:5–10.

1991. Two dogmas in retrospect. *Canadian Journal of Philosophy* 21:265–74.

Quinn, Warren S. 1990. The puzzle of the self-torturer. *Philosophical Studies* 59:79–90.

Ramsey, F. P. 1931. Truth and probability. In *The foundations of mathematics and other logical essays: Collected papers of F. P. Ramsey*, ed. R. B. Braithewaite. London: Routledge & Kegan Paul.

Rawling, Piers. 1990. The ranking of preference. *Philosophical Quarterly* 40:495–501.

Rawls, John. 1971. *A theory of justice.* Cambridge, Mass.: Harvard University Press.

1975. The independence of moral theory. *Proceedings of the American Philosophical Association* 48 (November):5–22.

1980. Kantian constructivism in moral theory: The Dewey Lectures 1980. *Journal of Philosophy* 77:515–72.

1982. The basic liberties and their priority. In *The Tanner Lectures on Human Values*, vol. 3, ed. S. M. McMurrin, 3–87. Salt Lake City: University of Utah Press.

1985. Justice as fairness: political not metaphysical. *Philosophy and Public Affairs* 14:223–51.

1987. The idea of an overlapping consensus. *Oxford Journal of Legal Studies* 7:1–25.

1989. The domain of the political and overlapping consensus. *New York University Law Review* 64:233–55.

1993. *Political liberalism.* New York: Columbia University Press.

Raz, Joseph. 1986. *The morality of freedom.* Oxford: Oxford University Press.

Reich, Robert B. 1988. Policy making in a democracy. In *The power of public ideas*, ed. Robert B. Reich, 123–56. Cambridge, Mass.: Ballinger.

Richardson, Henry S. 1986. *Rational deliberation of ends.* Dissertation, Harvard University.

1988. Commentary on Broadie. [On Aristotle on practical intellect]. In *The proceedings of the Boston Area Colloquium in Ancient Philosophy*, vol. III, ed. John Cleary, 253–61. Lanham, Md.: University Press of America.

1989. The logical structure of *Sittlichkeit:* A reading of Hegel's "Philosophy of right." *Idealistic Studies* 19:62–78.

1990a. Measurement, pleasure and practical science in Plato's "Protagoras." *Journal of the History of Philosophy* 28:7–32.

1990b. The problem of liberalism and the good. In *Liberalism and the good*, 1–28. See Douglass et al. 1990.

1990c. Specifying norms as a way to resolve concrete ethical problems. *Philosophy and Public Affairs* 19:279–310.

1991. Commensurability as a prerequisite of rational choice: An examination of Sidgwick's position. *History of Philosophy Quarterly* 8:181–98.

1992a. Degrees of finality and the highest good in Aristotle. *Journal of the History of Philosophy* 30:327–52.

1992b. Desire and the good in De Anima. In *Essays on Aristotle's De Anima*, ed. Amélie O. Rorty and Martha C. Nussbaum, 381–99. Oxford: Oxford University Press.

1992c. Review of Broadie, *Ethics with Aristotle. Mind* 101:358–61.

Roberts, Robert C. 1988. What an emotion is: A sketch. *Philosophical Review* 97:183–209.

Robins, Michael H. 1984. Practical reasoning, commitment, and rational action. *American Philosophical Quarterly* 21:55–68.

Rorty, Amélie O., ed. 1980a. *Essays on Aristotle's ethics.* Berkeley: University of California Press.

1980b. Explaining emotions. In *Explaining emotions*, ed. A. O. Rorty, 103–26. Berkeley: University of California Press.

1982. From passions to emotions and sentiments. *Philosophy* 57:159–72.

Rorty, Richard. 1979. *Philosophy and the mirror of nature.* Princeton: Princeton University Press.

1982. Overcoming the tradition: Heidegger and Dewey. In *The consequences of pragmatism,* 37–59. Minneapolis: University of Minnesota Press.

1987. Thugs and theorists. *Political Theory* 15:564–80.

1989. Solidarity or objectivity? In *Relativism: Interpretation or confrontation,* 35–50. See Krausz 1989.

Ross, W. D. 1930. *The right and the good.* Oxford: Oxford University Press.

1939. *Foundations of ethics.* Oxford: Oxford University Press.

Russell, Bertrand. 1989. Dewey's new "Logic." In *The philosophy of John Dewey,* ed. Paul Arthur Schilpp and Lewis Edwin Hahn, 137–56. La Salle, Ill.: Open Court.

Sartre, Jean-Paul. 1975. Existentialism is a humanism. In *Existentialism from Dostoevsky to Sartre,* Ed. Walter Kaufmann, 345–69. New York: Meridian-New American.

Savage, L. J. 1954. *The foundations of statistics.* New York: John Wiley.

Scanlon, T. M. 1982. Contractualism and utilitarianism. In *Utilitarianism and beyond,* ed. Amartya Sen and Bernard Williams, 103–28. Cambridge University Press.

1988. Levels of moral thinking. In *Hare and critics,* 129–46. See Seanor and Fotion 1988.

Schneewind, J. B. 1977. *Sidgwick's ethics and Victorian moral philosophy.* Oxford: Oxford University Press.

Seabright, Paul. 1987. Explaining cultural divergence: A Wittgensteinean paradox. *Journal of Philosophy* 84:11–27.

Seanor, Douglas, and N. Fotion, eds. 1988. *Hare and critics: Essays on "Moral thinking."* Oxford: Oxford University Press.

Searle, John R. 1964. How to derive 'ought' from 'is.' *Philosophical Review* 73:43–58.

Sen, Amartya. 1982. Rational fools. In *Choice, welfare, and measurement.,* 84–106. Cambridge, Mass.: MIT Press.

1984 [1970]. *Collective choice and social welfare.* Amsterdam: North-Holland.

1985. Rationality and uncertainty. *Theory and Decision* 18:109–27.

Sherman, Nancy. 1989. *The fabric of character: Aristotle's theory of virtue.* Oxford: Oxford University Press.

Sidgwick, Henry. 1981 [1907]. *The methods of ethics.* 7th ed. Indianapolis: Hackett.

Simon, Herbert. 1983. *Reason in human affairs.* Stanford, Calif.: Stanford University Press.

Sinnott-Armstrong, Walter. 1988. *Moral dilemmas.* Oxford: Basil Blackwell.

Solomon, Miriam. 1989. Quine's point of view. *Journal of Philosophy* 86:113–36.

Sorensen, Roy A. 1988. *Blindspots.* Oxford: Oxford University Press.

1991a. Rationality as an absolute concept. *Philosophy* 66:473–86.

1991b. Vagueness and the desiderata for definition. In *Definitions and definability: Philosophical perspectives,* ed. J. H. Fetzer, D. Shatz, and G. Schlesinger, 71–109. Dordrecht: Kluwer Academic Publishers.

Sperber, Dan. 1982. Apparently irrational beliefs. In *Rationality and relativism,* ed. Martin Hollis and Stephen Lukes, 149–80. Oxford: Basil Blackwell.

Stocker, Michael. 1979. Desiring the bad: An essay in moral psychology. *Journal of Philosophy* 76:738–53.

1990. *Plural and conflicting values.* Oxford: Oxford University Press.

Stump, Eleanor. 1989. *Dialectic and its place in the development of medieval logic.* Ithaca, N.Y.: Cornell University Press.

Sullivan, William L. 1990. Bringing the good back in. In *Liberalism and the good,* 148–66. See Douglass et al. 1990.

Tuozzo, Thomas M. 1991. Aristotelian deliberation is not of ends. In *Essays on ancient Greek philosophy,* vol. IV: *Aristotle's ethics,* ed. J. P. Anton and A. Preus, 193–212. Albany: State University of New York Press.

van Fraasen, Bas C. 1973. Values and the heart's command. *Journal of Philosophy* 70:5–19.

Velleman, J. David. 1989. *Practical reflection.* Princeton: Princeton University Press.

1992. The guise of the good. *Nous* 26:3–26.

Von Neumann, John, and Oskar Morgenstern. 1980 [1953]. *Theory of games and economic behavior.* 3d ed. Princeton: Princeton University Press.

von Wright, G. H. 1963. *The logic of preference.* Edinburgh: Edinburgh University Press.

1983. *Practical reason: Philosophical papers,* vol. I. Oxford: Basil Blackwell.

1989. A reply to my critics. In *The philosophy of Georg Henrik von Wright,* ed. Paul Arthur Schilpp and Lewis Edwin Hahn, 731–887. La Salle, Ill.: Open Court.

Waldron, Jeremy. 1987. Theoretical foundations of liberalism. *Philosophical Quarterly* 37:127–50.

Wallace, James D. 1988. *Moral relevance and moral conflict.* Ithaca, N.Y.: Cornell University Press.

Weiss, Anita M. 1986. Implications of the Islamization program for women. In *Islamic reassertion in Pakistan: The application of Islamic laws in a modern state,* ed. Anita M. Weiss, 97–113. Syracuse, New York: Syracuse University Press.

Wiggins, David. 1980a [1975–6]. Deliberation and practical reason. In *Essays on Aristotle's ethics,* 221–40. See A. Rorty 1980a.

1987. *Needs, values, truth: Essays in the philosophy of value.* Oxford: Basil Blackwell.

Williams, Bernard. 1973. Ethical consistency. In *Problems of the self: Philosophical papers 1956–1972,* 166–86. Cambridge University Press.

1981a. Internal and external reasons. In Williams 1981b, 101–13.

1981b. *Moral luck: Philosophical papers 1973-1980.* Cambridge University Press.

1985. *Ethics and the limits of philosophy.* Cambridge, Mass.: Harvard University Press.

Wittgenstein, Ludwig. 1958 [1953]. *Philosophical investigations,* trans. G. E. M. Anscombe. New York: Macmillan.

1960. *The blue and brown books: Preliminary studies for the Philosophical investigations.* 2d ed. New York: Harper & Row.

1969. *On certainty,* trans. Denis Paul and G. E. M. Anscombe. New York: J. & J. Harper.

1978. *Remarks on the foundations of mathematics,* 3d ed., ed. G. H. von Wright, R. Rhees, and G. E. M. Anscombe, trans. G. E. M. Anscombe. Cambridge, Mass.: MIT Press.

Wright, Crispin. 1984. Second thoughts about criteria. *Synthese* 58:383–405.
Ziadeh, Farhat. 1990. Integrity (*'ahlāh*) in classical Islamic law. In *Islamic law and jurisprudence*, ed. Nicholas Heer. Seattle: University of Washington Press.
Zwerdling, Daniel. 1990. Pakistani women repressed. In *All things considered*, radio broadcast, April 8. Washington, D.C.: National Public Radio.

Index

Abu Hanifa, 286, 287
abstraction, 245–6, 272
Ackerman, B., 280
Ackrill, J. L., 201n.
adequate representation, 115, 135, 253; conditions for, 106–111
Aeschylus, 113
Agamemnon, 113, 114–15
agglomeration, 41–3, 46, 136
aiming, 50, 52, 204–5
Aizpurua, J., 100n.
Albritton, R., 274n.
Ali Khan, Muhammad, 262, 263
Allais, M., 9, 25, 30; see also Allais paradox
Allais paradox, 28n., 29–30
Allan, D. J., 37
alternatives, see options
Amin, S. H., 241, 287
Anscombe, G. E. M., 23n., 32, 39–41, 204; see also Anscombe's fallacy
Anscombe's fallacy, 197–8, 200n., 202
Antigone, 114, 149
antisymmetry, see pursuit of x for the sake of y
Aquinas, T., 16, 25, 69n., 109
Aqvist, L., 80
Archimedean point, 306
Aristotle, xii, xiii, 120, 307; criticized by Dewey, 163, 164; on deliberation, 4, 14, 39n., 58, 185; on dialectic, 244–7; on ends and their pursuit, 6n., 16, 50, 54–5, 56n., 130, 201; holism of, 306; on the human good, 21, 69n., 306; on the particulars, 138; on perception, 36; on the practical syllogism, 33, 34n., 35n., 37, 62n., 74–7; psychology of action of, 23, 139; and Rawls, 219, 220; on reputable opinions (endoxa), 208; on the ultimate end, 194, 195,

202, 204–5, 211–18, 226; on virtue, 186, 293; see also happiness; practical wisdom
Arrow, K., 100
Audi, R., 19, 23n., 52, 193; see also syllogism: practical

Barnes, 299
barriers to mutual understanding, see cognitive ends; hardened propositions; tacit exemplars
Bender, J., 176
Bentham, J., 92, 106, 131
Berlin, I., 239
Bhutto, B., 240n.
bidirectionality, 141, 143, 176–7, 182
Bittner, R., 20, 150; on happiness, 155–6
Black, M., 38
Blum, L., 185
BonJour, L., 148
Bower, G., 186n.
Brandt, R., 110, 155n., 206
Bratman, M.: on deliberation, 60n.; on intentions, 39n., 53n., 78, 153; on motivational potential, 78–9; on reconsideration, 67
Broadie, S., 34n., 39n., 62n., 201, 210; on deliberation, 66; on the ultimate end in Aristotle, 194, 217
Broome, J., 10n., 20, 29, 94, 101, 118

Cachia, P., 242n.
charity: principle of, 254, 256–7; specified, 267–70
Charles, D., 76
circularity: epistemological, 293; in practical reasoning, 31, 209–10
cognitive ends, 282, 289, 292, 297–9, 304; contributing to disagreement's depth,

320

260, 264–5; susceptible of specification, 266–71, 280

coherence, *see* practical coherence; reflective coherence

commensurability, *see* conceptual commensurability; value commensurability

commensurans: coherence not as one, 195; the term, 15–16, 89; ultimate end as not one, 179, 226; as a useful measure, 104–7, 109; utilitarian versions, 121–2, 130

commitment: and emotion, 186–7, 188; as having loose implications for further action, 77–8, 80, 82; initial (*see also* starting point), 50; the notion of practical, as element of ends or reasons, 51–3

complementarities, *see* organic effects

completeness: postulate of practical, 123, 125; postulate inessential to Sidgwick's argument for commensurability; 132, 136; postulate rejected, 179; in practical systems, 44–5, in value rankings, 108, 118

conception of the good: articulated by ordering of finality, 149; notion glossed, 56; and practical theory, 86, 164–5; and regulatory structure, 53, 56, 226

conceptual commensurability, 250–2, 259, 282; defined 250–1; why conceptual commensurability not reducible to value commensurability, 266

conceptual scheme, 250; Davidson's attack on the idea, 254–6; the idea reconstructed, 263–5; and parochialism, 289

conflicts, practical: existence of irresolvable ones, 42, 149; gradations, 144–9; not ruled out by logic, 41–6; residue of, 81; as spur to systematization, 15, 90

Connolly, W., 298

considered judgment, 187–9

consistency, 91n., 93n.

constancy, 152, 154, 180, 182

continuity of someone's practical commitments, 169–74, 211

Cooper, J., 69n.

coordination, 152–4, 157

cost of pursuing an aim: as implicit limit, 39, 45, 163; as stand-in for all other ends, 66, 147

criteria, conceptual, 260–1, 274n.

Darwall, S., 25n., 51, 101n., 139n., 305

Davidson, D.: against conceptual schemes, 21, 254–9, 265, 278–9; holism of, 20n.; on practical reasoning, 51

Davis, W., xiii, 76, 176

decision theory: causal, 86n., 95n.; and commensurability, 15, 91, 119; multivalue, 166; as normative, 30; and relative rationality, 25–6; standard versions as excluding deliberation about ends, 8–9; *see also* Allais paradox

deliberation: episodes of, 14, 16, 59–60; general nature of, 4; not always a good idea, 4–5; political, xii, 234

Descartes, R., 32

desire, glossed, 51

de Sousa, R., 186n.

Dewey, J., 20, 171; against "ultimate ends," 162–5; on deliberation, 83–4, 159–62, 170, 174; Hurley and, 167, 168

dialectic: as a help in deliberation, 205–8, 216, 217; holistic, and its tools, 244–6; holistic, defended, 297–304; holistic, open to truth, 290–1, 299, 305; interpersonal, 247–8, 283, 285, 287–8, 294

dilemma, moral, defined, 41–2

disagreement: its depth, 254, 260–6; obstacle of, addressed 231–307; obstacle of, characterized, 232, 237–43

discursiveness: as informal mark of rationality, 31–3; limit to, 189; postulate of, 123–4, 127, 133–5, 175, 189–90

Doi, ʿA., 283, 284

Donagan, A., 166

Duhem, P., 255n.; *see also* Quine-Duhem thesis

Dunne, J., 184

education into deliberative freedom, 293–4

Elster, J., 157

embodiment of reasoning in a self, 178–9, 189; as making interpersonal extension difficult, 235, 247–8

emotions: deliberative role of, 6, 183–90; and passions, 62–3; as signs of reasoning's embodiedness, 178–9, 235, 258

end–means reasoning: as a form of relative rationality, 13–14, 305; left out by preference-based conceptions, 95, 99–

end–means reasoning (*cont.*)
   100; as nondeductive, 34, 37–8, 102;
   see also motivational transfer
end-norms, 50, 72–4, 190
ends: final versus nonfinal, 53–7; final
   versus ultimate, 195; in general, 49;
   and norms, 50; and reasons, 51; and
   regulation of pursuit, 51–3; *see also*
   cognitive ends; ultimate end
ethics, *see* morality
eudaimonia, 131, 202, 212, 220; *see also*
   happiness; ultimate end
Euripides, 117
Europa, Europa, 281
explanatory support, 150
extended reflective equilibrium, *see*
   reflective equilibrium: extended

Feyerabend, P., 21, 257, 277
Fodor, J., 20n.
Foot, P.: on goodness, 44; on "oughts,"
   43, 46
Foucault, M., 21, 298, 301
Frankfurt, H., 181, 269
Franklin, B., 7–9
Freud, S., 139, 141
friendship, 211–17
fungibility, 104n., 116–7
future contingents, 39n.

Gadamer, H.-G., 184
Galston, W., 295n.
Garcia, J. L. A., 44
Gärdenfors, P., 92, 180
Gauthier, D., 24–5, 27
Gewirth, A., 163
Gibbard, A., 23–4, 44, 71, 289
Gilligan, S., 186n.
Goethe, J. S. von, 117
good, whether the aim of all action,
   16n.
Goodman, N., 150n., 275
goodness, *see* conception of the good;
   organic effects
Gowans, C., 134
Greenspan, P., 42, 81n., 116n.
Greenwood, L. H. G., 201n.
Griffin, J., 90n., 93, 101, 112
Gutmann, A., 295n.

Habermas, J., 31, 280, 303
Hampshire, S., 300
Hampton, J., 92n., 102

Hansson, B., 92, 95, 96
happiness: as a potential commensurans,
   16, 109; and practical coherence, 154–
   8; as ultimate end, 92, 120–1, 130,
   201; *see also* eudaimonia
hardened propositions, 262–3, 265, 266,
   270–91, 304
Hardin, R., 101
Hare, R. M., 64n., 71n., 129, 155n.
Harman, G., 32, 41n., 150n.
Harsanyi, J., 20, 96
Hasan, A., 286–7
Hegel, G. W. F., 244, 296n.
Herman, B., 5n.
holism: and deliberation, 226, 277–9; in
   Dewey, 159–65; initial
   characterization, 141; interpersonal
   realization difficult, 234, 243; and
   motivation, 66–7; Quine's more
   demanding sort, 20n., 255, 257; and
   reflective coherence, 176, 178, 188;
   and specification, 171; *see also* dialectic
Hume, D.: on deliberation, xii, 15; on
   reason and passion, 13–14, 23, 25, 62–6
Hurley, S.: on conflicts, 180; on
   deliberation as theorizing, 150, 166–7;
   on disagreement, 258; on political
   deliberation, 234; on preference
   theory, 101; weighting model,
   167–9

Ibn Hazm, 287
ijtihad, 241, 286–7
incommensurability, *see* conceptual
   commensurability; value
   commensurability
incompossibility, 41, 238
independence axioms, *see* separability
indirect (two-level) conceptions, 129; of
   ultimate ends, 199; resisted, 53n.
institutional support of deliberative
   freedom, 295–6
instrumental rationality, *see* end–means
   reasoning
integrity: as an end competing with
   coherence, 136, 179–82, 200, 297;
   simply as an end, 58–60, 66
internalism regarding reasons, 19, 21, 34,
   62–8, 73
intuitionism: present-day, 133–4, 276;
   Sidgwick's three types, 124; *see also*
   discursiveness
Iqbal, M., 286

322

irrationality, 9, 12, 65, 202
Irwin, T., 244n.

Jalal, A., 285
Jeffrey, R., 93
Jonsen, A., 166, 184, 277–8
judicial appeal, 127, 139, 197, 198; *see also* superior validity
justification: and agreement, 302–4; antiholist, 133, 141, 198; bidirectional, 177, 182; broad use of the term, 175–6; and hardened propositions, 265; as not the role of the finality relation, 196–205; notion of involved in ends and reasons, 51, 200–1; open-ended, 189; as reflective coherence, 175–7, 189, 203; *see also* indirect conceptions; mutual support

Kant, I., xiii, 21, 164, 300, 306–7; on happiness, 155n.; on latitude, 71; moral psychology of, 19n., 51n., 306; partial commensurability in, 107, 109–10, 119–20; on simple conflicts, 237; on truth, 289
Kavka, G., 60n.
Keeney, R., 166
Khan, M., 285
Kirwan, C., 56n.
Kolnai, A., 69n.
Korsgaard, C.: on antisymmetry of pursuit, 202; on ends as sources of value, 21, 197, 203; on internalism, 68; self-conceptions in, 179n., 186
Kripke, S., 261n., 274–5
Kuhn, T., 254, 257, 260, 264n., 265, 276

Lance, M., 35
Larmore, C., 184, 245n., 280
Lepore, E., 20n.
Levi, I., 125
Lewis, D., 28n., 95, 257
liberty, 71, 219–27
Locke, J., 239
love, xiv, 116–7
Lovin' Spoonful, the, 135
Łukasiewicz, J., 35
Lukes, S., 251n., 264n.
Lyotard, J.-F., 298, 303

Mabbott, J., 146, 179
MacDonald, S., 69n., 198, 199n., 200n., 201n.

McDowell, J., 276n.
McFall, L., 180
MacIntyre, A.: on constancy, 152; on deep disagreement, 232, 233, 252, 307; on genealogy, 298n.; on narrative unity, 151; on social practices, 6
Marcus, R. B., 42, 134, 139, 145
Masud, M., 286
maximization models: preference-utility versons as ersatz, 94–6; as presuming commensurability, 15, 91, 120; rejected, 183; as unsettled by need for specification, 75, 220; *see also* conceptual commensurability; value commensurability
means–end, *see* end–means reasoning
Mele, A., 110
Mernissi, F., 286
Mill, J. S., 86, 92, 93, 106, 130, 131, 138, 155; argument for commensurability, 120–1, 132, 137; judicial metaphor, 140; secondary principles in, 164
Millgram, E., 10, 29
modus vivendi, 280–2
Moody-Adams, M., 178n.
Moore, G. E., 107, 110
moral dilemma, defined, 41–2
morality: as basis of fuller objectivity, 306–7; as constraining happiness in Kantian view, 219; equated with reasonableness by Sidgwick, 121, 125; *see also* Aristotle; considered judgment; Kant
Morgenstern, O., 93
motivational transfer: in end–means reasoning, 65; in reasoning about ends, 74–9
Muhammad, 240, 241, 242, 273, 283–4, 286–7
Murdoch, I., 185
mutual support, 140–2, 174–78, 181–4; gradations, 149–3; never total, 189; as route into theory, 207; *see also* practical coherence; reflective coherence

Nagel, T., 113, 305
narrative unity, 151, 302
Newton Smith, W., 264n.
Nietzsche, F., 148, 297–8, 300–3
Noori, A. Y., 241, 287
norms: absolute, 69–70; and ends, 50; *see also* end-norms
Nozick, R., 95n.

Nussbaum, M., xiii; on Aristotle, 38, 69n.; on commensurability, 8, 92, 110, 113, 114; on considered judgment, 187, 188n.; discursiveness in, 134n.; on emotion and perception, 184n., 185, 186n.; on human nature, 147; on love, 116, 117; on moral psychology, 64, 177, 189; on residue, 81n.

objectivity: not excluded, 19, 27, 209, 231, 299, 304–7; not striven for, 19, 24; *see also* rationality: relative; truth

obstacles to recognizing deliberation about ends, *see* disagreement; scope; source; system

O'Neill, O., 245

options, available, 77, 104, 185; their individuation, 10n., 100n., 101–2

ordinal tracking condition, 106–9

organic effects, 98, 100, 107–8

oughts, 41–6, 63–4, 125–6

overlapping consensus, 279–82, 290–1, 300, 303

paradigm, 171, 215–6, 260, 261, 276

Parfit, D., 10, 12, 108, 125, 126

Parodi, D., 161

perception: ineliminable role for, 76; helpful in deliberation, 183–90; *see also* self-perception

phronēsis, see practical wisdom

Pinkard, T., 296n.

Piper, A., 14n.

Plato, 106, 139, 244

pluralism, of conceptions of the good, 219, 232–3, 239, 282, 300

Pogge, T., 223

Popper, K., 276

possum norms, 36–7, 42–4, 81, 180, 184

practical coherence: as an end, 152–8, 179–83; gradations of, 144–51; not as commensurans, 195; postulate of, 123; postulate of transmuted, 189–90; *see also* reflective coherence

practical wisdom (*phronēsis*), 76, 166, 184, 194, 199, 210, 275–6, 293

pragmatism, *see* Dewey, J.

preferences, 9, 26, 30, 90–103, 107, 160, 305; intrinsic, 99–100

Prior, A. N., 80

promotion (of an end's finality), *see* specification

pursuit of *x* for the sake of *y*: antisymmetrical, 55–6; general account, 54–5; and ordering of finality, 201; reflexive case (final ends), 55

Putnam, H., 64n., 160, 168n., 267

Putnam, R. A., 160

Quine-Duhem thesis, 255, 257

Quine, W. V. O., 20n., 254–9, 267–8

Quinn, W., 100n.

Raiffa, H., 166

Ramsey, F. P., 93

rape victims: disagreement regarding, 240–43; hardened propositions regarding, 262–3; minimal agreement about, 246, 278–9; overcoming disagreement regarding, 282–4

rationality (of a process of practical thinking): postulates of, 122–3, 128, 132, 175, 189–90; relative, glossed 13; relative, and initial commitments, 50, 219; relative, and reflective sovereignty, 181, 183; relative, its norms, 30–1; relative, strategic restriction to, 26–8; relative, yet critical, 305–6; working gloss, 22–33; *see also* reasoning

Rawling, P., 103

Rawls, J.: on bidirectionality, 141, 142; on deliberative rationality, 203; on free public reason, 303; grass-blade counter example, 11, 200; holism of, 306; on justice, 21, 218–27, 245; on justification, 189; on life plans, 56, 151; on objectivity, 305; on reasonable and rational, 22n.; on reflection, 29; on simple conflicts, 237; on Sidgwick, 130; *see also* considered judgment; *modus vivendi*; overlapping consensus; reflective equilibrium; *Sittlichkeit*

Raz, J., 108n.

realism: about the good, 208; metaphysical, 267n.; *see also* truth

reasoning, practical vs. theoretical, 4, 22; *see also* rationality

reasons: lurking reasons, 98–9, 103, 118; motivating reasons, 64–5, 131

reflection, Socratic, 29–30, 140, 167, 176, 178, 189

reflective coherence: and dialectic, 244; and justification, 176–8; and objectivity, 305–6; and perception,

187–90; *see also* justification; practical coherence

reflective equilibrium, 178, 305–6; extended, 183–4, 188; shared, 234, 247, 307

reflective sovereignty: characterized, 178–9; difficult to model interpersonally, 235; its implications, 195, 203, 248

regulation by ends of pursuit: analyzed, 53–7; examples, 12, 50, 59–60; importance in deliberation, 61, 82, 85–6, 213–4, 225–7; and specification, 77; by ultimate ends, 202–5, 211; *see also* justification

Reich, R., 295n.

relative rationality, *see* rationality: relative

relevance: practical, 174–183; substantive, 72, 73, 79, 173, 245–6, 278; substantive distinguished from practical, 74

respecification, 224, 304; *see also* revisability

revisability, 20, 142, 159, 165, 178; *see also* bidirectionality; reflective coherence; self-evidence

Roberts, R., 186n.

Robins, M., 39n.

Rorty, A., 64n., 185, 186n.

Rorty, R., 277, 280; on Dewey, 161; parochial mood of, 289–90

Ross, W. D.: on Aristotle, 58, 244n.; on compunction, 81n; on moral conflicts, 42, 133–4; *see also* intuitionism; possum norms

Rousseau, J.-J., 236

Russell, B., 160n.

Sahlin, N.-E., 92

Sartre, J.-P., 44, 117

Savage, L., 29–30, 93

Scanlon, T. M., 71n., 302–3

Schneewind, J. B., 122, 125, 126–7

scope, obstacle of: addressed, 49–82; characterized, 14–15

Seabright, P., 258

Searle, J., 64n.

self-evidence, 137, 142, 176; *see also* reflective coherence; revisability

self-perception, 186, 210, 235, 296; *see also* emotions

self-sufficiency of the good life, 211–18, 226

Sen, A., 35, 92, 94–5, 101, 108

separability, 98, 101, 117; *see also* sure-thing principle

Sherman, N., 59, 184

Sidgwick, H.: on commensurability, 120, 129–32, 137, 159; on completeness, 123, 179; on happiness, 155; judicial imagery, 140; postulates of practical rationality, 122–8, 175, 189–90, 133; on practical conflicts, 136, 144, 198, 199; on superior validity, 126–8, 138, 176–7; on systematization, 20, 118, 121–2, 128–9, 138, 141, 142, 181; on ultimate end as source of value, 197

Simon, H., 63

Sinnott-Armstrong, W., 41, 43

Sittlichkeit, 296n.

Socratic, *see* reflection, Socratic

Solomon, M., 256n.

Sophie's choice, 42, 115–7

Sorensen, R., 28n., 32, 45

source, obstacle of: addressed, 193–227; characterized, 16, 193–5

specification: allowing room for judgment, 77–9; of cognitive ends, 266–70; and conflict, 185; and continuity, 169–83, 209–11; defined, 69–74; and dialectic, 245, 246; and division of labor, 234; examples of, 60, 214–18, 220; of hardened propositions, 261, 277, 285, 301; and promotion, 82–88, 224–6; and residue, 79–82; of a tradition, 293; *see also* abstraction; values

Sperber, D., 289

starting points, 184–6, 219; *see also* commitment: initial

Stocker, M., 90n.; on commensurability, 103, 104n., 117; on pursuit, 16n.; on residue, 81n.

Stump, E., 244

substitution effects, *see* organic effects

Sullivan, W., 295n.

superior validity: postulate of, explained, 123, 126–7, 129; postulate of, rejected, 132, 137, 138, 140, 189; *see also* judicial appeal

sure-thing principle, 30; *see also* separability

syllogism: Peripatetic, 35, 70, 77, 164, 169; practical, 19, 34–5, 37–8, 40, 74–5, 151

system, obstacle of: addressed, 89–190; characterized, 15–16

systematization: achievable without commensurability, 189–90; and

325